THE VATICAN
AND THE RED FLAG

THE VATICAN
AND THE RED FLAG

THE STRUGGLE FOR THE SOUL OF
EASTERN EUROPE

Jonathan Luxmoore and Jolanta Babiuch

GEOFFREY
CHAPMAN

Geoffrey Chapman
A Cassell imprint
Wellington House, 125 Strand, London WC2R 0BB
370 Lexington Avenue, New York, NY 10017-6550
www.cassell.co.uk

First published 1999

British Library Cataloguing-in-Publication Data
A catalogue record for this book is available from the British Library.

ISBN 0-225-66772-X

Typeset by BookEns Ltd, Royston, Herts.
Printed and bound in Great Britain by
Biddles Ltd, Guildford and King's Lynn

Contents

cɔcɔɔcɔcɔ

Acknowledgement

The 'red flag' is the flag of communism, but also a flag of warning. This book tells the story of the Roman Catholic Church's confrontation with communism from an East–West perspective, giving equal weight to the views and experiences of people on both sides of the old Iron Curtain. It owes a good deal to encouragement and advice from our late friend Peter Hebblethwaite, as well as practical support from his widow, Margaret Hebblethwaite, and the Librarian of Heythrop College, Michael Walsh.

We also wish to thank editors who have fostered our interest over the years, particularly Joop Koopman at the *National Catholic Register*, John Wilkins at *The Tablet*, Philip Walters at *Religion, State and Society*, Barbara Fraze at Catholic News Service, and Gabriele Burkhardt at Katholische Nachrichten-agentur.

While the book's factual content must speak for itself, the insights and judgements have drawn on conversations with many people whose influences, great or small, are traceable in the text. They include Andrzej Bardecki, Ladislav Hejdánek, László Lukács, Kastantas Lukenas, Emil Marinescu, Tadeusz Pieronek, Jacek Salij, Johannes Schasching, Karol Tarnowski, Józef Tischner, Miklós Tomka and Paul Zulehner.

೧ೲೲೲೲ

Introduction

When the Counsellor comes whom I shall send you from the Father, even the Spirit of Truth who proceeds from the Father, he will bear witness to me ... And when he comes, he will convince the world of sin and of righteousness and of judgment: of sin, because they do not believe in me; of righteousness, because I go to the Father and you will see me no more; of judgment, because the ruler of this world is judged. (John 15:26, 16:8–11 RSV).

The date is 1 December 1989. In the Vatican's Apostolic Palace, illuminated by television lights, two men are shaking hands, watched by their waiting retinues. Cardinal Agostino Casaroli can be seen in the background, the wiry architect of papal diplomacy. So, against a backdrop of soutaned priests and grey-suited diplomats, can Eduard Shevardnadze, the white-haired Foreign Minister of the Soviet Union.

Less than 600 miles to the north, students are dancing on the streets of Prague and Bratislava, celebrating the peaceful uprising which will profoundly affect their lives and fortunes. In Warsaw, Budapest and Berlin, communist power has already collapsed. In Bucharest and Sofia, Kiev and Vilnius too, the air is one of expectancy. All over Europe, as if by a miracle, there is talk of a new spring for the nations.

Yet today, attention has turned to this 'meeting of the century' in Rome, where Karol Józef Wojtyła and Mikhail Sergeyevich Gorbachev are greeting each other for the first time—a Pole and a Russian, a priest and a politician, a Christian and a Marxist, personifying visions of humanity locked for long decades in a bitter contest. Half a century has passed since Stalin ridiculed the Church with his famous retort, 'How many divisions has the Pope?' But today Stalin's successor has come cap-in-hand to the Vatican, fully aware that the power of the Pope is a force to be reckoned with, a force spanning the best defended borders, the mightiest State institutions.

Both men, Pope and General Secretary, have travelled a long way from simple origins at Wadowice and Stavropol. Both are decisive actors in a still-unfolding drama, creatures of their respective worlds who have also shaken and changed them. On such a day, who could still talk without irony of a Cold War between East and West?

That 'Cold War' was the name less for a historical period than for a state of mind—a system of rules and norms based on an assumption of permanent enmity. It began, historians say, on 4 February 1945, when a delegation of 600 British and American officials were taken in a convoy of cars over a winding mountain road down to the Crimean seaside resort of Yalta. 'We couldn't have found a worse place for a meeting if we had spent ten years looking for it', the British Prime Minister, Winston Churchill, reputedly confided to President Franklin D. Roosevelt that day, shortly before both men were introduced to their Soviet co-negotiator, Josif Stalin.[1]

Whatever the location's merits, it was at Yalta that Churchill, Roosevelt and Stalin put their signatures on a 3,000-word statement which was to have profound repercussions for the rest of the twentieth century. It confirmed plans for a final four-sided assault on the doomed Nazi Germany, and its division into occupation zones under a Berlin-based Allied commission. But the Yalta statement also contained two other important provisions. The first promised that governments responsive to the will of the people would be freely elected in countries liberated from Nazi occupation. The second reaffirmed that all three leaders wished to see a 'strong, free, independent and democratic Poland'.[2]

Western diplomats would later admit that Stalin had no intention of honouring the Yalta pledges. Soviet armies were poised to seize control of Poland, as well as Bulgaria and parts of Germany, and were advancing fast through Hungary and Czechoslovakia. A Soviet zone in Eastern Europe was already a *fait accompli*. So the Yalta Conference, diplomats would claim, was a damage-limitation exercise, intended to persuade the voracious Soviet ruler to accept a few constraints.

Yet critics maintain that Yalta also symbolized the triumph of *realpolitik*, and brought the Western powers into collusion with the continent's post-war division. The Crimean interlude, they say, merely gave diplomatic approval to a new type of international system emerging from the wreckage of the Second World War. The fate of Eastern Europe had already been sealed by events on the ground.

Perhaps it had been sealed on 23 August 1939, when a 'secret additional protocol' in the Nazi–Soviet Pact that month agreed to divide Polish territory between 'spheres of interest', allowing the Soviet Union to expand into the Baltic States and Bessarabia, as well as south 'towards the Persian Gulf'.[3]

Perhaps it had been sealed that September, when two words from Hitler on a telephone to Moscow—'Yes, agreed'—gave the green light to a Soviet invasion of Poland from the east two weeks after a German invasion from the west and allowed Vyacheslav Molotov, Stalin's foreign affairs commissar, to boast to the Supreme Soviet that the Wehrmacht and Red Army had jointly erased 'this ugly product of Versailles'.[4]

Perhaps Eastern Europe's fate had been decided in April 1940, when the massacre of 15,000 interned Polish officers by the Soviet NKVD at Katyn, Miednoje and Kharkov revealed Stalin's readiness to employ any means in eliminating East European statehood. Or perhaps it had been decided in December 1943 at the Teheran Conference, when Churchill agreed to cede territory to Stalin by shifting Poland's frontiers westwards in return for a commitment to maintain Poland's independence which was overruled by President Roosevelt.

Perhaps it had been sealed in 1944, when the great battles of Kursk and Stalingrad turned the tide of the war and launched the Soviet Army on its inexorable drive westwards. Perhaps the key moment came that August, when Stalin refused to allow aid to reach the embattled anti-Nazi insurgents of the Warsaw Uprising, and condemned the 'reckless adventure' which laid the city open to his own divisions.

What matters is how far Western governments came to connive in the Soviet Union's expansion into Eastern Europe by appearing to accept the principle that the internal affairs of countries could be controlled by external powers. No doubt their wartime alliance with Moscow contributed to an imbalance in Western thinking, according to which Stalin's crimes, though at least equal in magnitude and ferocity, were somehow never deemed as bad as Hitler's. But Western geopolitical calculations played their part as well, including an apparently sincere belief that Stalin could be persuaded by concessions to observe rules of good conduct, and that by signing a statement of intent he could be held to account before world opinion. 'The impression I brought back', Churchill told Parliament after returning from the Crimea, 'is that, so far as Stalin is concerned, I am quite sure he means to do well to the world and to Poland. I feel no doubt whatsoever in saying that Stalin has been sincere.'[5] Churchill's words encapsulated the 'spirit of Yalta'—of Soviet expansionism and Western connivance—which three generations of East Europeans would have cause to remember with bitterness.

One institution which resisted this East–West collusion was the Vatican. Pope Pius XII had courted British and American resentment by refusing to bless the alliance with Moscow. In 1945 he saw Yalta as betrayal. Yet Pope and Vatican appeared irrelevant to the emerging order of force and expediency. They were excluded from the post-war settlement because they seemed to have excluded themselves by failing to establish their role in a realistic, convincing way.

In a democratic era, the Vatican had only one claim to be taken seriously by the world's politicians—as the focus of spiritual loyalties within the world-wide Roman Catholic Church. But had Pius XII contemplated a resort to populism, he would have lacked a receptive audience. The Vatican's moral stature had been compromised in the war years by its preoccupation with uneventful diplomacy, at a time when forthright testimony and dynamic witness had been desperately needed.

The Pope spoke out repeatedly against the emerging post-war order. He showed its very premises were misconceived, that security and stability would not be achieved at the cost of suppressed rights and stifled aspirations. But he was unable to back this up with popular pressure. Instead, he persisted in seeing himself as a player at the diplomatic chessboard at a time when the world's great powers were controlling the game and inventing new rules. The Church's head had not yet realized how far spiritual loyalties can have political consequences.

This book tells the story of how this lesson came to be learned, and how those spiritual loyalties came to triumph over the worn-out *realpolitik* assumptions of East and West. Many factors help explain the collapse of communism: political deadlock, economic implosion, ideological break-down, technological advance, democratic ideas, Western pressure. None however can fully account for the unexpected turn of events in 1989, in which the role of the Pope and Vatican were universally acknowledged.

The Popes had been highlighting communism's dangers for 150 years. In the early nineteenth century, they had seen it as a conspiracy against the established order—a paternalistic order based on clearly delineated hier-archical structures, in which rich and poor, high and low were called to contribute to humanity's harmonious development. They saw the need to improve society—but without radically changing it. And they deeply distrusted talk of social movements which defied the customary constraints of authority and tradition.

By the 1930s, the Popes had analysed and refuted communism's pretensions. They knew it was an ideological system which offered beguiling answers to those moved by contemporary injustices. Yet Popes, even then, never fully understood communism. They saw it as a misguided reaction to the iniquities of industrial society, and believed the right response lay in corrective measures to safeguard the working population materially and spiritually. Their own reformist counter-postulates were sometimes novel, even radical. But they failed to see that communism was also a symptom of something deeper—a desire to escape not only from poverty and injustice, but also from indignity and humiliation which were the by-products of an irreversible rise in social consciousness and political emancipation. They failed to grasp the forcefulness of communism's all-embracing response, its capacity to offer a comprehensive way of thinking and living, a vision of new human beings freed forever from the stultifying prejudices and superstitions of history.

This failure helps explain why the Church found itself unprepared for Europe's growing economic and social disorders, and was unable to provide a convincing answer to emerging socialist and Marxist movements. It was in this way that a fault line opened up between radical social reformism and conservative Christian ethics, which contributed significantly to the disasters of twentieth-century totalitarianism.

Decades of trial and error would be needed before a fuller understanding of communism was matched by an effective response. This would be the achievement of Karol Wojtyła, the Polish Pope elected in October 1978. The forces for which he became a catalyst had already been emerging by the 1970s, but he ensured they were channelled in a positive direction. John Paul II could be thankful that new possibilities had been created by an evolution in Vatican thinking, combined with changes in the international climate. He had learned lessons from twentieth-century politics. One was that diplomatic agreements with communist regimes were worthless unless backed up by powerful pressure. Another was that Christians lacked the strength and self-confidence to exert this pressure by themselves, and had to find common ground with other 'people of goodwill'. He grasped something else as well: the modern world functioned not through governments but through people—people whose creative, revolutionary energies could be mobilized to accomplish God's work by breaking through the barriers of power and ideology.

The decade leading to 1989 marked a watershed in modern Church history, in which the Church realized its own power in relation to totalitarian regimes. To accomplish this it was forced to align itself clearly with the contemporary human rights struggle and find dynamic counter-propositions to communism's talk of social justice and emancipation—a view of the world in which the human person must always take priority over programmes, strategies and theories. It remained to be seen whether this commitment to human freedom and dignity would outlast the collapse of communism—or whether, under the turbulent sky of pluralistic democracy, the disastrous fault line of the past would open up again. By that 'meeting of the century' in

December 1989, when John Paul II and Mikhail Gorbachev came face to face in the Vatican's Apostolic Palace, communism had lost its self-declared war against the Church. But the conflict had taught lessons which needed to be pondered for the future.

In St John's account of the Last Supper, Christ promised to send 'another Counsellor', the Spirit of Truth, to 'declare the things that are to come' amid the vagaries and uncertainties of history. Pope John Paul II had entrusted his pontificate to this same Counsellor, as he took up the inheritance of his predecessors.[6] The liberating Spirit of Truth had been active in dramatic, unexpected ways in the intervening years.

Notes

1. Quoted in Michael Charlton, *The Eagle and the Small Birds: Crisis in the Soviet Empire from Yalta to Solidarity* (London: BBC Books, 1984), p. 11.
2. *Report of the Crimea Conference* (London: His Majesty's Stationery Office, 1945), pp. 4–5. Sections V and VI were titled 'Declaration on Liberated Europe' and 'Poland'.
3. Charlton, op. cit., p. 19.
4. Ibid. See also Krystyna Kersten, *Jałta w polskiej perspektywie* (London: Aneks, 1989).
5. Charlton, op. cit., pp. 42–3. See also Jan Karski, *Wielkie mocarstwa wobec Polski 1919–1945* (Warsaw: PiW, 1992).
6. *Redemptor hominis* (4 March 1979), no. 3.

1

⁊ᴄᴏᴄᴏᴄᴏᴄᴏ

The ravening wolves of Europe

Sometime in the eighteenth century, something profound began to happen to the refined civilization of Europe. It cannot be dated precisely, or even summarized satisfactorily. But its consequences were many and varied. It spawned an attitude of mind which refused to recognize any pre-ordained human or divine authority. It also brought an end to the unquestioned authority of the Roman Catholic Church.

What is known as the Enlightenment was a stirring of thoughts and ideas which pointed towards a coming age of social emancipation. It would be simplifying history to draw a direct connection between the Enlightenment and modern totalitarianism. But totalitarianism had its roots in a relativization of values, a belief in the primacy of a material world and the unlimited potential of liberated human capacities. For this, it had much to thank proponents of the Enlightenment vision. That vision gained expression in various movements, from liberalism to socialism, the latter later diversifying into Marxism and Leninism. The papal encounter with socialist ideas began in the early nineteenth century. But at that stage, there were no grounds for distinguishing between the various terms used for them. The French 'social Catholics', led by Félicité de Lamennais, were lobbying the Church by the 1820s to embrace positive elements from Enlightenment thought and help calm Europe's revolutionary chaos through a prudent combination of authority and liberty. But pressure from conservative powers, led by Austria-Hungary, ensured that their efforts were rebuffed in Rome.

'Keep out the ravening wolves who do not spare the flock of innocent lambs', Pope Pius VI demanded in May 1800, a decade after the fall of the Bastille.

> Unless the great licence of thinking, speaking, writing and reading is repressed, it will appear that the strategy and armies of wise kings and generals have

1

relieved us for but a short time from the evil which has crushed us for so long. So long as its stock and seed are not removed and destroyed, it will spread abroad and be strengthened to reach over the whole world. To destroy it later or to rout it out, legions, guards, watches, the armouries of cities, the defences of empires will not be enough.[1]

In his first formal reference to the 'unspeakable doctrine of Communism', in *Qui pluribus* (1846), the newly elected Pius IX dismissed it as 'most opposed to the very natural law', and warned that it would 'completely destroy men's rights, their property and fortune, even human society itself'.[2] The encyclical appeared two years after Marx had urged the destruction of religion—that 'sigh of the oppressed creature, the soul of a world without soul, the mind of a world without mind ... the opium of the people'. Two years later, in 1848, the year of revolutions, the *Communist Manifesto* would list the Pope with 'the Tsar, Metternich and Guizot, French radicals and German police spies', as one of the powers of the old Europe which had formed a 'holy alliance' to exorcize the 'spectre of communism'.[3]

At that stage, the Pope saw 'communism' as no more than a conspiracy, a radical wing of the republican movements making a bid for power in Rome, Paris and Vienna. He would have shown no interest in philosophical arguments purporting to distinguish 'communism' from 'socialism'. In December 1849, a few months after being forced to flee Rome's Quirinal Palace at night disguised as a servant, having seen his own secretary shot dead by besieging revolutionaries, the Pope suggested for the first time that 'proponents of the pernicious fictions of socialism and communism' were using different methods to subvert the working classes. But he still blamed both jointly for attempting to 'seize supreme control to the ruin of all'.

> If the faithful scorn the fatherly warnings of their pastors and the commandments of the Christian Law, and if they let themselves be deceived by the present-day promoters of plots, deciding to work with them in their perverted theories of Socialism and Communism, let them now and earnestly consider what they are laying up for themselves ...
>
> The final goal shared by these teachings, whether of Communism or Socialism, even if approached differently, is to excite by continuous disturbances workers and others, especially those of the lower class, whom they have deceived by their lies and deluded by the promise of a happier condition. They are preparing them for plundering, stealing and usurping first the Church's then everyone's property. After this they will profane all law, human and divine.[4]

In 1864 the First International met in London to debate the rival ideas of Marx, Bakunin and Mazzini. It was also the year which saw publication of Pius IX's *Syllabus Errorum*, with its famous proposition rejecting the notion that 'the Roman Pontiff should reconcile himself or reach agreement with "progress", liberalism and recent departures in civil society'. This again warned against 'communism' and 'socialism', listing them with secret societies, Bible societies and liberal clerical associations as 'pestilences' of the day.[5]

It would have required severe blindness not to see a link between the rise of socialist agitation and the excesses of the Industrial Revolution. And from the late 1860s onwards, papal pronouncements encouraged economic and social reforms to offset alienation and disaffection among the workers of Europe. But the emphasis remained firmly on the need for a balance between component parts of the body politic—a solidarist vision of an unequal, but harmonious and just, social order.

By mid-century, the growth of an industrial society in Europe had brought growing prosperity for a rising middle class of owner-entrepreneurs, but no positive benefits for the expanding worker population, among whom atheist and revolutionary sentiments were being fostered by socialist groups. A start had been made to help the workers in Germany by 'social Catholics' under Wilhelm von Ketteler. But those who sympathized, like Ketteler, with certain socialist demands were careful not to translate their activities into a political stance. When the first organized labour movement emerged during the decade, it came under the influence of the First International and turned its back on the Church.

In France, the Church had conspicuously taken the side of 'order' in the conservative backlash which followed the failed revolution of 1848. Inevitably, this had eroded the creditworthiness of Catholic social initiatives, like Frédéric Ozanam's Société de Vincent de Paul which sought to recreate the Church's frayed bonds with new worker communities. Anti-Church feeling was to reach its bloody apogee in the murder of the Archbishop of Paris and at least 50 priests in the short-lived 1871 Commune. 'Religion was looked on by the masses as a political weapon', the French Cardinal Ferrata wrote in his memoirs, attempting to explain the outburst of hatred which had marked the months of the Commune—'as a monopoly of the aristocracy, a relic of the *ancien régime*.'[6]

As before, no attempt was made in Rome to distinguish between moderates and extremists. When Wilhelm Liebknecht and August Babel formed a German Social Democratic Party in 1869, it provided a model for European Marxists favouring parliamentary methods over the proletarian dictatorship advocated by revolutionary socialists. But socialists, whatever their coloration, were viewed as conspirators and subversives. No one bothered to come to grips with their ideas, since no one saw them, at that stage, as posing a coherent challenge to the established order.

In several countries, Catholic social reformers continued to advocate a range of philanthropic and charitable initiatives, as part and parcel of an attempt to re-evangelize depressed worker communities. But the Church's hierarchy was firmly identified with the interests of power and property, and highly fearful of radical social movements.

By the advent of Leo XIII in February 1878, Church assumptions were coming under pressure. Clearly, socialist agitation was growing rather than receding, as worker communities throughout Europe continued to demand a fair share of national wealth. The revolutionary theories of Marx were winning converts as never before. *Das Kapital*, appearing in its first volume in 1867, had been widely read in France and Germany. Its ideas were making steady progress despite the collapse of the First International in 1876. They offered a scientific explanation of the world and human life which was far more precise than the prometheanism of Nietzsche and positivism of Comte, not to mention the idealistic musings of Saint-Simon, Proudhon and Blanc.

At the same time, the Church's alliance with Europe's ruling regimes was looking shakier. The savage suppression of the 1863 January Uprising in Poland, co-led by Catholic priests, had strengthened the hand of imperial Russia. Protestant Prussia had gained a dominant position through the unification of Germany, and had defeated the Catholic powers of Austria and France. In Italy, the Risorgimento swept away the Papal States and left Rome occupied in 1870. In a final indignity to Pius IX, a mud-throwing mob on Rome's Sant' Angelo bridge waylaid the cortège taking his body for burial at midnight and tried to throw it into the Tiber.

There were many who believed the time was coming for the Church to realign itself more wholeheartedly with social reform—if need be at the cost of slackening its traditional alliance with Europe's old absolutist regimes— and to build up its social influence rather than relying on the wielders of power. The thought of Lamennais, condemned by Gregory XVI in *Singulari nos* (1834), had tendered the vision of a union between the forces of popular emancipation and Catholic spirituality against corrupt monarchical states whose secular outlook had become increasingly hostile to religious truth. The Breton priest had been dead for three decades, but a similar line of reasoning had lived on.

In March 1870, four months before the adoption of the dogma of Papal infallibility, a *postulatum* at the First Vatican Council had openly acknowledged for the first time that the 'evil of socialism' had its root cause in the greed of employers, and had urged the Council to clarify Church teachings on employer–worker relations.[7] Pope Leo XIII was to be just as resolute in condemning modern anti-Christian political doctrines. But he would combine this with an awareness of the need for a clearer Christian model of the social order, which could permit necessary changes.

In December 1878, the Pope's encyclical *Quod apostolici muneris* again denounced 'that sect of men who, under various and almost barbarous names, are called Socialists, Communists or nihilists', and whose 'wicked confederacy' had originated in doctrines which had waged a 'deadly war' against the Catholic faith in the name of reason. Although successive popes from the Enlightenment on had warned of the consequences, Leo XIII added, guardians of the public weal had 'looked upon the Church with a suspicious and even hostile eye'.[8]

Yet anti-clerical liberalism and unrestricted capitalism were as much to blame, the Pope continued. God intended that there should be various orders in civil society, 'differing in dignity, rights and power'. But he also required that rulers 'use the power conceded to them to save and not to destroy'. He held over the heads of the rich 'the divine sentence that unless they succour the needy, they will be repaid by eternal torments'.

In 1885, *Immortale Dei* switched the emphasis to 'liberalism' entirely, pointing out how it endangered moral norms and social stability. The Church was not opposed to democracy and intellectual enquiry, the encyclical made clear. But it believed popular sovereignty led to violent revolution. 'To despise legitimate authority, in whomsoever vested, is unlawful, as a rebellion against the Divine Will.'[9]

Finally, in 1891, the Pope put the record straight with a document showing that Catholic teaching could offer an alternative to both liberalism and socialism. *Rerum novarum* appeared two years after Leo XIII had proclaimed his famous *Ralliement*, urging French royalists to make their peace with the Third Republic. It came two years before the formation of a Second International again focused attention on a Europe-wide socialist movement.

As Nuncio to the Kingdom of Belgium in the 1840s, the Pope had witnessed intolerable working conditions. He had set up a study group in Rome under Cardinal Ludovico Jacobini to work out the Church's response. But the encyclical also drew on the pioneering work of Catholic social reformers abroad and offered some fresh thinking about the Church's relationship with modern society. Although accepting the Church's political subordination to the State, it insisted the Church had a right to make moral demands and powerfully reaffirmed a link between economics and ethics.

The condition of the working classes, Leo wrote, was now 'the pressing question of the hour'.

> By degrees it has come to pass that working-men have been surrendered, isolated and helpless, to the hard-heartedness of employers and the greed of unchecked competition. The hiring of labour and the conduct of trade are

concentrated in the hands of comparatively few; so that a small number of very rich men have been able to lay upon the teeming masses of labouring poor a yoke little better than slavery.[10]

Yet if abusive capitalism was the root cause of modern poverty and misery, socialist proposals—a community of goods, abolition of private property, a classless society—also violated Christian teaching and natural law. In fact, Leo XIII insisted, they would make the working classes poorer still. It was a mistake to believe classes were naturally hostile and 'intended by nature to live in mutual conflict', the encyclical added. 'Capital cannot do without Labour, nor Labour without Capital.'[11]

What the Pope offered instead was a reaffirmation of the harmonious Christian order in which workers received a living wage and had their interests protected by associations or unions. The human dignity and equal rights of the working-class majority had to be fully respected. Workers were 'members of the state equally with the rich'.

It was said that Rerum novarum helped inspire early legislation on social security. Unlike previous papal pronouncements, it firmly stressed the need for distributive justice, calling this the 'first duty of rulers'. It also accepted that the Church's concerns extended to 'temporal and earthly interests', as well as spiritual ones. Yet if Catholics were exhorted to improve the social order, they were not expected to change it. Rerum novarum's definition of the Church's role was founded, as before, on the paternalistic principle of charity. The Pope was aware of the nineteenth century's social and economic disorders and was encouraging Catholics to be aware of them too. But his diagnosis stopped a long way short of recognizing the full anthropological dimensions of the crisis, with all the corrosive consequences flowing from social and economic structures which destroyed human dignity. The task of Christians was, in the end, humanitarian rather than political.

This largely explains why, although some contemporaries praised Rerum novarum as signalling a shift in the Church's position, others saw it as a ruse, with far more in common with Pius IX's social conservatism than with any new-found commitment to social justice. In Germany, the socialist paper Vorwärts praised Leo XIII for having 'stolen a march on secular governments',[12] while in France, the socialist Jean Jaurès called the encyclical a 'Socialist manifesto in its decisive parts'.[13] But Jaurès, for one, believed the Catholic Church would continue to 'cast its lot with the forces of political and social reaction'.

Sure enough, there was no shortage of Catholics who sympathized with the socialist struggle to safeguard worker rights, and who welcomed Rerum novarum as providing some much-needed justification. But Leo XIII's accompanying exhortation to priests—'not to shut themselves up within the walls of their church or presbytery, but to go to the people and concern themselves wholeheartedly with the workers, the poor, the men of the lower classes'[14]—clearly required a certain qualification, coming twenty years after the doctrine of papal infallibility had strengthened the Church's centralized authority, and when liberal pressures in the Church were being countered by conservative Ultramontane tendencies.

The Church's defence of private property continued to set Catholics at odds with socialists—whose 'false doctrines' about eliminating it threatened, in Leo's words, to 'spew the paths they travel with blood'.[15] Confrontation was growing with anti-clerical liberals too. Far from bringing the sides closer, the passage of time was polarizing divisions.

In 1901, Leo XIII reaffirmed the Church's position with *Graves de communi*. The encyclical sent a shot across the bows of 'Christian Democrats', who had attempted to give Catholic social reformism a more political direction since *Rerum novarum*. 'This expression offends many virtuous people', the Pope said. 'They fear it may indicate a preference for popular government over other forms of government, that it may restrict the virtue of the Christian religion to the interests of the people alone.'[16]

Meanwhile, although the accompanying criticism of socialism was moderate in tone compared to earlier documents, *Graves de communi* reminded Catholics that socialist aims, whatever practical programmes they might give rise to, ultimately posed a threat to the Church. 'The Church teaches that the different social classes remain as they are because it is obvious that nature demands it', Leo XIII noted the following year.[17]

By the advent of Pius X, there were plenty of would-be Catholic reformers who still regarded all socialists as conspirators, and resented their evident success in mobilizing the working classes. But their own organizations were weak by comparison, and hidebound by their Church alignment. In 1906, two years after Romolo Murri's Opera dei Congressi had been suppressed at papal directive, Catholic labour organizations in Italy could claim just 70,000 members, compared to the 570,000 enrolled in the socialist-dominated General Confederation of Labour and Chambers of Labour. By 1910, Catholic groups still accounted for no more than 12.5 per cent of the country's organized labour-force.[18]

Pius X soon put paid to any remaining attempts to interpret his predecessor's teachings in some kind of political direction. Catholic intellectuals who had responded to Leo XIII's perceived reformism by attempting to bring Catholicism up to date were brought to book by the condemnation of 'Modernism'—that 'synthesis of all heresies'—in *Pascendi* (1907). 'It is in conformity with the order established by God in human society that there should be princes and subjects, employers and proletariat, rich and poor, instructed and ignorant', the new Pope reiterated. One

Catholic movement explicitly formed in response to Leo XIII's social teaching, Marc Sangnier's Sillon, which had sought to educate young French workers in a spirit of democracy and social justice, was duly condemned in 1910. 'The true friends of the people', Pius X retorted, 'are neither revolutionaries nor innovators, but traditionalists.'[19]

By the late nineteenth century, socialist agitation had intensified in Eastern Europe too, particularly among disaffected worker populations in Austrian-ruled Hungary and Bohemia. The more austere, repressive conditions in Russian-ruled territory had delayed economic advancement, impeding the emergence of a native bourgeoisie and industrial working class. But everywhere, the rise of national feeling, social frustration and political polarization had caught the Church off-guard and created fertile ground for revolutionary ideas.

It was, however, in backward, undeveloped Russia that the agitation reached its apex. Ironically, when Tsarist rule was overthrown in 1917, the Vatican appeared to react with a curious equanimity. Chaos prevailed inside Russia, while foreign armies were pressing at its borders. Rome was convinced that the new Bolshevik regime could not last.

Historians have argued that the Vatican even saw advantages in the new situation. Besides crippling the Russian State, the revolution had swept away the traditional privileges of the Orthodox Church, creating an opening, in theory at least, to missionary activity by the Catholic Church—an unprecedented chance to win long-lost Eastern Christians back to Rome. If forced to choose between a resurgent imperial Russia, and the revolutionary forces hell-bent on destroying it, was it perhaps tactically expedient to opt for the lesser, more temporary evil?[20]

This is a simplification. But there were dilemmas to be faced. The Catholic Church had had ample warning of the Bolsheviks' hostility. Lenin had argued the case for allowing religious workers and even priests to support the Communist Party's programme, and had urged against imposing atheism as a rigid requirement for members. But he had constantly reiterated the Party's 'resolute hostility to religion', seeing it as the logical extension of Marx's dialectical materialism. 'Religion is the opium of the people, a kind of vodka by which the slaves of capital blacken their human figure and their aspirations for a more dignified human life', Lenin declared in 1909. 'Religions, modern churches, religious organizations of all kinds—Marxism considers them always as organs of bourgeois reaction.'[21]

Sure enough, by the end of 1918, the Bolsheviks had seized Church properties and massacred thousands of Orthodox priests, religious and laity. But the new regime had shown a readiness to maintain ties with the Vatican, at a time when other states were also establishing diplomatic relations after the First World War. Within months of October 1917, some Vatican sources claimed to see signs of a 'positive evolution' in Moscow.[22] The optimism was called in question soon enough by evidence that Catholics were being persecuted too. But by then, the Vatican was in contact with Russia's new rulers.

In any case, maintaining links with as many regimes as possible was a Vatican priority. By the end of the nineteenth century, the Papacy had been deprived of its Italian possessions for close on three decades. It had been weakened by continuing Church conflicts with Italy, as well as with Bismarck's Prussia and the French Third Republic. With the collapse of the Austro-Hungarian monarchy likely to give birth to a chain of hostile independent states, it seemed essential to maintain a high profile on the international stage. In August 1917, Benedict XV's peace proposals had been ignored by Europe's warring sides. Two years later, the Pope found himself excluded from the Versailles Treaty, amid disagreements with the US Wilson Administration over the future map of Europe.[23] But the Vatican was determined to remain a factor in international relations.

Added to this, the Catholic Church had over 150 parishes in Russia, giving it a direct stake in the new regime's policies. It had a chain of churches, built mostly by Polish and German deportees and settlers, stretching to Irkutsk and Vladivostok. Meanwhile, the Church's dioceses of Tyraspol and Mogilev each had its own seminary. St Petersburg, where the Bishop of Mogilev resided, was home to no fewer than 72 Catholic schools. With half a million members in European Russia and more in Siberia, the Church was producing holy people like St Rafał Kalinowski (1835–1907) and Blessed Jurgis Matulaitis (1871–1927).

The Papacy had enjoyed an uncertain but not unreasonable relationship with the Russian Tsars. Tsar Paul I had visited Pope Pius VI in 1781. He had a chapel built in St Petersburg in honour of the Knights of Malta, of which he was Grand Master. In 1801, when the Pope was deported from Rome by Napoleon, he sent him a message pledging that he could count on 'the hospitality of the Tsar of all the Russias, who would treat him as a true father'.[24]

Since traitors to the Orthodox faith were also branded enemies of the State, Catholic conversions had required civil courage in Russia. But they had occurred nonetheless, symbolizing an escape from Tsarist despotism, with prominent converts such as Princess Zinaida Volkonskaya and Prince Ivan Gagarin establishing something akin to a mid-nineteenth-century Catholic court-in-exile in Rome. Though intolerant of anything which questioned their power in religious matters, the Romanov dynasty took the

Papacy more seriously than its own Orthodox Synod. Nicholas I visited Gregory XVI in 1845, allegedly to thank him for defending the Russian Empire's rights against Poland's 1830 November Uprising. In 1881, when Alexander II was assassinated in St Petersburg, Leo XIII sent a message to his heir, Alexander III, condemning the revolutionaries and urging Christian unity against the 'evil of Socialism'.[25]

In 1882, the Tsar had regulated the Catholic Church's affairs in an agreement with the Vatican and sent a permanent representative to Rome. In 1905, Nicholas II's Edict of Toleration gave equal rights to Catholics and Orthodox throughout the Russian Empire.

But Moscow had been engaged, in the meantime, in a bitter struggle to Russify Catholic Lithuania and Poland. It had also attempted to suppress the Ukrainian Greek Catholic Church in Galicia. By the outbreak of war in 1914, there had been talk of a Russian drive to the Bosporus and Adriatic, reuniting Eastern Europe's traditional Orthodox territories within a single Russian-ruled bloc. Hence the Vatican's dilemma. Great Catholic nations— Lithuania, Poland, Hungary, Croatia—would be in the firing line of any new-born Russian expansionism. Here too, spurred on by the first Communist International, formed in Moscow in March 1919, revolutionary groups were agitating in response to the Bolsheviks' seizure of power. But the new regime wanted legitimacy, or at least some tempering of its violent image. A window of opportunity existed.

In 1920, a Papal Commission in Rome began studying Russian affairs and training missionaries. In August the following year, with the Russian civil war at an end, the Moscow government agreed in talks with the Secretary of State, Cardinal Pietro Gasparri, that a Vatican mission under Fr Eduard Gehrmann could organize famine relief, on condition that it refrained from proselytism. Quaker, Baptist, Jewish and Mennonite missions were already at work in Russia, so this was hardly a concession. Meanwhile, the Bolshevik regime was rapidly gaining strength. After a few months' notional independence, Byelorussia and Ukraine had been swallowed up into the newly proclaimed Soviet Union. An invading Bolshevik army, en route westwards, had been narrowly turned back by Poland's Marshal Piłsudski at the 'Miracle on the Vistula'.

But there were still voices in the Vatican who believed Soviet rule would be temporary, and that relations should be maintained in expectation of better times.[26] In December 1921, Rome announced an apostolic vicariate for the estimated 75,000 Catholics of Siberia. And in February 1923 it even created a new diocese at Vladivostok. The Soviet regime went out of its way to give the impression of closeness with the Vatican. At the 1922 Genoa Conference, when the Vatican delegate, Mgr Giosue Sincero, drank toasts with the Soviet representative, Georgi Chicherin, aboard the *Dante Alighieri*, White Russians abroad complained bitterly about the show of 'cordiality'. Chicherin himself claimed ostentatiously that Pius XI had 'flirted' with him at Genoa.[27]

Evidence suggests the Bolsheviks exploited the famine which racked post-Revolution Russia and Ukraine as a pretext for grabbing Church wealth. In March 1922, Lenin sent a top-secret message to members of the Politburo:

> Now and only now, when people are being eaten in famine-stricken areas, and hundreds, if not thousands, of corpses lie on the roads, we can (and therefore must) pursue the removal of Church property with the most frenzied and ruthless energy, without hesitating to put down the least opposition ... The greater the number of representatives of the reactionary clergy and reactionary bourgeoisie that we succeed in shooting on this occasion the better, because this 'audience' must precisely now be taught a lesson in such a way that they will not dare to think about any resistance whatsoever for several decades.[28]

But it was to take time for the Vatican to relinquish its expectations that Bolshevik policies were about to be moderated. In March 1923, Archbishop Jan Cieplak of Mogilev and his vicar-general, Mgr Konstantin Budkiewicz, were condemned to death for supporting a 'counter-revolutionary organiza-tion'. Budkiewicz was shot on Good Friday, whereas Cieplak's sentence was commuted to ten years. But twelve other Catholic priests were jailed at the same time. Soviet propaganda organs spoke of the Pope's support for a confederation of 'Black Internationals', which had allegedly brought Mussolini to power in Italy and were posing a deadly threat to the new communist order.

In early 1924, when the Vatican relief mission was expelled and its supplies seized by the Soviet authorities, Fr Gehrmann told the Pope he saw no possibility of the regime collapsing. But this, paradoxically, seemed to make some kind of contact even more necessary. Talks were soon under way in Berlin about sending an Apostolic Delegate. And when Moscow agreed, the French Jesuit, Mgr Michel d'Herbigny, entered the country in October 1925. 'The result of the struggle is uncertain, my friend. What *is* certain is that it will be long', Chicherin reputedly told d'Herbigny after his arrival.

> We communists feel pretty sure we can triumph over London capitalism. But Rome will prove a harder nut to crack. If Rome did not exist, we could deal with the various brands of Christianity. All would finally capitulate before us. Without Rome, religion would die. But Rome sends out propagandists of every nationality in the service of her religion. They are more effective than guns or armies.[29]

Perhaps Chicherin's words really did reflect a grudging Soviet realization that the Catholic Church's moral authority posed a concrete obstacle to communist power. But they may also have been intended to flatter the Vatican's naivety. After the 1923 trials, the open persecution of religion was replaced by administrative measures designed to harass and intimidate without creating martyrs. The Vatican was encouraged to believe it would be allowed to continue its activity. 'It was a source of pleasure to read more than once in the reports of the Soviet authorities', Pius XI told Odo Russell, Britain's Vatican representative, 'that the Church of Rome remains the most formidable barrier to revolutionary ideas, and that so far no breach in Russia has been made in its position.'[30]

Yet the naivety was gradually receding. The more the Vatican conceded, the more Moscow demanded. In 1926, when the Soviet regime handed Archbishop Eugenio Pacelli, the Nuncio to Berlin, a plan to guarantee the Church's position, the Vatican agreed that its own dispatches could be monitored and censored as a *quid pro quo*. But by the following year, Moscow had ruled out any possibility of giving Church rights treaty-level protection. The affairs of the Catholic Church were to remain subject to the political whims of Soviet law-making.

In 1927 came Pius XI's condemnation of Action Française, an event which put in doubt claims that the Vatican automatically sympathized with right-wing forces. But in the same year Britain and United States finally signed conventions recognizing the new Soviet regime (in the US case, with President Roosevelt's insistence on a clause guaranteeing religious freedom) and a tactical Soviet *rapprochement* was reached with the Russian Orthodox Church under Metropolitan Sergei of Novgorod. The Soviet government had gained a measure of international respectability. It had less need of Rome's approval. 'We are conducting and we will conduct a campaign against religious prejudices', Lenin's successor, Josif Stalin, a former Georgian Orthodox seminarian, reaffirmed the same year.

> The legislation of our country allows each citizen to practise any religion whatsoever. This is a matter of conscience for each individual. It is exactly for this reason that we have realized the separation of the Church and the State. But by realizing this separation and by proclaiming the liberty of worship, we have nevertheless maintained for each citizen the right to fight by way of persuasion, propaganda or agitation against this or that religion, or against all religion. The Party cannot be neutral in relation to religion; it conducts a campaign against all religious prejudices, since it is in favour of science.[31]

In April 1929, this 'campaign' became a full-scale offensive again, when all religious instruction was banned by decree, unleashing a violent programme of atheization. The following February, faced with incontrovertible evidence that savage persecution was again occurring, Pius XI denounced the 'horrible, sacrilegious outrages' in an open letter. A Mass of expiation in St Peter's a month later was attended by 50,000, but boycotted by diplomats from countries enjoying relations with the Soviet Union.[32]

In 1931 the Pope declared that

Communism teaches and pursues a twofold aim: merciless class warfare, and complete abolition of private property. This it does, not through secret, hidden methods, but openly, publicly and by every means, even the most violent. To obtain these ends, communists shrink from nothing and fear nothing; and when they have acquired power, it is monstrous beyond belief how cruel and inhuman they show themselves to be.[33]

Moscow's propaganda channels responded with open abuse, accusing the Vatican of plotting against Moscow with a coterie of Mensheviks, Western bankers and White Russian army remnants. 'The motive force behind any anti-Soviet crusade will henceforth be the Vatican', the Soviet Foreign Minister, Maxim Litvinov, announced in Geneva.[34] 'We hate Christianity and the Christians. Even the best amongst them must be considered our worst enemies', was the verdict of the Soviet commissar of public education, Anatoli Lunacharski.[35]

The effects of Soviet persecution were felt most clearly by the Russian Orthodox Church. Before 1917, the Church had boasted 54,000 parishes, 50,000 schools, 1,000 monasteries and 40 seminaries. By the late 1930s, it had lost roughly two-thirds. At least 45,000 churches had been left in ruins, 200,000 priests, monks and nuns executed, and half a million more imprisoned or deported, in the greatest persecution in Christian history.[36] Most of the 614 Catholic churches registered on Soviet territory in the early 1920s had been closed as well. Any earlier notion that the Catholic Church might somehow benefit from the Bolshevik revolution had been exposed as a fantasy.

By now, the Vatican had evidence from other countries too of what awaited the Church once hostile socialist or communist regimes came to power. In France, a 'Separation Law' in 1905 had been followed by socialist governments under Émile Combes and Édouard Herriot, both committed to rigorous anti-clerical policies. In Budapest and Munich, Béla Kun and Kurt Eisner had proclaimed proletarian dictatorships in 1919, while in neighbouring Austria, guided by Otto Bauer's 'Red Vienna', the Church was reputedly losing 30,000 members a year to new socialist and Marxist organizations.

The flirtation with revolutionary rule proved temporary. In Hungary, Kun's 'Republic of Councils' was displaced by Admiral Horthy's dictatorship, while in Austria the Church-backed governments of Ignaz Seipel and Engelbert Dollfuss kept socialist parties out of central government for more than a decade. Meanwhile, anti-Church measures were soon relaxed under popular pressure in France and working relations restored with the Vatican.[37]

But that still left Russia, now joined in what was dubbed the *terribile triangolo* by Mexico and Spain. In Mexico, the revolutionary movement turned violent in 1926, when a socialist president, Plutarcho Calles, attempted to implement the country's anti-clerical Queretaro Laws of 1917 by expelling Spanish priests and closing Catholic schools and convents. Calles's aim was to curb the Church's land ownership, as well as restricting American economic influences. The Queretaro legislation was modelled on the 1905 French Separation Law, although it was claimed that Calles had also commissioned a study of the Soviet Union's penal legislation as a model. But within a year, 40,000 Cristero rebels took up arms in western Mexico, with the apparent support of local Church leaders. Atrocities were committed by both sides.

Pius XI circulated a record of anti-Church measures to foreign governments, citing evidence that priests had been turned into 'outlaws and criminals', and endorsing the right of Catholics to armed resistance.[38] An even more comprehensive condemnation followed in the March 1927 encyclical *Nos es muy conocida*. But most European governments looked the other way.

In Spain, a republic was declared in April 1931 after the abdication of King Alfonso XIII. The Church was declared a public corporation. Its privileges were abolished, schools secularized and religious processions banned. 'With these measures', the socialist premier, Manuel Azaña y Díaz, told Parliament, 'Spain ceases to be Catholic.'[39]

The measures were followed by anarchist attacks on Church property around the country, as well as efforts to eradicate Christian cultural influences. The result, from July 1936, was a full-scale civil war, in which thousands of priests, monks and nuns were slaughtered. Events in Mexico and Spain were a stark reminder of the fragility of the social order, and the Church's vulnerability to mass popular uprisings driven or manipulated by socialist and communist agitators. The spectre of violence was not confined to Russia: it had appeared right in the heart of Europe.

It would be argued later that Pius XI was too obsessed with the dangers of communism, and failed to make necessary distinctions between violent revolutionary groups and parliamentary socialist movements like the British Labour Party which were committed to peaceful, legal methods. Because of this, the argument runs, the Pope neglected to support a tactical alliance between Catholics and moderate socialists which might have succeeded in holding back the rise of Nazism and Fascism.

Certainly, there were precedents to hand for this kind of tactical co-operation. Germany's Catholic Centre Party had achieved a good showing in every election since 1871, and had voted with socialists in the late nineteenth century against laws restricting left-wing organizations which were also thought to pose a threat to centrist parties. The Italian Popular Party, formed in November 1918 under Don Luigi Sturzo, had also worked for an understanding with socialists and left-wing trade unions after the rise of Mussolini.

Meanwhile, the Pope had made it clear he had no objection to necessary social and economic reforms, and would condemn no doctrines which maintained basic Christian values. In Spain, he condemned anti-Church measures in *Dilectissima nobis* (1933). But he did not denounce the Spanish Republic, and even gave the impression of favouring a moderate Catholic republicanism against Spanish Church objections. General Franco styled himself 'El Generalisimo Cristianisimo de la Santa Cruzada'. But his requests for the Pope to bless his 'crusade' were repeatedly ignored. 'The Church is never bound to one form of government more than to another, provided the Divine rights of God and human consciences are safe', Pius XI noted in the encyclical.

> She does not find difficulty adapting herself to various civil institutions, be they monarchies or republics, aristocratic or democratic. Evident proof of this lies in the numerous Concordats and agreements concluded in recent years, and in the diplomatic relations the Holy See has established with different states since the Great War.[40]

Yet the criticism tends to ignore contemporary conditions. Even allowing for the British exception, most European socialist parties were still anti-clerical and Marxist in orientation in the 1930s. In France, a group of Catholic thinkers associated with the journal *L'Esprit* were attempting to find common ground between Christianity and the demands of social emancipation—a point of departure for the emerging philosophical school of Personalism. But although Emmanuel Mounier and colleagues had forged links with socialists and communists, their work found little if any reflection in the attitudes of Church leaders.

The Vatican still persisted in seeing socialism as no more than a tempered version of communism. And its fear of communism was founded on empirical evidence. As Archbishop Achille Ratti, Pius XI had been the Vatican's Nuncio in Warsaw when the Red Army's attempt to strike westwards was turned back in 1920. Had it succeeded, the Bolsheviks would almost certainly have continued into war-weakened Germany. On becoming Pope, Pius XI had sent his future successor, Archbishop Eugenio Pacelli, to

15

represent him in Munich and Berlin, where he took charge of negotiations with Moscow. He was a man who knew what it was like to be under direct threat from communist expansionism—at a time when corresponding threats from Fascism and Nazism were only just becoming apparent.

Nine months after Ratti became Pope, the Italian Fascists took power under Mussolini, and began constructing a new type of state. It was a one-party system, combining emotional nationalism and social collectivism. But it also departed from previous totalitarian models by attempting to accommodate the Catholic Church, to which most Italians belonged. The 1929 Lateran Treaty and Concordat finally settled the 'Roman Question' which had hung over the Papacy's head for 60 years. It also restored the Vatican's status as an independent territory, and proclaimed Catholicism the 'sole religion of the Italian State'.[41] Later events would show that the Fascist opening to the Church had been a subterfuge. But it seemed, at the time, much more than could be expected in Soviet Russia, now facing the terror of mass purges, or in socialist-ruled Mexico and Spain.

In Germany, likewise, Hitler's National Socialist Workers Party assumed power in January 1933, proclaiming an ideology which mixed socialist and Fascist elements with racist, neo-pagan innovations. But Hitler was aware of the failure of Bismarck's *Kulturkampf* 60 years earlier and reacted cautiously towards the Catholic Church. His July 1933 Concordat with the Vatican presaged the dissolution of the Catholic Centre Party and all non-Nazi political formations. But it promised the Church important concessions. Although it was widely suspected that these promises would not be kept, there was still room for hoping Nazi policies would be modified to maintain internal unity against the Soviet threat from the east.

In the early 1930s, in short, Pius XI could have been forgiven for thinking Church and humanity had more to fear from communism and socialism than from Fascism and Nazism. He could foresee the weakness of the Western world in the face of new radical movements of both Left and Right. But the key priority, he believed, was to defend the Church and Christianity against tactical fudges which might weaken their identity or spread confusion. This meant doing everything possible to maintain the Church's position. But the emphasis would be on internal Catholic consciences, rather than on external political action. All of this helps explain why, when a new encyclical appeared in May 1931, the fortieth anniversary of *Rerum novarum*, it forcefully reiterated the Church's earlier warnings against any purported alliance with socialists. *Quadragesimo anno* showed the Vatican had come a long way from the conspiracy theories of Pius IX and Leo XIII. In the era of the Great Depression, the Pope was aware of the drastic economic and social hardships on which extremes were feeding. They were, he believed, the ultimate consequence of the 'idols' of liberalism about which his predecessors had warned since the mid-nineteenth century.

> Free competition has destroyed itself; economic domination has taken the place of the open market. Unbridled ambition for domination has succeeded the desire for gain; the whole economic regime has become hard, cruel and relentless in ghastly measure.[42]

Pius XI knew—it was painfully obvious—that Catholic social reformers had failed to find a convincing answer to poverty and exploitation. He also knew that exhortations to charity would not be enough to meet the 'urgent necessity of uniting forces to combat the massed ranks of revolutionaries'. Finally, he was conscious that socialism had undergone a division over the previous half-century—between communism of the Soviet kind, and the social democracy common in Western Europe, which had renounced violent class warfare and no longer condemned private property. Many Catholics saw possibilities of co-operating with the second, believing a 'reformed socialism' was compatible with Christian principles.

> It would seem as if socialism were afraid of its own principles and of the conclusions drawn from them by communists, and were tending in consequence towards the truth which Christian tradition has always held in respect; for it cannot be denied that its opinions sometimes closely approach the just demands of Christian social reformers ... If these changes continue, it may well come about that these tenets of mitigated socialism will no longer be different from the programme of those who seek to reform society according to Christian principles.[43]

Yet if these Catholics now hoped for some kind of papal endorsement, *Quadragesimo anno* disappointed them. Pius XI acknowledged a distinction between socialism and communism. But all forms of socialism, democratic or not, the Pope emphasized, denied the supernatural destiny of men and women, subordinated the individual to the collectivity, and were based on the same materialist conception of the world as communism.

> If, like all errors, socialism contains a certain element of truth (and this the Sovereign Pontiffs have never denied), it is nevertheless founded upon a doctrine of human society peculiarly its own, which is opposed to true Christianity. Religious socialism, Christian socialism, are expressions implying a contradiction in terms. No one can be at the same time a sincere Catholic and a socialist properly so called.[44]

At the same time, the encyclical's emphasis should be noted carefully. Pius XI was writing against a different background from Leo XIII. But he saw an obvious continuity in the social and economic conditions which confronted the Church then and now. On the one side, the 'growing division of the population into two classes' had unleashed a yearning for socialist solutions which would expose society to 'still graver dangers'. On the other, liberal dogmas had prevented 'effective interference' by governments, generated 'dangerous individualist ideas', and shown their 'utter impotence' to find a solution to social problems.

This was why the Church's intervention was needed. The Pope urged lapsed Catholics who had teamed up with socialists to rejoin the Church. When it came to cause and effect, the Church was quite clear. 'Cultural socialism'—the kind of socialism being instilled into the minds of unsuspecting citizens through educational initiatives—pointed towards Bolshevism. But its 'parent' was liberalism. The Church regretted the 'indolent apathy' of governments who allowed the propagation of socialist doctrines. But it condemned *even more severely* the foolhardiness of those who neglect to remove or modify such conditions as exasperate the hearts of the people, and so prepare the way for the overthrow and ruin of the social order'.[45]

So much for the prognosis: what could Pius XI suggest by way of a cure? The Pope offered what he thought was the blueprint for a harmonious society—a 'community of communities' which depended on neither liberalism nor socialism. Its instruments would include a living wage and improved work conditions. Its pillars would be voluntary associations, vocational groups and 'committed young men', all interacting in the cause of social reconstruction according to the principle of subsidiarity, which barred higher bodies from usurping functions properly performed by lower ones. The Pope spoke vaguely of 'social justice' too. But despite his earlier disclaimer, he stressed that its 'soul' must be 'social charity' and a sense of common good.

Quadragesimo anno was, in short, a missed opportunity. It correctly recognized that socialism and communism were misguided reactions to the abuses of modern liberal capitalism, and that they would go on exerting an appeal until these abuses had been neutralized. But its dreamy, paternalistic vision underestimated the radical forces which were seizing the initiative by the 1930s. Its concluding exhortation to Christians—'lay aside internal quarrels, link up harmoniously into a single battle-line, and strike with united forces towards the common aim'—could hardly compete with the militaristic rhetoric coming out of Berlin and Rome, whose attractiveness was felt by Church members too. The Pope had again condemned socialism and communism. But he had failed to offer counter-arguments capable of convincing a sceptical world.

Perhaps Pius XI realized this, but concluded that it was already too late, and that the Church's only realistic option was to guard its doctrine and stand firm. In any event, the coming half-decade was to call in question the supposition that Fascism and Nazism posed fewer direct dangers than communism and socialism.

Barely a month and a half after *Quadragesimo anno*'s appearance, the Pope addressed a new encyclical to the Church in his native Italy. *Non abbiamo bisogno* recognized that the 1929 Lateran Treaty and Concordat had legitimized Mussolini's Fascist state. The guarantees given to the Church on paper had been chipped away in practice. Catholic schools and organizations, including the Popular Party and Catholic Action, were being closed and intimidated.

The encyclical blamed 'masonry and liberalism' for the rise of anti-clericalism in Italy. But it also roundly condemned the 'pagan worship of the State', as well as the Fascist regime's brutality, and the 'inventions, falsehoods and calumnies' diffused by its press.[46]

It was to take six more years for a corresponding papal condemnation of events in Germany. The 1933 Concordat extended earlier Vatican treaties with the *Länder* of Bavaria, Prussia and Baden, and contained guarantees for the Church. But Catholic objections to the Nazis' sterilization law and racist programme had been registered before the year was out by Cardinal Michael Faulhaber of Munich. An open campaign against the Catholic Church soon dispelled any illusions Pius XI might have had about Nazi intentions.

Germany's Catholic bishops faced a dilemma, even so. Hitler's regime saw the Church's role as being to underwrite Nazi foreign policy by highlighting the communist threat. And in August 1936, meeting in Fulda, the bishops duly obliged with a pastoral letter endorsing the Führer's claim to be saving Europe from Soviet expansionism. Once Germany had regained its strength, they added, 'a Europe cleansed from Bolshevism and the entire rescued civilized world will be thankful to us'.[47]

A second letter, read in churches in January 1937, warned that the Soviet Union had begun its advance on Europe. 'The Führer and Chancellor of the Reich, Adolf Hitler, has sighted the advance of Bolshevism from afar, and his thoughts and aspirations aim at averting the horrible danger to our German people and the entire West', the pastoral added. 'The German bishops consider it their duty to support the head of the German Reich by all means at the Church's disposal.'[48]

The Vatican did not share this view of events. In September 1936, *L'Osservatore Romano* had warned that historic international enmities were being exacerbated by a 'war of ideologies' between 'autocracy and communism'. However, it had identified 'racial intolerance' as a second destabilizing factor, calling it the 'powder keg of Europe'. 'War on the

Catholic Church is a war in alliance with communism', the Pope warned Hitler the same month. Cardinal Pacelli, now Secretary of State, had also spoken of 'the need to combat paganism, whether in the form of international Bolshevism or nationalist-religious movements'.[49]

In March 1937, Pius XI followed this up with *Mit brennender Sorge*, reaffirming the teachings of Christianity against the corruptions of Nazi ideology. The encyclical, distributed secretly to Catholic churches throughout Germany, was written in a mood of resignation, as if already anticipating some inevitable cataclysm. The Church's moderate attitude to the Nazi regime, the Pope insisted, had not been guided by expediency or weakness—but by a determination 'not to deny definitely the loyalty of others to their pledged word, before the iron language of facts had torn away the veil which by deliberate camouflage covered and still covers the attack on the Church'.[50]

Yet it was evident, even then, that the Vatican still saw communism as a greater menace. *Non abbiamo bisogno* and *Mit brennender Sorge* had vigorously denounced the practices of the Fascist and Nazi regimes. They had also condemned aspects of their respective doctrines, such as the 'statolatry' of Fascism, and Nazism's 'idolatrous cult' of a 'national God'. But neither encyclical had attempted to dissect and denounce them as ideologies. Just as crucially, both had concluded with the hope that the Fascist and Nazi regimes were reformable. 'We did not conclude that they were the expression of a programme properly so called', Pius XI said of Mussolini's policies.

> We have not said we wished to condemn the party as such. Our aim has been to point out and condemn all those things in its programme and activities which have been found contrary to Catholic doctrine and Catholic practice, and therefore irreconcilable with the Catholic name and profession.

Even in the case of the Nazis, the Pope prayed that those who had 'erred' would be granted 'an hour of enlightenment like that given to Saul on the way to Damascus'.[51]

This had never been said of communists. Whereas Fascism and Nazism were viewed as temporary fits of madness, luckily confined (for now) to Italy and Germany, communism was, by contrast, a fixed ideological system which could neither be moderated nor restrained. Modern socialist variants, as the Pope had acknowledged in 1931, might show themselves open to democratic practices. But communism was inherently aggressive and had a long record of atrocities.

This was the essential message contained in *Divini Redemptoris*, issued in March 1937 just five days after the encyclical on Germany. Pius XI was an old man by now. A year had passed since the Soviet Union's new Stalinist constitution promised 'freedom of worship' alongside 'freedom of anti-religious propaganda'—a 'trifling change', the Pope noted, which gave the superior rights of atheists constitutional legitimacy. It was time to go beyond familiar reassertions of Church teaching to a more comprehensive exposé of communism's fallacies. This was what *Divini Redemptoris* was intended to provide for the first time.

The 'revolution of our own time', Pius noted, was 'now either already raging or else frowning its menace in nearly every part of the world, exceeding in violence and magnitude any persecution which the Church has ever sustained, and threatening to reduce whole nations to a state of barbarism'.[52] The Vatican, of all the world's authorities, had been most insistent in its condemnations. This was why the Church was a communist target: the sovereign reality of God offered an 'utter and complete refutation' of communist theories.

> Communism is intrinsically evil, and therefore no one who desires to save Christian civilization from extinction should render it assistance in any enterprise whatsoever. Those who allow themselves to be duped and who connive at the establishment of communism in their own countries will be the first to pay the penalty.[53]

Despite everything, Pius XI predicted that communism would fail. It was already falling short, he said, of its 'lavish promises' in Russia, where much of society had been reduced to slavery under a 'criminal and terror-ridden conspiracy'.[54] Yet he was well aware of communism's attractiveness, particularly among European intellectuals, some of whom—H. G. Wells, George Bernard Shaw, André Gide and others—had visited Moscow on stage-managed tours and allowed themselves to be used as Stalin's propaganda tools. Pius XI knew communism offered a 'pseudo-ideal of justice, equality and brotherhood', and a 'counterfeit mysticism' which thrived in the current climate of exploitation and poverty. It promised to remedy the abuses of 'economic liberalism', resolve social conflicts and bring peace. In the world of the 1930s, the Pope recognized, these were 'legitimate objectives'. Communists claimed to have improved economic conditions—although this had more to do with forced labour than with any genius in communist planning. Their doctrine advocated class warfare, a 'godless human society'. But it worked through 'skilful agitators' and a 'diabolically efficient system of propaganda, probably unparalleled in history'.

Thanks to this, *Divini Redemptoris* acknowledged, there was also no shortage of Catholics among the ranks of what Lenin had called 'useful idiots'. Communists had concealed their real intentions by posing as champions of peace, and by proposing schemes and programmes seemingly in accordance with Church teachings. They had infiltrated Catholic organizations and made bogus promises of religious freedom.

> Like every other error, communism contains some element of truth, and its adherents make adroit play with this in order on occasion to disguise the repulsive cruelty which is intrinsic to the doctrine and its methods. They thus succeed in duping persons of more than ordinary integrity, these in their turn becoming apostles of error and instilling it in the minds of others.[55]

The Pope made it clear that the Church condemned communism not only because it was anti-Christian. It was, he stressed, 'a doctrine full of error and sophistry, contrary to revelation and reason alike', which destroyed the foundations of civil society, and refused to acknowledge the true origin, nature and purpose of the State. But he still believed, like his predecessors, that it was the 'policies of economic liberalism', elevating selfish interests over community loyalties, which had caused communism's rise in the first place. There could be no hope of saving society unless the economic and social order was inspired by Christian charity.

Yet the Pope also acknowledged that this charity needed 'translating into action'. And here *Divini Redemptoris* was at its weakest. It urged priests to be active in industrial areas, called on organizations like Catholic Action to step up their efforts for the poor, and appealed to the State to ensure that property owners show greater responsibility. It also defended the principles of social justice, defining them as 'arrangements enabling every single member of society to receive all it needs to fulfil its own functions' in line with the common good.[56]

Finally, in a flourish of rhetoric, the encyclical called on every social class to take part in the Church's 'mission to repel the attacks of communism', and committed the Church's campaign against communism's 'monstrous and hateful blasphemies' to the protection of St Joseph the Worker.[57]

Yet all of this represented little more than a rekindling of the same paternalistic Christian tradition. Like his predecessors, the Pope was looking for the best means of upholding what he saw as a divinely ordained social order. Urgent social and economic reforms were needed to curb abuses and injustices—a fact acknowledged since the nineteenth century. But when it came to practical insights, the same fear of radical change predominated.

The Church had rejected communism and socialism because neither offered the right answer to contemporary problems. But the Church, for its own part, had not yet found the right medium for supporting just and authentic human demands. Those who recognized and accepted these temporal demands—but who also rejected communism and socialism—had no clear and convincing concepts to describe what was really needed. That had been the main shortcoming in Catholic social teaching from Leo XIII onwards. The Church lacked master-notions capable of holding the imagination of wavering multitudes. The fault line between radical reformism and paternalistic Christian ethics remained as wide as ever.

In the late 1930s, the Vatican failed to recognize that, with or without communism, a century's social and political emancipation had generated unstoppable demands which could only be met by a comprehensive rethinking of the Church's attitude to contemporary disorders, and of Christianity's response to current philosophical and ideological challenges. This failure had characterized the Vatican's most comprehensive statement on communism to date. It was the mentality with which the Church approached the cataclysm of 1939.

Notes

1. Pius VI, *Diu satis* (15 May 1800), nos 14, 16, 25.
2. Pius IX, *Qui pluribus* (9 November 1846); in *Acta Pii IX*, vol. I, p. 13.
3. Statement from the first paragraph of *The Communist Manifesto*, published in February 1848; Friedrich Heer, *Europe, Mother of Revolutions* (New York: Praeger 1972), pp. 110–43.
4. Pius IX, *Nostis et nobiscum* (8 December 1849), nos 18, 25.
5. Sidney Z. Ehler and John B. Morrall (eds), *Church and State Through the Ages* (London: Burns and Oates, 1954), pp. 281–5.
6. Quoted in Henri Daniel-Rops, *L'Église des Révolutions: Un combat pour Dieu* (Paris: Fayard, 1964), p. 83.
7. William Purdy, *The Church on the Move* (London: Hollis and Carter, 1966), p. 88; Klaus Schatz, *Vaticanum I 1869–1870*, Band III: *Unfehlbarkeitsdiskussion und Rezeption* (Paderborn: Ferdinand Schoningh, 1994), pp. 207–96.
8. Leo XIII, *Quod apostolici muneris* (28 December 1878), nos 4, 6–7, 9–10.
9. Leo XIII, *Immortale Dei* (1 November 1885); in Ehler and Morrall, op. cit., p. 303. The Pope also condemned Naturalism and Rationalism.
10. Leo XIII, *Rerum novarum* (15 May 1891), no. 2.
11. Ibid., nos 15, 27.
12. Daniel-Rops, op. cit., p. 149.
13. Paul Misner, *Social Catholicism in Europe: From the Onset of Industrialisation to the First World War* (London: Darton, Longman and Todd, 1991), p. 218.
14. Quoted in Bill McSweeney, *Roman Catholicism: The Search for Relevance* (Oxford: Basil Blackwell, 1980), p. 61.
15. To a workers' pilgrimage, October 1889; ibid., p. 77.
16. Leo XIII, *Graves de communi* (18 January 1901). See Daniel-Rops, op. cit., p. 126.
17. Quoted in McSweeney, op. cit., p. 83. See also François Houtart and André Rousseau, *L'Église face aux luttes révolutionnaires* (Paris: Editions Ouvrières,

1972).

18. Sandor Agocs, *The Troubled Origins of the Catholic Labour Movement, 1878–1914* (Detroit: Wayne State University Press, 1988), pp. 126–31. See also John M. Molony, *The Emergence of Political Catholicism in Italy* (London: Croom Helm, 1977); Pino Guiliana, *Mario Sturzo: vescovo uomo di Dio* (Rome: Edizione Oreb, 1993).

19. Quoted in McSweeney, op. cit., p. 84.

20. See, for example, Leon Tretjakewitsch, 'Bishop Michel d'Herbigny SJ and Russia', *Das Ostliche Christentum*, vol. 39 (Wurzburg: Augustinus-Verlag, 1990), showing misguided Vatican notions; and Antoine Wenger, *Rome et Moscou 1900–1950* (Paris: Desclée de Brouwer, 1987).

21. V. I. Lenin, 'The attitude of the Workers Party to religion', *Collected Works*, vol. 15 (Moscow, 1972), pp. 405–10. Also Arto Luukkanen, *The Party of Unbelief: The Religious Policy of the Bolshevik Party 1917–1929* (Helsinki: Studia Historica, 1994), pp. 193–5.

22. Hansjakob Stehle, *Eastern Politics of the Vatican 1917–1979* (London: Ohio University Press, 1981), pp. 11–33; Józef Mackiewicz, *W Cieniu Krzyża* (London: Kontra, 1972), pp. 3–32.

23. Dragan R. Zivojinovic, 'The Vatican, Woodrow Wilson and the dissolution of the Habsburg monarchy 1914–1918', *East European Quarterly*, vol. III, no. 1 (March 1969), pp. 31–70; Anthony Rhodes, *The Power of Rome in the Twentieth Century* (London: Sidgwick and Jackson, 1983), pp. 239–48.

24. Mackiewicz, op. cit., p. 27; Charles E. Timberlake (ed.), *Religious and Secular Forces in Late Tsarist Russia* (Seattle: University of Washington Press, 1992).

25. Ibid., pp. 27–8. Claims that the nineteenth-century Popes resisted Poland's demands for independence also partly derived from Tsarist propaganda.

26. Mackiewicz, op. cit. See also Sergio Trasatti, *La Croce e la Stella: La Chiesa e i regimi comunisti in Europa dal 1917 a oggi* (Milan: Mondadori, 1993), pp. 9–87; Johann Kraus, *Im Auftrag des Papstes in Russland* (Siegburg: Steyler, 1970); Angelo Tamborra, *Chiesa Cattolica e Ortodossia Russa: due secoli di confronto e di dialogo* (Milan: Edizioni Paoline, 1992).

27. In Anthony Rhodes, *The Vatican in the Age of the Dictators* (London: Hodder & Stoughton, 1973), p. 133. See also Chicherin's cynical remarks, in Trasatti, op. cit., p. 24.

28. *Political History of Russia*, vol. 4, no. 1 (New York: Nova Publishers), pp. 6–9; Boleslaw Szczesniak (ed.), *The Russian Revolution and Religion: Documents Concerning the Suppression of Religion by the Communists 1917–1925* (Notre Dame, IN: University of Notre Dame Press, 1959).

29. From German dispatches, in Rhodes, op. cit., p. 135. See also Stehle, op. cit., pp. 34–42.

30. Rhodes, op. cit.

31. Josif Stalin, *Collected Works*, vol. 10; Christel Lane, *Christian Religion in the Soviet Union: A Sociological Study* (London: Allen and Unwin, 1978), pp. 27ff.

32. The text of the Pope's letter was published in *L'Osservatore Romano* (9 February 1930). See also Stehle, op. cit., pp. 133–7.

33. Pius XI, *Quadragesimo anno* (15 May 1931), no. (a) 112.
34. Rhodes, op. cit., p. 140.
35. From Lunacharski's 'New Anti-Religious Manual' (1933); C. Read, *Religion, Revolution and the Russian Intelligentsia* (London: Macmillan, 1979).
36. Figures from the Russian Presidential Commission on the Rehabilitation of Victims of Political Repression; *The Tablet* (23–30 December 1996).
37. The same pattern was evident elsewhere. See Jonathan Luxmoore and Jolanta Babiuch, 'Truth prevails: the Catholic contribution to Czech thought and culture', *Religion, State and Society,* vol. 20, no. 1 (1992); Helmut Gruber, *Red Vienna: Experiment in Working Class Culture 1919–1934* (New York: Oxford University Press, 1991).
38. Pius XI, *Nos es muy conocida* (28 March 1927), nos 26–27.
39. Rhodes, op. cit., p. 116.
40. *Dilectissima nobis* (3 June 1933), no. 4.
41. Full text (Articles 1 and 2 of the Lateran Treaty) in Ehler and Morrall, op. cit., p. 386.
42. Pius XI, *Quadragesimo anno* (15 May 1931), no. 109.
43. Ibid., no. (b) 113, 114.
44. Ibid., no. 120.
45. Ibid., no. (a) 112, 122.
46. Pius XI, *Non abbiamo bisogno* (29 June 1931); in Ehler and Morrall, op. cit., pp. 464, 475, 480.
47. Guenter Lewy, *The Catholic Church and the Third Reich* (London: Weidenfeld and Nicolson, 1964), p. 206. See also Peter C. Kent, 'A tale of two Popes: Pius XI, Pius XII and the Rome–Berlin Axis', *Journal of Contemporary History*, vol. 23 (1988), pp. 593–4.
48. Lewy, op. cit., pp. 209–10.
49. Kent, op. cit., p. 594.
50. Pius XI, *Mit brennender Sorge* (14 March 1937), no. 7.
51. Ibid., para. 51; *Non abbiamo bisogno*, in Ehler and Morrall, op. cit., pp. 479–80.
52. Pius XI, *Divini Redemptoris* (19 March 1937), no. 2.
53. Ibid., no. 82.
54. Ibid., no. 34.
55. Ibid., no. 24.
56. Ibid., nos 71, 61–67.
57. Ibid., paras 100, 108, 112.

2

❦❦❦❦

In the eye of the post-war storm

It is summer 1945. Much of Eastern Europe lies in ruins. Stalin's Red Army has bulldozered its way to Berlin in pursuit of the fleeing Wehrmacht. Poland's once-vibrant capital, Warsaw, has been reduced to a heap of rubble. The roads are clogged with refugees, demobbed soldiers, returning prisoners and forced labourers. As remnants of Poland's wartime underground Armia Krajowa go to ground, the Soviet-controlled paramilitary police begin rounding up potential opponents. The Nazi concentration camp at Majdanek has been reopened—this time for 'enemies of the people'—and forms part of a huge network of communist-run detention centres. With Poland's borders shunted 200 miles westwards by an East–West agreement, stranded German civilians are being slaughtered *en masse*, while Ukrainians, Lithuanians and Byelorussians are herded east to seal the redrawn Polish–Soviet border.

Further south, Russian Cossacks and Yugoslav royalists are being forcibly repatriated by the Allies to the Soviet Union and Yugoslavia. Tito's communist Partisans are withdrawing from north-eastern Italy under Stalin's orders. But the Soviet Union has grabbed defeated Romania's northern Bessarabia province. Romania and Slovakia are expelling ethnic Hungarians, the Czech Republic expelling Sudeten Germans.

In Poland, it is widely known that rows erupted over the Yalta Conference that February. The London-based government-in-exile has complained to Churchill and Roosevelt about the talk of 'spheres of influence'. Five years of German occupation have cost Poland a third of its wealth and a fifth of its population. Some kind of division is clearly opening up in the centre of Europe. The East's war-scarred inhabitants look set to become its first victims.

Yet terror and helplessness are by no means the only prevalent emotions this summer. There is also a sense of guilt—not least over the disappearance of Poland's 3 million Jews, a crime devised and conducted by Germans, but perpetrated on Polish territory. There is a feeling of new energy too, replete with dreams and illusions, a sense that the savagery of war has purified the world, pointing to a new order of peace and justice.

It was against this background that a 25-year-old Roman Catholic theology student had been called in to help rebuild his local seminary in the southern city of Kraków. Born on 18 May 1920, three months before Marshal Piłsudski's Polish Legions drove the Red Army from the gates of Warsaw at the 'Miracle on the Vistula', Karol Wojtyła had sensed his priestly vocation late.

Wadowice was a town of 10,000, nestling in the Carpathian foothills a few dozen kilometres south-west of Kraków. Most local families, Karol's included, were descended from peasant stock. But Wadowice had enterprising young inhabitants and could not be called provincial. Karol's father was a military administrator, holding the rank of lieutenant, and was known to neighbours as a silent, self-disciplined man with few social contacts. As for Emilia, his mother, Karol would remember her suffering from constant infirmities, often travelling away from home for medical treatment, always in need of rest.[1] Emilia's early death on 13 April 1929 robbed Karol of a traditional Polish family upbringing, in which inculcating religion, education and culture were overwhelmingly a mother's responsibility. It also deprived him of the commanding authority of a typical Polish father, since Karol senior was left to perform a woman's duties, right down to the cooking and sewing. Socially and culturally, this gave Karol a kind of autonomy, and forced him to learn the arts of judgement, self-reliance and discernment by himself.

In December 1932, Karol's only brother, Edmund, who was 14 years older, died of scarlet fever in Bielsko hospital. He had contracted the disease from a patient just weeks after starting his career as a doctor. By then, contemporaries were noticing Karol's religiousness. He attended church daily, prayed between school classes, and paid frequent visits to Kalwaria Zebrzydowska, a local centre of popular spirituality. He had also encountered the authoritarian Catholicism strong in towns like Wadowice, which had helped preserve the national identity even in the relatively mild conditions of Poland's pre-1918 Austrian Partition. By the age of 15, Karol was an active member of the conservative Sodalicja Mariańska, a school association with ties to Roman Dmowski's nationalist Endecja party. He was also performing works in the school's theatre group by Mickiewicz, Słowacki and Krasiński, Poland's great nineteenth-century Romantic poets.

Wadowice was a meeting place for political and ideological movements

27

besides Endecja. Some families supported the Ludowa Lewica, or 'Peasant Left', of Wincenty Witos. Some were socialists, inspired by Józef Putka, an activist from nearby Chocznia, who held meetings to canvass support for Poland's Socialist Party, the PPS.

The town also had a strong, industrious Jewish minority comprising a third of its population. Karol had at least three close Jewish friends, as well as Jewish teachers and a Jewish landlord. But if he was ever tempted by the anti-Semitism widespread in social circles like his, Karol never revealed it. His thinking had been shaped in a conservative Catholic environment. It was to be exposed to radical alternatives when he moved to Kraków with his father in September 1938 and enrolled at the Jagiellonian University.

The philosophy faculty course which Karol signed on for was known as *Polonistyka*, and was usually chosen by poorer students lacking science and language skills (most of whom went on to become teachers), or by those believing they possessed literary potential. With around 250,000 inhabitants, Kraków had sent deputies to the Vienna Parliament under the Austrian partition. So it had experience of democracy, and fewer advocates of violent revolution than Warsaw and the cities of western Poland.

But in 1938 the atmosphere at the Jagiellonian was fraught with anxiety. Since the mid-1930s, many students had concluded that they faced a choice between Soviet-style communism and Fascist-style nationalism. Everything in between—from socialist to liberal—was liable to be attacked as lacking in vision. All students were aware of the growing conflict between political ideas and values. At this tense juncture in Polish history, it was shaping identities and outlooks.

Karol quickly came into contact with supporters of the right-wing Endecja and its more extreme offshoot, the Falanga, with its proclaimed aim of destroying communism 'with the power of ideas and fists' and of enshrining a 'Polish Catholic totality'. Marshal Piłsudski had curbed the power of the Polish Right after his May Coup twelve years before. The action had alienated right-wing groups, making them enemies of the Sanacja regime which retained power after Piłsudski's death.

But among Kraków students, the Left was predominant. In addition to the communists, groups like the Independent Socialist Youth were also listed on police files. But although this meant they had more passive sympathizers than declared members, the Left had successfully tapped into the mood of disaffection which was particularly marked among students of the humanities.

Karol attended the seminars of Kazimierz Wyka, a 'progressive' Polish literature historian kept under surveillance by the local Sanacja office, and was present at political discussions which ended in fist-fights with the Falanga. He also had close left-wing friends: Tadeusz Holuj, who survived

Auschwitz and became a Communist Party activist; Stanisław Pigoń, who belonged to the left-wing peasant movement, the PSL; Wojciech Żukowski, who fought with the Armia Krajowa and later served as a Polish press correspondent in China and Vietnam. Some fellow-students even called Wojtyła 'the Socialist'. He was discreet and sparing with his opinions. And the traditional style of his poetry was criticized at readings as out of step with contemporary fashion. But he was regarded as an unconventional character, with progressive, even radical views. The fact that he never wore a tie was viewed as an anti-establishment gesture.[2]

But Wojtyła was finding his own way, and was in touch with right-wing groups as well. The Jagiellonian's student self-help association, Bratniak, had been controlled by the PSL for more than a decade. But in 1937, it was taken over by Endecja, supported by the Sodalicja Mariańska and reputed funds from Kraków's Church leader, Cardinal Adam Sapieha. In late 1938, during his first term, Karol was elected to Bratniak's council.

The mainstream Endecja was not to be confused with the extremist Falanga, which in November 1938 demanded that the university institute 'Days without Jews and Ukrainians'. Falanga confrères in Warsaw, 220 miles north, put up banners over the gates of Piłsudski University denouncing 'Jew-communism' and demanding segregation. This was happening two years after Cardinal August Hlond, Poland's Catholic Primate, had proclaimed in a 1936 pastoral letter that Jews 'represent the avant-garde of the atheist movement, the Bolshevik movement and subversive action'. Hlond had warned that an anti-Jewish stance, 'imported from abroad', would be contrary to Catholic ethics, acknowledging that many Jews were also 'outstanding, noble and upright'.[3] Like other Church leaders, however, he had failed to confront anti-Semitic feeling.

Fellow-students later remembered that Wojtyła disapproved of the anti-Jewish atmosphere. Like Bratniak, the Polonistyka Circle had also been taken over by the Endecja before Karol's arrival. And in 1938–39, members were demanding the expulsion of Jewish students. But Karol hung around with a Jewish student, Anka Weber, to protect her from right-wing thugs. Friends saw the gesture as a sign of opposition to anti-Semitism.[4]

Wojtyła was beginning his second year when the Germans invaded from the west on 1 September 1939, and the Soviet Army from the east 17 days later. In October, Hans Frank established his headquarters at Kraków's historic Wawel Castle, pledging to turn Poland into an 'intellectual desert' cleansed of 'nobles, priests and Jews'. In November, the Jagiellonian's professors were rounded up and herded to concentration camps.

The autumn events destroyed the myth that it was possible to remain on the sidelines, vainly hoping the era of extremes would pass. For Karol, it was also a time for self-questioning—for asking how Poland could have left itself so vulnerable. 'Were we really liberated?' he wrote to his Wadowice friend Mieczysław Kotlarczyk in late 1939, in a letter which berated Poland's failure to live up to Romantic ideals. 'The nation was misled and lied to. Its sons, as during the Partitions, were scattered to the winds around the world. Why? Because they didn't want to waste away in the homeland's prisons.'[5]

The occupation put an abrupt end to Karol's university life. He continued his studies secretly over the next three years—enduring his father's death in February 1941. But he had to have a work document to avoid being press-ganged by the Germans. So he got a job at the Solvay chemical factory in Kraków and the adjoining Zakrowiek quarry. In the meantime, he and Kotlarczyk helped set up an underground acting group, the Rhapsody Theatre, modelled on the 'Drama of the Word' associated with the Romantic writers Norwid and Wyspiański. Cultural and intellectual life was as much part of the national resistance effort as military conspiracies. It was often as dangerous too.

Perhaps it was this which best equipped Wojtyła to withstand the seductions of communist propagandists. His theatre involvement taught him the importance of words and concepts, used in particular circumstances to project the personality and stir the imagination. Meanwhile, his factory and quarry job also taught him something about the world of work.

But the war impressed other things on Karol too. The destruction of Kraków's Jews reached its head on the night of 13–14 May 1943, when 2,000 were killed and 3,000 were sent to the camps of Auschwitz and Płaszow, with none of the spectacular resistance encountered in the Warsaw Ghetto. It revealed, as never before, the destructive potential of power misapplied in the service of fanatical ideologies.

In the end, tossed in all directions by competing ideas and values, Wojtyła chose the Church. He joined Kraków's underground seminary in October 1942, the hardest possible time for answering a vocation. By then, he had seen both the conservative popular Christianity of the countryside and the more liberal Catholic culture of the city. Kraków was a centre for order life and offered higher training standards than other towns. Students and seminarians came to study here from Silesia and eastern Poland, bringing elements of the contrasting Church traditions forged in Poland's Russian and German partitions.

As a devotee of the Romantic poets, Karol would have been aware of the Polish intelligentsia's traditional scorn for the Church's passivity. But like most seminarians from small-town origins, he would have had little knowledge of the unsavoury aspects of Poland's pre-war Church. In his letter to Kotlarczyk in 1939, he had enthused about an 'Athenian Poland, enriched with all the greatness of Christianity'.[6]

Even at the war's end, when the Church had largely redeemed itself, there were many who failed to share Karol's enthusiasm. Communism had been brought to Eastern Europe on the bayonets of Stalin's Red Army. But the communist programme, with its mythological content and primitive metaphysics, encountered positive public responses. Disorientated intellectuals and workers were lured by its promises of security and justice. After the chaos and destruction, the myth that humankind had at last found a blueprint for bringing conflict and division to an end had no shortage of ardent believers.

Poland had lacked a strong communist movement of its own. But many pre-war intellectuals had professed socialist sympathies. And although these reflected little more than a vague desire for a society without poverty and intolerance, it was enough to create an opening for post-war communism. In 1945, most intellectuals looked back at pre-war Poland as a bad memory, characterized by unemployment, nationalism and anti-Semitism. Even when Marxism was vigorously propagated, very few would ever get around to reading *Das Kapital*. But the idea of a Marxist avant-garde, with a mission to lead the nation, chimed in well with Poland's home-grown intelligentsia tradition. The party called itself the Polish Workers' Party (PPR) to avoid associations with the ill-fated pre-war Communist Party, whose leaders had been rounded up and executed by Stalin in 1939. Though built from the top down, it offered rapid advancement to those drawn by the vision of a 'People's Poland' at a time when the mass of the population was excluded and powerless.

The year 1947 saw the new order consolidated. In January, rigged elections gave the PPR and its allies over 80 per cent of the popular vote. In July, collectivization began against earlier promises. In September, the 'Nativist' PPR leader, Władysław Gomułka, was shunted from office and jailed by the 'Muscovite' Bolesław Bierut, heralding full-scale Stalinism. In December, the PPR was merged with the Polish Socialist Party to form the Polish United Workers' Party (PZPR). Many who declared support were simple careerists, who saw opportunities in joining or dangers in not. But many were also persuaded that communism was a political necessity, and that the new regimes should be accepted for the sake of stability in Eastern Europe.

This 'acceptance' of communism was assisted by a silent terror campaign. At the war's end, Poland's AK resistance army, the largest in Europe, had split into at least 50 underground groups, which continued to harass and disrupt the imposition of communist rule. As the communist-controlled Polish Army tightened the noose, many young fighters fled westwards to escape capture. The dirty war was to continue well into the 1950s.

The Red Army liberated Czechoslovakia in early 1945 and withdrew by the year's end, annexing part of Ruthenia to Ukraine as 'rectification'. In May 1946 elections, the Communist Party won 38 per cent in Czech Bohemia and Moravia, and 30 per cent in Slovakia. And on 25 February 1948, led by Klement Gottwald, it seized sole power when Social Democratic ministers resigned from the government. Pro-Communist workers seized public buildings amid a propaganda barrage. When the Foreign Minister Jan Masaryk, the son of the Czechoslovak state's founder, was found dead beneath his office window a week later, it also symbolized the death of Czechoslovak democracy. May elections were said to have given the Communist Party 90 per cent in Bohemia and Moravia, and 86 per cent in Slovakia. By the summer, Stalinist purges were under way.

Yet the imposition of communist rule was not just a story of force and violence. In the inter-war First Republic, Czech intellectuals had acquired radical sympathies. The liberal playwright Karel Čapek had deplored the 'pessimism and dismal hatred being pumped artificially into the working class'. But by the late 1930s, the Czechoslovak Communist Party had become Europe's largest after that of France, as disaffection was spurred on by the 1938 Munich débâcle and collapse of liberal values.[7] Most Czech intellectuals, buoyed by the Marxist challenge not to interpret the world but change it, supported the 1948 takeover.

The Red Army reached Budapest in February 1945, after over-running the devastated Hungarian countryside. By the end of March, a land reform decree had allowed over 600,000 landless peasant families to benefit from the first phase of redistribution. Here too, with communists forming a minority in a provisional Independence Front government, many hoped for far-reaching changes. November 1945 elections, organized by the Allied Control Commission, gave the conservative Independent Smallholders Party 58 per cent—far ahead of the Communists, who scored 17 per cent. The Communists held only four ministries in a new coalition government. But their 'Left Bloc' with the Social Democrats gave them added political weight, while the presence of Soviet troops put pressure on the Smallholders. In January 1946 much of Hungary's heavy industry was declared nationalized. In February, the monarchy was abolished and the country proclaimed a republic. And in March, a 'Law for Protecting the Democratic System', popularly dubbed the 'Hangman's Law', prescribed draconian penalties for alleged spies and subversives.

Communist propagandists exploited the unjust provisions of the Paris Peace Treaty of February 1947, which ordered heavy reparations, upheld the territorial losses conceded at the 1921 Treaty of Trianon, and ignored the rights of Hungarian minorities in Czechoslovakia and Romania. They fostered the view that only communists could mediate with the Soviet occupiers, and attempted to divide their opponents by fabricating plots and scandals. Fresh elections in August 1947 only slightly increased the communists' share to 22 per cent. But they were now the largest party, making it possible to consolidate power. In June 1948, communist and social democratic groups were forcibly merged to produce a Hungarian Workers Party. Mass arrests began.

Surveying the historical scene from the 1990s, the Russian writer Alexander Solzhenitsyn would see weakness and confusion in his country's predominant church as a key factor in the communist seizure of power in 1917. Could the same be said of Eastern Europe in the 1940s?

Unlike in Hungary and the Czech lands, the Catholic Church in Poland had not been used as a tool of foreign imperial rulers; but a gulf between the Church and secular intelligentsia had opened up in the nineteenth century, leaving most of the greatest thinkers and writers outside the Church's embrace. Although spiritual interests had lingered on, the intelligentsia's ethos was positivist and non-conformist.

The country's Catholic priests were a mixed bag. The largest element looked to the *Polak-Katolik*, the citizen instinctively identifying his Polishness with Catholicism, as the embodiment of all virtue. By the early twentieth century, helped by Tsarist attempts to assimilate the Poles by abolishing religious teaching and the use of Polish in schools, culture and society were divided between the traditional popular Catholicism of the countryside and the secularism of an educated city élite. The division was disastrous for both: for the Polish intelligentsia, by accentuating its alienation from other social groups; and for the Church, by identifying Catholicism ever more deeply with conservative interests.

There were priests who offered help to lay intellectuals seeking an opening to the Christian faith, such as Fr Władysław Korniłowicz at the Franciscan centre of Laski. There were also renewal movements, such as Odrodzenie, whose aim was a 'Christian humanism' capable of bridging the gap between reform-minded Catholics and socialists.

But these initiatives had no visible impact on the Church's conservative hierarchy. The Church's leaders defended the national identity alongside their own rights and privileges. But their philanthropic efforts, although extensive, barely touched the surface of current needs. Since secularization was less advanced here than in Czechoslovakia and Hungary, the Church remained Poland's only coherent source of moral authority. But it was an authority tainted with intolerance, which was incapable of assimilating new Catholic thinking from the wider world.

The Catholic Church had also ignored Poland's ethnic minorities. 'Hunger and unemployment are the greatest tools of agitators from the communist and extremist camps', warned the Ukrainian Catholic Metropolitan Andrei Sheptycky of Galicia in the late 1930s. 'Polish society, with few exceptions, lives completely segregated from us, and does not realize how deeply the present crisis is affecting the Ukrainian masses ... This is a generation without a future.'[8]

In 1945, Poland had lost most of its minorities anyway, and was now, thanks to the border changes, 95 per cent Catholic. After 150 years of foreign partition, the Church had had just 20 years of independence to rebuild and reorganize, before losing a third of its clergy and much of its infrastructure during the war. But even without the wartime decimations, it would have been unprepared for the confrontation with communism. Its own intellectuals were incapable of conducting an effective polemic against the new doctrines.

Poland's pre-war secular intelligentsia had been marked out for extermination by both invading powers. The young professionals and administrators who emerged in its place after the war often brought with them the folk religiousness of a traditional upbringing. But this fragile inheritance was easily eroded by the atheism of the new ruling establishment. This formed a natural ingredient of the enthusiasm effused by communist converts.

Things had looked much the same in neighbouring Czechoslovakia. In Slovakia, part of predominantly Lutheran Upper Hungary till 1918, the Catholic Church could claim to have helped preserve a national language and culture against Magyarization. But in Czech Bohemia and Moravia, it was widely seen as an Austrian imposition, the spiritual purveyor of a repressive imperial order which had endured since the seventeenth century. Whereas Slovak Catholicism belonged to the popular Slavic model, seeing the nation as a supreme value, the Catholicism of the more secularized Czechs was forged on an anvil of cultural conflict.

Reforming priests had helped import Enlightenment ideas to the Czech lands. Many had fought for Czech self-rule in the 1848 uprising, as well as supporting a national reawakening and backing calls for the redistribution of Church wealth. But by the late nineteenth century, greater freedom had accentuated political and social divisions, leaving education, art and literature dominated by a secular anti-Catholic perspective. 'Nothing can be expected of even reformed Catholicism', Czechoslovakia's founder-president, Tomáš Garrigue Masaryk, asserted later. 'For us, ecclesiastical religion, and Catholicism in particular, are things surpassed.'[9]

In 1918, independence was accompanied by anti-Catholic riots, during which statues of the Virgin Mary and St John of Nepomuk, installed by Habsburg designers in the age of baroque Catholicism, were torn down by the Prague crowd. The Czech First Republic became a liberal democracy, based on the rule of law. But its cultural and political establishment were hostile to Catholicism. Church–State separation was enshrined in law, and citizens encouraged to leave the Catholic Church. A new 'Czechoslovak Church', founded by Fr Karel Farský in 1920, soon boasted 800,000 members.

Despite Masaryk's intentions, the First Republic was to witness a substantial Catholic revival. The majority of priests welcomed the new state and Pope Benedict XV established relations within a year—a conciliatory gesture lauded by Masaryk himself. By the accession of President Edvard Beneš in 1935, the anti-Catholic struggle had virtually petered out. The People's Party, composed of committed Christians, rejected both laissez-faire capitalism and communism in the spirit of Pius XI's *Quadragesimo anno*. Meanwhile, two Moravian centres for Christian exploration at Olomouc and Starou Říši acquired a reputation for open-minded theology and attracted some of the best-known Czech writers and poets—Jaroslav Durych, František Křelina, Jakub Deml, Jan Zahradníček—whose contacts with French Personalism placed them in the forefront of European Catholic thinking.

Yet movements like this enjoyed an ambivalent relationship with the Church's still-conservative hierarchy, and were not sufficient to hold back the sweeping radicalization of the late 1930s.

The positive role of reform-minded Czech Catholics was to be partly eclipsed anyway by events in Slovakia. Since 1918, many Slovak Catholics had felt closer to the Catholic traditionalism of Poland than the liberal humanism of Masaryk. Under the presidency of a Catholic priest, Mgr Josef Tiso, these differences reached a head. Slovakia spent its first six years of independence for half a millennium as a German client-state.

Tiso's political miscalculations were protested against by both the Church hierarchy and the Vatican, while the prestige of independent Slovakia was substantially redeemed by a heroic uprising in 1944. Many Slovaks would later argue that Tiso had never received a fair hearing, since he was condemned for war crimes by a Soviet-directed military court and his death sentence was signed by a Czech president. But the priest's disastrous legacy tarnished the image of Catholicism and provided a rich fund for communist anti-Church propaganda.[10]

In Hungary, the Church was institutionally stronger. But here too, the Catholic hierarchy's high profile had depended on its subservience to Habsburg power. It was the Piarists and Jesuits who educated the generation of political and cultural leaders dominant in Hungary's early nineteenth-century Reform Age. But the Church's upper ranks were hostile to reformist ideas and opposed Hungary's social emancipation laws later in the century. When spiritual themes were taken up by poets like Imre Madách and Mihály Vörösmarty, it was usually with a deep pessimism born from the defeat of Hungary's 1848–49 independence struggle, a national trauma in which the Austrian-dominated Catholic hierarchy had stood on the side of the imperial reaction.

By the turn of the century, a rift had opened up between Hungary's modern Budapest-based urban intelligentsia, much of it of Jewish origin, and the backward, conservative countryside. With its roots firmly in the latter, Catholicism remained a weak force in Hungarian life and culture. 'Give us priests who identify with the poor, whose apostolic life leaves no room for doubt!' declared the Catholic social reformer Fr Ottokár Prohászka in 1900. 'For the Gospel, with its resignation and suffering, is but an empty shadow.'[11]

Prohászka's own case illustrated the dilemmas facing those campaigning for change. In 1911, six years after he had been appointed Bishop of Székesfehérvár, three of his books were placed on the Index by Pope Pius X. But Prohászka's paternalistic Christian reformism, mixing theological modernism with anti-Semitism, was viewed as a voice from the conservative establishment by Hungary's political Left. More radical Catholic figures, such as Sándor Geisswein and Sándor Horváth, lacked the strength of organization to win popular support.

In 1920, Hungary was forced to cede most of its territory at the Treaty of Trianon. By then, helped by the wartime collapse of its administrative class, Béla Kun's communist regime had seized power and unleashed a five-month reign of terror, only to be overthrown by troops loyal to Admiral Miklós Horthy, the Habsburg 'Regent'. The authoritarian backlash which ensued, during which communists were imprisoned and executed, dashed hopes of social change. By 1935, four million rural inhabitants and 600,000 industrial workers, more than half the Hungarian population, were living below subsistence level, in conditions of poverty and injustice vividly described by writers like Zsigmond Móricz and Dezső Kosztolányi.[12]

It would be claimed later that the Hungarian Church's traditional alignment with the upper classes had weakened under the Lutheran Horthy. Archbishop János Csernoch, Catholic Primate in the early twentieth century, came from Slovak peasant stock, while his successor, Cardinal Jusztinián Serédi, was the son of a tiler. In 1923, the Church even offered to give up some of its own massive holdings to aid a land reform programme, only to have the offer blocked by the government. But these were small lights on an otherwise bleak horizon. With 57 million acres, a third of all arable land, the Catholic Church remained Hungary's richest landowner. Its bishops and order heads held *ex officio* seats in the Senate, while its lower clergy enjoyed high living standards and numerous civic privileges. Although Catholics comprised 70 per cent of the pre-war population, with at least half practising regularly, the clergy had little in common with the ordinary people.

In the 1930s, a spiritual revival among Hungarian intellectuals had brought a proliferation of new Catholic publications. The Church-owned monthly *Vigilia*, founded in 1935, began publishing Western philosophers and theologians, and could claim links with great Hungarian writers such as Endre Ady and Mihály Babits. But *Vigilia*'s best Catholic writers could hardly place themselves in the same league as their secular counterparts.

Meanwhile, new religious movements had launched a range of social initiatives. Yet these belonged to Church tradition and offered few answers to the great questions of the day. *Rerum novarum* was left unpublished for 40 years in Hungary. The Church was unable to exert an effective counter-influence when the drift to extremes became apparent in the late 1930s.

As in Poland and Czechoslovakia, the Hungarian Church partially redeemed itself during the war years. Cardinal Serédi publicly opposed Admiral Horthy's alliance with Germany and Italy. And although anti-Semitism had been a Church feature since Béla Kun's Jewish-dominated Republic of Councils, voices were raised against anti-Semitic measures after the Nazi occupation of March 1944.

Some Church leaders belatedly recognized the need for a Catholic organization committed to social reform. Two Jesuit priests, Béla Kovrig and Jenő Kerkai, who had co-founded the pre-war KALOT youth movement, proposed giving land to labourers and creating a universal social welfare system. But the Church had no reformist wing which could seriously contest ideas with the new communist élite.

'Socialism, at least at the beginning, was Christianity's bad conscience.'[13] The words of the Polish Catholic writer Tadeusz Mazowiecki, who would become Poland's first post-communist head of government four decades later, described the dilemmas facing the Church throughout Eastern Europe. It had lost the loyalty of workers and intellectuals, and was ill-prepared for ideological challenges, at a time when many would have concurred with Marx's maxim that Christianity's social principles 'preach the necessity of a ruling and an oppressed class, and all they have for the latter is the pious wish that the former will be charitable'.[14]

Once in power, Eastern Europe's communist parties followed a three-tiered policy: to destroy the Church's social influence and economic independence; to secularize society; and to divide the clergy between 'progressive' and 'reactionary' wings, severing their links with Rome.

In Hungary and Czechoslovakia, communist propagandists exploited the Church's authoritarian, anti-national image. All Catholic books were removed from public libraries, writers silenced or driven abroad. Hundreds of thousands of hectares of Church land were expropriated under land reform laws.

In Hungary alone, 200 Catholic journals and at least 3,000 Catholic schools, 60 per cent of Hungary's pre-war total, had been suppressed or nationalized by 1948. So had Catholic organizations—beginning with those, like KALOT, which had worker links. Czechoslovakia's post-1948 regime resurrected the Habsburg policy of paying priests' salaries from the State budget, ostensibly to compensate for the seizure of Church properties, but also to ensure clerical subservience. Religious teaching, although never banned in State schools, was tightly restricted. Most Catholic publications and associations were closed or taken over.

Repression was even more intense elsewhere. In Bulgaria, Georgi Dmitrov, a Comintern veteran, returned from the Soviet Union in 1946 to establish a communist state. A 1949 law proclaimed the majority Bulgarian Orthodox Church a 'people's democratic Church' and demanded that religious associations with foreign headquarters, including Catholics, terminate their activities.

Albania's communist leader, Enver Hoxha, who had been educated at the Sorbonne, saw Islam, Orthodoxy and Catholicism as channels for the respective interests of Turkey, Greece and Italy. Out of 160 Catholic clergy, as many as seven bishops and archbishops, 65 diocesan priests, 33 Franciscans and 15 Jesuits died in the ensuing persecution.

In countries like this, it was not difficult to see why local communists, many ill-educated, found the well-endowed, highly disciplined Catholic Church intimidating. But what of the Soviet Union? By 1939, the Soviet regime had virtually eradicated the Latin Catholic Church on its territory, closing all but three of around 1,000 pre-1917 Catholic churches and chapels, and eliminating all but ten of 912 priests and religious. In 1945, new states had been incorporated into the Soviet Union. The anti-religious campaign started over again.

Pope Pius XII had called Lithuania 'the northernmost outpost of Christian Europe' shortly before its two decades of inter-war independence ended with an invasion by the Red Army in 1940. Lithuanian intellectuals had traditionally been lukewarm in their Catholic loyalties. But the pre-war Communist Party had notched up barely 1,700 members. In summer 1944, when the Red Army recaptured most of the country from the Germans, anti-religious measures were delayed to avoid a head-on clash with public opinion. By the time repressions began in earnest the following year, the new

Soviet rulers faced determined guerrilla resistance. At least 30,000 'Forest Brethren' were operating in the Lithuanian countryside, while 100,000 others supported them through local self-defence groups. Church leaders resisted regime demands that they urge the partisans to lay down their arms. But they discouraged Church involvement, and only 30 of the 700 priests working in the republic in 1947 had active links with the freedom fighters. Despite this, a third of priests and all but one bishop were in jail by mid-1947.[15] Conciliatory gestures cut no ice whatever with the Soviet rulers.

If comparisons could be drawn, it was the Greek Catholic Church in Ukraine which faced the harshest persecution of all. The Greek Catholic rite had been founded at the 1596 Union of Brest, when the Orthodox Metropolitan of Kiev and most Ukrainian bishops, pressured by the Austrian occupiers, had agreed to return to Roman jurisdiction while retaining their eastern traditions. Russia's Orthodox Church had always been hostile to what it pejoratively dubbed the *Uniaty*. So were Russia's rulers, whether Tsarist or Soviet, who saw the Greek Catholics as purveyors of a hostile Western influence.

But the Church had strong roots. In 1939, when Polish-ruled western Ukraine was annexed to the Soviet Union, it had four million members, served by 2,500 priests and 4,119 churches. The Church's leader for forty years, Metropolitan Andrei Sheptycky, a veteran of Siberian labour camps, was 80 when Red Army tanks rolled in. But when western Ukraine was captured by the Germans a year later, he protested at the mistreatment of Jews and publicly denounced the use of Ukrainian slave labour.[16]

None of this could save the Church when the Soviets reoccupied the region in 1944. When Sheptycky died that November, his successor, Josif Slipyi, sought a *modus vivendi* and donated 100,000 roubles for Soviet war-wounded. But plans to liquidate the Greek Catholic Church had already been prepared. In April 1945, Slipyi and four other bishops were deported to labour camps on charges of Nazi collaboration.

The Russian Orthodox patriarch, Alexei I, enthroned with Stalin's consent in 1943, sent a message urging Greek Catholics to repudiate their bishops' 'pro-fascist line'. In March 1946, a 'Pioneer Group' of Greek Catholics was recognized by the Soviet regime as the Church's only administrative organ. It convened a synod in Lviv and proclaimed the Church's 350-year union with Rome annulled. Only 42 Ukrainian priests declared support for the 'Pioneer Group', and less than half accepted its decision. Of the rest, at least 800 were arrested before 1946 was out. The rest fled abroad or went underground.

The assault on Greek Catholics was just as intense in neighbouring Romania, where the Church, founded 100 years after Ukraine's, was suppressed in 1948. Slovakia's Greek Catholic minority was forcibly merged with the Orthodox Church in 1950, landing all but 28 of its 300 priests in communist prisons. In Poland, the Church was never formally banned, but its churches were seized and most members deported. In Hungary and Bulgaria, the Church managed a tentative existence, although subject to rigid controls.

Could the Catholic Church, in these circumstances, devise a coherent response? Each national hierarchy believed in a strong, uncompromising stance. But they differed over how to achieve it.

Cardinal Stefan Wyszyński was 47 when he became Primate of Poland in October 1948. The Church was struggling to recover from the destruction of the war. Returning to Poland in 1945, after being liberated by US troops from a Gestapo prison, Cardinal Hlond had urged Poles not to be afraid 'of modernity, social change or the people's form of government'.[17] As a sociology lecturer at Włocławek seminary in the 1930s, Wyszyński had supported social reform. But he took office 'with an outline of a programme, not fully completed or clarified'.[18]

> Together with many others who had long fought for social justice, I came to consider that altering the socioeconomic structure was a necessity ... Poland had no shortage of social forces—among clergy as well as lay Catholics—who were spiritually prepared to rebuild the system. Nor were these forces altogether opposed to socialist aims, although the atheism that socialism spawned was a harmful hindrance. Had it not been for this narrow atheism, which carried us to the brink of religious war, Polish society, with its cultural, historically democratic tendencies, would have been a most fertile field for a wise government to work with ... If Marxism had come directly from the West, without Eastern intervention, it would undoubtedly have been accepted with greater trust.[19]

Wyszyński was aware that the Polish communists' initial lack of legitimacy made them reliant on manipulation and subterfuge. Whatever their leaders said and did, they were certain to view the Church as an obstacle to their plans. But they could only act against it once its social support had been weakened. In this situation, the Church's best hope lay in refusing to be sidelined and isolated. The primate travelled around the country, celebrating Masses and leading pilgrimages. He ensured that local priests remained politically uninvolved, while maintaining good relations with their parishioners. At the same time, he was ready to negotiate points of disagreement with the regime, without allowing himself to be out-talked or pushed into rhetorical overreactions.

The strategy paid off. Even at the height of Stalinist rule, the Polish Church was too well supported for the regime to risk a head-on collision.

Wyszyński sensed that the State would sooner or later overreach itself, and be forced to recognize that, even under communism, a strong Catholic Church was a permanent feature. After years of trial and struggle, this is precisely what happened.

Wyszyński's Czech neighbour, Cardinal Josef Beran, had survived three years in Nazi concentration camps, earning the Military Cross and Czech Resistance Medal. When he was named Archbishop of Prague in November 1946, the Church-backed People's Party was governing in coalition, and his enthronement was attended by the communist Klement Gottwald and other government members. Beran trod a conciliatory path. In February 1948, when the communists seized power, he welcomed promises that the new government would do nothing to disrupt Church–State relations.

The regime needed coming elections to confirm its legitimacy, and was well aware that the Church could prevent this by urging Catholics to spoil their votes. So it asked the new Archbishop to adopt a 'positive attitude' to the takeover. Beran responded by urging Czechs not to risk a civil war by resisting. The Catholic Church would accept a socialism, he added, which conformed with legal structures. But unlike Czech Protestant leaders, Beran insisted his hierarchy would stay neutral. When communist newspapers put it about that the Church was supporting communism, he responded with an angry letter. 'Christianity and communism cannot be reconciled', Beran insisted. 'Anyone who tries to accomplish this is either ignorant of history or playing comic games.'[20]

When Gottwald was inaugurated as President after the election of May 1948, the Archbishop agreed to celebrate the traditional *Te Deum* in Prague's St Vitus cathedral, but he warned priests not to accept official positions. When the ruling was ignored by Fr Josef Plojhar, a fellow veteran of Dachau, now acting as communist Health Minister, he was suspended. The communists saw Beran as a centrist figure between the Church's 'reactionary' and 'progressive' bishops, who would co-operate under certain conditions.[21] But he was believed to be under pressure from 'anti-Communists' in the Vatican. The regime wanted Plojhar's suspension lifted since this could deter other priests from collaborating. Since Beran would not bow to their demands, conflict became inevitable.

By mid-1949, Beran and the Vatican's Prague Nunciature were being depicted as ringleaders in a plot to disrupt Church–State co-operation. On 15 June, secret police agents stole an official seal from the Archbishop's chancery in Hradčanská Square, and dispatched a message to priests ordering them to disregard previous instructions not to support the regime. They also installed an official to control Church documents. Three days later, preaching at Corpus Christi, Beran vowed he would never 'capitulate' or sign agreements which violated Church laws. 'He who refuses to betray God cannot be a traitor to his country and people', the Archbishop declared in a letter smuggled out his palace. 'We are insignificant and helpless amid these raging, satanic powers. But although we are powerless, we can help by our attitude to keep the evil from our people.'[22]

On 19 June 1949, Beran was shouted down by communist agents when he tried to preach again in St Vitus cathedral. The outrage marked the end of his active role in Church life. Although the Czech bishops refused to sign a loyalty oath to the regime, they advised ordinary priests to accept the terms demanded.

Beran would have liked to see some kind of Church–State agreement, accepting the communist system in return for a guarantee of Church rights. Instead, he had found himself pushed into opposition, mostly by communist actions infringing vital Church interests, but partly also by Vatican pressure to resist compromise. This gave the regime an excuse for even harsher reprisals. The Archbishop was finally forced from his post in March 1951. Perhaps because of Western pressure, his planned treason trial never took place. But he was detained at a remote monastery till 1964, after which, on visiting Rome to receive his Cardinal's hat, he was barred from re-entering the country.

Beran's Hungarian counterpart was to encounter a similar fate, even though his style and approach were very different. József Mindszenty was enthroned, aged 53, at Esztergom cathedral on 7 October 1945 following the death of Cardinal Serédi. He had been arrested by Hungary's Nazi-allied Arrow Cross government in June 1944, and could point to a sound war record—something his communist opponents attempted to cover up. Nor did he oppose—initially at least—the country's land reform programme. But Mindszenty embodied a highly conservative image of the Catholic Church, and had a record of opposing left-wing policies. In 1919, after just four years as a priest, he had managed to get himself arrested twice—for speaking out against the 'socialist policies' of Hungary's centrist Mihály Károlyi government, and later for opposing Bela Kun's 'Republic of Councils'. 'The dog was the same', Mindszenty later remarked, 'only his collar was now redder.'[23]

This had turned Mindszenty into a staunch opponent of communism. It had also made him, like many Hungarians, sceptical about social and economic change. In his memoirs, he regrets no land reform had been attempted in Hungary before 1920—but only because this might somehow have delayed the loss of Hungarian territory at Trianon. He planned to sell off half his Veszprém diocese's 24,000 acres in 1944—but only since the Church's land-holdings were already endangered and the proceeds could be used to set up new parishes.[24]

As Hungarian Primate, Mindszenty saw his task as twofold: to defend the faith and unmask communism. 'Communist ideology can achieve lasting effects only where a nation's religious foundations have been undermined', the Cardinal wrote in his memoirs, 'so that reason, faith in God and morality do not offer sufficient resistance.'[25]

With Hungary occupied by the Red Army and the communists poised to assume power, many felt the Church had no option but to conciliate its opponents. But the Primate believed that, in the end, Hungary's future would be decided by popular loyalties. Vigorous testimony, he sensed, could still force the regime to back down. Even if this never happened, the Hungarian Church must maintain its identity: persecution was a necessary price for keeping values and principles intact.

In a pastoral letter written before the elections of August 1947, Mindszenty wrote:

> We trusted those who had taken over the reins of government. We overlooked their abuses of authority, believing such abuses were the inevitable accompaniment of change and hoping they would cease with the passage of time. Now the time has come for elections, we can no longer keep silent. We must publicly declare that no Christian voter can support a party that rules by violence and oppression, and tramples underfoot all natural laws and human rights.[26]

By the time Mindszenty was arrested in December 1948, several senior prelates, including Archbishop Gyula Czapik of Eger, had taken part in discussions with the communist regime, as it attempted to drive a wedge between the Primate and more accommodating Church figures. The following February, after a three-day trial, Mindszenty was sentenced to life imprisonment on charges that included espionage, currency speculation and attempting to overthrow the government. There were voices in the Hungarian Church who believed he should have been more accommodating.

In reality, the truth is more complex. In his memoirs—written 'so that the world may see what fate communism has in store for mankind'—Mindszenty says he recognized the dangers from the start, at a time when other Church leaders were inclined to believe radio propaganda that communism had changed and no longer threatened the Church. The regime, Mindszenty believed, was determined to crush the Church. And it would have done it anyway, whether the Church's leaders were co-operative or confrontational. The fate of the Russian Orthodox Church in the 1930s had shown what happened when religious leaders attempted to appease hostile communist powers.

Ironically, this was the opposite of what Cardinal Wyszyński had concluded in Poland, after also studying the Russian Orthodox example.

But Mindszenty had thought his position through, concluding that the best to be hoped for, if it came to it, was that he himself would go down fighting, bequeathing a legacy of strength and integrity which future generations might find edifying.

By the time the Cardinal's sentence was being read out, amid a chorus of unheeded international protests, his Croatian counterpart, Alojzije Stepinac, had served more than two years of a 16-year sentence, on charges of conspiring to overthrow the Yugoslav government. After forming a government in 1944, Tito's communists had launched a campaign against supposed Nazi collaborators within the Church. It was intended to weaken national identity in Croatia and Slovenia, Yugoslavia's most homogeneous and defiant provinces. But it was ideologically motivated too: the Catholic Church was expected to pose a key obstacle to communist power.

Born into a peasant family, Stepinac had been a 36-year-old Austro-Hungarian Army veteran when he was named the world's youngest archbishop in 1934 after just four years as a priest. He was 39 when he became full Archbishop of Zagreb, one of Europe's largest archdioceses. Before the war, he had set up a committee to help Jewish refugees from Nazi Germany. In April 1941, when an Independent State of Croatia was proclaimed from the ruins of the Yugoslav kingdom, the Archbishop welcomed it as a sign of the 'hand of God at work'. But Stepinac's relations with the regime of Ante Pavelić were tense from the outset. In private and later public protests, he warned that atrocities by the Ustaše party were driving the population into the hands of Tito's Partisans. He urged priests to avoid politics, and turned down a request by Pavelić to help form a provisional government in 1945.[27]

Stepinac's mother and brother—the latter executed by the Germans in 1943—were said to have had Partisan links. But where the Archbishop erred was in attacking communism more stridently than Fascism, thereby making it easier for opponents to equate the Church with the Ustaše. 'The communist movement is not only the Church's greatest enemy in all centuries, but also the greatest enemy of human freedom', Stepinac declared in April 1945, in a Zagreb cathedral sermon. It contained no comparable condemnation of Nazism. 'The Church's attitude towards communism is clear, towards those who deny its very right to exist, who raise monuments to Satan and Judas Iscariot.'[28]

Stepinac could hardly be blamed to standing up for Croatia, particularly at a time when it was hard to separate fact from propaganda about Ustaše crimes. But like Mindszenty in Hungary, he believed he could rally Catholic support and underestimated the strength and ruthlessness of the forces ranged against him.

Whether Stepinac was pushed into intransigent opposition, or had deliberately chosen this path for himself, the result, in September 1945, was a pastoral letter and circular to clergy, co-signed by seventeen Yugoslav bishops, which gave the regime its best pretext yet for direct action. Both documents condemned anti-Church measures, as well as the notion of Church–State separation and the communist regime's materialist philosophy. Some priests were said to have refused to read them, believing them too confrontational. After securing victory in November elections, the regime redoubled its attacks.

The Archbishop was finally arrested on 18 September 1946, after being incriminated by his own secretary. In court, Stepinac denied that the Church had opposed social reform, and insisted he had only acted in the spirit of papal encyclicals. But the trial had a political purpose. Tito knew the Catholic Church was the only social force capable of rallying opposition. Some Church diehards—Archbishop Ivan Šarić of Sarajevo was a good example—had fled fearing communist reprisals. Since Stepinac had refused, he had to be destroyed. Stepinac was 48 when he was sentenced to sixteen years' hard labour after a show trial that saw death sentences passed on two co-defendants. The relative leniency was widely attributed to the regime's unwillingness to create top-level martyrs. Stalin and the Comintern were to denounce Tito eighteen months later. Yugoslavia needed Western support and internal unity.

Can historical judgements be applied to the four Church leaders in question? All attempted to serve the Church according to their understanding of local conditions. And all spent time in prison—a sure sign that the co-operative stance of Wyszyński and Beran or the confrontational attitude of Mindszenty and Stepinac made no essential difference to the inherent hostility of communist regimes. But personal skills played a part too, as did the readiness to speak and act independently of papal directives.

Mindszenty and Stepinac had based their response to communism on the strictures set out a decade before in *Divini Redemptoris*. Indeed, their sermons and homilies contained rhetorical passages which might well have been extracted verbatim from the standard version of Pius XI. This made conflict hardly surprising. For how could Catholics attempt to coexist with a doctrine which was 'intrinsically evil'? How could they tolerate governments whose 'repulsive cruelty' was innate? How could they engage in discussion with those whose theories were 'utterly and completely refuted'? In 1945, this was what Catholics were supposed to believe. If they really did, could they credibly engage in moral resistance but draw the line at political opposition?

It was Wyszyński's achievement that he failed to be hidebound by pre-war definitions. There were occasions, he concluded, when principles were eroded more quickly by unbending rigour than intelligent flexibility. If the communist regimes were brutal, they were also clever, with a keen grasp of the strengths and weaknesses of potential friends and enemies. This was something the peasant stubbornness of Mindszenty and Stepinac, for all their courage, could not countenance. Unlike them, Wyszyński was ready to believe communists were open to forms of persuasion like anyone else. He was prepared to study every decision in minute detail, acknowledging promises kept as well as condemning those broken, never prejudging and never allowing himself to be pushed into the straitjacket of committed opposition.

Ironically, this was what the Czech Beran had tried to accomplish too. Beran was unlucky that, unlike its Polish neighbour, his Church was more susceptible to divisions, and that anti-Church measures never risked the same public backlash in Czechoslovakia as in Poland.

By the time of Wyszyński's appointment, Karol Wojtyła was in his third year as a priest in Kraków. Ordained on 1 November 1946 by Cardinal Sapieha in his private chapel, Karol had left for Rome by train fifteen days later. Sapieha, who had talent-spotted Wojtyła during a visit to Wadowice's school back in 1938, had emerged from the wartime occupation as Poland's greatest Church leader, with a personal authority outstripping that of the Primate, Cardinal Hlond, who had spent the war years abroad. But he had been shocked into depression by the Red Army's arrival in early 1945. The premonition of what was coming had undoubtedly rubbed off on his brightest pupil.

Rome gave Karol his first contacts with theologians and Church leaders from abroad. He attended an audience with Pius XII shortly after arriving, as well as a meeting with Cardinal Hlond and the city's resident Polish Jesuits and Marians. He met professors such as the Frenchman Pierre-Paul Philippe, an expert on the Eastern Churches, at the Dominican-run Angelicum, his place of study, and mixed with the sixteen French-speaking students at the Belgian College, where he was assigned a room.

It was at the Belgian College that Karol also met Fr Joseph Cardijn, founder of the Jeunesse Ouvrière Chrétienne, whose Mission de France headquarters at Lisieux he visited during a tour of France and Belgium in the summer of 1947. The trip, made with a Polish fellow-student, Fr Stanisław Starowieyski, gave Wojtyła first-hand experience of the methods of the Mission's 'worker priests' and the pastoral problems facing post-war Western society. It caused a deep personal impression. In an enthusiastic article, written after his return to Kraków on 15 June 1948, he described the

Mission's key challenge—to keep in daily touch with the poor, while also maintaining its intellectual and philosophical character. The 'worker priests' offered a 'living testimony', Wojtyła stressed—not as an 'act of resistance or opposition', but as a 'positive, constructive attempt to create activity'. The young priest wrote that

> This school, as very often happens with new trends in the Church, is making an effort to return to the Gospel's simplicity, its spirit and engagement. The proletariat does not accept new teaching without a struggle. But this should not disappoint the lay and clerical pioneers. They understand that some types of culture are disappearing, that certain once-vibrant traditions are now just empty sand.[29]

The article, Wojtyła's first, covered a sensitive topic—the Church's links with workers—at a time when the lines of Church–State confrontation were being drawn in Poland. But it was published uncensored, suggesting it was considered acceptable as a 'progressive view' from within the Catholic clergy. By then, Wojtyła had gained considerably more experience of life and ideas than the average Polish priest. In Italy, he had witnessed discussions of the Vatican's wartime stance, as well as the desperate struggle to prevent a post-war communist election victory. It gave him an insight into the Vatican's dilemmas in responding to totalitarian threats. At a time when other priests had been left without clear signposts against the communist programme, he had been given the chance to devise his own antidotes to the alienation and disaffection on which Marxism thrived.

Wojtyła had arrived back in Poland with a divinity doctorate at the start of the Stalinist period. By the time Wyszyński took over as Primate at Hlond's death that October, the Church's educational and charitable infrastructure had already been partly rebuilt. But Karol was lucky to be in Kraków. Unlike Warsaw, the city had survived and kept most of its pre-war population, with the obvious exception of the Jews from its Kazimierz ghetto. The stable atmosphere provided a good background for reaching mature judgements. Wojtyła had not read Marxism extensively by then. But he was conversant with its claims, and had more or less made up his mind about the ideological movement controlling his homeland.

A contributory factor had been his doctoral thesis, 'The idea of faith in St John of the Cross', completed in Rome. Wojtyła had for a time considered joining the Carmelite order in honour of this sixteenth-century Spanish mystic. But he had concluded that the real test of morality comes with deeds. His study had taught him the value of contemplation—of that 'self-emptying' which allowed the believer to attain purity of faith, hope and love. But the fullness of the religious experience, Wojtyła sensed, required contemplation to be matched by action.[30]

What kind of action? Karol had been looking for the answer since 1944, when he began work on his play *Brat Naszego Boga* (Brother of our God). Completed in 1949, it was a work which revealed the steady evolution of his thinking. It was also to be left unpublished for 30 years, perhaps out of fear of the censor, but more likely because Wojtyła considered it too personal and self-revealing to entrust to a wider public.

The play's real-life subject, Adam Chmielowski (1845–1916), had a leg amputated, aged 18, without anaesthetic while fighting the Russians in the 1863 Polish January Uprising. As a noted painter, Chmielowski became well-known in the high society of Kraków. But at the century's end, after a religious conversion, he devoted himself to the poor and founded a new Franciscan order, taking the name Brother Albert. His life had thus been dedicated to two senses of charity—the charity of armed struggle for an oppressed nation, and the charity of care for the wretched. When he died, two years before Poland's independence, he was buried in Kraków's Discalced Carmelite church.

In *Brat Naszego Boga*, Adam rejects the paternalistic philanthropy of the nineteenth-century Church. He is full of venom for those like his own uncle who appease their consciences with donations to charity—who demand 'for a złoty here, a złoty there, the right to lock up quietly inside oneself all these upheavals, all these tensions'.[31]

He also rejects the advice of his liberal artist friend Maks, who advises him to close his eyes and stick to his painting. Maks believes 'society' is constituted from the interaction of freely competing forces—people are 'like a multitude of atoms, revolving each in his own sphere'. Instead, Adam concurs with another shadowy character, Nieznajomy, who tells him he has a duty to act—revolutionary upheavals are products of social injustice, of the 'great, boundless anger' of the masses. Nieznajomy personifies Europe's revolutionary socialist movement. His ideas of social justice come straight out of Polish Romantic literature, echoing those of the failed rebel Pankracy in Krasiński's *Nieboska komedia*, and with accents from Dostoevsky.

But Chmielowski parts company with Nieznajomy when it comes to revolutionary methods. For one thing, Nieznajomy's approach to suffering is anonymous and indiscriminate. He believes in common responsibility—whole classes are to be branded guilty for social evils. Nieznajomy manipulates emotions to harness the destructive anger of the exploited. But it is clear that agitators like him know little of the misfortunes of the 'street people' in whose name they claim to speak. The poor are not ready for the revolution Nieznajomy has in mind. It fuels demands that cannot be satisfied, and brings new injustices and divisions.

In its place, Adam attempts to work out his own idea of mercy, defending his 'path to God' against the frustrated taunts of his own followers. Through suffering, he attempts, as Christ did, to identify with his fellow-men. Poverty and injustice should indeed awaken a 'great just anger'. 'But there's a difference between summoning forth this righteous anger, letting it ripen and emerge as a creative force—and exploiting the anger, abusing it as a material tool', Chmielowski concludes. 'Man's poverty is deeper than the resources and goods we're talking about ... Here anger is no good: charity is essential.' The rejection is mutual. For Nieznajomy is contemptuous of Adam's charity, believing it appeases revolutionary passions and erodes the power of the people. 'Watch out for those apostles of mercy: they are our enemies' is the revolutionary's final response.[32]

Wojtyła retraces his own thinking through the protracted anguish of the artist. Like Brother Albert, he himself had given up art in favour of a more committed life as a priest. Like most of his generation, he was aware of contemporary injustices and had thought through Marxist options, at a time when the 'new science' was locked in a mortal struggle with Christianity. But in the end, Wojtyła declined to offer social solutions of his own, and retreated instead to the high ground of personal integrity and conscience—of Christian liberation from within rather than temporal liberation from without. As a priest, he knew he had to align himself with Church teachings and live up to his vocation as a guardian of souls—hoping, with Brother Albert, for a 'captivity which turns into freedom'. But he was also aware that this otherworldly response would be constantly challenged by the radical, revolutionary currents of the age—by new societies which no longer accepted the passive, worn-out formulations of the past. *Brat Naszego Boga* made little direct reference to Catholic doctrine and was imbued with anti-clerical accents. It showed how close Christian mystics and Marxist revolutionaries could come in their burning frustration with the state of the world.

Notes

1. These reminiscences are taken from Juliusz Kydryński (ed.), *Młodzieńcze lata Karola Wojtyła* (Kraków: Oficyna Cracovia, 1990), pp. 129–32.
2. Ibid., pp. 165, 170; Adam Boniecki (ed.), *Kalendarium życia Karola Wojtyły* (Kraków: Znak, 1983), p. 43; Kazimierz Wyka, *Patrząc ku młodości* (Kraków: Uniwersytet Jagielloński, 1964).
3. 'Głos Prymasa Polski', *Rycerz Niepokolanej* (May 1936), p. 140; Andrzej Pilch, *Studencki ruch polityczny w Polsce w latach 1932–1939* (Kraków: Zeszyty Naukowe Uniwersytetu Jagiellońskiego, 1989), pp. 151–67; Ronald Modras,

The Catholic Church and Anti-Semitism: Poland 1933–1939 (London: Harwood, 1994), pp. 343–80.

4. Boniecki (ed.), *Kalendarium*, p. 40.
5. Ibid., pp. 47–8.
6. Ibid., p. 48.
7. See Jacques Rupnik, 'Czechoslovak Communists and the State (1928–48)' in N. Stone and E. Strouhal (eds), *Czechoslovakia: Crossroads and Crises 1918–88* (London: Macmillan, 1989), pp. 169–82.
8. Quoted in Oksana Hayova, 'Andrey Sheptytskyi and the social role of the Church under the occupational regimes', *The Ukrainian Review*, vol. 41, no. 4 (1994), p. 15.
9. Tomáš G. Masaryk, *Modern Man and Religion* (London: Allen & Unwin, 1938).
10. Bohdan Cywiński, *Ogniem Próbowane: I was prześladować będą* (Lublin: Redakcja Wydawnictw, 1990), pp. 217–74.
11. Address (1 January 1900). See also Leslie A. Murray, 'Modernism and Christian Socialism in the thought of Ottokár Proházka', *Occasional Papers on Religion in Eastern Europe*, vol. 12, no. 3 (1992).
12. For contemporary social conditions, see Péter Hanák, *The Corvina History of Hungary* (Budapest: Corvina, 1988), pp. 181–4, 191–200.
13. Tadeusz Mazowiecki, 'Spotkania Chrześcijaństwa z ideami socjalistycznymi i kontrowersje między nimi' in W. Wesołowski (ed.), *Losy Idei Socjalistycznych i Wyzwania Wspołczesności* (Warsaw: Polskie Towarzystwo Wspołpracy z Klubem Rzymskim, 1990), p. 46.
14. David McLellan, *Marxism and Religion* (London: Macmillan, 1987), p. 23.
15. Cywiński, op. cit., pp. 155–61.
16. Hayova, op. cit., pp. 19–21.
17. From *Tygodnik Powszechny*, no. 35 (1945); quoted in Andrzej Micewski, *Kościoł-Państwo 1945–1989* (Warsaw: Wydawnictwo Szkolne Pedagogiczne, 1994), p. 9.
18. *A Freedom Within: The Prison Notes of Stefan Cardinal Wyszyński* (London: Hodder & Stoughton, 1985), p. 12.
19. Ibid., p. 18.
20. Beran's letter to Justice Minister Aleksej Čepička; in Cywiński, op. cit., pp. 234–5.
21. Ibid., pp. 243–4. See also Karel Kaplan, 'Church and State in Czechoslovakia from 1948–1956', *Religion in Communist Lands*, vol. 14, no. 1 (1986), pp. 59–72.
22. Trevor Beeson, *Discretion and Valour* (London: Collins, 1982), pp. 237–8.
23. József Cardinal Mindszenty, *Memoirs* (London: Weidenfeld and Nicolson, 1974), pp. 6–7.
24. Ibid., pp. 14, 22–32.
25. Ibid., pp. 45–6.
26. Pastoral Letter (1 November 1946); Mindszenty, *Memoirs*, op. cit., p. 267.
27. See Stella Alexander, *Church and State in Yugoslavia Since 1945* (Cambridge: Cambridge University Press, 1979), pp. 20–1. Stepinac and his bishops also denounced 'all opinions and doctrines, whether of rightists or leftists, which

violate divine precepts and deprive others of human rights'.

28. Alexander, op. cit., p. 40.
29. Karol Wojtyła, 'Mission de France', first published in *Tygodnik Powszechny*; in *Aby Chrystus się nami posługiwał* (Kraków: Znak, 1979), pp. 13–14.
30. Wojtyła, op. cit., pp. 16–27; 'O humanizmie św. Jana od Krzyża', *Znak*, vol. 6, no. 1 (1951), pp. 8–20. Wojtyła developed his reflection in *Miłość i Odpowiedzialność* (Lublin: Towarzystwo Naukowe Katolickiego, 1960) and *Osoba i Czyn* (Kraków: Polskie Towarzystwo Teologiczne, 1969).
31. Karol Wojtyła, *Brat Naszego Boga* (Kluczbork: Antykwa, 1996), p. 28.
32. Ibid., pp. 74, 79, 102.

3

ເວເວເວເວເວ

The agonies of Pius XII

The Vatican had emerged from the Second World War to find the Catholic Church mortally threatened. In the east, Stalin's Soviet Union had swallowed up 3 million Catholics with the reoccupied Baltic States, 10 million more with eastern Poland, and half a million with eastern Prussia. New regimes were being installed under Soviet Army pressure in Eastern Europe. From Berlin to Bucharest, Szczecin to Sofia, the Church's fate lay in the balance.

Powerful communist parties seemed poised for power in Western Europe too—by force of arms in Greece, by the ballot box in Italy. Western communist hardliners had complained of a sell-out at Yalta too—not of East European democracy to Soviet communism, but of Western socialism to US capitalism. Most saw the Vatican as an ally of the latter.

A common front forged by Italy's revolutionary Left during the war had enabled the Communist Party to emerge as the West's strongest. Armed communist bands killed 52 priests in Emilia province alone between the 1944 liberation of Rome and the declaration of an Italian republic in 1946, in a wave of attacks paralleling the murders by Mussolini's Fascists in the 1930s. Having lived under anti-clerical governments since 1870, and a Fascist regime since 1922, the Vatican viewed the prospects of a communist team in Rome's Palazzo Quirinale with understandable alarm.

But Pius XII was aware of communism's attractiveness to idealistic intellectuals, especially in Western Europe, where the motives were purely ideological, without the external Soviet pressure seen in the East. The standard papal denunciation of communism, *Divini Redemptoris,* though signed by Pius XI, had been approved by Eugenio Pacelli, his Secretary of State. When Pacelli became Pope on 2 March 1939, his first encyclical, *Summi pontificatus* (20 October 1939), duly reaffirmed the Church's condemnation of totalitarianism. But he was also a diplomatist, who had negotiated with the Soviet regime and France's communist-backed Popular Front. He believed agreements and understandings could be patched together even between enemies.

Pius XII was aware of plans for a Soviet–German deal allowing for the carve-up of Poland at least three months before the Molotov–Ribbentrop Pact was signed on 23 August 1939. His Secretary of State, Cardinal Luigi Maglione, went on attempting to defuse tension diplomatically until German armies crossed the Polish border on 1 September. But the Pope's eve-of-war broadcast, with its famous appeal—'Nothing is lost by peace; everything may be destroyed by war'—illustrated the uselessness of traditional diplomacy in a new world order of force and power. Perhaps this was why Pius XII attempted no more full-scale peace initiatives. There were to be good aspects to Vatican wartime conduct—such as the help provided by its Information Service and the charity dispensed to fugitives and refugees. But the Pope's persistent attempts to cling to the diplomatic high ground of impartiality were widely resented.

Hitler had spoken in the Reichstag of German armies crossing the frontier 'to forestall a Polish attack'. The Vatican was said to have blamed Poland for refusing to cede Gdańsk or make gestures to its German minority. It took the Pope till Christmas to speak of a 'premeditated aggression against a small, hard-working, peaceful people, under the pretext of a non-existent threat'.[1] By then, he could just as easily have been referring to Czechoslovakia, carved up by Hitler the previous March, or to Finland, invaded by the Soviet Union in November. Complaints that he failed to react would go on—as Denmark, Norway, Holland, Belgium, Luxembourg, Yugoslavia and Greece fell victim to German invasions. In May 1940, the Pope allegedly admitted to Italy's ambassador to the Vatican, Dino Alfieri, that he had been 'too discreet' about events in Poland. 'Catholicism seems to have failed completely when confronted with the judgement of history', an underground Polish Catholic newspaper declared in 1941. 'In the person of the Pope, we have found neither a great apostle nor a father.'[2]

Even more would be said about Pius XII's alleged failure to denounce the German slaughter of Jews. An unofficial US government *démarche* on the matter was sent to Rome in 1942, followed by others from Britain, Belgium and several Latin American states. But the Pope's position was that he had already condemned Nazi outrages, and would merely intensify the suffering by being more specific.

Before his death on 13 February 1939, Pius XI had prepared an encyclical, *Humani generis unitas*, denouncing racism and distancing the Church from the 'unjust, unforgiving campaign against the Jews under the cloak of Christianity'. The new Pope had used parts in *Summi pontificatus*. But the text as a whole had been left unpublished. Pius XII believed diplomatic pleading would achieve more than public denunciations. According to some accounts, Pius XI had died a day before convening a meeting of Italian bishops to repudiate the Vatican's 1929 Concordat with Mussolini. It was even rumoured he had been poisoned by Nazi agents to pre-empt the encyclical's appearance.[3]

In a letter to Archbishop Konrad von Preysing of Berlin in April 1943, the Pope left it to local bishops to decide whether local circumstances 'recommend them to show reserve'.[4] Evidence suggests some Church leaders in Eastern Europe shared Pius XII's view that speaking out would be unwise. Cardinal Sapieha of Kraków was said to have torn up a collection of documents about the Holocaust smuggled to him from Cardinal Maglione in August 1942, warning that the Nazi governor, Hans Frank, would 'kill all of us' if they were found. 'What would be the use of saying what all the world knows?' Sapieha reputedly added.[5]

But others did not agree. Hungary's Cardinal Jusztinian Serédi warned fellow-senators they would stand accused at the Day of Judgement if they voted for an anti-Semitic law.[6] No one doubted that Jews were being killed on a huge scale. The general outline of what was happening was noted in a Vatican Secretariat of State memorandum, issued in May 1943, two weeks after the outbreak of the Warsaw Ghetto uprising.

> Jews: terrible situation. 4½ million Jews in Poland before the war, plus many deported there from other countries. Number of Jews in Poland now 100,000. Warsaw had a ghetto of approximately 650,000—today, only 20–25,000 ... The disappearance of so many is only explicable by death ... There are death camps at Lublin (Treblinka) and near Brest-Litovsk. It is said that they are put by hundreds in gas-chambers. Transported there in cattle wagons hermetically sealed.[7]

But incontrovertible evidence from Auschwitz did not reach the Vatican until mid-1944. Until then, with wartime propaganda mingling with facts, many Western Church leaders had also doubted whether atrocities were occurring on such a scale. The Hungarian Bishop Apor Vilmos of Győr still deplored the lack of guidance. 'Our flock does not know what to abide by', noted Bishop Vilmos, who was machine-gunned in 1945 by a drunken Soviet soldier while attempting to protect local women. 'In the confessional, they ask if they are allowed to feel sorry for these poor tortured Jews. A devout elderly woman told me almost in fear and whisper, as if she'd committed a crime, that she'd given bread for the people in the ghetto.'[8]

Vatican diplomats later claimed that the Pope saved at least 15,000 Hungarian Jews by personally intervening with Admiral Horthy, as well as tens of thousands through Church channels in Italy. Yet the real question was not whether Pius XII did anything—evidence confirms he did many things—but whether he did all he could. That question could be asked of every wartime leader. But the Pope's moral authority made it particularly important.

Pius XII was not the only contemporary figure to believe formal protests served little purpose. The British premier, Neville Chamberlain, had argued the same during a meeting with Pius XI after the Munich débâcle of 1938.[9] But if the Pope really believed he would worsen the suffering by speaking out, this was the weakest of all his arguments. The historical record confirms overwhelmingly that totalitarian regimes are least likely to respond to diplomatic appeasement. This was certainly the case with communism. But Hitler too, like Stalin, was not above relaxing his religious repressions to gain public support. He did so after *Mit brennender Sorge* in 1937, and when the annexation of Austria and the Czech Sudetenland in 1939 raised the proportion of Catholics in Third Reich territory. To claim that a public denunciation of Nazi crimes would have created a crisis of loyalty and conscience for German soldiers misconceives the respective roles of diplomacy and testimony. No reasonable observer could have expected the Pope to save people just by saying things. But even mere words could have brought comfort to those sentenced to die unnoticed and unmourned in silent anonymity.

A better argument is that Pius XII knew words of condemnation would not be heeded anyway—and that he would merely waste his authority by devoting repetitive verbiage to the daily atrocities. 'If I have to speak one day, I shall do so, but I shall say everything', the Pope remarked to Italy's ambassador in September 1941.[10] To 'say everything' was hardly possible. If it was difficult to obtain firm evidence of Nazi misdeeds, it was even harder with Soviet ones. But the Pope knew enough to be certain that Stalin's cruelty at least equalled that of Hitler—and that his words would cut even less ice with Soviet leaders than with the Nazis. By the time of Hitler's invasion of Russia in 1940, attempts to build a communist paradise had left a peacetime death toll of 20 million. 'When you cut down the forest, woodchips fly', Stalin's NKVD police chief, Nikolai Yezhov, a man known as the 'Bloody Dwarf', had declared in 1936, paraphrasing Lenin. 'Better that ten innocent people should suffer than one spy get away.'[11] Against such a background, would not words of condemnation merely be held up to ridicule?

When the Red Army invaded Poland in 1939, two weeks after the Germans, the Pope warned Lithuania's ambassador that the 'sinister shadow' of the ideology and actions of the 'enemies of God' was growing 'daily closer and more threatening'.[12] Statements like this were taken by some as proof of a one-sided tendency to condemn the Soviet Union. This was unjust. Pacelli had also helped draft *Mit brennender Sorge* and numerous protests against Nazi policies. He was said to have instigated the Vatican's boycott of Hitler's Rome visit in May 1938, an event which dished Hitler's claim to be waging a Church-backed 'anti-Bolshevik crusade'. In 1939, the new Pope was pilloried as the 'Popular Front candidate' by Nazi propagandists. Germany was one of few states which sent no representative to his coronation.

Yet the claim persisted that Pius XII had failed to speak out against Nazi crimes. It was levelled against him by Rolf Hochhuth in *The Representative* (1963). In the early 1970s, it was extended by Carlo Falconi to a wider charge that he had knowingly ignored the fate not only of the Jews, but of Poles, Serbs, Russians and Gypsies as well. Falconi blamed Pius XII's 'bureaucratic, legalistic mentality' and 'over-temporalistic conception' of the Church.[13] Epithets aside, the Pope's stance did indeed cost the Vatican dearly.

Having spent thirteen years as Nuncio in Munich and Berlin, Pius XII was reluctant to admit that Germany was lost to the civilized world. The likes of Himmler and Rosenberg had made clear what an ultimate Nazi victory would mean for the Church, dashing vain expectations that Christianity might somehow benefit from German advances against communism. But the Pope erred in believing the Vatican wielded diplomatic influence in its own right, and that by exercising reserve it could continue to play a decisive part on the international stage. The Vatican's role had already been unclear in 1939. Was it, in the end, just a state with its own temporal interests—albeit whose citizens happened to be spread around the globe? Or was it something much more—the nerve-centre of a world-wide social force, whose power derived from its position as the world's highest moral authority? The Vatican had attempted to be both—and failed to be either. By 1945, many viewed it as little more than an irritating blot on a war-scarred horizon where, as Stalin joked at Yalta, real power was measured only by military divisions.

The Pope's apologists believed he had kept the Vatican aloof from the warring parties, by refusing to confer the mantle of righteousness on either side. But for many, it all looked too much like prevarication and insensitivity. No serious observer could have doubted his repugnance for the 'satanic spectre of Nazism', or his hope that the Western democracies would prevail.[14] But the US Administration wanted more than this. For the benefit of world opinion, it needed Pius XII to bless its wartime alliance with the Soviet Union. And to achieve this, it had to convince Church leaders that religious freedom had been re-established there.

Stalin obliged the Administration with a series of tactical concessions. The Soviet government had slightly modified its treatment of the Russian Orthodox Church by 1938. There was, after all, little left to destroy. With all but 28 bishops either dead or interned, the Church was finished as an opposition force. But Stalin knew it retained an influence, which could be harnessed to highlight his own statesman-like moderation. In 1942, the first Church publication for six years, *The Truth About Religion in Russia*, was issued in various languages, denying claims of religious discrimination. That March, it was reported that Stalin had sent a hand-written letter to Pius XII urging the resumption of Soviet–Vatican ties. The bogus letter, originating in Romania, was an Italian propaganda stunt to discredit the Pope. But it was eagerly seized on by the Allies as proof of a change in Soviet policy.[15] Roosevelt was annoyed that 'certain bishops in the US' were still denouncing collaboration with communists.

'In so far as I am informed, churches in Russia are open', the President wrote to Pius XII on 3 September 1941.

> I believe there is a real possibility that Russia may as a result of the present conflict recognize freedom of religion, although, of course, without recognition of any official intervention on the part of any church in education or political matters ... I believe the survival of Russia is less dangerous to religion, and to the church as such, and to humanity in general than would be the survival of the German form of dictatorship.[16]

In his reply, the Pope studiously avoided taking up Roosevelt's fantasy about religious freedom in Russia, only expressing his hope for 'a true and enduring peace'. But the US government persisted. 'It would seem logical, both from a moral as well as a practical standpoint, that the effort should be made to bring Russia more and more completely into the world family of nations, with identical aims and obligations', the President's envoy, Myron Taylor, wrote to Cardinal Maglione, the Vatican Secretary of State, in 1942.[17]

Stalin went out of his way to give Roosevelt's claim a measure of plausibility. On the night of 4–5 September 1943, the Russian Orthodox Church's three surviving metropolitans were summoned to the Kremlin and offered help in arranging the first meeting of the Church's Synod since 1935. Under the ensuing 'Compromise', nineteen barely living Orthodox bishops were plucked from their gulags and flown to Moscow, to elect Metropolitan Sergei as Patriarch on 8 September. In return for unquestioned subservience to the Soviet state, the Orthodox Church gained *de facto* concessions, including the release of many priests and the reopening of 20,000 churches. The official seat of the Orthodox Patriarchate was moved from a shed on Moscow's outskirts to the former German Embassy.

Significantly, the 'Compromise' was reached several months after the battle of Stalingrad had turned the tide of war in Stalin's favour. The customary view that the Soviet dictator took the surprise initiative at a moment of vulnerability is therefore open to question. A likelier explanation is that Stalin realized the terrorized Orthodox leadership had already, in Lenin's words, been 'taught such a lesson' that it could now be used as a tool in the coming Soviet expansion, particularly against the strong Catholic cultures of Eastern Europe.

Stalin's gesture also chimed in perfectly with Allied arguments that the Soviet Union was a cut above Nazi Germany in civilized standards. But Pius XII still refused to be hoodwinked. The Vatican had an American representative, Fr Leopold Braun, in Moscow throughout the war, as well as scattered observers in Ukraine and Byelorussia, who agreed there were signs of change[18]. But Vatican officials were amazed that the Roosevelt Administration apparently took Soviet claims to heart, and appeared intent on accepting Stalin's assurance that anti-religious policies were being reconsidered.

By the turn of the tide in 1943, the Vatican had antagonized the United States. Something broadly similar had happened during the First World War, when Woodrow Wilson believed Rome was siding with the Central Powers to preserve the Catholic Austro-Hungarian monarchy. The Vatican could argue, as Cardinal Gasparri did then, that neutrality did not mean indifference. It could justify its fear that an unconditional German surrender would, as in 1918, leave Eastern Europe open to the Soviet Union. But the US Administration concluded that the Pope was fanatically anti-Communist, and that his irrational judgements should not be taken seriously when it came to working out the post-war order.

When British and American leaders arrived at Yalta in February 1945, they agreed to Germany's 'complete disarmament, demilitarization and dismemberment'.[19] It would have been hard to imagine how the Vatican could be excluded more comprehensively. Yet even after the Yalta negotiators had carved up Europe, the worn-out Pope still hoped to make his influence felt. In October 1945, Pius XII set out two principles to guide Church–State relations. First, it was the State's duty to secure the common good by allowing unity through diversity—something impossible under totalitarian or authoritarian regimes. Second, the Church's own authority derived from divine precepts and had nothing in common with secular states. The Church would henceforth always support democracy. But the fate of pre-war Europe had shown that democracy was far from foolproof. It required, at the very least, a secure foundation in the Christian faith.[20]

Whatever was said about the Pope's 'obsession with communism', the October allocution, like most of his statements in the 1940s, made no direct reference to it, and had Nazism as much in mind when condemning totalitarianism and authoritarianism. Addressing the cardinals in June 1946, the Pope warned against 'forces of subversion and atheism', and lamented that 'two sister-nations' (Italy and France) now faced 'the unyielding power of a materialist state'. However, the Church's task, he went on, was to 'point out clearly the limits beyond which, to right and left, the rocks and whirlpools stand ready'.[21] This was hardly evidence of a one-sided obsession. Nor was it as far as some Church leaders wished the Pope to go in denouncing communism.

But in Eastern Europe, the Vatican emerged from the war an easy target for communist propagandists.

In independent Croatia, the dictator, Ante Pavelić, had attempted to tie his Ustaše party's nationalistic ideology to Catholicism. The Pope and the Croatian Church were accused of failing to condemn the regime's crimes—which included the massacre of Serbs, Jews and Gypsies, and the forced 'conversion' of 250,000 Orthodox laypeople. It was hard to tell truth from disinformation, especially when Tito's communist Partisans were using collaboration charges as their main weapon against the Church. But certain facts were undeniable. The Pope had received Pavelić in Rome just six weeks after the Croatian state's proclamation. Vatican diplomats were adamant that he had met him as a Catholic, not as a head of State. They also pointed out that, despite Italian pressure, the Pope had never formally recognized the new state—a fact which angered Pavelić, who knew Rome had recognized independent Slovakia. But these were technical details which Tito's propagandists made short work of.

Telling truth from fiction posed equal problems in Slovakia. When Mgr Josef Tiso had become President under German tutelage in 1938, Pius XI had sent a personal blessing. Seven years later, in April 1945, the Catholic priest found himself in handcuffs, deported home by American troops after fleeing across the border to Austria. When his trial opened in December 1946, Tiso cited evidence that he had offered to resign rather than see Nazi laws applied against Slovakia's Jews, and had only consented to stay in office in the hope of using his power to save them. But before he was hanged at 5.30 a.m. on 18 April 1947, the deposed President told a fellow-priest his real aim had been to 'save Christian civilization from communism'.[22] This was hardly a man who could expect justice from a Soviet-directed military court.

The Vatican had recognized Nazi-allied Slovakia on 25 March 1939—as had the Soviet Union, on 16 September. Pius XII had refused to confirm Tiso's monsignorial title, and had ordered the Vatican's chargé d'affaires to protest when the Bratislava parliament passed anti-Jewish legislation in 1941. But these were diplomatic incidents which few people were aware of. They were more likely to remember the Slovak bishops' pastoral letter in April 1942, defending the State's attempts to impede the 'pernicious' and 'dangerous' influence of Jews; or the words of Bishop Karol Kmetko of Nitra, who told Slovakia's Chief Rabbi in 1943 that Jews deserved to be slaughtered and could expect no help without embracing Christianity.[23] 'It is a great misfortune that the President of Slovakia is a priest', the Vatican's deputy Secretary of State, Mgr Domenico Tardini, conceded that July. 'Everyone knows the Holy See cannot bring Hitler to heel. But who will understand that we cannot even control a priest?'[24]

That question would be asked many times. Initially at least, the Vatican had sound reasons for believing the Church's best hopes lay with small states which had tied their reborn national identity to the Catholic faith. In pre-war Yugoslavia, the Serb-led government had looked with hostility at the Catholic Church, seeing it as a natural defender of the separate identity of Croats and Slovenes. In Czechoslovakia, President Masaryk's anti-Catholic culture struggle had cut Church membership by a quarter before petering out. But with the war over, it was clear that Croatia and Slovakia had made poor allies.

Voices of optimism could still be heard in Rome. Cardinal Francis Spellman of New York described how Pius XII's strictures against 'falsehood, imperialism, atheism and contempt for the human person' had a special resonance at a Rome consistory held in February 1946 in the presence of many one-time Nazi and communist victims.[25] It was hoped something might be salvaged in countries not yet fully controlled by Soviet-installed communists.

In Poland, religious worship was unhindered and war-damaged churches reconstructed with State funding, while even the Moscow-trained President Bierut saw an interest in attending occasional church ceremonies. So did Czechoslovakia's communist premier, Klement Gottwald—a man who had bragged to Parliament that his party's headquarters were in Moscow, where he and his colleagues were learning how to 'wring the necks' of their opponents.[26] In Romania and Bulgaria, Vatican nuncios stayed at their posts. Even in Soviet-occupied eastern Germany, the new authorities seemed conciliatory.

The Vatican's Nuncio to Hungary, Archbishop Angelo Rotta, who had vigorously opposed the wartime Arrow Cross government's anti-Jewish measures, was ordered to leave on 5 April 1945, a day after proclamation of the country's liberation. In his memoirs, Cardinal Mindszenty says he travelled to the 1946 Rome Conclave with a letter from Prime Minister Zoltán Tildy, a Calvinist minister, requesting that Rotta be sent back. However, he persuaded Pius XII this was just a stunt to improve the government's image.[27] Pius XII had sharp enough instincts to see that real power already lay with the Soviet-backed parties of Eastern Europe, and that their ideological hostility to the Church would show as Moscow's stranglehold tightened. He knew the war had given way to the *machismo* of geopolitics, and that no Western government would risk further conflict for the sake of human rights.

Yet the fate of millions of Catholics was at stake. To find its place in the post-war order, the Vatican would have to ask itself searching questions. How had Europe's Christians been capable of inflicting such suffering on each other? How could the Church offer hope to a world scarred by Auschwitz and Stalin's purges? Without compromising on principles, the Pope had to exploit whatever practical opportunities existed, while avoiding provocative moves which could give the regimes an excuse for attacking the Church. He also had to rely on local Churches which had a far better knowledge of the rapidly changing situation in Eastern Europe.

If this was the case, Pius XII showed a questionable adroitness when it came to striking the right balance. When Cardinal Hlond arrived back in Poland on 20 July 1945, he announced that he had been given 'special powers' (*facultates specialissimae*) by Pius XII to put the Church's affairs in order 'throughout Polish territory'. By August, 'Polish territory' included rich tracts of eastern Germany, ceded under the Postdam agreement as compensation for Stalin's annexation of Polish lands in the east. The scene in these 'Recovered Territories', Hlond told Mgr Tardini at the Vatican's Secretariat of State, was one of 'total disorganization'. The newly installed Polish authorities consisted of 'communists, uneducated people and Jews seeking revenge'. All German civilians were seen as war criminals, and Soviet troops were grabbing everything they could lay hands on. The German Church's leader in the region, Cardinal Adolf Bertram, had died that July. This made it essential, Hlond argued, for the Polish Church to take over.[28]

The Polish Primate realized that Pius XII could not appear to be taking sides, since the new Oder–Neisse border had not been ratified by an official treaty. Local German bishops had not recognized the border, and could not be seen to have renounced their jurisdiction voluntarily. But they would have no choice if this jurisdiction was revoked by a higher Church authority. This was why, Hlond reasoned, he had been given 'special powers'—to get the Pope off the hook.

The plan ran into trouble. Hlond was unable to brief Cardinal von Preysing of Berlin or provide proof of where his powers extended. When new Polish Church administrators began work on 1 September, the German Church accused him of acting uncanonically. Poland's provisional government was growing angry too. Formed in June under the Yalta agreement, its priority was to consolidate its authority—not least by having Poland's new borders accepted. But although the US, Britain and Germany had recognized the government, the Vatican had maintained ties with Poland's government-in-exile, based in London. Against this background, President Bierut saw Hlond's special powers as a papal dodge to avoid conferring recognition, and as proof of Pius XII's 'well-known liking for Germany'.

Under any other circumstances, the Stalinist party boss would not have cared about the Vatican's position one way or the other. But he saw very quickly that he could use the Pope's ambivalence towards the 'Recovered Territories' against Poland's Catholic Church, by straining its links with Rome and sowing doubts about its patriotism.

On 12 September, the government announced it was terminating Poland's 1925 Concordat. Pius XII had violated the treaty himself, it argued, by nominating German bishops for Polish dioceses during the Nazi occupation. He was now refusing to nominate Polish bishops for the 'Recovered Territories' or even recognize Poland's post-war government.

The Pope insisted his wartime appointments had been made when the Polish dioceses were annexed to the Reich and most Polish priests had fled. But the acrimonious rupture in relations put the Polish Church in an impossible position. How could it combine loyalty to Rome with patriotic concern for the interests of Poland?

Bierut had no intention of allowing a free Church in Poland. But in 1946–47, communist power was not yet secure. Could the Vatican not have played the government at its own game, by holding it to its promises of religious liberty—if need be at the cost of withdrawing its recognition at a later stage?

This, at any rate, was the view of Cardinal Hlond. Bierut's only real interest, Hlond knew, was in playing the Vatican against the Polish Church. But everything suggested, the Primate told Cardinal Sapieha of Kraków, that 'the Church could obtain many things as a price for supporting the government'.[29]

If true, the Vatican's refusal to reopen relations dampened hopes of progress. Poland's bishops knew their authority and autonomy—and personal safety—depended on their connection with the Pope. So there could be no talk of disregarding Vatican directives. But their subservience to Rome gave communist propagandists a field day: here was a Church which questioned its state's borders and betrayed the nation's interests. The bishops could lamely point out that, while the Vatican had not formally recognized Poland's Oder–Neisse frontier, it had not publicly questioned it either. They could also detail the work of integration being done by Polish Church personnel in the 'Recovered Territories'. But in the end, Hlond was in no doubt that he and his colleagues had been used.

> In 1945, none of the German bishops could resign his jurisdiction of his own free will without incurring his society's disapproval. So when the Polish administrators were appointed, the bishops presented their formal objection to the Holy See. But in reality they were pleased the appointments had been made without their needing to resign voluntarily. They are now basking in the glory of martyrdom and public injury, while the whole responsibility rests on me.[30]

Atomic bombs had been dropped on Hiroshima and Nagasaki on 6 and 9 August, within days of the Postdam agreement; so Pius XII had had other matters on his mind. He was convinced Europe needed a strong post-war Germany, and had chosen to stay diplomatically aloof between the Polish and German Churches. But the impression remained that he had merely washed his hands of a murky situation, leaving the Polish Church dangerously exposed and accelerating confrontation with Eastern Europe's communist-dominated regimes.

By the late 1940s, Poland was not the only country to have turned overtly hostile to the Vatican. In Romania and Ukraine, the campaign against Greek Catholics highlighted the extent to which Orthodox hierarchies were being used as tools of communist policy. 'The Vatican's activity is directed against the popular masses', declared Patriarch Justinian Marina of Bucharest at a Moscow conference. 'It has become a centre for international intrigues against the interests of the peoples, particularly the Slavs, and a centre of international fascism.'[31] In December 1945, Pius XII addressed a special letter, *Orientales omnes Ecclesias*, to Greek Catholics for the 350th anniversary of their Church's creation at the Union of Brest. No Pope could have failed to feel deeply for those now suffering and dying for no other reason than that they wished to maintain ties with the Holy See.

But Pius XII was soon grappling with another danger too. With most Church–State agreements now annulled, the new regimes were cajoling priests and laity to throw in their hand with the communist programme. If 'representative' Catholic bodies could be set up, they could elect their own bishops and declare 'national Churches' independent of papal jurisdiction. This threatened to undermine the Church more than any act of persecution. 'To be with Christ or against Christ: that is the whole question', the Pope declared at Christmas 1948. Only 'traitors and deserters' could lend their services to 'parties that deny God, put might in the place of right, threats and terror in the place of liberty, and turn lying, opposition and incitement of the masses into weapons of policy, thus rendering national and international peace impossible'.[32]

When it came to figureheads, there were two men who had the kind of qualities Pius XII expected—Archbishop Stepinac and Cardinal Mindszenty. At his trial in 1946, Stepinac had conspicuously stood behind the Pope's authority. When he was sentenced, *L'Osservatore Romano* published a decree excommunicating those who had taken part in his trial. The Pope expected other bishops and archbishops to meet the same fate—Cardinal Wyszyński said he could sense this 'in every document' emanating from Rome.[33] When Hungary's Cardinal Mindszenty was charged with treason in 1948, it therefore caused little surprise.

In his memoirs, Mindszenty insists he too was interpreting the Pope's will in concluding that shallow compromises would not help the Church. Pius XII had met Mindszenty first during a visit to Budapest in 1938. He had been so impressed that in 1945, after just a year as a bishop, the country's youngest prelate was named Primate of Hungary. It was the Pope's 'robust confidence' in him, Mindszenty says, which persuaded him to accept.[34]

Mindszenty's arrest came six months after the Cominform's denunciation of Tito, when Stalin was baying for blood. But Pius XII was not intimidated. A decree from Rome's Consistorial Congregation excommunicated Catholics involved in the Hungarian Cardinal's detention and urged international pressure. When Mindszenty appeared in court, the Pope called it a 'mock trial'.

It was now 'well known', he declared at a Mass of expiation in St Peter's Square, what totalitarian states would extract as their price for tolerance. They wanted a Church which 'waters down the law of God' and 'slavishly stays shut within its four walls'. The text of Matthew 22:9 ('Go therefore to the thoroughfares . . .') was, Pius XII added, a 'good passage to go back to when we drink a little too deeply of the heady spirit of accommodation'.[35]

The Pope had concluded that tough rhetoric was merited everywhere, irrespective of local conditions. In Czechoslovakia, where anti-Vatican propaganda was mounting in ferocity, he condemned the 1948 communist coup and demanded the disciplining of 'political priests' against the advice of local bishops. The Catholic clergy were depicted as traitors in the service of foreign powers. 'If you obey the government, you will get this and that. If you obey the Vatican, you will get nothing', President Gottwald reputedly told priests in July 1949.[36]

The strong Vatican reaction had some effect. Even 'progressive' priests in Czechoslovakia became reluctant to support the regime's initiatives, and the once-defiant Health Minister, Fr Plojhar, began staying away from government sessions. The communist regimes were aware that priests in disrepute with their own Church were of limited usefulness. As word got around about the Pope's condemnations, most found themselves ostracized by ordinary Catholics.

Yet if Pius XII's forceful stance weakened elements attempting to undermine the Church from within, it did not remove them. In early 1949, Pius XII was still certain most Church leaders were about to be martyred. Meeting that February, Cominform delegates urged a continued offensive to break the Church's links with Rome. The best response, the Pope believed, was to steel one's courage for whatever lay in store. History had justified Tertullian's adage, 'the blood of martyrs is the seed of the Church'.

It was, however, the prospect of a split in the East European Church between pro-regime and pro-Rome groups which prompted the Vatican's next move. In a dramatic, unexpected decree, dated 1 July, the Holy Office said it had been asked whether it was 'lawful to join Communist Parties or favour them', and to distribute publications supporting the 'teaching or action of Communists'. A ruling had also been requested, the Holy Office continued, as to whether Catholics who 'knowingly and freely' did so should be given the sacraments, and whether Catholics who 'profess, defend or propagate' communist doctrine should be excommunicated as apostates.

The answers were clear. No, it was not lawful: the sacraments were to be refused and communists excommunicated.

> Communism is materialistic and anti-Christian; and the leaders of the Communists, although they sometimes profess in words that they do not oppose religion, do in fact show themselves, both in their teaching and in their actions, to be the enemies of God, of the true religion and of the Church of Christ.[37]

The Decree was intended to remove any doubts about a possible change in the Vatican's position. Corruption from within had been the fear behind Pius X's condemnation of Modernism in the early twentieth century—an alleged conspiracy which, unlike communism, had never progressed beyond intellectual abstractions. Then as now, the reasoning went, the Church's greatest danger lay in internal subversion. It had to impose discipline on its members.

Although brief, the Decree contained potentially important nuances. The phrase 'knowingly and freely' (*scienter et libere*) offered room for interpretation, as did words like 'profess', 'defend' and 'propagate'. But most readers simply saw it as restating the 1937 strictures of Pius XI's *Divini Redemptoris*— 'Communism has treacherously attempted to worm its way into the bosom of the Church and has been thrown out', exulted the Jesuit-edited *Civiltà Cattolica*.[38] That reaction summed up the mood in conservative Vatican circles.

Pius XII was alarmed at the threat from Western communist parties as well. As the Soviet grip on Eastern Europe tightened, it seemed ever more important to prevent the communist 'contagion' from spreading. The Decree would hardly discourage militant, committed communists. But it might dissuade some communist waverers, or at least wean them in the direction of less threatening alternatives.

Yet if the Decree was intended to drive wedges, this was no more than a surmise. The condemnation of socialism remained on the doctrinal statute-books from *Quadragesimo anno* in 1931. If existing doctrine was taken seriously, socialists and communists were equally unacceptable.

There was evidence that views were divided in the Vatican over the wisdom of Pius XII's move. At the Secretariat of State, Mgr Tardini thought the Decree lacked 'psychological preparation' and voiced 'sincere dissatisfaction at the work methods of the Holy Office'.[39] It met mixed reactions from Church leaders elsewhere too—not least in France and Germany, where some form of co-operation between reforming Catholics and moderate communists was being widely canvassed. But the most serious charge against Pius XII related to Eastern Europe, where he had made Catholics appear disloyal *en masse*. There had been no decree barring Catholics from working with Nazis and Fascists. Since all areas of public life were already under communist control, the Decree amounted, in effect, to an injunction against any Catholic social activity.

If anyone pointed this out to Pius XII, however, the Pope took no notice. A follow-up decree on 11 August required special dispensations for marriages between Catholics and communists. Another, in July 1950, barred children in communist youth groups from the sacraments. This third document conceded that some Catholics had joined communist organizations to save their lives or jobs. But it added a new provision, excommunicating Catholics who collaborated with communists in Third World anti-colonial movements for plotting against the 'lawful authority' of Church and state.

This was the kind of polarization which suited the communist mentality, at a time when 'soft targets' like the Church were needed to help the new regimes consolidate. Pius XII had made no effort to understand the fears and illusions on which communism was feeding. Rather than entering the battle for hearts and minds drawn to the utopian dream of a new world order, he had resorted to legalistic injunctions. In the daily reality of life, Eastern Europe's Catholics were on their own.

Notes

1. Quoted in William Purdy, *The Church on the Move* (London: Hollis & Carter, 1966), pp. 32–4. See also Léon Papeloux, *Les Silences de Pie XII* (Brussels: Vokaer, 1980), pp. 93–122.
2. Papeloux, op. cit., p. 38; Jonathan Lewis, 'Pius XII and the Jews: the myths and the facts', *The Tablet* (25 February 1995), p. 250; Jean Chelini, *L'Église sous Pie XII* (Paris: Fayard, 1989), pp. 261–88.
3. Georges Passelecq and Bernard Suchecky, *L'Encyclique cachée de Pie XI* (Paris: Éditions La Découverte, 1995); *Ecumenical News International* (6 October 1995), pp. 7–9.
4. Text in Saul Friedlander, *Pie XII et le IIIe Reich—Documents* (Paris: Éditions du Seuil, 1964), p. 129.
5. Quoted in Purdy, op. cit., p. 259.
6. Ibid., pp. 263–4; Andor Csimadia, *Rechtliche Beziehungen von Staat und Kirche in Ungarn vor 1944* (Budapest: Akadémiai Kiadó, 1971).
7. P. Blet, R. Graham et al. (eds), *Actes et documents du Saint-Siège relatifs à la seconde guerre mondiale* (Vatican City, 1967–82), vol. 9, no. 174, p. 274.
8. Quoted in Lewis, op. cit., p. 250.
9. Purdy, op. cit., p. 29.
10. From *Documenti Diplomatici Italiani* (Rome), series IX, vol. 7; in Italo Garzia, 'Pope Pius XII, Italy and World War II', unpublished paper (1991), p. 11.
11. Extracts from Yezhov's speech in Roy Medvedev, *Let History Judge* (New York: Columbia University Press, 1989), p. 603.
12. Carlo Falconi, *The Popes in the Twentieth Century* (London: Weidenfeld and Nicolson, 1967), p. 255.
13. Carlo Falconi, *The Silence of Pius XII* (London: Faber and Faber, 1970), pp. 46–65; Rolf Hochhuth, *The Representative* (London: Methuen, 1963).
14. Purdy, op. cit., p. 43.
15. Antoine Wenger, *Rome et Moscou 1900–1950* (Paris: Desclée de Brouwer, 1987), pp. 587–91.
16. Myron C. Taylor (ed.), *Wartime Correspondence Between President Roosevelt and Pope Pius XII* (New York: Macmillan, 1947), pp. 61–2.
17. Ibid., p. 63.
18. Wenger, op. cit., pp. 577–9. The minutes of Stalin's secret meeting with the three metropolitans, taken by Georgi Karpov, were published for the first time by the Russian daily *Sievodnia* in 1994; see *Ecumenical News International* (14 October 1994).
19. Michael Charlton, *The Eagle and the Small Birds* (London: BBC Books, 1984), pp. 11–52; Pierre de Senarclens, *Yalta* (Paris: Presses Universitaires de France, 1984).
20. Allocution to the Roman Rota (2 October 1945); in Sidney Z. Ehler and John B. Morrall (eds), *Church and State Through the Ages* (London: Burns and Oates, 1954), p. 604.

21. Purdy, op. cit., p. 91.
22. 'Dokumentý o procesu s Jozefem Tisem', *Listý* (Bratislava), vol. 22, no. 5 (1992), pp. 49–58.
23. Lewis, op. cit., pp. 251–2.
24. Blet et al. (eds), *Actes et Documents*, vol. 8, no. 426, p. 598.
25. Robert Gannon, *The Cardinal Spellman Story* (London: Robert Hale, 1963), p. 292.
26. Jacques Rupnik, 'Czechoslovak Communists and the State (1928–48)' in N. Stone and E. Strouhal (eds), *Czechoslovakia: Crossroads and Crisis 1918–88* (London: Macmillan, 1989), p. 171.
27. József Mindszenty, *Memoirs* (London: Weidenfeld & Nicolson, 1974), p. 43.
28. Peter Raina (ed.), *Kościoł w PRL—Dokumenty 1945–1959* (Poznań: W Drodze, 1994), p. 15.
29. Ibid., p. 77; Kazimierz Papee, *Pius XII a Polska 1939–1949: Przemówienia, Listy, Komentarze* (Rome: Editrice Studium, 1954).
30. Quoted in Mikołaj Lizut, 'Błąd kardynala', *Gazeta Wyborcza* (2 December 1995).
31. Mireille Macqua, *Rome–Moscou: L'Ostpolitik du Vatican* (Louvain-la-Neuve: Cabay, 1984), p. 150.
32. Carlo Falconi, *The Popes in the Twentieth Century*, op. cit., p. 266.
33. Stefan Wyszyński, *A Freedom Within* (London: Hodder & Stoughton, 1985), p. 4.
34. Mindszenty, op. cit., p. 33.
35. Purdy, op. cit., pp. 92–3.
36. Karel Kaplan, 'Church and State in Czechoslovakia from 1948 to 1956, Part II', *Religion in Communist Lands* (Keston), vol. 14, no. 24 (1986), p. 181.
37. Text of the Decree in Ehler and Morrall, op. cit., p. 611.
38. Andrea Riccardi, *Il Potere del Papa: da Pio XII a Giovanni Paolo II* (Rome: Editori Laterza, 1993), p. 97.
39. According to Vladimir d'Ormesson, France's ambassador to the Vatican; Riccardi, op. cit., pp. 97–8. See also Carlo Felice Casula, *Domenico Tardini 1888–1961: L'azione della Santa Sede nella crisi fra le due guerra* (Rome: Edizioni Studium, 1988), pp. 153–268.

4

୧ଽ୧ଽ୧ଽ୧ଽ

Post-Stalinism and its discontents

Ironically, it was the East European regimes themselves which did most to publicize the 1949 Decree at a time when local Church leaders would have preferred to keep quiet about it. Perhaps the Pope hoped it would have a similar effect to Pius XI's sanctions against Action Française in 1927, which were relaxed a decade later at the pleading of the movement's now-humbled leader, Charles Maurras. But if he expected a show of contrition by communist regimes, Pius XII plainly misjudged them.

The campaign against the Church in Eastern Europe long predated the Decree. But the Pope's latest 'hostile act' was used as a pretext for stepping up repression.

In Poland, where the government branded the document an 'act of aggression against the Polish state', the Catholic bishops tried to deflate the Decree's importance. It had brought 'nothing new', they insisted, only 'clarification of ambiguities'. It was a 'purely religious document' for Catholics wishing 'to act consistently' with Church teachings. 'The Decree evaluates communism not from a social or economic perspective, or with reference to the struggle for a new social order, but as a materialistic and anti-Christian world-view', the bishops continued. 'So we can conclude it has no real political character. It does not attack any state or struggle against any government.'[1] Church leaders were aware that Poland's communist rulers would tolerate differences of opinion. But if they could show these were being politicized, the rulers would take action. This was the real danger underlying the 1949 Decree.

The Polish regime had been negotiating a 'freedom of conscience' law with Church leaders. But on 5 August, it went ahead and issued the law unilaterally, nationalizing Church lands and barring religion from schools. Even now, Church leaders attempted to play down the Vatican document. 'Because the Decree merely recalls Church law and clarifies internal religious sanctions, the bishops did not think it was necessary to inform the public about it', the Bishops' Conference secretary, Bishop Zygmunt Choromański, told the government. 'But since the Polish press has begun to mislead society, we decided out of necessity to inform priests through private channels—not about how to implement the Decree in Poland, only about the current state of affairs.'[2]

Reactions were harsher elsewhere. In Hungary, Cardinal Mindszenty's life sentence was confirmed by the appeal court on 6 July, a few days after the Decree. In Romania, Bishop Augustin Pacha of Timişoara was arrested on 19 July and jailed for eighteen years as a 'Vatican spy'. In Bulgaria, the Decree was labelled a 'medieval provocation' and followed by new measures against orders and seminaries. Moves to break the Church's ties with Rome were intensified in Lithuania and other Soviet republics. 'The Pope revealed his anti-Christian face in all its ugliness by his recent decree excommunicating communists', the Orthodox Moscow Patriarchate concurred with the Soviet government.[3] In far-away China, the proclamation of Mao's Tse-tung's People's Republic in October was accompanied by ruthless persecution of organized religion.

The Czechoslovak government had already asked the Vatican to recall its chargé d'affaires, Mgr Gennaro Verolino, whose 'conspiratorial actions' had been mentioned at the Mindszenty trial in Budapest the previous February. On 13 July, he was ordered out. 'On the evening of Verolino's departure forever from our country, which he wished to plunge into civil war, a decree over the Holy See's radio announced the excommunication of all Catholic communists', Justice Minister Aleksiej Čepička exulted two days later. 'This is only an expression of rage at the success of the workers in their struggle against exploiters. Those who try to carry out orders from the Vatican are without doubt traitors to the state and the people.'[4]

Even in Czechoslovakia, there were grounds for supposing the Vatican's tough line could yield dividends. Threat of excommunication deterred many priests from collaborating with the regime's organizations. When a 'peace congress' was arranged in 1951 by the notorious Fr Plojhar, many objected to attacks being made on the Vatican.

But by then Archbishop Beran had been ousted and over 3,000 priests were under lock and key. 'Action K', planned by Klement Gottwald, had closed 247 monasteries on the single night of 13–14 February 1950, while the country's Catholic seminaries had been reduced from seven to two. Bishops who stayed loyal to the Pope, such as Ján Vojtaššák of Spiš and Pavol Gojdič of Prešov, were imprisoned for treason. But subservience was no defence either. Those who tried to conciliate the regime by signing its loyalty oath soon encountered a similar fate.

Similar stories of persecution could be heard throughout the region. A combination of wartime suffering and communist pressure had diminished the Catholic Church's association with historic injustices, making communist claims about its alliance with reactionary forces sound distinctly outdated. But the Vatican Decree appeared to reaffirm the stereotype—that all Catholics were enemies of communism. It reimposed a fixed position on Church leaders, at a time when they needed to take their own case-by-case decisions. This was a point stressed by Cardinal Wyszyński in Poland. It was, predictably, Wyszyński who became the first to break ranks.

At the time of the Decree's appearance, Fr Karol Wojtyła had been at his first Kraków parish for less than four months. He had arrived at St Florian's on 17 March 1949, and had poured his energy into the job. Youth associations were not permitted by Poland's communist rulers, so pastoral work among the young was particularly important. That was where Karol excelled. Being a priest under Stalinist rule implied a certain heroism—the heroism of publicly representing a faith which contradicted the invincible ideology of state and party. It required a tight self-discipline, and a sensitivity to the complex moral choices confronting all citizens.

Perhaps Karol had gained these qualities mostly from his wartime experiences, as well as his travels among the worker priests of France and Belgium. Many people were struck by the young priest's novel style of preaching. The language of most sermons was stiff and declaratory, learned by rote from official Church handbooks. But Karol's were more philosophical. He preached a Gospel for everyday life, for those scared and bewildered by the new conditions around them.

One other Kraków priest was similarly known for his open, approachable style—Fr Jan Pietraszko. Like him, Karol was sometimes criticized for being too contemplative and cerebral. This seemed to encourage followers to flee the world rather than confront the challenge of communism. But in the prevailing atmosphere, contemplation was a form of resistance. It was a kind of resistance which contrasted sharply with the loud, defiant noises coming out of Rome.

At the time, few priests had much awareness of the controversies over the Vatican's wartime role. But those who did generally assumed Pius XII had been misinformed. Similarly, few priests heard about the Holy Office Decree. But those who did hear about it tended to believe the Vatican had underestimated the real-life complexities of societies under the Stalinist yoke.

The Polish Church had traditionally enjoyed a kind of love–hate relationship with Rome, which touched Karol Wojtyła as it touched other priests. In the nineteenth century, when Poland was partitioned, the Vatican had offered moral support. But it had also counselled acquiescence and let the Poles down at key moments, as in 1830 when Gregory XVI condemned the Polish cadets' November Uprising. No doubt, this reflected Rome's strategic relations with Russia, Austria and Germany, as well as its fear that an anarchic Polish Parliament would corrupt Slavic Catholicism.

The Vatican had recognized Poland in 1919, seeing it as a Catholic bridgehead after the collapse of the Habsburg monarchy. But as late as 1916, its Secretary of State, Cardinal Gasparri, had dismissed Polish independence as 'a dream, an impossible goal!'[5] Although the future Pius XI, as Achille Ratti, was one of few diplomats who remained in Warsaw during the 'Miracle on the Vistula', he was disliked by the Polish Right and its Church hierarchy allies during his 1918–21 term as Vatican representative. For one thing, he was close to the ex-socialist Marshal Piłsudski. For another, he insisted on staying neutral in Poland's dispute with Germany over Silesia, at a time when many suspected the Vatican of supporting Berlin's claims.

Though dubbed 'Il Papa Polacco' (the Polish Pope) at his election in 1922, Ratti was not considered a friend of Poland. His support for eastern Poland's Greek Catholic minority was said by Foreign Minister Józef Beck to have 'weakened the Polish state and Catholic life'.[6] Meanwhile, the Vatican's advice to appease Hitler's territorial ambitions in the 1930s was particularly resented. It was an issue which seriously damaged the Polish view of his successor, Pius XII, as well.

Karol Wojtyła would have known the scene from Słowacki's Romantic-era drama *Kordian*, where a feeble pontiff, parrot perched on shoulder, ignores the pleas of a Polish visitor. It conveyed the view inherited by Polish priests—although needed as an advocate on the international stage, the Vatican was an ally who could not be relied on.

But the young priest from Kraków had reasons for seeing things a little differently. Wojtyła had been at the Vatican and seen something of its inner workings. He had had a chance to sense for himself how Rome's power could be used. Karol's mentor, Cardinal Adam Sapieha, had once worked in the Vatican Curia. In 1918, when a meeting of Polish bishops was called at Częstochowa, Achille Ratti had hurried down from Warsaw, only to be told rudely by Sapieha that they wished to confer *alone*. But Sapieha's relations with Pacelli were different. He shared Pius XII's aristocratic disdain for deals and compromises, and wielded greater influence in Rome than Poland's Primate, Cardinal Hlond. 'He was full of power and strength, unafraid of any persecutions', the Pope said at Sapieha's death in 1951.[7]

By the 1950s, Wojtyła's thinking had been shaped by Nazi occupation and Stalinist repression. His study of St John of the Cross had taught him the virtue of contemplation, while his seminary training had introduced him to the traditional Thomism which dominated Polish Catholicism. Wojtyła recalled later that his first encounter with the Thomist philosophical system caused an 'intellectual shock'. Although required to learn from old-fashioned textbooks, he came to see it as 'in some senses perfect'. But it still left gaps when it came to understanding the contemporary perplexities of communist-ruled Poland.[8]

In 1951, Wojtyła left St Florian's for the Jagiellonian University's Theology Faculty, to work on his 'Habilitation' (associate professorship) thesis: 'The possibility of building Christian ethics on the assumptions of Max Scheler's system'. Scheler (1874–1928) had worked with the German philosopher Edmund Husserl. Like Husserl's other assistant, Edith Stein, a Jew who became a Carmelite nun and died at Auschwitz, he had converted to Catholicism. But he had later discarded the idea of a personal God in favour of a deeper metaphysical reflection.

Scheler studied the ethical codes upheld by different societies in history, in an attempt to show that absolute, objective values were the outcome of a cumulative process. Wojtyła's purpose was to ask whether this approach was useful for the study of Christian ethics too. The conclusion of his thesis was negative. But he was impressed by Scheler's accompanying notion of the human person as a 'searcher for God', who achieved full development by gradually recognizing the divine. The philosopher's work taught something about the strengths and limitations of Christianity. It also showed how the Phenomenological method of enquiry could help clarify the internal life of the human person.

Phenomenology—the philosophical school associated with Husserl—maintained that it was possible to look beyond everyday 'objective' experiences and recognize the 'subjective' essence of phenomena perceived by the human mind. This meant 'putting the world in parenthesis' and being free to examine the 'stream of consciousness'. The Jagiellonian's principal Phenomenologist, Roman Ingarden, who had worked closely with Husserl, was dismissed by the communist regime in the early 1950s. But as a 'philosophy of conscience', Phenomenology helped Wojtyła reflect on the social and psychological experiences of those around him, and on how these experiences had shaped personalities and the understanding of values.

There was an obvious contrast here with Thomist metaphysics. Thomism was a universal system, existing above and beyond historical contexts. It was less open to the specific dilemmas of people living through particular periods. By contrast, Phenomenology could help non-believers understand the 'experience' of Christianity. It could even lead them to Christianity through its values, if not through its dogmas. It also offered an antidote to the official ideology of communism. Whereas Marxism stressed the duty to change the world through revolutionary destruction, Phenomenology taught that it was necessary to understand the world first—but this time in a methodical way which took full account of human nature's complexities. Whereas the Stalinist system encouraged citizens to believe the person 'exists through acting', Phenomenology introduced an element of modest, detached reflection. It offered tools for analysing the contrast between Marxist theory and practice. It also referred to traditions of thought stretching back to antiquity, whereas the Marxist emphasis was on violent discontinuity—a new beginning after wasted centuries.

Karol Wojtyła's pastoral work among young people at St Florian's inevitably carried certain political implications. But if this was a form of opposition, it was the kind of persistent 'space-creating' opposition within the system which was favoured by Cardinal Sapieha. In the early 1950s, Polish Marxism still claimed to be a 'total theory', an all-embracing science which would create a 'new Man' to inhabit a new social order. Outright priestly defiance was not allowed by the Church any more than it was by Poland's communists.

At that stage, most priests had only a vague awareness of the Polish Communist Party's ideological claims. Only in 1950, when Poland's Bishops' Conference agreed to place the Party's *Trybuna Ludu* in seminary libraries, could they even read a daily newspaper. Although issues like agricultural collectivization provoked lively discussions, most had never read Marxism. They knew it only from its visible impact—the daily anxieties generated by the Party's expanding dogmatism.

Better informed priests might challenge Marxism over its interpretation of religion. But they often ran into trouble when they questioned its more complex theories of oppression and alienation. Many were left confused, unable to tell whether Marxist pretensions were good or bad. For priests like Karol Wojtyła, with a sensitivity to social injustice, discretion was often the better part of valour if one was to avoid dangerous entanglements in words and definitions.

Wojtyła was still at St Florian's when Cardinal Wyszyński signed an 'Understanding' with the Polish government on 14 April 1950. This, the first accord with a communist regime reached independently of the Vatican, had been approved by the Polish Bishops' Conference after a lengthy debate. But it was Wyszyński's in conception. 'We had no foreign models to look to, and it would have been unwise not to realize the gravity of our situation', was the Primate's explanation.

It was up to the Bishops' Conference to conduct the Church's affairs in the context of the 'Polish reality', in such a way as to spare the Church new losses—all the more since we could expect these to be merely the *initia dolorum*, the first of our sorrows. The whole development of social change was certain to produce conflict: Christianity versus Godlessness. To make certain such a conflict did not find us unprepared, we had to gain time to build up strength to defend God's positions.[9]

The Understanding embodied a simple bargain: the State would protect the Church's rights, while the Church would recognize the State's secular competence. It committed the Church to 'encourage support for national reconstruction and respect for the State authorities'. In return, it appeared to provide the Church with a degree of institutional protection.[10]

Church leaders knew the regime would see the Understanding as no more than a stage in its *realpolitik*, enabling it to exploit the Church's authority before finally crushing it once communist power was secure. But they believed the risk was worth taking. The Understanding established no more than a few vague quasi-legal precedents. But without them, Church–State relations would have no legal basis whatever. With the Church acknowledged in this way, it would be harder to justify future repression.

Wyszyński sensed the regime had staked its legitimacy on social and economic advance. Until this was achieved, it would be unable to risk the head-on conflict occurring in Czechoslovakia or Romania. Of course, the government's record warranted a deep mistrust. But history—anti-clerical France, Bismarck's Germany, Mexico, Spain, Russia—showed the Church never turned down the possibility of agreement. 'I was not opportunistic', Wyszyński insisted. 'I believed a compromise in relations was absolutely necessary, just as it was inevitable that this country with a Catholic viewpoint must coexist with its official materialism.' [11]

This was to be more or less the claim advanced by Hungary's bishops too, when they signed their own agreement with the regime of Mátyás Rákosi on 30 August 1950. Hungary's Calvinist, Lutheran and Jewish communities had obtained similar security-for-subservience promises in 1948. With Mindszenty jailed and resistance emasculated, most bishops believed the Catholic Church had no choice but to follow suit.

Yet the agreement, signed four months after Poland's, was weighted heavily against the Church. It guaranteed 'full religious freedom'. But this was already guaranteed in Hungary's new Stalinist constitution of 1949; and it could mean whatever the communist authorities wanted it to mean. The regime made only two practical concessions. First, out of 3,000 pre-war Catholic schools, it consented to restore just eight. Second, it agreed to continue the Habsburg policy of subsidizing the Church financially—for eighteen years, with gradual reductions, 'until the Church develops its own means of support'. Just how the Church would do that, in a State-controlled economy, was anyone's guess. In reality, the provision merely gave the State a material stranglehold.

Perhaps even this was better than nothing. But the *quid pro quo* extracted from the Church was far more wide-ranging. It required the bishops to 'recognize and support' the government and constitution, back the regime's 'peace movement', and discipline priests 'obstructing the peaceful development of the Hungarian People's Republic'. It also noted that Hungary's Stalinist Five-Year Plan was 'designed to raise our living standard and ensure social justice', called on Catholics to 'do all in their power' to implement it, and instructed parish priests not to oppose the enforcement of collective farms—that 'voluntary union of farm workers based on the moral principle of human solidarity'. 'The bishops sternly condemn any sort of political activity designed to overthrow the present social order', the document stipulated. 'Furthermore, they will not tolerate the debasement of the Catholic Church and laity into instruments of treason and revolution.'[12] That was just about as far as down the road of subservience as any Church hierarchy could have gone.

Rákosi himself had described Poland's 'Understanding' as a model. But he had openly rejected Church demands for an end to State interference. With 2,800 interned monks and nuns threatened with deportation to Siberia, the bishops had clearly acted under duress. What had emerged was a document slanted overwhelmingly in the State's favour, with none of the checks and balances evident in the Polish case.

The bishops' subservience was to produce few benefits anyway. In May 1951, a State Office was set up with powers to supervise Church appointments. And in June, the agreement's main Church signatory, Archbishop József Grősz of Kalocsa, was arrested for 'espionage and conspiracy' and jailed for fifteen years. That July, surviving bishops went ahead and took a loyalty oath to the constitution.

Writing later, Grősz's successor at Kalocsa, Archbishop József Ijjas, would defend the 1950 agreement as expressing the Church's 'subservience to the dynamics of a historical juncture'. Besides quoting Leo XIII's distinction in *Immortale Dei* (1885) between the respective goals of Church and State, he offered numerous biblical texts to justify the bishops' stance, such as Romans 13:1-2: 'Let every person be subject to the governing authorities. For there is no authority except from God, and those that exist have been instituted by God.' The Archbishop cut short his New Testament exegesis before St Paul went on to describe rulers as 'ministers and servants of God'. Not even Ijjas had the nerve to suggest this applied to the likes of Rákosi.[13]

Cardinal Mindszenty, not surprisingly, saw things differently. The agreement had been a 'profound humiliation' for the Church, the Primate wrote. The letters and sermons which followed it were 'caricatures of religion'. Mindszenty was surprisingly mild towards the 'kind and loyal' Archbishop Grősz, noting only that his 'vacillations weakened rather than secured his situation'. But the agreement was another matter. 'Of course, the humiliation was part of the communists' plan', Mindszenty declared. 'But the most outrageous thing of all was that priests were now forced to take a line directly contrary to their own inclinations. . .They now had to ask citizens to collaborate with the atheists.'[14]

Ironically, Stalin's death on 3 March 1953 was followed by fresh crackdowns in Eastern Europe, as efforts were made to suppress expectations of change. But it also brought the first signs of crisis in world communism.

By now, both sides in Poland were accusing each other of flouting the 1950 understanding. That September, Cardinal Wyszyński was arrested for 'abusing ecclesiastical functions'. Having failed to harness the Church's authority, the regime had resorted to direct action.

Although the Cardinal was held for three years, he was never formally charged. But an authoritative article in the Communist Party's daily, *Trybuna Ludu*, on the day of his arrest (25 September) accused him of exerting an 'unreasonable influence' over other Polish bishops, and ignoring a 'solemn promise' to dissociate himself from 'hostile American–Vatican actions'. 'For Primate Wyszyński, the Understanding was only a manoeuvre, designed to mislead the government and public opinion', the paper asserted.[15] It was something of a backhanded compliment to Wyszyński's political astuteness.

During the month of the Cardinal's detention, another bishop, Czesław Kaczmarek of Kielce, after being held without trial for 32 months, was jailed for twelve years for allegedly collaborating with the Germans. By then, five other bishops and 900 priests had been arrested too. Catholic university faculties, newspapers and seminaries faced drastic new restrictions.

The pattern was repeated throughout Eastern Europe. In July 1953, the Vatican confirmed that seventeen bishops in neighbouring Czechoslovakia were in prison or detention, leaving a single auxiliary still at large. In the German Democratic Republic—the Soviet-occupied state proclaimed in 1949—the ruling Socialist Unity Party (SED) maintained the orthodox Marxist view that industrialization would destroy religion more effectively than outright repression. But dozens of Catholic priests and Evangelical ministers had also been jailed. The savage suppression of an uprising in June 1953 reinforced the regime's power.

Support for communism was nevertheless eroding. In Poland, it was clear that Sovietization had no mass constituency. Stalin's system was hostile to bourgeois freedoms and cut across the attachment to national statehood. Having rebelled against Russian domination since the eighteenth century, the Poles were rejecting Soviet rule too.

Meanwhile, the Catholic Church was re-emerging as a social force. The communist offensive had strengthened its popular identification with national history and culture. The hopes aroused by the post-war communist programme had been squandered by Bierut's Stalinist brutality. In 1954, the Communist Party admitted Poland's rural inhabitants had resisted collectivization. No one had managed to deter demands for a more democratic, accountable system.

Many older Polish communists had nursed a covert resentment of Stalin's Soviet Union, remembering the murder of their pre-war communist colleagues in the Moscow show-trials of the late 1930s. Information about the incident had long since been suppressed. But by the mid-1950s, some Communist Party members had begun to speak about it again. In any case, the communist stranglehold on information, science and culture had never been absolute in Poland. Although freedom of expression was severely restricted, it was becoming possible to criticize more openly. As awareness of communism's shortcomings spread, Western books were being smuggled into the country—George Orwell, Arthur Koestler, Albert Camus, Jean-Paul Sartre—which explored the inside workings of the system and its ideology.

When the General Secretary of the Soviet Communist Party, Nikita Khrushchev, denounced Stalin's crimes at the Twentieth CPSU Congress in February 1956, it came less as a sudden revelation than as confirmation of what had been sensed for some time. It would take three decades for Khrushchev's 'Secret Speech' to be published officially in the Soviet Union. But in Eastern Europe, the text was circulated to Party cadres and broadcast by the US-funded Radio Free Europe in Munich. The eradication of Stalin's personality cult became official policy here also.

'How rapid is the decline of gods wrought by human hands!' Cardinal Wyszyński mused in his prison diary. He added that he had invoked God's mercy for Bolesław Bierut, who died suspiciously on a visit to Moscow the same month. Although the communist President had died under an excommunication decree for his part in the Primate's arrest, Wyszyński forgave him, and even said Mass for him in his prison cell.[16]

In June 1956, when Tito visited Moscow for the first time since Yugoslavia's break with the Soviet Union in 1948, Khrushchev acknowledged that 'roads to conditions to socialist development are different in different countries'. The half-garbled sentence appeared to suggest the Soviet Union would allow national regimes greater leeway. The era of purges and show-trials was at an end. The term 'revisionist' was touted to describe those yearning to return to the original communist vision, freed of its latter-day Stalinist corruptions.

The first sign of open unrest came that June, when local workers took to the streets of Poznań in western Poland demanding 'bread and freedom'. The demonstration was savagely put down and the news quickly suppressed. But spontaneous disturbances followed in Warsaw, suggesting the discontent was more widespread. In both cases, the demonstrators raised national emblems and sang Catholic hymns. Władysław Gomułka, the post-war Party rival of Bierut, who had been arrested in the early 1950s, was brought back to power, skilfully presenting himself as symbol of a popular revolt against Moscow and Stalinism. In a three-hour speech to the Communist Party's Eighth Plenum on 20 October, Gomułka defended the 'honest Poznań workers' They were merely protesting, he said, against 'distortions of the basic rules of socialism, which is their ideal'.[17]

Ironically, the 'Polish October' marked the highpoint of the Communist Party's social influence. It was symbolized by the crowd of 400,000 which assembled in Warsaw's central Plac Defilad, and rapturously applauded as Gomułka promised to restore the 'ideas of socialism, steeped in the spirit of human freedom'. Gomułka knew a show of Church approval could be a vital asset. And given the right inducement, the Church was ready to respond. 'The previous regime caused harm and injustice not just to Catholics, but also to honest people of a different world-view', the bishops noted in a letter. 'Your Plenum speech gave constructive directions for the future.'[18] Cardinal Wyszyński was released and arrived back in Warsaw the following day, urging Poles in the courtyard of his Primate's residence to be ready to 'give long years of trouble, hardship, pain and suffering'. 'Working magnificently' could be a greater heroism, Wyszyński added, than 'dying magnificently'.[19]

A new Church–State accord followed in December. The communiqué noted that

> Episcopate representatives stated that as a result of changes in public life aimed at consolidating legality, justice, peaceful existence, raising social morality and righting wrongs, the government and authorities will find in the Church hierarchy a full understanding. [In return,] the government representatives emphasized their readiness to remove remaining obstacles to realizing the principle of full freedom for religious life.[20]

That was a bit over the top. But some 'obstacles' were removed. Religion was reintroduced to schools and Church appointments freed from government scrutiny. Meanwhile, five Catholics were allowed uncontested seats in the 1957 election to Poland's assembly, the Sejm. The Sejm had 460 seats, so this was not power. It did signify, however, a tiny but legal Catholic presence within the legislature. As a further concession, the Gomułka regime allowed small 'Catholic Intelligentsia Clubs' to provide a discreet outlet for non-Marxist intellectuals in Warsaw, Kraków, Poznań, Wrocław and Toruń. The Church extended the pastorates it had set up for different social groups. A nine-year Novena of spiritual preparation was announced for the millennium of Christianity in Poland in 1966.

The 'concessions' did not last. By late 1957, the Communist Party had regained confidence and begun re-establishing its hold over society. The method this time was not secret police terror, but remorseless 'administrative measures'. For those on the receiving end, it made little difference. Gomułka set about purging revisionists from the Party, and made clear that 'harmful phenomena' would now be eliminated. The visionary hopes of 1956 looked more like naive illusions.

By then, however, the international climate had changed under the impact of events further south. Hungary had been praised by Stalin as a country 'in the vanguard of socialism'. It could be argued that its inhabitants had merely attempted to rebuild communism on humane foundations rather than overthrow it completely. Unlike the Poles, however, the Hungarians had been driven into open revolt against Soviet occupation.

Having unsuccessfully attempted to ignore the reformist lead given by the February 1956 Soviet Communist Party congress, Mátyás Rákosi resigned as party leader on 27 July, allowing the readmission of Imre Nagy, a former prime minister who had been condemned as a 'Right deviationist'. On 6 October, the communist Foreign Minister, László Rajk, whose execution in 1948 had been the pretext for savage purges, was declared innocent and given a state funeral. Over 200,000 Hungarians attended it, pledging solidarity with the Poles and demanding Soviet troop withdrawals. At 10 p.m. on 23 October, a few hours after Gomułka had waved to cheering Warsaw crowds 400 miles to the north, the first shots of the Hungarian uprising were fired in front of Budapest's radio station.

Archbishop Grősz of Kalocsa, released the previous May, appealed for order. But on 30 October, the day the Soviet regime promised to reassess its ties with the People's Democracies, Grősz found himself upstaged when Cardinal Mindszenty's charges were annulled and the old firebrand was freed. Mindszenty's cavalcade reached Budapest in triumph at 4.00 a.m. the following morning, having been forced to stop and sign autographs by applauding villagers along the way. By evening, there were reports that Soviet troops had re-entered Hungary after staging a tactical withdrawal, and were converging on the capital. The Nagy government denounced the Warsaw

Pact and appealed to the UN. But on 3 November, as troop movements continued, the government's negotiating team was arrested by the Soviet Army. The uprising approached its *dénouement*.

That night, Mindszenty made a radio appeal to the world from the Budapest Parliament. Communist rule had been swept away, he declared, by the 'entire Hungarian people'. Today, Hungarians wished to live in peace with all nations, deciding their fate through free elections. 'The entire civilized world has stood by us', Mindszenty pleaded. 'Let everyone in the whole country know this fight was not a revolution but a fight for freedom.'[21] It was the speech of a man who had just spent eight years in detention. But the text was poorly put together. It contained enough hawkish language to give the impression that Mindszenty was hostile to the Nagy government. Although rejecting 'old-fashioned nationalism', it also fostered an illusion, shared by many uprising participants, that Western governments were offering support.

Mindszenty had barely got home when the Soviet bombardment of Budapest began. He hurried back to Parliament and stayed there till a white flag was run up. Then he made his way in disguise between columns of Soviet tanks to the nearby American Embassy. A cable authorizing his asylum arrived from President Eisenhower in 30 minutes. By morning, hundreds of dead and wounded lay in the surrounding streets. In Budapest alone, 5,000 died in eight days of fighting. Mass executions and deportations followed.

The Soviets had prevaricated over Hungary. What had clinched the argument, in the end, were the likely knock-on effects. Officials in Romania and Czechoslovakia had reported growing public sympathy for the Budapest government, while the East German Party had warned that 'enemy forces' were looking for further 'weak spots in the socialist camp'. Meanwhile, British and French entanglement in the Suez crisis had conveniently distracted world opinion. Gomułka had succeeded in persuading Khrushchev that Poland would remain, despite everything, a 'loyal member' of the Warsaw Pact. But Nagy and his supporters had given no such assurances.

The reimposition of communist rule also brought a clampdown on the Church. Appointments made without government approval in 1956 were annulled by decree, and 'unreliable' priests replaced. Forced to salvage what they could, the bishops declared their readiness to support the new regime of János Kádár if certain Church rights were maintained. But the pre-uprising *status quo* was gradually reimposed. In 1959, the regime claimed the power 'to take necessary steps to ensure the priestly ministry, proper Church administration and the training of priests'. That took subservience beyond what even the 1950 'agreement' had envisaged.

Kádár had initially made a show of support for Nagy's 'counter-revolutionary demands', even telling Soviet Party leaders in secret talks that Hungary's communists had been 'compromised in the eyes of the masses'. Once in power, however, he left little doubt what Cardinal Mindszenty could expect if he ever ventured out of the US Embassy. 'It was Mindszenty who worked out the programme of the counter-revolution', Hungary's latest communist strongman declared. 'Mindszenty is an enemy of our democratic and social achievements.'[22]

The repression in Hungary steeled the determination of hardliners elsewhere too. In Poland, the concessions of 1956 continued to be rescinded. Gomułka blamed the Vatican. 'We admit with satisfaction that Cardinal Wyszyński and the rest of the Episcopate did not follow the path of the Hungarian Cardinal Mindszenty—a path which would have brought the worst consequences', the Party leader told the Polish bishops. 'But the Vatican hasn't changed its hostile attitude to Poland.'[23]

Yet the events of 1956 had brought the first real challenge to communist power. They had also produced the first stirrings of a dialogue between its intellectual critics. Leszek Kołakowski, Poland's leading Marxist ideologue, met Wyszyński for the first time in 1957, during a discreet visit to Laski, the sprawling Franciscan centre north of Warsaw. The Party's Control Commission found out and accused him of conspiring behind its back. But the meetings and encounters continued. Wyszyński sought out critical-minded party insiders who might provide useful allies.

In 1958 Warsaw's Catholic Intelligentsia Club was allowed to launch a monthly journal, *Więź*, which aimed for dialogue with intelligent Marxists. If *Więź* had an idol, it was the French philosopher Emmanuel Mounier, whose 'Personalist' school had attempted to bridge the gap between Catholics and socialists in pre-war France. Mounier had visited Poland in May 1946, while still editor of *L'Esprit*, and voiced regret that Polish Catholics remained 'sunk in bourgeois traditionalism' and had not used their 'historic opportunity' to 'reconcile the Church and socialism'. He believed communism owed its success to its *mystère*—'the central force which established its power in men's hearts'. It had brought a kind of redemption. Christianity and communism were bound together 'in a rigour and fraternity which goes well beyond power struggles'.[24]

For *Więź*, this meant Christianizing communism 'from within', rather than opposing it outright. 'What are the values in contemporary life we wish to serve above all?' the journal declared in its first editorial. 'We reply without hesitation: in the temporal order, the supreme value is Man ... The goal of our socio-political institutions is to make possible each man's complete personal development.'[25] Although claiming to be independent of both Church and State, *Więź* was heavily censored. The 'Left Catholics' who filled its columns were marginal numerically. But it offered an outlet for Catholic writers to develop their talents and ideas.

Another forum attempting the same job was the Catholic *Tygodnik Powszechny* in Kraków. Founded in 1945 by Cardinal Sapieha, the weekly's founder-editors—Jerzy Turowicz, Stanisław Stomma, Stefan Swieżawski and Antoni Gołubiew—were veterans of Poland's pre-war Odrodzenie renewal movement, and had tried to find common ground between French-style Personalism and the 'open Marxism' talked about by moderate Polish communists. This made it, like *Więź* in Warsaw, an exception to Polish Catholicism's conservative mainstream. The post-war communist regime had tolerated the paper as a concession to the Church. But hardliners were keen to suppress it—and succeeded in suspending its editors in 1953–56, when they refused to print Stalin's official obituary. To be credible as a Catholic paper, *Tygodnik Powszechny* had to tell the truth. To survive, it also had to obey the demands of the communist censors.

That meant a precarious existence, based on cautious everyday compromises. Some criticized the weekly's apparent subservience and passivity. But by the late 1950s, it had become a small but important sanctuary of ideas. Besides giving a forum to leading Catholics unable to publish elsewhere, it carried articles by sympathetic Marxists such as Jan Strzelecki and Antoni Słonimski.

This kind of dialogue was quite different from what was being offered by Bolesław Piasecki's 'Social Movement of Progressive Catholics', better known as Pax, which had attempted since the late 1940s to win Catholic support for the communist State. Aided by lavish State funding, Pax had published the Church Fathers and carefully selected Catholic works from the West. It had produced at least one writer of note itself—Jan Dobraczyński, whose *Letters of Nicodemus* was acclaimed a genuine achievement in spiritual writing. But Pax was hydra-headed. It combined a rigid Catholic conservatism, complete with elements of nationalism and anti-Semitism, with a ruthless commitment to communist aims. Its membership was clan-like and had secret police links. In 1953, besides taking over *Tygodnik Powszechny*, it defended the imprisonment of Cardinal Wyszyński with a shrillness which outdid even the communist press. Pax recruited young intellectuals keen for a chance to talk and write. But the dialogue it offered was false, since its outcome was pre-determined. In Pax's hands, there was little to distinguish totalitarian communism from totalitarian Christianity: both were just as hostile to the rights and needs of the individual.

The Church was still isolated from Poland's budding opposition. Non-communist thinking remained dominated, as in the pre-war years, by the liberal, secular outlook personified by men like the revered social scientist

Stanisław Ossowski. Cardinal Wyszyński himself claimed to have studied Marx's *Das Kapital* three times, 'beginning when I was still at seminary'.[26] He had gone on defending freedom through the Stalinist years, and knew the Church must offer alternatives, rather than just attacking communism.

But Wyszyński was an exception. Most Polish intellectuals, disillusioned with Marxism, still saw the Catholic clergy as backward and parochial. Dogmatism and authoritarianism seemed much the same whether they came from the Church or the Party.

The picture was similar in neighbouring countries. Czechoslovakia's communist regime had resisted reforms after Stalin's death, and had denounced Gomułka's 'Polish road to socialism' in 1956. The critics were becoming bolder. Karel Kosík, the Communist Party's key propagandist, had enthusiastically joined in the denunciation of 'cosmopolitan bandits and wreckers' in November 1952, when Rudolf Slánský and eleven Party officials were sentenced to death in Eastern Europe's biggest show-trial. But by the late 1950s, Kosík had changed. He was now denouncing the 'vulgarized Marxism' which saw human beings as mere objects.[27] This was a voice from the ideological establishment. And the Party responded by sacking Kosík from his post at the Academy of Sciences. But from the relative safety of Prague University, other Marxist philosophers—Milan Machovec, Václav Černý, Ivan Sviták—were also discussing communism's failures, as well as the values to be found in other traditions, including Christianity.

Yet there were no real interlocutors on the Christian side. Josef Hromádka, a Protestant theologian, had welcomed the imposition of communist rule. He saw it, not unlike Mounier, as the culmination of a historical struggle for freedom, and believed ruthless repression was a necessary price for laying the foundations of a just society. Once communism was secure, Hromádka was certain, the system would conform with humane values. The challenge of Christians was to ensure this happened as soon as possible. Hromádka was never a simple collaborator. But he misjudged the workings of communist power, and became one of the 'useful idiots' whose good intentions Lenin had urged his henchmen to exploit.

With over 400 Czech and Slovak priests still in prison, and others detained without formal charges, it was hardly surprising that offers of dialogue, wherever they came from, were ignored by most Church leaders. But the more critical atmosphere after 1956 also gave the Church opportunities. In a 1958 report, the Czechoslovak government admitted it had observed a 'large illegal network' of Catholic groups. The bishops had been compromised by collaboration, it pointed out. But the growing activities of laypeople posed dangers.[28] For all the quislings and turncoats, the Church's loyalty to Rome remained intact.

In Hungary, the Kádár regime coined a slogan, 'Who is not against us is with us'—reversing the hostile rhetoric preached in Stalinist times. The aim was to make conformism easy, by convincing the population that change was both impossible and unnecessary. Kádár worked to give the impression that national unity had been achieved behind basic communist objectives. Once the Church had been marginalized as a social force, there would be no problem in allowing private Catholic devotions to survive.

The policy showed signs of paying off. By the late 1950s, priestly vocations had dropped sharply and religion was fading from Hungarian life. Church leaders had failed to anticipate the demoralizing effects of trading subservience for survival. Marxist thought was in the ascendant, led by the 'Budapest School' of György Lukács. In June 1956, Lukács had angered the Communist Party by condemning 'Stalinist dogmatism'. But he remained a devout communist—a cynical, destructive personality with a wide following among young intellectuals. By contrast, the Church was isolated and lacked the social and cultural outreach to hold back secularization.

Tamás Nyíri, one of few top Catholic philosophers still at large after 1956, believed Hungarian Catholicism needed new 'methods of activity'. Marxists had criticized religion, Nyíri argued, more because of the abysmal record of religious organizations than through any innate hostility. And Christians needed to respond by 'incorporating the Marxist critique'—by refuting the argument that 'faith needs misery and injustice to survive' and becoming a 'force for liberation'.[29] This was easier said than done. Like *Więż* in Poland, the Church's monthly, *Vigilia*, had tried to find Catholics a place in communist society, in which a contribution could be made to the common good without betraying beliefs and principles. But although *Vigilia* drew good writers, its influence was limited.

The same basic strategy, promising the Church a secure future after destroying it as a social force, was followed elsewhere with varying degrees of success. In Lithuania, scattered units of the 'Forest Brethren' were still fighting skirmishes with the Soviet Army in 1958, even though 96 per cent of land had been collectivized and a quarter of the population deported. But the purges and executions had ended. Amnesties in 1953 and 1955 brought 130 exiled priests home. Though constantly harassed, Church life limped on.

In East Germany, the Berlin Wall had not yet separated the churches east and west. The country's communist boss, Walter Ulbricht, believed he could use them to enhance the Communist Party's image. 'It seems to me that capitalism and basic Christianity are irreconcilably opposed', Ulbricht told Church leaders. 'I am increasingly concluding that socialists, communists and Christians, despite differences in philosophy, must work together in shaping society and ensuring peace.'[30]

The East German was articulating what had become established policy throughout the communist world. After 1956, most regimes had discarded the Stalinist illusion that Church and religion could be eradicated, and were instead seeking out 'progressive' Christians who could be made to serve Party aims. In November 1954, sixteen months before Khrushchev's 'Secret Speech' lifted the lid on Stalinist repression, a Soviet Communist Party resolution had confessed to 'serious errors' in the policy towards religion. It had been directed by 'persons barren of science', the resolution noted, who had often done no more than repeat 'stupid stories and fables'. The Party was still committed to 'liberating citizens from their religious errors'. But 'patience, profoundness and judiciousness' would henceforth be in order. 'Administrative measures ... illegal attacks' merely strengthened religious prejudices.[31]

By the time of Khrushchev's speech, the 'new methods' were supposedly in place. The new General Secretary was no liberal. And by the decade's end, he had consolidated his power and a fresh anti-religious drive was under way. But the carrot-and-stick approach continued. Having proved its loyalty to Soviet foreign policy objectives, the Russian Orthodox Church was allowed to join the Geneva-based World Council of Churches. A steady trickle of Western theologians ventured to Moscow in search of 'Catholic–Marxist dialogue'.

The dynamics of the post-Stalinist era clearly demanded a more discerning attitude if Eastern Europe's official Marxism was to be challenged effectively. The 'revisionists' of 1956—Leszek Kołakowski, Karel Kosík and others— were taking advantage of their party positions to forge contacts with like-minded thinkers abroad. Catholics also looked for ways of confronting communist abuses in a way which took prudent account of the system's strengths and weaknesses.

By 1958, Fr Karol Wojtyła had been teaching at Poland's Catholic University of Lublin for four years. He had joined the staff at the recommendation of the lay philosopher Stefan Swieżawski, after the forced liquidation of the Jagiellonian University's theology faculty. Wojtyła had obtained the 600-year-old faculty's last 'Habilitation'. Its closure by the regime drastically reduced the opportunities for priests to acquire higher education and was a severe blow to the Church.

Students at the Catholic University, known by its initials as KUL, considered Wojtyła unconventional. A priest from Puszcza Augustowska complained to his bishop when the new lecturer and a group of students turned up in swimsuits to see his church during a summer excursion. Wojtyła applied to study sexual ethics at the Catholic University of Leuven in Belgium, but was refused a Polish passport. He caused minor outrage when he recommended a nun, Karolina Kasperkiewicz, for a department post when nuns were not supposed to teach priests, and when he asked a KUL literature professor, Irena Sławińska, to lecture priests on improving their pastoral language.

With his Phenomenology background, Wojtyła was an exception at KUL, where most staff-members were born and bred in the 'Lublin School' of classical Thomism. His own Thomist training gave him a foundation for expressing thoughts and ideas in universally recognized Christian categories. But Thomism had its limitations. Disputes within the KUL fraternity were usually scholarly affairs. The fact that they were hardly heard about outside was only partly because Catholic academics were kept isolated by Poland's communist rulers. A 'properly understood Thomism', it was also said, needed no external partners. Wojtyła became known as someone who wished to make the 'Lublin School' more open to current issues.

An 'engagement with modernity' was the aim of Kraków's *Tygodnik Powszechny* too. Since publishing his first article here in 1949, Wojtyła had become increasingly involved in editorial policy. Working with Jerzy Turowicz's team opened up new horizons. It gave him the experience, unusual among priests, of a close partnership with talented laypeople. It taught him how to communicate, drawing on personal insights and feelings. In addition, it put him in touch with various philosophical trends— particularly Personalism, with its affirmation of the primacy of the human person over theories and ideologies.

By the late 1950s, French Personalism had evolved into an important counter-proposition to Marxism. It boasted a similar axiological structure: social justice, human emancipation, engagement with the world. But it gave these principles a Christian meaning and offered answers to troubling questions about the Church's place in modern society. This was the approach Wojtyła had tried to follow in his lectures on Catholic ethics. Though remembered as dry and academic, the classes were well attended.

For most Polish priests, it was the exciting events of 1956 which provided the first real *entrée* to Marxist writings, as well as showing how Marxist theories about state and society clearly contrasted with those of the Church. Wojtyła was an exception. As a KUL lecturer, he had been sparing in his public remarks about Marxism. But he had talked about it in private, and his notes and articles contained copious references to Marxist analysis, particularly those elements which had caught the imagination of his own generation.

When a collection of Wojtyła's essays was printed in two underground *samizdat* volumes in 1953–55, they proved that he had read Marxism exhaustively, to the extent of being able to debate its claims from an expert Christian standpoint. The text of *Catholic Social Ethics* ran to 336 closely typed pages, and contained sections on Personalism, Liberalism and Individualism, as well as 'Totalism' and 'Solidarism'. Much of it, however, was written as a polemic with Marxism. A detailed contents table, listing Wojtyła's main theses, included subtitles such as 'Communism in its historical dimension' and 'The issue of revolution'.

Catholic Social Ethics was, however, an unusual kind of polemic. Instead of rejecting Marxist concepts, Wojtyła traced their historical origins in Christian tradition, showing the different meaning given to them by figures stretching back to St Thomas Aquinas. His aim, he stated clearly, was not a 'total criticism' of Marxist philosophy, but an analysis of how it had used or misused 'ethical categories'.[32]

Class struggle was the starting point. Catholicism could not 'agree with materialism', Wojtyła said. But it recognized that 'various facts and historical processes' were economically determined, and that 'the evil which is class struggle' was sometimes justifiable to ensure a 'just distribution of goods'.

> The realization of social justice is an element of the realization of God's kingdom on Earth ... In the name of this principle of justice, every person has an undeniable right to struggle to defend what rightly belongs to him. So does a social class. In a well organized society, orientated to the common good, class conflicts are solved peacefully through reforms. But states that base their order on individualistic liberalism are not such societies. So when an exploited class fails to receive in a peaceful way the share of the common good to which it has a right, it has to follow a different path.[33]

Wojtyła differed from Marxism, however, in the meaning he attached to 'class'. Whereas Marx had defined classes economically, and the German sociologist Max Weber as a cultural phenomenon, Wojtyła saw them as a compound of both. A class was 'a community of people linked by a similar attitude to the means of production and a similar form of cultural life'.[34]

Wojtyła's notion of struggle was different as well. In Marxism, class struggle was a means of liberation, the 'sacred duty of the proletariat'. But if Catholicism accepted the need for it, it did not see it as a 'supreme ethical imperative'. Class struggle could help achieve the common good 'only indirectly and marginally'.

> Although Catholicism is aware of the importance of material and economic factors in the life of individual and society, it also postulates the freedom of the human will. For this reason, it sees the possibility of solving burning social and economic issues in an evolutionary way. The struggle of suppressed classes against exploiting classes should be a stimulus ensuring this evolution occurs more quickly ... But despite all the factors which divide people in society

(such as cultural levels), or even set them against each other (such as attitudes to the means of production), Catholic social ethics assumes there are other deeper, more fundamental factors which unite them and build solidarity.[35]

When it came to demanding justice, however, Wojtyła had no doubt. Society had 'a strict right, even a duty', to ensure just governance, by controlling the exercise of power and criticizing its mistakes. When this failed, it had a right to passive resistance. And when *this* failed, it had a final option—'active resistance against a legal but unjust power'. As the authoritative text, Wojtyła cited Pius XI's 1927 encyclical, *Nos es muy conocida*, written in response to anti-Church violence by Mexico's socialist regime. As with a defensive war, active resistance could be justified as a 'necessary evil'.[36]

Wojtyła also drew a careful distinction between 'active resistance' and revolution. Catholic moral theologians had denied that 'political revolution'—the kind envisaged by Marx—could be ethically justified. They had done so not out of 'conservatism or opportunism', but out of concern for the common good. The Church would never accept the 'fatalistic conception of revolution' put forward by such thinkers as Nikolai Berdyaev. Violent upheavals could not be ethically justified as a means of 'changing systems or political powers'.[37]

Wojtyła traced communism back to Christian tradition too, even subtitling one section of his text 'The objective superiority of the communist ideal'. But he made clear he was using the term generically to mean common ownership. This was the kind of 'communism' idealized by philosophers all the way back to Plato—'liberation from the range of vices connected with principle of private property'.

'In the contemporary communist movement, the Church sees and acknowledges an expression of largely ethical goals', Wojtyła wrote. 'In *Quadragesimo anno*, Pius XI writes that criticism of capitalism, and protest against the system of human exploitation of human work, is undoubtedly "the part of the truth" which Marxism contains.' Yet the Church believed it was possible to 'enfranchise the proletariat' and change the social and economic system while keeping private property.

> According to patristic tradition and the centuries-old practice of monastic life, the Church acknowledges the ideal of communism. But it considers, given the current state of human nature, that universal implementation of this ideal— while protecting the individual's complete freedom—meets insurmountable difficulties. Human nature suits private property. We should attempt to ensure that reforms are implemented for a realization of social justice within an economic system based on private property.[38]

In his *Tygodnik Powszechny* articles, Wojtyła showed he also had a distinctive view of Marxism's 'atheist utilitarianism'. Whereas other priests were trained to view it as a form of sinfulness, he saw it rather as the product of a mistaken conception of the person—of a person located 'in a material world of impulses which does not see anything further'. He was aware that atheists faced personal dramas. The confrontation between faith and non-faith was a confrontation between two stages of consciousness, two ways of being a human being. This made it an anthropological problem, which deserved to be understood rather than condemned.[39]

Wojtyła studied the work of contemporary atheists, particularly the French prophet of Existentialism, Jean-Paul Sartre. Sartre's notion of freedom contradicted the Christian conception. He saw it as a personally willed liberation from outside constraints, whereas Christianity saw freedom as the capacity to fulfil objective values. But although he rejected Sartre's notions, Wojtyła learned something from him too. Sartre's idea of the person as a 'law-creator' charged with upholding the rights of humanity suggested a sense of moral responsibility could be found among committed atheists too.

The Marxist argument that Christianity impeded social progress by spreading 'idealistic illusions' could just as easily be used against communists, Wojtyła concluded. Christianity's 'social programme', it was true, was 'based on religious motives'. But religion itself was 'socially motivated'. It had a 'society-building character', against which its Marxist antagonists often appeared to be the 'real individualists'.

But as practitioners of one form of 'independent ethics', Marxists were open to conversion. Whereas Christian ethics advocated a struggle for justice based on the commandment of love, Marxism restricted the struggle to one between a righteous class and its exploiters. But the ethical intentions of Marxists could be acknowledged. Marxist and Christian ethics represent 'two ways of responding to human fate in every dimension'. The principles and ideals found in Marxist ethics 'are those of Christian ethics, minus the reference to God which gives Christian ethics a religious character'.

'In this sphere, the materialist assumptions of Marxism are undoubtedly enlightened by the idea of justice, and this idea has attracted many supporters who were conscious that the division of material goods is unjust and harmful', Wojtyła pointed out. 'Christian ethics cannot be based on class, since it must be universal. But it understands the struggle for justice. Without exaggeration, we can say that Jesus Christ engaged in this struggle himself— but within a dimension greater than that of those who wish to see Him only as a "first socialist".'[40]

In short, it is the 'ideology proclaimed by the Gospel' which offers the best means of survival. But Wojtyła concurred with Marxism that an analysis of the causes of social suffering—of work, property, the distribution of goods—also provided a key to understanding human history. Thanks to his forays into a comparison of Christianity and Marxism, he already had a clear idea of what should be done to counter communism's stranglehold, as well as of the terms and concepts—responsibility, participation, solidarity—which would form the rudiments of a Christian counter-programme. They were acquiring their own force and authority, and would be perfected in the years ahead.

Notes

1. 'List Episkopatu do Rządu' (1 August 1949); in Peter Raina (ed.) *Kościół w PRL—Dokumenty 1945–1959* (Poznań: W Drodze, 1994), pp. 163–4.
2. 'Oświadczenie Sekretarza Episkopatu bp. Z. Choromańskiego' (12 August 1949); ibid., p. 178.
3. Quoted in William Fletcher, *Religion and Soviet Foreign Policy 1945–1970* (Oxford: Oxford University Press, 1973), p. 33.
4. *Rudé Právo* (17 July 1949).
5. From Roman Dmowski, *Polityka polska i odbudowanie państwa* (Warsaw: Parzyński, 1925), pp. 136–7.
6. Neal Pease, 'Poland and the Holy See, 1918–1939', *Slavic Review*, vol. 50, no. 3 (Fall 1991), p. 527; Zygmunt Zieliński and Stanisław Wilk (eds), *Kościół w II Rzeczpospolitej* (Lublin: Wydawnictwo KUL, 1980).
7. Letter to Polish bishops *Cum iam lustri* (1 September 1951); in *Nauczyciel i Pasterz: Listy pasterskie, Komunikaty, Zarządzenia* (Rome: Ośrodek Dokumentacji, 1987), p. 213.
8. Karol Wojtyła, *Osoba i czyn, oraz inne studia antropologiczne* (Lublin: Katolicki Uniwersytet Lubelski, 1994), pp. 424–30.
9. Stefan Wyszyński, *A Freedom Within* (London: Hodder and Stoughton, 1985), pp. 13–14.
10. 'Porozumienie zawarte' (14 April 1950); in Raina, op. cit., pp. 232–5.
11. Wyszyński, op. cit., pp. 14–15.
12. Text of agreement in Gyula Havasy (ed.), *Martyrs of the Catholics in Hungary* (Budapest: privately published, 1993), pp. 82–3.
13. József Ijjas et al., *Ensemble pour une bonne cause: L'État socialiste et les Églises en Hongrie* (Budapest: Corvina, 1978), p. 61.
14. József Mindszenty, *Memoirs* (London: Weidenfeld and Nicolson, 1974), pp. 189, 205.
15. Quoted in Wyszyński, op. cit., *p. 224.*
16. Ibid., pp. 235–6.
17. Nicholas Bethel, *Gomułka: His Poland and His Communism* (London: Longmans, 1969), pp. 218–19.

18. 'List Episkopatu Polski do I Sekretarza KC PZPR' (27 October 1956); in Raina, op. cit., p. 565.
19. *Słowo Powszechne* (5 November 1956). Wyszyński listed the reasons for communism's failure in Poland in *A Freedom Within*, op. cit., pp. 18–19.
20. 'Komunikat Komisji Wspólnej przedstawicieli Rządu i Episkopatu' (8 December 1956); in Raina, op. cit., pp. 575–6.
21. Full text in Mindszenty, op. cit., pp. 331–3.
22. József Közi-Horváth, *Cardinal Mindszenty* (Devon: Augustine Publishing, 1979), pp. 93–4. Kádár made clear that Mindszenty's sentence was considered still valid.
23. 'List I Sekretarza KC PZPR W. Gomułki do Episkopatu Polski' (27 May 1959); in Raina, op. cit., p. 722.
24. Roy Pierce, *Contemporary French Political Thought* (London: Oxford University Press, 1966), pp. 49–88. See also *Écrits* (Paris), vol. 3, p. 64. Mounier's major works included *Révolution personnaliste et communautaire* (1935) and *Le Personnalisme* (1950).
25. Andrzej Bukowski, 'Rozdrosz i wartość', *Więż*, no. 1 (February 1958).
26. *A Freedom Within*, op. cit., p. 66.
27. Karel Kosík, *Dějiny filosofie jako filosofie: Filosofie v dějinách českého národa* (Prague: CSAV, 1958). See also Peter Hruby, *Fools and Heroes: The Changing Role of Communist Intellectuals in Czechoslovakia* (London: Pergamon, 1978), pp. 188–95.
28. Karol Kaplan, 'Church and State in Czechoslovakia from 1948 to 1956, Part III', *Religion in Communist Lands*, vol. 14, no. 3 (1986), p. 280.
29. Ijjas et al., op. cit., pp. 112–14.
30. Quoted in Trevor Beeson, *Discretion and Valour* (London: Collins, 1982), pp. 214–15.
31. *Pravda* (Moscow; 11 November 1954).
32. Karol Wojtyła, *Katolicka Etyka Społeczna*, vol. I (Lublin: *samizdat*, 1953), p. 64. Very few of the estimated 200 copies illegally printed of the book survive and *Catholic Social Ethics* is not listed in anthologies of Wojtyła's writings. Volume I (154 pages) is unmarked and untitled, perhaps reflecting a fear of communist reprisals. Volume II (182 pages) carries the title and author's name, and is labelled 'Part 2—Detailed'. Attention was drawn to the book's existence by the US journalist Jonathan Kwitny in *Man of the Century* (New York: Henry Holt, 1997).
33. *Katolicka Etyka Społeczna*, pp. 63–4.
34. Ibid., pp. 62–3.
35. Ibid., p. 65.
36. Ibid., pp. 131–3.
37. Ibid., p. 133.
38. Ibid., pp. 62, 68.
39. *Tygodnik Powszechny* articles 'Christmas 1958' and 'An ethical foundation' in Karol Wojtyła, *Aby Chrystus się nami posługiwał* (Kraków: Znak, 1979), pp. 71, 166.
40. *Aby Chrystus*, pp. 169–79.

5

᠙᠙᠙᠙

An old order hangs on

Few of the modest advances made by Christians in Eastern Europe by the late 1950s could have been directly attributed to Vatican diplomacy. But Pius XII's record had been a complex one. He had been right to foresee the thoroughness with which communism, controlled and co-ordinated by the Kremlin, would emerge as the main menace after the defeat of Nazism. He had also been right to reject the Western illusions in the Yalta agreement of 1945, with its naive prediction of a 'continuing and growing understanding between East and West'.[1] That 'lasting peace' had turned out to be an unjust and unstable international order, achieved at the cost of humane principles. It was not the sort of peace Pius XII had called for in the desperate months of 1939.

Writing in the 1960s, Carlo Falconi would accuse Pius XII of having allowed his anti-communism to become 'irrational and fanatical', paralysing his actions and retarding world peace.[2] He blamed a 'psychological complex' born from Pius XII's experiences as Nuncio in Munich during the 'Red Days' of 1919. His residence had been raked by gunfire and his car stolen by Spartacist revolutionaries—an experience the Pope was said to have relived in recurring nightmares. But 'irrational and fanatical' were inappropriate adjectives. As Secretary of State in the 1930s, Pacelli had personally monitored the grim excesses perpetrated against the Church in Mexico, Spain and the Soviet Union. His fear of communism was empirical. Where he erred was in believing he could fight a totalitarian ideology with traditional diplomatic methods, and that his authority was strong enough by itself to isolate and discredit it.

Pius XII was not the reactionary his critics claimed. At various stages in his pontificate, he spoke passionately about social reform and safeguarding liberties. But he failed to understand the deeper impulses behind communism's expansion, as well as the psychological disorientation which

93

held sway in Eastern Europe, where the pressure exerted on citizens often made considered choices impossible. Those who saw it as a conflict between state and society more often than not got it wrong. In reality, society was permeated by dreams and terrorized illusions. Some were ready to die fighting communism; others saw communism as the promise of the future. There were no reliable criteria for determining who found themselves in either camp. Both included heroes and villains, intellectuals and workers, Left and Right. Both—as Wyszyński and Mindszenty acknowledged—included Christians and atheists. To pose as architects of emancipation, the communist regimes needed the Church to be as backward as possible. The last thing they wanted was a Church which had rid itself of bad associations and was responding imaginatively to the problems of modernity.

Yet Pius XII appealed to a model of Christian society which took too much for granted. Far from isolating the communist regimes, his no-compromise policy played into their hands. Instead of buttressing the self-confidence of local churches, he left them dangerously exposed, raising the stakes in a confrontation they could not hope to win. He might also have concurred with Cardinal Wyszyński that communists could be persuaded to keep promises as well as break them, and that differences of opinion could occur in communist parties as in other human organizations. But the general anathema reaffirmed in the 1949 Decree made practical discernments impossible.

Above all, Pius XII lacked the will to go beyond legalistic formulations. As Mgr Domenico Tardini later recalled, whereas Pius XI had 'outwardly enjoyed a fight, Pius XII visibly suffered'. He was 'by natural temperament, mild and rather timid ... not born with the temper of a fighter'.[3]

Pius XII rejected charges that he had made the Vatican an instrument of the Cold War, and insisted his aim was to hold Europe together rather than divide it. In 1941, Tardini had predicted to Roosevelt's envoy, Myron Taylor, that communism would be the war's main beneficiary, and would quickly emerge as an even deadlier enemy than Nazism. Deploying resources to counteract this enemy became a key Vatican preoccupation. When the Paris Conference was convened in 1947 to draw up a European response to the reconstruction programme outlined by the US Secretary of State George Marshall, its objective of 'economic solidarity' was eagerly supported by *L'Osservatore Romano*.[4]

Yet there were limits to the Pope's pro-Western stance. He resisted attempts to gain his backing for NATO in April 1949, and made it clear that a 'united Europe' should also be predominantly a Catholic Europe—an idea given weight by the Catholic founding fathers: Konrad Adenauer, Jean

Monnet, Robert Schuman and Alcide De Gasperi. Meanwhile, although the Vatican shared the interest of the United States in 'containing' communism—a concept outlined in the 1947 Truman Doctrine—it did so in the name of Christianity, not of 'Western' or 'liberal' values. The Pope counted on American help in preventing communist takeovers in France and Italy when both seemed poised 'to commit their future to the unyielding power of a materialist state, without an other-worldly ideal, without religion, without God'.[5] But since his first visit in 1936, Pacelli had felt little admiration for the US. It shared with France the dubious heritage of having pioneered modern notions of Church–State separation. Although the Church was legally free there, it was hidebound by a materialistic culture, as well as by the anti-Catholic bias traditionally pervading the 'White Anglo-Saxon Protestant' establishment.

Cardinal Francis Spellman of New York had first met Pacelli as a clerk at the Secretariat of State in the late 1920s, and had played a key role as errand boy extraordinary between the Vatican and US Administration. In 1931, he had helped smuggle *Non abbiamo bisogno*, Pius XI's encyclical on Mussolini's Fascists, out of Italy to the world's press. And in 1936, he had personally organized Pacelli's US tour, which culminated in a meeting with Roosevelt two days after his inauguration. The US President even joked about his 'patriotic Army chaplain' to Stalin at Yalta in February 1945, reputedly drawing another sarcastic remark about the Church's 'divisions'.[6]

Rumours of Spellman's covert influence were seized on in Eastern Europe. At Archbishop Stepinac's trial in 1946, he was said to have blackmailed the US government into cutting aid to Tito's regime. When Mindszenty appeared in the dock in 1949, he had plotted to restore the Habsburg monarchy. And at the Polish Bishop Kaczmarek's trial in 1953, he was said to have tried to force the US to ally with Hitler against the Soviet Union.

Calumnies aside, Spellman was undoubtedly an enemy of communists—those 'God-hating, freedom-hating puppets now terrorizing, brutalizing and tyrannizing half the world'.[7] When the Vatican maintained a discreet silence, he praised Senator Joseph R. McCarthy's efforts to 'make America aware of the danger of communism', insisting that 'no American uncontaminated by communism has lost his good name because of the Congressional hearings on un-American activities'.[8] But it was open to question how much practical impact Spellman's troubleshooting really had. Truman himself denounced Mindszenty's trial as the 'infamous proceedings of a kangaroo court'. But not all American public figures shared Spellman's concerns. For all his efforts, he failed to remove the blockage in US–Vatican relations. When President Truman tried to send General Mark Clark as permanent ambassador in 1951, he was rebuffed by Congress. The Vatican Secretary of State, Archbishop Giovanni Battista Montini, condemned the 'vulgar, bitter and entirely unjustified attacks on the Holy See' still being heard in the US. He accused Spellman and the American Church hierarchy of failing to 'react adequately'.[9]

In Eastern Europe, the view of the Vatican as nerve-centre of a US-led anti-communist campaign nevertheless persisted. It was in part to strengthen the Church's image of independence from hostile powers that Pius XII took steps to reassert unity in Catholic ranks. In the encyclicals *Mystici corporis* (1943) and *Mediator Dei* (1947), he reaffirmed the identification of the Body of Christ with the Catholic Church. Similarly, *Humani generis* (12 August 1950), published when millions of Catholics were flocking to Rome for a Holy Year, strengthened the authority of the Magisterium against modern theological innovations. The dogma of the Assumption (1 November 1950), establishing the Virgin Mary's bodily translation to heaven, reasserted Catholic orthodoxy's intuitive basis and appealed to the loyalty of the Catholic masses.

But if Pius XII believed he was asserting the Vatican's role as a spiritual force above the East–West division, he had not yet found a credible way of achieving this. The Vatican had never acted against Russia, the Pope said in a letter to 'the most dear Russian peoples' in July 1952.

> When in 1941 some people tried to persuade us to approve war against the Russian people, we never did ... Our office compels us to condemn and reject the errors preached by atheistic communism. But we have your good in mind in doing this. We know how many of you still nourish the Christian faith in your hearts.[10]

Yet in political terms, the assumption that the Vatican was aligned with the 'capitalist' West against the 'communist' East was rarely called into question.

In Western Europe, the Vatican's backing for Christian Democratic parties had considerable effect. In Germany, France, the Netherlands and Belgium, they held up to two-thirds of national legislature seats by 1955. Italy's Christian Democrats, founded in 1943 under Alcide De Gasperi, had inherited the lower middle class and peasant constituencies of the pre-war Partito Popolare. Catholic Action, a movement launched in the 1860s in reaction to the Risorgimento, had also survived the Second World War with 3 million members, building on the guidelines laid down by *Quadragesimo anno* in 1931.

But the Vatican had failed to anticipate the resilience of Italy's Communist Party, which in 1945 had been the largest and best-disciplined communist movement in Western Europe. The party claimed to have abandoned the idea of seizing power through violent revolution, in favour of a 'long march through the institutions' to the 'progressive democracy' envisaged by Antonio Gramsci. Its leader, Palmiro Togliatti, still insisted on seeing Italian communism as a 'complete religion of man'. But he was convinced the party could win power without the help of Moscow. To do so, some form of expedient relationship was inevitable with the Church. 'Even in the Communist Party, there are Catholic citizens—perhaps even the majority' was Togliatti's explanation.[11]

The Italian Communist Party's calls for an accommodation were widely discounted. After all, even Lenin and Stalin had proclaimed their party open to religious members. Eastern Europe's communists were saying much the same. In May 1947, Vatican officials urged Alcide De Gasperi, who had spent the war under the Pope's protection, to expel Communist Party ministers from his national unity government. But the communists gathered strength. As elections neared the following year, fears of civil war grew.

In February 1948, the Irish ambassador to the Holy See, Joseph Walshe, found Pius XII 'in a mood of deepest pessimism', lamenting 'the imminent danger to the Church throughout Western Europe' and declaring his own readiness 'to be martyred for Christ in Rome'.[12] It was the month Czechoslovakia's communists seized power in Prague. Stalinist rule was being consolidated in the East. 'All organized Catholicism in Italy, both inside and outside the Vatican, has turned its activities to the one purpose of defeating the communist menace', Walshe wrote in his report. 'Never before has the Vatican led such a powerful movement in this country.'[13] The 'movement' was a 2 million-strong network of semi-secret groups led from Rome by Luigi Gedda, a 45-year-old medical doctor. Branches of the Comitato Civico were active in two-thirds of Italy's 27,000 Catholic parishes. Their aim was to organize votes for the Christian Democrats. But Gedda's ambitions went well beyond acting as a support arm for De Gasperi. Like other Catholic zealots, he believed the Christian Democrat leader was too concerned with tactical compromises. The evils of the day, Gedda was convinced, were all traceable to a basic flaw in European civilization, which had led from Protestantism, via the French Revolution, to liberalism and communism—a communism now poised to 'cross the borders of Italy and poison our people'.[14]

Although Gedda enjoyed privileged access to Pius XII, views differed over the extent of the Pope's personal involvement. Archbishop Montini, who co-ordinated the Vatican's pre-election stance, believed the relative success of Italian communism reflected 'a facile, supine following' of foreign thought. But Montini distrusted Gedda's aggressive style. He was confident

Italian electors had already grasped that 'there were but two alternatives: communism or anti-communism'.[15]

In the event, De Gasperi's Christian Democrats trounced the combined forces of communists and socialists with 48.3 per cent to 31 per cent when Italians voted on 18 April 1948, suggesting the 'Red Italy' scare had been exaggerated. But fears that Togliatti could still attempt a Czechoslovak-style coup persisted until the summer. There was talk of the Pope fleeing Rome; of 80,000 young Catholics preparing for armed resistance; of gun-running across the Adriatic, Soviet infiltration, US intervention.

As in Eastern Europe, some observers believed the Church had failed to rise to the communist challenge. It had lost pastoral contact with worker communities, whose hardships were exploited by communist agitators. The estimated million workers on Catholic trade union books in 1948 were outnumbered six-to-one by communist-backed labour organizations. Even now, the Vatican maintained its traditional fear of mass social movements. It was reluctant to sanction Christian Democrat attempts to generate mass pro-Church pressure.[16]

In 1949, although the Holy Office Decree barred Catholic co-operation with communists, voices in De Gasperi's Christian Democratic party argued that a limited 'opening to the Left' might still be attempted by approaching moderate followers of Giuseppe Saragat in Italy's Socialist Party. In 1924, when Popular Party leaders had proposed a similar coalition to stop Mussolini, Pius XI had opposed the idea, urging the faithful to put their trust instead in the 'great principles of faith and religion'. In 1949, Pius XII reacted to talk of an *apertura a sinistra* with much the same platitudes. He saw the need for an alliance of anti-communist forces. But socialists, however 'moderate', were still 'anti-Christian'.

On the contrary, many conservative Catholics believed the Christian Democrats had betrayed their principles, and that a balance had to be restored through a *unione sacra* of Right-wing forces. In April 1952, with the Communist Party again poised to do well in municipal elections, Luigi Gedda launched 'Operation Sturzo' with the aim of bringing the Christian Democrats into a Right-wing alliance. Pius XII put De Gasperi under pressure. The Christian Democrat leader's daughter Maria recounted how the Pope's Jesuit confidant, Riccardo Lombardi, a man dubbed 'God's Microphone' for his decade-long anti-communist crusade, had threatened to force De Gasperi's resignation. 'The Pope would rather see Stalin and his Cossacks in St Peter's Square than the communists victorious in the elections', Lombardi reputedly told De Gasperi's wife during an angry encounter at the family home.[17]

In the event, Pius XII was persuaded not to support Gedda openly against

De Gasperi, and thus risk dividing his party. The Christian Democrats prevailed in the election; but the episode disrupted De Gasperi's relations with the Pope until his death in 1954.

There were some, like the Milan theologian Don Carlo Colombo, who saw dangers in anathematizing the Italian Communist and Socialist Parties, believing it would widen the gulf between the Church and Italy's workers and 'increase the strength and attractiveness of communism'.[18] There were voices in the Vatican too who believed an approach could be made to 'good elements' on the Left. Archbishop Montini's hand was detectable in Pius XII's conciliatory message for Christmas 1955. There was nothing 'providential' or 'historic' about communism, the Pope declared. Nevertheless, 'we warn Christians in an industrial era not to be content with an anti-communism based on the defence of a liberty empty of content. They should rather build a society in which man's freedom rests on the moral order.'[19]

Yet this was something of an exception. From 1954 onwards, Pius XII was on his sick-bed, and this boosted the power of Vatican conservatives. The timing was unfortunate. By the mid-1950s, a whole decade had elapsed since the dying shots of the Second World War. Trade was expanding, democracy consolidating, popular culture reviving. A happier, better-ordered world was emerging from the chaos and destruction of the past.

But if this had accentuated the conflict between modern pluralistic cultures and older systems of authority, the Vatican remained firmly aligned with the latter. It had yet to find a language comprehensible to wavering contemporaries. Cardinal Alfredo Ottaviani, who took charge of the Holy Office, was adamant the 1949 Decree should be applied in all its vigour. Convinced the Christian Democrats had been soft on communism, Ottaviani was even said to favour having Togliatti's Communist Party outlawed, as had been its counterpart in Franco's Spain. Pius XII rejected this. 'Such an action would encourage a revolution and be inconceivable in the light of democratic procedures', was the Pope's response.[20] But the view predominated that even to speak of an 'opening to the Left' represented a comprehensive betrayal of Catholic tradition.

Togliatti, for his part, made a distinction between the Vatican and Church hierarchy on one side—'poisoning, perturbing, lacerating mankind with their empty controversies, ridiculous condemnations and senseless persecutions'[21]—and the honest Catholic masses who he believed were ready to defy the Church and endorse communist objectives. At the Party's Eighth Congress in 1956, convened after Khrushchev's 'Secret Speech', there was talk of an 'Italian way to socialism', supported by 'anti-capitalist Catholic forces'. But the potentially sympathetic Catholic public, Togliatti had concluded, was in reality too subservient—to a Church still deeply allied (in the Party's view) with capitalist interests.

Fear of communism continued to dominate the Vatican's approach to international issues. When the UN Charter was signed in San Francisco on 26 June 1945, pledging 'human rights and fundamental freedoms for all without distinction as to race, sex, language or religion', the Pope had praised the 'unprecedented experience, goodwill, political wisdom and organizing power' going into the task of a secure international system.[22] But the Soviet Union's veto power in the Security Council made him doubt the UN's peace-making capacity. In the Third World, Pius XII defended the rights of small nations to a share of the world's economic resources. But with revolutionary movements emerging during de-colonization in the 1950s, the Third World became a region of East–West confrontation. When a Non-Aligned Movement was proclaimed at Bandung in 1955, the Vatican detected the hand of communists.

The Pope was similarly hawkish when it came to the emerging geostrategic balance. The Soviet Union exploded its first atomic bomb on 23 September 1949, while the US tested a 'fusion bomb' in 1951, a year after a stepped-up policy of 'aggressive containment' had been outlined by the National Security Council. Pius XII had doubts about the theory of deterrence. But the key to peace, he was sure, lay not in disarmament, but in freedom. Although arms reductions were a moral duty, especially when weapons of mass destruction might evade control, they were subject to the principle of legitimate defence.

When plans for a European Defence Community collapsed in August 1954 over France's hesitation, the Pope lamented that 'a nationalist state ... unstable in its alliances'[23] appeared to have single-handedly set limits on European unification. The reference to France had a certain irony. In the pre-war years, Cardinal Jean Verdier of Paris—a man dubbed the 'Red Cardinal' by the French Right—had attempted unsuccessfully to build up the Church in new worker suburbs. In 1943, two priests from the Jeunesse Ouvrière Chrétienne, Godin and Daniel, had presented a report, La France— Pays de Mission?, to Verdier's successor, Archbishop Emmanuel Suhard. It painted a dire picture of a declining Church which had lost contact with the industrial population, and proposed that specially trained pastoral teams be sent to new city areas. The first 'mission' was functioning in Paris by the end of 1944.

Advocates of the worker priests could cite Pius XI's injunction in the 1937 encyclical Divini Redemptoris: 'Unless the priest goes among the workers and the poor to put them on their guard against prejudice and false doctrine, and correct their wrong impression, they will fall easy prey to the preachers of communism.'[24] But some went much further, arguing that the Church needed *désembourgeoisement* and should learn from Marxist analysis. The movement was in contact with the communist-dominated Confédération Générale du Travail (CGT) and campaigned against France's presence in Indochina. With supporters like the Dominican Dominique Chenu pushing for the movement to have greater autonomy, it was seen as a threat to parish structures.

Cardinal Suhard received his first note of caution from the Vatican in June 1945. His death in May 1949 robbed the worker priests of their protector. The Vatican was worried that the campaign against communism in Italy would be compromised by the French Church's apparent tolerance of left-wing priests. In a 1950 exhortation to priests, the Pope deplored the 'alarming spread of revolutionary ideas' among 'certain priests not highly distinguished for learning or austerity of life'.[25] The wording caused widespread offence, and an attempt by Cardinal Gerlier to draw up guidelines was resisted. But the Pope dug his heels in. 'He errs who thinks he can serve worker interests with the old methods of class struggle', Pius XII told Italian Catholic Action on May Day 1953, 'or who believes he must justify his efforts to go on exercising religious influence over the world of work.'[26]

Despite the forewarnings, the attempted curbing of worker-priest activities the following September caused uproar. The decree restricted priests to part-time work and did not ban the Mission de France outright. But the worker priests blamed right-wing political pressure. The Pope's supporters could argue that, while the movement's aims were worthy, its members had exceeded their calling to bring the Church closer to the poor. But many believed the Pope had allowed himself to be pushed into condemning the first vigorous Church attempt to tackle working-class alienation.

In Eastern Europe, the Pope had expected the 1949 Holy Office Decree to be obeyed with a stoical defiance, as faithful Catholics readied themselves for whatever fate God had prepared for them. But in April 1950, news came of Wyszyński 's 'Understanding' with the Polish regime. It was, in the words of the French ambassador, Vladimir d'Ormesson, 'completely unexpected', and seemed to fly in the face of the Polish bishops' previously rigid, uncompromising stance.[27]

Writing after his arrest three years later, Wyszyński admitted his own uncertainties. But there was one point he was sure about: if any kind of martyrdom was needed, it was 'the martyrdom of work, not of blood'. The Cardinal had impressed this on Vatican officials, even describing it as the 'guiding thought for the Church in Poland'. Since *causae maiores* (major issues) were reserved to the Holy See, he acknowledged, the Polish bishops had no right to negotiate full-scale agreements. But 'understandings'—a term which 'came up at the last moment'—could at least establish contacts between Church and State. Pius XII had excluded the Vatican from any possible negotiations. So Wyszyński had been left with no option but to devise these contacts himself.[28]

This was not how the Vatican saw it. In a report to Paris, d'Ormesson said it was believed that the Polish bishops had been guided by 'material concerns', and had failed to understand what they were up against. What they had produced was an empty text which would 'sow confusion and conflict' among Polish Catholics. 'The Secretariat of State concludes that the Soviets have obtained their aim, which was to remove the means of contact between the satellite countries and the Holy See', d'Ormesson noted. 'It believes the bishops, because of their lack of contact with the Holy See, are losing their independence of thought, which would have enabled them to evaluate correctly these events and the propositions made to them.'[29]

Wyszyński's Understanding had also implicitly questioned the Vatican's attitude to Poland's 'Recovered Territories'. Even when Poland and the new German Democratic Republic formally recognized their Oder–Neisse border in a 1950 protocol, Pius XII still refused to nominate Polish bishops. He bitterly objected to clauses in the Understanding which committed Poland's bishops to 'make representations' in Rome and counter German Church 'revisionism'. Ambassador d'Ormesson told his Foreign Ministry:

> The Holy See was particularly shocked since it had believed it could count on the toughness of the Polish clergy, and had placed hopes on them which it could not place initially on the clergy in Hungary and Czechoslovakia. Tardini said the Holy See had made a mistake. It would now be stressing the faithfulness and unity of priests and bishops in these two other countries.[30]

Although Wyszyński had acted against the Pope's will, Pius XII still made him a Cardinal in January 1953, and ensured that the Consistorial Congregation excommunicated those responsible for his arrest. Poland's communist propagandists, showing little discernment, still branded him a 'rowdy pupil of the Vatican'.

Meanwhile, the praise for Hungary and Czechoslovakia soon wore thin. Wyszyński had the unique conditions of Poland to thank for the relative even-handedness of the Understanding. In Hungary, Church leaders had also spoken of the need to avoid martyrdom, and had also acknowledged the same distinction between *causae maiores* and *causae minores*. But the Hungarian agreement was vaguer and made no mention of Church links with Rome. Though taken aback by Wyszyński's action, the Pope at least saw him as a capable man with formidable public backing. In Hungary, Cardinal Mindszenty's imprisonment had broken Church resistance. The situation was quite different.

'News of the agreement caused the Pope great anxiety', a senior Vatican official, Mgr Angelo Dell'Acqua, wrote to Archbishop Grősz on 9 October. 'Even if we do not take notice of everything, it is well known that only the Apostolic Holy See is competent to define the basic political principles between the Church and the different nations.'[31] However correct, it was an unwise reaction. Dell'Acqua's letter was cited by the Rákosi regime as a pretext for arresting Archbishop Grősz on 22 June 1951 on charges of abusing his functions and conspiring against the government.

Grősz's fate confirmed Pius XII's view that there was no point attempting to conciliate communist regimes. In March 1951, the Consistorial Congregation had pronounced a general excommunication against all those who violated Church rights by 'bringing a bishop before a secular judge, attacking his person, hampering the exercise of ecclesiastical jurisdiction, plotting against ecclesiastical authorities or occupying a post or function without legitimate appointment'.[32] That covered just about everything being done against the Church in Eastern Europe. Since excommunication was the Church's final sanction, the Pope had shot his last bolt.

In his Christmas message that December, Pius XII coined the phrase 'Church of silence'. 'Hands tied, lips sealed, the Church of silence responds to our invitation. She shows with her gaze the still fresh graves of her martyrs, the chains of her confessors ... her silent holocaust.'[33] When the Bulgarian Passionist Bishop Eugen Bossilkov was arrested with two dozen Catholic priests in July 1952, the Pope denounced the 'wave of terror' sweeping across Bulgaria. He had met Bossilkov in 1948, a year after appointing him a bishop. Bulgaria's Catholic bishops, under communist threats, had written to the UN Secretary General, insisting religious freedom reigned in their country. When Bossilkov's trial opened, *L'Osservatore Romano* denounced it as 'an alibi for premeditated murder'. The bishop was shot with three other priests on the night of 11–12 November 1952, although confirmation reached Rome only in 1975.

In Czechoslovakia, the first group of bishops had taken a loyalty oath to the state in March 1951, the month of the excommunication order. Many saw the oath as a necessary price for the Church's survival. But this was not Rome's view. In May, the Vatican agreed that the oath could be taken—but only to the government, not to Czechoslovakia's communist constitution. Anything more would be 'treason against the Church'.[34]

In Yugoslavia, Tito's anti-religious excesses had begun to modify after his break with Stalin. The Church's resistance had been broken and the communist leader needed to patch up his image. In June 1951, he offered to release Archbishop Stepinac on condition that he leave the country. When Stepinac refused, the government released him anyway, allowing him to return to his home village.

But anti-Church violence continued, along with press attacks on the Vatican. Knowing Tito needed Western backing against the Soviet Union, Pius XII was determined not to give ground. In November 1952, the regime said it was willing to negotiate a 'satisfactory agreement'. But the message received no Vatican reply. Instead, on 29 November—Yugoslavia's National Day—Stepinac's name appeared on a list of 24 new Cardinals.

The Belgrade government claimed the nomination was timed to prevent an improvement in relations. On 17 December, the Belgrade Nunciature's chargé d'affaires, Mgr Silvio Oddi, was duly told to pack up and leave. There was 'no further reason', the government added, for maintaining diplomatic ties.[35] When new anti-religious measures were introduced in May 1953, Yugoslavia's Interior Minister, Aleksandar Ranković, sought to justify them with reference to the Vatican's 'acts of interference'. Tito opened fresh discussions with Church representatives during the year. But talk of a Polish-style understanding was overshadowed by the new restrictions and Vatican opposition. 'Without approval by the Holy See, the Church's leaders must not in any way promise anything or confirm anything', Mgr Tardini wrote to Archbishop Josip Ujčić of Belgrade, '—not even orally, and this includes the draft or concept of any agreement. This is not only against Canon Law, but harmful to the Church and to souls.'[36]

In the last three years of his life, Pius XII had reason to feel bitter. Khrushchev's 'Secret Speech' in February 1956 was greeted with caution in the Vatican. Whatever pledges the Soviet leader might make, there had been no concrete improvement in religious rights. On 29 June 1956, Pius XII sent a letter to the four jailed Cardinals—Stepinac, Wyszyński, Mindszenty and Beran—urging their followers to stay loyal. The text was intended to parallel Pope Calixtus III's Bull 500 years earlier, announcing prayers against the Turkish infidel. It was dispatched a day after the worker riots in Poland had been crushed by communist tanks.

'Beware a false coexistence!' the Pope told the Katholikentag festival in Germany that September. 'The Catholic Church does not force anyone to belong. It asks only freedom to live according to the State's constitution and laws, ministering to her faithful and preaching Christ's Gospel openly.'[37]

The unexpected momentum of events in Poland caused cautious optimism in Rome. On 26 August, a million pilgrims arrived at the national shrine of Jasna Góra to mark the start of the nine-year Novena in preparation

104

for the country's Christian millennium. When Cardinal Wyszyński was freed two months later by Gomułka's reformist regime, the Pope wired an apostolic blessing for the Polish nation 'on the path which seems to be leading it towards the good'.[38]

But the optimism was short-lived. When Imre Nagy had been Hungary's communist premier in 1953–55, religion had enjoyed 'an almost privileged position', according to Vatican Radio, 'while faith in God and fidelity to the Church had been strengthened in the people's soul'.[39] In October 1956, Nagy was back in power and the fighting started.

Pius XII responded with three short encyclicals in the space of a week. The first, *Luctuosissimi eventus*, was issued on 28 October, the day Nagy acknowledged the uprising's patriotic aims and demanded the withdrawal of Soviet troops. It called for prayers and solidarity with the Hungarians, who were 'moving the hearts of all those attached to the rights of civilization, human dignity and the freedom due to persons and nations'.[40]

When Cardinal Mindszenty was released two days later, the Pope immediately sent a telegram, assuring him 'the whole Catholic world rejoices in sympathy with your motherland'. A day later, the second encyclical, *Laetamur admodum*, voiced hope that justice would return through 'dialogue and understanding'. But on 5 November, the niceties ended. János Kádár declared the 'counter-revolution' suppressed, and the third encyclical, *Datis nuperrime*, proclaimed 'the blood of the Hungarian nation cries out to God for vengeance'. In a radio address, Pius XII condemned Western inaction and urged a defence pact. 'Can the world remain indifferent', he demanded, 'when the blood of so many innocents has been shed?'[41]

The uprising's savage suppression came as a cold shower for those naively hoping Soviet power could be overcome by popular resistance. Moscow was ready to despatch divisions to crush anti-Soviet rebellions. There would be no Western backing for attempts to overturn the *status quo* decreed at Yalta. In his Christmas 1956 broadcast, Pius XII attacked the 'softness' of the UN and Western powers, and the 'false realism' conjured up by the idea of 'peace at any price'. No one expected the impossible, he conceded. But the fitting UN response should have been to strip the Soviet Union and Hungary of membership. Both had shown they had 'a conception of sovereignty which undermines the UN's very foundations'.

> It is manifest that in present circumstances, once all other efforts have proved vain, a war of effective self-defence with hope of success against unjust attacks could not be considered 'illicit'. The sad reality obliges us to define the terms of struggle in clear language. No one can honestly reproach us with wishing to harden the opposing fronts. If we remained silent, we would have far more to fear from God's judgment.

The Pope then added that he had always avoided calling Christians to an anti-communist crusade; but where religion was long-established, it was natural that people should view the struggle unjustly imposed on them in these terms. Christians could not sit at the tables of God and his enemies simultaneously. 'What aim can be served by reasoning where there is no common language? How can divergent paths be reconciled, when on one side absolute common values are rejected, making "coexistence in truth" impossible?'[42]

The Pope was speaking after the Suez crisis had revealed further flaws in Western unity. When the Treaty of Rome was signed three months later, on 25 March 1957, setting up a Common Market, it was welcomed as the dawn of a new era by Vatican Radio.

In September 1957, when the Pope ordered Hungarian priests to refrain from political activity, the Kádár regime accused him of interference. Three 'peace priests' ignored the ban by accepting parliamentary seats, and were duly excommunicated. The excommunication of one, Fr Richárd Horváth, was lifted after the Hungarian bishops ruled that he had 'met with submission all the stipulated conditions'.[43] But the others looked with scorn at the Vatican's anguished warnings.

The Pope was unshaken in his conviction that no accommodation was possible with communist regimes. In December 1956, when the wily Cardinal Wyszyński of Poland signed a fresh 'understanding' with Gomułka's reformist regime, it was viewed as an act of disloyalty. Arriving in Rome that May to receive his cardinal's hat four years late, Wyszyński was kept waiting for a week before being granted a papal audience. Even then, Pius XII had no more than fifteen minutes to spare.

Polish conditions were an obvious exception. In the Soviet Union, the Church was virtually defunct. In 1955, when the Pope had named Julijonas Steponavičius assistant bishop for Vilnius in Lithuania, the regime had deported him to a remote village. It did the same when Pius XII tried again in 1957, naming Vincentas Sladkevičius suffragan of Kaišiadorys. When Bishop Kazimieras Paltarokas of Panevėžys died in 1958, there were no resident bishops left.

By Pius XII's final months, the view of the Vatican as an institution on the defensive was widely shared.

Catholic Europe had ended up becoming nothing but Atlantic Europe; Christianity was identified with Western civilization; and the marriage of religion and politics became once again very close, while the condemnation of atheist communism served the interests of capitalism, imperialism and colonialism. It was precisely this identification of the Church with a specific social and political side that condemned Pope Pacelli's line to failure.[44]

This was the view of communists East and West. It was, of course, one-sided. The Pope had supported Europe's Christian Democrats as a means of holding back communism. But he had also viewed them as a necessary check on the re-emergence of pre-war injustices—the very abuses which had spurred the rise of extremism in the first place.

Where the Pope had erred was in failing to provide a sufficient antidote for the stereotypes abounding by his death on 9 October 1958—especially regarding the perceived imbalance between his attitudes to communism and Nazism. The image of Pius XII as an obsessed anti-communist—a proponent of Cold War confrontation—was in part of his own devising and had impeded the Church in its efforts to resist the ideological onslaught from the East. When it came to demands for human rights and social justice, the Church still had little to offer. The gulf between popular emancipation and paternalistic Christianity still seemed uncomfortably wide. Changes were clearly needed. And they would not be long in coming.

Notes

1. *Report of the Crimea Conference*, no. 9.
2. Carlo Falconi, *The Popes in the Twentieth Century* (London: Weidenfeld and Nicolson, 1967), pp. 275, 278.
3. William Purdy, *The Church on the Move* (London: Hollis and Carter, 1966), pp. 20–1; Domenico Tardini, *Pio XII* (Vatican: Tipografia Poliglota, 1960).
4. P. Blet, R. Graham et al. (eds), *Actes et Documents du Saint-Siège relatifs á la seconde guerre mondiale* (Vatican City, 1967–82), vol. 5, pp. 206–8; Carlo Felice Casula, *Domenico Tardini 1881–1961* (Rome: Edizione Studium, 1988), pp. 260–8.
5. *L'Osservatore Romano* (27 July 1947). The Plan was also backed by *Il Quotidiano*, the paper of Catholic Action (3 August 1947).
6. Address (1 June 1946); in Purdy, op. cit., pp. 67–8.
7. Andrea Riccardi, *Il Potere del Papa: da Pio XII a Giovanni Paolo II* (Rome: Editori Laterza, 1993), p. 109.
8. Press statement (18 September 1953); quoted in Robert Gannon, *The Cardinal Spellman Story* (London: Robert Hale, 1963), p. 346.
9. Ibid., pp. 348–50.
10. Montini's letter to Spellman (12 March 1953); from Gerald P. Fogarty, 'The United States and the Vatican 1939–1984', unpublished paper, University of Virginia (1985).
11. Purdy, op. cit., pp. 90–1.
12. Rosanna Mulazzi-Giammanco, *The Catholic–Communist Dialogue in Italy* (New York: Praeger, 1989), pp. 55–9.
13. Quoted in Dermot Keogh, *Ireland, The Vatican and the Cold War: The Case of*

Italy, 1948 (Washington, DC: Occasional Paper no. 10, Woodrow Wilson Center, 1992), p. 35.

14. Ibid., p. 13.
15. Purdy, op. cit., p. 64.
16. Keogh, op. cit., pp. 15–16; Enrico Manfredini, *Giovanni Battista Montini* (Brescia: Istituto Paolo VI, 1985), pp. 90–1.
17. Mulazzi-Giammanco, op. cit., pp. 91–4.
18. Falconi, op. cit., p. 275; Giancarlo Zizola, *Il Microfono di Dio: Pio XII, padre Lombardi e cattolici italiani* (Milan: Mondadori, 1990).
19. Quoted in Sandro Magister, *La politica vaticana e l'Italia, 1943–1978* (Rome: Editori Riuniti, 1979), pp. 184–5.
20. Purdy, op. cit., p. 95.
21. Andrea Riccardi, 'The Vatican of Pius XII and the Catholic Party', *Concilium*, no. 197 (1987), p. 47.
22. Mulazzi-Giammanco, op. cit., p. 61. See also Carlo Corradini, *Atteggiamenti del PCI verso la Chiesa Cattolica e la Religione* (Rome: Rovigo, 1978).
23. From the UN Charter, Article 13. Pius XII's statement in Purdy, op. cit., p. 137.
24. Christmas Message (1954); in Christine de Montclos-Alix, 'Le Saint-Siège et l'Europe' in Joël-Benoît d'Onorio (ed.), *Le Saint-Siège dans les Relations Internationales* (Paris: Éditions du Cerf, 1989), p. 143.
25. *Divini Redemptoris* (19 March 1937), no. 86.
26. Purdy, op. cit., pp. 228–9; J. Derek Holmes, *The Papacy in the Modern World* (London: Burns and Oates, 1981), p. 185.
27. Purdy, op. cit., p. 230.
28. 'List Ambasadora Francuskiego w Watykanie'; in Peter Raina (ed.), *Kościół w PRL—Dokumenty 1945–1959* (Poznań: W Drodze, 1994), p. 295.
29. Stefan Wyszyński, *A Freedom Within* (London: Hodder and Stoughton, 1985) pp. 11–12, 14–16.
30. 'Raport Ambasadora Francji w Stolicy Apostolskiej'; in Raina, op. cit., pp. 236–7.
31. Ibid.
32. Gyula Havasy (ed.), *Martyrs of the Catholics in Hungary* (Budapest: privately published, 1993), p. 85.
33. Quoted in Jean Chelini, *L'Église sous Pie XII: L'après-guerre* (Paris: Fayard, 1989), p. 451.
34. Ibid.
35. Karol Kaplan, 'Church and State in Czechoslovakia from 1948 to 1956, Part III', *Religion in Communist Lands*, vol. 14, no. 3 (1986), pp. 277–8.
36. Mireille Macqua, *Rome–Moscou: L'Ostpolitik du Vatican* (Louvain-la-Neuve: Cabay, 1984), p. 177.
37. Ibid.; Stella Alexander, *Church and State in Yugoslavia Since 1945* (Cambridge: Cambridge University Press, 1979), pp. 144–5.
38. Purdy, op. cit., p. 118.
39. Bohdan Cywiński, *Ogniem Próbowane: I was prześladować będą* (Lublin: Redakcja Wydawnictw, 1990), p. 447.
40. Quoted in Macqua, op. cit., p. 107.

41. Chelini, op. cit., pp. 451–2.
42. József Közi-Horváth, *Cardinal Mindszenty* (Devon: Augustine, 1979), p. 85; Cywiński, op. cit., p. 451; Mindszenty, op. cit., p. 216.
43. Chelini, op. cit., pp. 452–5.
44. Ibid., p. 452.
45. Mulazzi-Giammanco, op. cit., pp. 83–4.

6

cɔɛɔɛɔɛɔ

John XXIII and the signs of the times

When Angelo Giuseppe Roncalli succeeded Pius XII on 28 October 1958, it took him just three months to announce the Rome diocese's first ever synod, as well as a revision of Canon Law and an ecumenical council. The aim was a 'fuller and deeper recognition of truth, a renewal of Christian morals, and a restoration of unity, harmony and peace'.[1] But at 76, John XXIII was seen as a transitional Pope, not one to question the premises and practices of established Catholic social doctrine.

As a papal diplomat in Turkey, Bulgaria and France, Roncalli had loyally followed Pius XII's vigorous line on communism. When he was elected, the Holy Office was still in the hands of Cardinal Ottaviani, a man who publicly derided those eager to 'shake hands and exchange friendly smiles' with communist 'new antichrists'. The whole Vatican machine was geared to his predecessor's no-compromise policy. It was rumoured that alternative papal candidates had even included Cardinal Spellman of New York, who had backed McCarthy's purges and denounced communist rulers in 1956 as 'God-hating lustful beasts masquerading as men'.[2]

John XXIII's first encyclical, *Ad Petri cathedram* (29 June 1959), did not mention communism directly. But it denounced the 'despicable business' purveyed by enemies of truth, and warned against 'errors which enter the recesses of men's hearts and the bloodstream of society as would a plague'. Those wishing to remain Christians, the Pope went on, must avoid the 'false principles' which the Vatican had always condemned. Their proponents threatened to 'destroy the basis of Christianity and civilization'.[3]

On the social order, *Ad Petri cathedram* focused on Leo XIII's link between divine authority and human order. It defended class inequalities as essential 'laws of nature', and urged 'harmony and agreement' to maintain the 'balance of the body politic'. Social improvements were needed—the encyclical urged just wages and fair treatment for employees. But this was less for moral

110

reasons than because poor conditions risked 'rioting mobs, wanton destruction of property and sometimes even bloodshed'.[4]

In Italy, the encyclical was widely viewed as an encouragement to the Christian Democrats. High Vatican figures like Ottaviani poured scorn on talk of a 'religious thaw' in Khrushchev's Soviet Union, and were incensed at President Giovanni Gronchi's plans to visit Moscow in January 1960. The Soviet regime responded in kind. The air was thick with harsh anti-Vatican propaganda.

Yet even before *Ad Petri cathedram* appeared, there were hints of a certain change. In January 1959, to a chorus of *émigré* protests, the Vatican downgraded the embassies representing Polish and Lithuanian governments-in-exile, where Kazimierz Papee and Stanislovas Girdvajnis had remained defiantly since the war. That April, in a boost to Church hardliners, the 1949 Holy Office Decree, barring co-operation with communists, was republished. But in a commentary, Vatican Radio said Catholics who disobeyed it would 'face penalties but not excommunication'. On 19 April, *L'Osservatore Romano* suggested it might not apply to Eastern Europe at all, since it was concerned 'with Catholics acting on their own free will'.[5]

In its reference to Eastern Europe, *Ad Petri cathedram* took up Pius XII's phrase, the 'Church of Silence', and voiced solidarity with those suffering for their faith. But the Church was 'ready to forgive all freely and beg this forgiveness of God', the encyclical added. 'Forgiveness' was a new word in the Vatican's lexicon on communism. At least one East European newspaper claimed to detect 'a certain restraint in tone'.[6]

Hints of change continued. On 26 September, *Grata recordatio* said there were grounds for hoping purveyors of 'sterile postulates and assumptions' would set them aside and return to Christianity. The implication that communists could repent was something new, too. For the time being, there would be no more talk of 'intrinsically evil' doctrines or exhortations to 'vast campaigns'—the language in which Pius XI had set the tone for the Church's post-war confrontation with communism.

On 28 November, *Princeps pastorum* acknowledged that the Church itself was guilty of faults. It quoted St John Chrysostom: 'There would be no need for sermons if our lives were shining; there would be no need for words if we bore witness with our deeds; there would be no more pagans if we were true Christians.' The coming council, John XXIII said, would depend more on 'fervent prayer' than on 'diligent application'.[7] Witness and testimony would have pride of place over threats and injunctions.

By 1960, the Vatican's role on the world stage was growing. Pius XII had received ten heads of state in nineteen years; John XXIII was to receive 34 in five. Meanwhile, the number of Cardinals was allowed to increase beyond its previous limit of 70. The Church was expanding in the Third World and looking further afield. It would have to identify with cultures and societies beyond its narrow Western confines, and cope with new responsibilities generated by a post-colonial era of national emancipation.

John XXIII's next encyclical, *Mater et magistra* (15 May 1961), appeared on the 70th anniversary of Leo XIII's *Rerum novarum* and contained enough sharp language about injustices and inequalities to suggest a real change in the Vatican's position. It recalled Marx's charge that the Church took no interest in social matters 'other than to preach resignation to the poor and generosity to the rich'. It also reaffirmed Pius XI's condemnation of communism and socialism.[8] But the 'radical transformation' of the past twenty years, John XXIII added, had made it necessary to rethink the application of Catholic social principles. In some countries, 'the unbridled luxury of the privileged stands in violent, offensive contrast to the utter poverty of the vast majority'. A vigilant effort was needed to ensure that 'social inequalities, so far from increasing, are reduced to a minimum'.[9]

The Pope defended private ownership as a key to freedom and 'true social order'. But it should be extended, he added, 'to all classes of citizens', if necessary by increasing State and public ownership. He conceded that there would always be a 'vast field' for 'Christian charity': but beyond that he hardly mentioned it. Instead, the emphasis in *Mater et magistra* was on structural solutions, another new departure. The Pope urged developing countries to avoid the mistakes of wealthier nations, by ensuring 'social progress keeps pace with economic progress'. The time had come, he added, for advanced countries to abandon their plans for 'world domination'. A lasting peace would be impossible 'as long as glaring economic and social imbalances exist'.[10]

This implied link between equality and peace brought *Mater et magistra* close to endorsing the claims of socialists. So did its stress on social and economic development as a precondition for human rights. The Pope did not specify which system offered greatest hope. But poverty was being exacerbated in the Third World, he said, by 'a deficient social and economic organization'. The 'only possible solution' was one which 'respects and promotes true human values'. There were theories to hand about how to achieve the 'organic reconstruction of society'. But Catholic teaching could also help solve present-day difficulties if applied actively and analytically. Christians should be educated in a spirit of commitment. It was a 'gross error' to suppose Christian perfection was achieved by fleeing the world.

John XXIII returned to communism towards the end of the encyclical, deploring the 'bitter persecution' of Christians and the 'refined barbarity of their oppressors'. To view religion as an 'obstacle to human progress' was, he added, 'the most fundamental modern error'. But *Mater et magistra* did not point fingers. Although communism was a perversity, it was only one of many facing the modern world.[11]

It was easy to see why John XXIII's new emphasis on justice and equality attracted the attention of communists. At the Twenty-Second Soviet Communist Party Congress in October 1961, Khrushchev described 'peaceful coexistence' as the main aim of Soviet foreign policy. This was the logical consequence of geostrategic developments. Soviet expansionism was blocked by the creation of NATO and the rearming of Germany, while a growing rift with China had divided world communism. In short, war with the West could no longer be seen as inevitable. Communism's ultimate victory was assured. But care had to be taken to prevent a capitalism in its death throes from unleashing a nuclear catastrophe. Nascent anti-war movements in the US and Western Europe offered certain opportunities. So did the Catholic Church—in the hands of an 'anti-Western' Pope.

Khrushchev had reasons for seeing John XXIII that way. On the night of 12–13 August 1961, with up to 30,000 fleeing westwards each month, the East German regime had finally sealed off Germany's Soviet-occupied sector and begun building an 'anti-fascist wall', shooting at civilians who attempted to cross the intervening death strip. Less than a week later, the Pope named a new Archbishop of Berlin. The 40-year-old Alfred Bengsch asserted that he wished to stay politically neutral, neither praising nor criticizing the regime's policies. On 10 September, John XXIII appealed for peace and disarmament from his summer residence at Castelgandolfo. The Soviet Union had just broken a nuclear moratorium with three tests in Kazakhstan. There was talk of a serious new downturn in East–West relations. So the Pope's gesture was eagerly seized on in Moscow. In a press statement, Khrushchev wondered if 'fervent Catholics' like Kennedy and Adenauer would 'grasp the Pope's admonition'. It was the first time a Soviet Party boss had spoken this way about a Pope.

> The head of the Catholic Church takes into account the feelings of millions of Catholics in all parts of the world who are uneasy about the military preparations of the imperialists. John XXIII honours reason when he exhorts governments against a general catastrophe and makes them aware of the immense responsibility they have towards history.[12]

On 25 November, Khrushchev went a step further, and sent the Pope a message for his 80th birthday, praising his 'noble ambition to contribute to reinforcing and consolidating peace'. Something had clearly changed. Soviet propagandists were no longer presenting the Vatican as the feeble lap-dog of

Western capitalism. Reputedly, the Pope saw Khrushchev's message as a 'sign of divine providence'.[13]

The romance with Khrushchev was to reach its zenith a year later. In October 1962, the Soviet Union's installation of missile bases in Cuba brought an ultimatum from the Kennedy Administration which appeared to take the world to the brink of war. Both sides indicated a readiness to consider papal mediation, using messages relayed by Norman Cousins, the pacifist editor of the US weekly *Saturday Review*. And on the early morning of 24 October, as fears reached fever pitch, John XXIII's appeal was duly delivered to the US and Soviet embassies in Rome. It spoke passionately of the 'anguished cry that comes from all points of the land, from innocent babes to the old', and urged both sides to show 'maximum wisdom and prudence'. A return to negotiations would, the Pope added, testify 'to each party's conscience and stand as evidence before history'.[14] The text was published in *Pravda* on 26 October. Two days later, Khrushchev backed down and agreed to pull the missiles out.

In a Kremlin meeting with Cousins that December, Khrushchev insisted the Pope's face-saving appeal had been 'the only gleam of hope', adding that he now wished to 'extend contacts' with the Vatican. The Church's aim, the Soviet leader acknowledged, was to 'serve all humanity', not only Catholics. In his Christmas Message John XXIII spoke of 'unmistakable signs of deep understanding', of 'new prospects for fraternal trust and the first glimmers of a calm future with true social and international peace'.[15]

By then, the Second Vatican Council was in its third month. In January 1959, the Pope had listed restoring Christian unity as its chief aim.[16] A Secretariat for Christian Unity was one of twelve bodies set up to prepare the Council agenda. A key priority was to persuade the world's largest Orthodox Church—in Russia—to take part.

The Moscow Patriarchate refused. The Pope had no right to call an ecumenical council, it insisted; so sending observers would wrongly imply recognition of his primacy. The Ecumenical Patriarch of Constantinople, Athenagoras I, turned down the invitation too. But in October 1962, when the Council opened, two Russian Orthodox officials, Archpriest Vitaly Borovoi and Archimandrite Vladimir Kotliarov, suddenly showed up among 48 observers. There had been some backstage manoeuvring.

The likeliest explanation was that the Kremlin believed the Vatican was ready to make return gestures and had pressed Patriarch Alexei I to send representatives. During a discreet meeting in Metz, the Dean of the Sacred College of Cardinals, Cardinal Eugène Tisserant, had reputedly promised Metropolitan Nikodim, head of the Moscow Patriarchate's foreign relations department, that the Council would be 'non-political' and avoid anti-communist pronouncements. Mgr Jan Willebrands, the Dutch secretary of Cardinal Augustin Bea's Christian Unity Secretariat, had visited Moscow in September to give 'direct information' about Vatican II's agenda. 'The Council will not speak out against any one country—for example, England, Germany or Russia', Willebrands told Borovoi. 'If the Church must warn its members against certain errors ... it does not, in so doing, condemn a people or nation, although the authors of the error may belong to a specific nation.'[17]

This seemed to reassure Russian Church leaders. Khrushchev claimed to be impressed by Vatican II's opening pledge that the Church would 'loyally collaborate with every sincere effort in favour of peace'.[18] In his talks with Cousins, he made much of the robust peasant temperament he shared with John XXIII. Both were would-be reformers, the Soviet leader said, of their own respective worlds. A new-look, post-Stalinist Soviet Union was making common cause with a new-look, 'realist' Vatican, which was now an important point of entry for gaining acceptance in the Western world.

The Pope, for his part, saw relations with Moscow as the key to wider contacts with Eastern Europe. If the Soviet Union modified its attitude, other communist governments would follow suit. It was the right hunch. Most regimes allowed Catholic bishops to go to Rome. Poland sent 17 out of 64, Yugoslavia 24 out of 27, while Czechoslovakia granted passports to four. Even Bulgaria, where John XXIII had been the Vatican's Apostolic Visitor in 1925–34, permitted a bishop to travel west.

Just why so many permits were handed out was a matter for speculation. Were the East Europeans really interested in Church reforms—and if so, which did they believe would suit communist interests? Did they conclude that Vatican II's 'opening to the world' would in reality weaken the Church? Did they, like Khrushchev, see the Vatican as a potential ally in the expansion of world communism?

In some cases, East European participation was accompanied by signs of change at home. Conditions had begun to ease in Yugoslavia while Pius XII was still alive. A delegation of bishops had attended John XXIII's coronation in November 1958. In December 1959, Tito had again talked of 'normalizing' relations with the Vatican. When Cardinal Stepinac died in suspicious circumstances the following February, the regime showed a conciliatory face by allowing him to be buried in Zagreb cathedral. Speaking at a requiem Mass in St Peter's, the Pope said he now hoped for 'civil and religious peace'.[19] There were reports of exploratory contacts between Rome and Belgrade.

Yet the mere presence of East Europeans did not necessarily imply any slackening in anti-Church policies. The Kádár regime in Hungary saw contacts with the Vatican as a way of legitimizing the post-1956 order. Vatican officials, visiting in October 1962, were said to see Hungary as the test-bed for a new *Ostpolitik*. But its Church hierarchy was already totally subservient. In March 1961, 200 priests were arrested for illegal youth teaching. Instead of defending them, a Church statement warned that 'irresponsible persons' would not be allowed to use the Church for 'seditious acts'.[20] Even in Poland, *L'Osservatore Romano* hit out at anti-Church measures, insisting these were following the 'paradigm' established by the persecution of Russian Orthodoxy. Polish communists, the paper added, had tried to create an 'internal destructive dialectic' within the Church, by presenting Wyszyński's 1950 agreement as a 'rebellion against the Holy See'.[21]

Similar reservations could be expressed towards the more spectacular gestures made to John XXIII by Khrushchev. The Soviet government allowed three Lithuanian priests to attend Vatican II's second session, and raised no objection when two new bishops were consecrated for Lithuania and Latvia. There was more to come. The presence of Russian Orthodox observers was bitterly criticized by exiled bishops from the outlawed Ukrainian Greek Catholic Church, at a time when their own leader, Metropolitan Josif Slipyi, was still in a Soviet labour camp. A plea for Slipyi's release was passed to the Moscow Patriarchate via Archpriest Borovoi. And when Norman Cousins met Khrushchev in December 1962, the Soviet leader agreed in principle, on condition that 'no political case' was made of his 'act of goodwill'. It was to remain no more than that. 'One more enemy in freedom doesn't scare me', Khrushchev retorted.[22] But Slipyi's 'crime against the Soviet people' was not being forgiven. This was not a pardon.

Slipyi, not surprisingly, was reluctant to accept the Soviet leader's largesse, and insisted he would only return if immediately reinstated in his Lviv archdiocese. In the end, the 71-year-old Metropolitan was prevailed on to leave the country by Mgr Willebrands. He arrived in Rome, via Vienna, on 9 February 1963, having seen the last of Lviv through the windows of a speeding train. Though this was billed in the West as a major Soviet concession, Slipyi felt humiliated. He had promised never to leave Ukraine 'unless under forced escort'. 'But the voice of Pope John XXIII summoned me to the Vatican Council. His call was an order, for in it I saw the incomprehensible intention of God's wisdom.'[23]

Slipyi's release suggested a conflict between the twin priorities of diplomacy and testimony. Diplomacy could rescue occasional Church leaders, whose cases symbolized the struggle for truth and justice. But it could not rescue whole Church communities, who would go on suffering just as before. The move did, however, set the pace for Khrushchev's next 'concession'. On 7 March, the Soviet leader's son-in-law, Alexei Adzhubei, arrived at the Vatican with his wife. Adzhubei was editor of the Soviet Communist Party's *Izvestia* daily, and the visit officially formed part of a larger audience for newspaper editors. But when the audience ended, the Russians were led to the Pope's library. The couple had come as Khrushchev's envoys, and the encounter was widely seen as the possible prelude to a visit by the Soviet leader himself. Once again, there was talk of 'new openings'.

But the latest conciliatory escapade attracted stiff opposition. Vatican Radio ended its news bulletin the day before with material on Soviet anti-religious persecutions. It also pointedly requoted a message from John XXIII after his election in 1958, lamenting the 'slavery of individuals and masses' under 'atheistic and materialistic' regimes. 'Communist tactics have truly changed, so changed as to succeed sometimes in lodging doubt', the broadcast continued. 'Unfortunately, the reality is different than the propaganda. Communism remains what it was: atheistic and materialistic, both theoretically and in practice.'[24]

Some commentators complained that the Adzhubei visit lacked any clear purpose. The Pope himself was said to have turned down suggestions that Moscow and the Vatican could establish formal relations. Had the unusual episode not merely spread confusion among Catholics—as well as losing Italy's Christian Democrats 'a million votes', as the right-wing *Il Borghese* put it?

Perhaps John XXIII's real purpose had merely been to offer a paternalistic embrace to Eastern Europe's communist rulers. A report from the Vatican's Secretariat of State spoke of Adzhubei's 'visibly emotional air and damp eyes'.[25] It was a crude, sentimental image, not one for the practitioners of geopolitics. Yet in its way, it also put Europe's Christian unity back on some kind of agenda, and conveyed the impression that the Pope's *offensive de charme* had elicited a show of Soviet fealty. When Italy's authoritative Jesuit magazine *Civiltà Cattolica* submitted its report on the meeting for Vatican approval, according to normal procedure, the text was turned down. According to one account, the Pope was advised to reject it by Mgr Dell'Acqua, the same official who had reprimanded Hungary's bishops for their 1950 agreement. Dell'Acqua's arguments indicated how divided the Church had become in its response to communism:

I would not use the term 'enemy from always' ... I would not dare say definitely that the reasons determining the communist turn are tactical and political in nature. It may be true, but why should it be the Church who says so? It is like turning away one's adversary without further recourse ... Pius XII himself always spoke of 'atheistic communism', not simply of communism.

Moreover, he always carefully avoided seeming to be associated with international crusades against communism.[26]

There was one more top-level release before 1963 was out—that of the Czech Cardinal Beran. By then, John XXIII had issued a new encyclical, justifying the revised attitude to communism. In *Ad Petri cathedram*, four years before, he had sternly reminded seekers of peace that they 'must make no concessions to error'. In *Mater et magistra*, he had reminded Catholics that they should always accept the Church hierarchy's 'authoritative judgement' when dealing with those 'who do not share their view of life'.[27] But in *Pacem in terris* (11 April 1963), a document conceived during the Cuban Missile Crisis, John XXIII went much further. There could be no doubting that the Vatican's stance had changed significantly.

Peace on earth could never be guaranteed, the Pope acknowledged, without observing the 'divinely established order'. This was an order based on the fundamental principle that 'each individual is truly a person ... endowed with intelligence and free will',[28] whose rights were economic and social (the kind of rights stressed by communist regimes), as well as cultural and political (the rights most often talked about in liberal democracies).

The Pope defended the 'progressive improvement' which had occurred in the life and activity of working people. It should always be remembered, he added, that the exercise of power was conditional. People had the right to choose their rulers and draw up constitutions. The Church's teaching was 'perfectly consistent with any system of genuine democracy'.

> In view of the fact that the power to rule lies in the moral order and comes from God, if ever those holding authority in the State issue laws or commands contrary to this order, and therefore contrary to the will of God, the citizens cannot in conscience be bound by them ... If any officers of State violate or neglect to take account of human rights, they not only fail in their duty, they lose all authority to command obedience.[29]

Pacem in terris leant heavily on Popes stretching back to Leo XIII. But its general defence of the right of resistance was new. So was its vigorous condemnation of nations which 'exert unjust political domination over others', or take actions which constitute 'an unjust oppression of other countries or an unwarranted interference in their affairs'. Not surprisingly, given his experiences the previous autumn, John XXIII had strong words about the East–West military confrontation, even if he appeared to accept the logic of nuclear deterrence. The arms race should be stopped and nuclear weapons banned. But disarmament must also 'reach into men's very souls'. Interstate relations must be regulated not by armed force, but by 'truth, justice and vigorous and sincere co-operation'.

The encyclical went on to flirt with the idea of world government—a notion which *Mater et magistra* claimed to have traced back to Pius XI's *Quadragesimo anno* of 1937. Whereas Pius XII had distrusted the UN, John XXIII saw it as a model. He believed the 1948 Universal Declaration of Human Rights was a 'step in the right direction' towards a 'juridical and political ordering of the world community'.[30]

It was at this point that John XXIII added a statement which was to have far-reaching repercussions. The time had come, he said, for Catholics to co-operate in good causes with non-Christians who retained a 'natural moral integrity'. Helped by God's grace, even those who had 'fallen into error' could still 'regain the path of truth'. Their human dignity should always be respected.

> We must make a clear distinction between false philosophical theories about the nature, origin and purpose of the universe and of man, and the practical measures that have been put into operation as a result of these theories, in social and economic life, in cultural matters and in the management of the state. For whereas theories, once formulated, remain unalterably fixed and frozen in the words that express them, the measures to which they give rise are constantly subject to alteration as circumstances change. Besides, who will deny that good and praiseworthy elements can be found in such measures in so far as they conform to the rules of right reason and reflect the lawful aspirations of men?[31]

The Pope added a caution: prudence was needed in deciding when and how co-operation was possible. For Catholics, such decisions must be taken by 'leading figures in the community and authorities in the matter being dealt with'—not necessarily by the Church's hierarchy.[32]

This was a long way from the formularies of John XXIII's predecessors. The encyclical's distinctions—error and victim, theory and practice—could be traced to St Augustine, although some observers also detected the influence of Maritain and Mounier. Whatever the origin, *Pacem in terris* marked a clear departure from the gloomy, Manichaean outlook of Pius XII. False doctrines should be left to fade away, not hardened by condemnations. Sinful practices were best remedied by conversion, rather than by anathemas. It was a good and saintly postulate. But it raised an obvious question: did changes of heart by individuals, however important and influential, affect the performance of states and power-structures?

In any event, *Pacem in terris* set the tone for the rest of Vatican II—and for the 3,500 bishops, experts, auditors and observers who prayed daily in St Peter's for sound judgement. The statement, *Humanae salutis*, announcing the Council on Christmas Day 1961, had optimistically used the words *segni dei tempi* ('signs of the times'). Vatican II's objective was to 'bring the modern world into contact with the vivifying and perennial energies of the Gospel', while making the supernatural order 'reflect its efficiency' in the temporal one.[33] When it came to enacting this vision, the Council went well beyond expectations.

John XXIII's notion of a 'dialogue' between the Church and the world was the dominant theme of the 'Pastoral Constitution', *Gaudium et spes* (7 December 1965), whose opening pledge of 'deep solidarity' with man— 'considered whole and entire, with body and soul, heart and conscience, mind and will'—confirmed a decisive shift from the 'fortress Church' mentality of the past.

Gaudium et Spes spoke of the dawn of a 'new age of human history', an age of moral extremes and sharp dichotomies, in a world 'at once powerful and weak, capable of doing what is noble and what is false, disposed to freedom and slavery, progress and decline, brotherhood and hatred'. It was a world of social and economic changes in which 'traditional institutions, laws and modes of thought and emotion do not always appear in harmony'. So the Church was forced to re-examine its assumptions and ask funda- mental questions. It had to be open to far-reaching changes—not only to the changes in hearts and attitudes urged by previous Popes, but also to changes in structures and institutions. The social order required 'constant improvement' if it was to 'grow in freedom towards a more humane equilibrium'.[34]

In a chapter on 'The political community', *Gaudium et spes* acknowledged that cultural, social and economic progress had generated a desire for greater political responsibilities. People had a right to choose their rulers and defend their freedoms. They were repudiating political systems which hindered liberty, victimized citizens or abused authority to the benefit of 'political parties or governing classes'. Faithful to the Gospel, today's Church proclaimed the 'rights of man' and respected the 'dynamic approach' which was fostering these rights worldwide.[35] 'True peace' could only be obtained when human welfare and dignity were respected and safeguarded.

Gaudium et spes went well beyond repudiating the Church's political alignments under Pius XII. To the traditional principle of 'charity', it now added 'justice', so that 'justice and charity' became a recurrent catchphrase. It recalled the rights and duties of workers and owners, and set out a vision of a mixed economy, in which decision-making was neither left to 'a few individuals or groups possessing too much economic power, nor to the political community alone'. Meanwhile, it denounced doctrines which opposed reform 'on the pretext of a false notion of freedom', and those which subordinated personal rights to the 'collective organization of production'.[36]

Although private property was 'an extension of human freedom', *Gaudium et spes* continued, it was subject to the 'universal destination of earthly goods'. There were occasions when the common good called for expropriation or nationalization. The Church had always taught that the rich must aid the poor. Every person had a right 'to possess a sufficient amount of the earth's goods for himself and his family'. So those 'in extreme necessity' had the right to a share in the riches of others.

The Church's 'Dogmatic Constitution', *Lumen Gentium*, dated 21 November 1964, used the concept of a 'Pilgrim Church', ready to enter communion with all forms of culture which were based on authentic values.[37] The Church had to undergo changes to fulfil its 'earthly responsibilities'. It had to be aware of its faults and recognize that it could not answer every question. No one could 'identify the authority of the Church exclusively with his own opinion'.

> The Church is the faithful spouse of the Lord and will never fail to be a sign of salvation in the world; but it is by no means unaware that down through the centuries there have been among its members, both clerical and lay, some who were disloyal to the Spirit of God. Today as well, the Church is not blind to the discrepancy between the message it proclaims and the human weakness of those to whom the Gospel has been entrusted. Whatever history's judgement on these shortcomings, we cannot ignore them and must combat them earnestly. The Church also realizes how much it needs the maturing influence of centuries of past experience in order to work out its relationship to the world ...
>
> By reason of her role and competence, the Church is not identified with any political community nor bound by ties to any political system. It is at once the sign and the safeguard of the transcendental dimension of the human person.[38]

This acknowledgement of past failures was unprecedented. It caught the imagination of many people outside the Church, and encouraged them to look again at an institution they had once shunned. Meanwhile, Vatican II's Decree on Ecumenism, *Unitatis redintegratio* (21 November 1964), recognized the rich heritage of the Eastern Churches, and Catholicism's debt to them in liturgy and doctrine. The Decree on Religious Liberty, *Dignitatis humanae* (7 December 1965), defended 'free enquiry' in matters of faith and ruled out discrimination against minority religions.

A similar spirit of penance and openness characterized Vatican II's treatment of communism. Two preparatory commissions had debated the forms of pastoral care which could be used in countering its influence. But when Vatican II's Central Commission amalgamated their two reports into a single schema, it deleted the reference to communism and used the phrase 'errors of materialism' instead.

This was deliberate. Several East European participants had argued against a direct condemnation of communism. The youthful Archbishop Bengsch of Berlin had put their case forcefully in May 1962. Communism, Bengsch argued, was 'only one form of atheism and materialism'. If it was to be denounced by name, it would also be necessary to condemn 'every materialistic ideology', including those flourishing in the West. To maintain the Council's dignity, the 'language of the mass media' should be avoided— especially phrases like 'free nations' and 'iron curtain'.

> Certainly, the Church has the right and duty to condemn in candid language any heresy, especially atheistic communism ... In spite of this, I would briefly like to explain why I, exercising my office of Archbishop in East Germany, thus under the reign of the communists, do not like the proposed draft. It is very well stated in the draft that the activity of the Church must be clearly differentiated from political or economic anti-communism ... However, if the Council now ceremoniously proceeds exclusively against communism ... the communists would have an easy and very welcome opportunity to misuse the Council's words in their propaganda and prove to the inexperienced that the Church is engaging in political actions.[39]

Bengsch wanted to delete references to the 'Church of Silence' too, believing they would 'absolutely surely occasion new oppression'. It would be 'considerably more helpful', the Archbishop retorted, 'if the Church in other nations would keep silent about the Church of Silence'.[40]

Some participants vigorously disagreed. A Slovak bishop, Pavel Hilnica, recently released from labour camp and sent into exile, was attacked by Prague Radio after calling dialectical materialism the 'mystery of Satan'. Meanwhile, Paul Yu Pin, the exiled Archbishop of Nanking, appealed with 70 others for communism to be condemned along with fashionable illusions about 'peaceful coexistence' and 'extended hands'.[41]

But others went even further than Bengsch in opposing a confrontational stance. Although Vatican II's drafts contained impressive statements on social justice, it was argued, the Church had always recognized the importance of social justice too late. It had taken half a century for *Rerum novarum* to confront the theories of Marx, while the errors of some other radical figures had been 'condemned unthinkingly'. Cardinal König of Vienna believed Marxism's atheistic character had a lot to do with 'distorted expressions of religion'. Communists were wrong to see religion as a form of alienation. But religion would nevertheless have to be 'purged continually of certain alienating features'.[42]

That argument was heard from Eastern Europe too. Cardinal Franjo Šeper of Zagreb believed that the 'egotism of Christians' was largely to blame for both communism and atheism. If the Gospel had been 'lived and preached to the full', the Croat Cardinal argued, and if those defending the established social order had not 'falsely invoked the name of God', the world would have been spared.[43]

It was the view that condemnations merely reinforced opposition without changing anything in practice which won through at Vatican II. There were those in the middle, like Cardinal Slipyi, who saw the point in avoiding provocative declarations but also objected to the suggestion that Christian abuses had helped spur the rise of communism. Yet their voices were gradually drowned. 'We know how many people have embraced atheist Marxism today' was the argument of Cardinal Bernard Alfrink of Utrecht. 'But it is useless to repeat the condemnation of communism, since the whole world knows the Church's position on this subject. The Council should promote and encourage dialogue with all men of goodwill, and not issue condemnations.'[44]

During Vatican II's final session in autumn 1965, 334 participants signed a *démarche* demanding that communism be treated more forcefully. But this was no more than a tenth of the assembled Council Fathers.

The final version of *Gaudium et spes* was prepared by a commission under König and Šeper, which included the Jesuits Henri de Lubac and Jean Daniélou, as well as Bishop Hilnica and the Polish Archbishop Bolesław Kominek of Wrocław. It made no reference to communism or Marxism. Instead, three sections on atheism were inserted in a chapter on 'The dignity of the human person'. These drew certain distinctions—between agnosticism, indifference, conscious atheism and the rejection of absolute truth. However, they acknowledged that atheism often derived from 'a violent protest against the evil of the world', as well as a 'critical reaction against the Christian religion'.

> Believers can thus have more than a little to do with the rise of atheism. To the extent that they are careless about their instruction in the faith, or present its teaching falsely, or even fail in their religious, moral or social life, they must be said to conceal rather than reveal the true nature of God and religion.[45]

The document made one clear allusion to communist regimes—which looked 'for man's autonomy through his economic and social emancipation', and held that religion thwarted this emancipation by 'raising man's hopes in a future life'. But even then, it went out of its way to be conciliatory.

> Although the Church altogether rejects atheism, she nevertheless sincerely proclaims that all men, those who believe as well as those who do not, should help to establish right order in this world where all live together. This certainly cannot be done without a dialogue which is sincere and prudent ... The Church demands effective freedom for the faithful to be allowed to build up

God's temple in this world. She courteously invites atheists to weigh the merits of the Gospel of Jesus Christ with an open mind.[46]

Talk of dialogue with the Church's opponents was something new. Meanwhile, other reasons were offered for avoiding any direct mention of communism. One was that communism had a 'multiplicity of meanings', another that it comprised political and economic views not under discussion in *Gaudium et spes*. A third was that Marxism was a 'philosophical system, needing far-ranging interpretation': it was better not to mention it at all than risk labelling it one-sidedly and incompletely.[47]

As a concession to hard-line objectors who had signed the autumn *démarche*, a footnote was added to Article 21 listing previous papal statements on communism. This mentioned Pius XI's *Divini redemptoris* of 1937 and Pius XII's *Ad Apostolorum principis* of June 1958 (denouncing the Church schism in China), as well as *Mater et magistra* and *Ecclesiam Suam*, the first encyclical of the new Pope, Paul VI. But it made no reference to the Holy Office's 1949 Decree prescribing excommunication for communist collaborators. Clearly, Catholic teaching was still in motion. Each text would have to be read within its historical context. While distancing itself from communism, the Church had acknowledged that its own record was at fault, and that it still had to find an effective answer to the ideological challenges confronting it. The Council Fathers had endorsed the moral postulate of dialogue. They had also recognized that communism and Marxism often had the dimensions of a quasi-religious faith, and would not be undermined by denunciations and sanctions alone. All that could be done was to counter them patiently with a more convincing ethos and with the power of truth.

When John XXIII died on 2 June 1963, two months after *Pacem in terris*, Vatican II had only just begun. But there could be no doubting that his vision of a Catholic Church adapted to modern times, guided by soulful intuitions rather than legal formulations, had significantly moved hearts and minds shaped by the confrontations of the 1950s. The Pope had encouraged Christians to ask searching questions about their own motives and actions. 'It was not given to believers faithful to Catholic dogma, but to atheistic communists, to abolish the absolutism of private profit in Russia', one of several critical Catholic thinkers rehabilitated by Vatican II, Jacques Maritain, had recalled. 'This process would have been less vitiated by the force of error, and would have occasioned fewer catastrophes, if it had been performed by Christians.'[48]

In the early 1960s, many still claimed to see evidence of the 'humanization of communism' prophesied by Hromádka and others after the Second World War. The Soviet Communist Party's 1961 programme listed the values expected from good Soviet citizens: patriotism, conscientious work for the community, helpful and humane attitudes, respect for others, honesty, moral integrity, protection of the family ... Were these not, for the naive and gullible—for Lenin's 'useful idiots'— precisely the values of liberal democracy, the very same Judaic–Christian virtues underlying Western civilization? It required a sense for the ways of disinformation to see that these high-sounding Soviet ideals lacked grounding in objective laws and ethics. They were only words, whose meaning and sense depended on the ideological whims of communist officials.

John XXIII had been too worldly-wise to fail to see this for himself. But even before his death, the charges had piled up against him. Some said he had allowed Soviet propaganda to triumph without securing any real Church advances. Others claimed he had opened the door to Marxist influences within the Church itself. While Pius XII had denounced communist tyranny, John XXIII had talked of 'peace'. Had he not thereby helped legitimize Soviet rule, identifying the Vatican, less than two decades after Yalta, with a permanent East–West division?

In reality, the Pope had been gazing over a broader historical landscape. His predecessors had condemned the French Revolution and the Enlight-enment ideals of reason and democracy. Yet these movements had all, in time, abandoned their destructive fanaticism and become inescapable components of modern society. Could the same occur with communism? That was a question over which views and convictions were bitterly divided. John XXIII did not answer the question: but he did succeed in posing it. The struggle which he had unleashed would shape the course of coming years.

Vatican II had recognized belatedly the awesome reality revealed by two world wars—that conventional statecraft could no longer guarantee peace and stability, and that a secure future would depend on the acceptance of ethical standards in international affairs. As globalization advanced, the Church could no longer limit itself to the interests and concerns of Catholics alone. It had to respond to the myriad of thoughts and ideas being exchanged around the world, as the Cold War gave way to a search for mutual contacts, to talk of 'convergence' and '*détente*'. Pius XII, like Popes before him, had tried to combat communism head-on from a position of strength, by rallying the Church around a concentration of tradition, authority and loyalty. By contrast, John XXIII saw communism as an outgrowth of modernity with its own roots and rationale—a 'sign of the times' which had to be read and interpreted if it was to be countered by a prophetic witness. Just how these worthy axioms were to be put into practice was another question. The citizens of Eastern Europe were not yet in a position to demand changes on their own terms. The

Pope had lacked the means of obtaining a deep understanding of the region's real conditions, and of seeing how the power of the Church and Vatican could be used to challenge communism on its home ground.

Notes

1. *Ad Petri cathedram*, no. 3.
2. All Saints address in the Philippines (28 November 1956); in Robert Gannon, *The Cardinal Spellman Story* (London: Robert Hale, 1963), p. 398. For Ottaviani, see Ernest Milcent, *A l'Est du Vatican: La papauté et les démocraties populaires* (Paris: Éditions du Cerf, 1980), pp. 8–9.
3. *Ad Petri cathedram*, nos 7, 130.
4. Ibid., no. 36.
5. See Józef Mackiewicz, *W Cieniu Krzyża* (London: Kontra, 1972), pp. 9–17.
6. *Polityka* (Warsaw: 22 August 1959); *Ad Petri cathedram*, no. 137.
7. Ibid., no. 88. See also *Grata recordatio*, nos 17–18; *Princeps pastorum*, no. 34.
8. *Mater et magistra*, no. 34.
9. Ibid., nos 69 and 73.
10. Ibid., nos 120, 157 and 168.
11. Ibid., nos 216 and 256.
12. Giancarlo Zizola, *The Utopia of Pope John XXIII* (New York: Orbis Books, 1978), pp. 120–1.
13. Ibid., pp. 117–18; Peter Hebblethwaite, *John XXIII: Pope of the Council* (London: Geoffrey Chapman, 1984), pp. 392–4.
14. Zizola, op. cit., p. 8.
15. Quoted in Stjepan Schmidt, *Augustin Bea: The Cardinal of Unity* (New York: New City Press, 1992), p. 581.
16. The Pope added later that the Council's aim would be to 'attract the gaze of the great majority of Christians of every denomination'; *Aeterna Dei sapientia* (11 November 1961), no. 62. See also Hebblethwaite, op. cit., pp. 306–24.
17. Schmidt, op. cit., p. 362; Antoine Wenger, *Les Trois Rome: L'Église des années soixantes* (Paris: Desclée de Brouwer, 1991).
18. Zizola, op. cit., p. 4. Archpriest Borovoi told a Polish newspaper that John XXIII and other Church figures had 'all spoken of their great admiration for our state and people, and our struggle for peace'; *Słowo Powszechne* (Warsaw: 30 November 1962).
19. The Croatian Catholic weekly *Glas Koncila* cited evidence in February 1998 that Stepinac died as a result of prolonged poisoning; *KAI Biuletyn* (7 February 1998). See also Mireille Macqua, *Rome–Moscou: L'Ostpolitik du Vatican* (Louvain-la-Neuve: Cabay, 1984), p. 177. For Yugoslav participation at Vatican II, see Stella Alexander, *Church and State in Yugoslavia Since 1945* (Cambridge: Cambridge University Press, 1979), pp. 243–5.

20. Gyula Havasy (ed.), *Martyrs of the Catholics in Hungary* (Budapest: privately published, 1993), pp. 108–9.
21. Article signed by Chief Editor Federico Allessandrini, *L'Osservatore Romano* (16 December 1962).
22. According to the verbatim record of Cousins; in Zizola, op. cit., p. 140.
23. Wasyl Lencyk, 'Iosyf Slipyi—Patriarch and martyr', *The Ukrainian Quarterly*, vol. 45, no. 3 (Fall 1989), p. 255; Jaroslav Pelikan, *Confessor Between East and West* (Grand Rapids: William B. Eerdmans, 1990).
24. Zizola, op. cit., p. 156.
25. The report was written by the interpreter, Fr Alessandro Koulic; see Zizola, op. cit., p. 160. The Pope was allegedly disappointed that details of the meeting were not published by the Vatican; Hebblethwaite, op. cit., pp. 481–4.
26. Zizola, op. cit., p. 164.
27. *Ad Petri cathedram*, no. 95; *Mater et magistra*, no. 239.
28. *Pacem in terris*, no. 1.
29. Ibid., nos 49–50 and 61.
30. Ibid., nos 114 and 144.
31. Ibid., nos 158–159.
32. Ibid., nos 160 and 191–192.
33. Quoted in Herbert Vorgrimler, *Commentary on the Documents of Vatican II*, vol. 5 (London: Burns and Oates, 1969), p. 7. See also Hebblethwaite, op. cit., pp. 397–9.
34. *Gaudium et spes*, nos 9 and 26.
35. Ibid., nos 41 and 73–75.
36. Ibid., no. 65.
37. The title of chapter VII of *Lumen Gentium*; *Gaudium et spes*, no. 62.
38. Ibid., nos 43, 55 and 76.
39. Hansjakob Stehle, *Eastern Politics of the Vatican 1917–1979* (London: Ohio University Press, 1981), pp. 443–4. The German journalist claimed to be the first to publish Archbishop Bengsch's *Non placet*, translated from the signed Latin original, dated 4 May 1962.
40. Ibid., p. 444.
41. Sergio Trasatti, *La Croce e la Stella: La Chiesa e i regimi comunisti in Europa dal 1917 a oggi* (Milan: Mondadori, 1993), p. 234; William Leahy and Anthony Massini (eds), *Third Session Council Speeches of Vatican II* (New York: Paulist Press, 1966), pp. 158–9.
42. Vorgrimler, op. cit., pp. 147, 164–8. Several of the earlier points were made by Archbishop D'Souza of Bhopal in India; see Jean-Yves Calvez, 'Le Marxisme au Concile' in *Le Deuxième Concile du Vatican* (Rome: École Française de Rome, 1989), pp. 689–702.
43. Ibid., p. 692; Vorgrimler, op. cit., p. 145.
44. Calvez, op. cit., p. 691.
45. *Gaudium et spes*, no. 19.
46. Ibid., nos 20–21.

47. For example, by Cardinal Gabriel-Marie Garrone of Toulouse; Vorgrimler, op. cit., p. 64.
48. Quoted in Zizola, op. cit., pp. 125, 142.

7

cacacaca

Great expectations and broken promises

Khrushchev's romance with John XXIII had effects in the West. In Spain, where the Communist Party's 5,000 members faced constant police harassment, the two Santiagos—Alvarez and Carrillo—saw 'progressive Catholics' as potential recruits for an anti-Franco alliance. In France, Roger Garaudy's 1965 book *De l'Anathème au dialogue* was intended as a communist answer to *Pacem in terris*. Through dialogue with Christians, Garaudy maintained, Marxists could 'rediscover beneath the myths the aspirations that brought them forth', while Christians could transform their faith from Nietzsche's 'Platonism for the masses' into a vehicle for social and political commitment.[1] The French communist believed Vatican II had largely answered this need.

Yet Garaudy was to be expelled from the French Communist Party in 1970, five years before announcing his Christian conversion. Like him, those open to the Church were hardly representative.

In Italy, the Communist Party was said to have seen Roncalli at his election as a decrepit reactionary, and to have advised the Soviet Party against attempting contact. If true, the Party leadership's view had changed by 1963, when Palmiro Togliatti spoke at the Pope's birthplace, in Bergamo: 'We no longer accept the naive and erroneous conception that the extension of knowledge and a change in social structures suffice to determine radical modifications of religious consciousness', he confirmed.[2] Yet he added that communism was still 'certain of victory'. Improved relations with the Catholic Church must take the form of a 'reciprocal understanding and search for common goals'. There could be no question of any philosophical *rapprochement*.

John XXIII's conciliatory message was taken up in Eastern Europe too. Yet the 'dialogue' urged on the Church by pro-regime groups was never a true one. Its goal—strengthening communism—was predetermined and unnegotiable. Those delegated for the task were not seeking truth. They were merely serving the Party's interests.

In Poland, even the government admitted that Bolesław Piasecki's Pax Association, formed to enlist Catholic support for communism, had tried to be 'more socialist than the Party, and more devout than the Pope', when its only real interest was to 'relive the good times of 1949–56'.[3] Here too, 'dialogue' was seen, as Togliatti saw it, as practical co-operation behind communist goals. 'Dialogue with Catholics does not signify ideological compromise or coexistence', the Soviet philosopher L. N. Velikovich noted in 1965. 'Communists recognize the deep ideological differences between Marxism and Catholicism, but do not consider them an obstacle to joint activity.'[4]

Ironically, John XXIII himself had made a similar distinction between 'false theories' and 'practical measures'. But the Pope had not called this dialogue, only 'deliberations'.

The Vatican's Secretariat for Unbelievers was aware that important distinctions were involved. Vatican II's Pastoral Constitution had acknow-ledged that differences over religion need not rule out practical agreements. But 'dialogue' was a two-way process. It required an 'open and benevolent mind', which 'acknowledges the dignity and worth of the other person'. It made sense only if it obeyed the rules of 'truth and liberty', was undertaken by experts, and avoided 'manipulated doctrinal discussion for political ends'.[5]

Even by that exacting definition, gestures of genuine dialogue occurred in Eastern Europe, among those capable of thinking and talking with a degree of independence. It was a patchy encounter. The early 1960s brought a renaissance of Marxist thought in Hungary, as the followers of György Lukács—Eastern Europe's most advanced Marxist group—came into contact with the 'Frankfurt School' of Habermas and Adorno, and Western 'New Left' writers like Sartre and Marcuse. Communist reformers experimented with market theories, allowing pragmatism to scratch at the margins of ideology. Yet the 'liberals' of the Budapest School were no more than a minuscule element of the Hungarian élite. They had no contact with Hungary's Churches and showed no interest in its Christian traditions.

In Yugoslavia, Belgrade University's 'Praxis Group' of Marxists were looking again at concepts of alienation and exploitation found in the Young Marx to explain current discontent. But their tentative theories were viewed, as in Hungary, as an internal party affair.

Yet there were some brighter lights on the horizon. In Czechoslovakia, a semi-independent journal of art and literature, *Tvář* (The Face), launched in 1964, offered a forum for Christian as well as Marxist writers. In Poland, the five newly co-opted Catholic deputies claimed to be acting out the exhortations of *Pacem in terris*. 'Members of the Polish United Workers Party say proletarian internationalism; but we say universality in the Christian spirit', explained its leader, Stanisław Stomma. 'Although this shows a different philosophical foundation, the final conclusions are somewhat similar and can lead to common goals. This means an injunction to struggle for peace, for coexistence, a struggle with a moral quality.'[6]

Of course, statements like this had to be seen in the light of restricted options. But on the communist side too, there were possible openings. Leszek Kołakowski, Poland's leading Marxist philosopher, had concluded that he should re-evaluate European culture's debt to Christianity. Those advocating social justice, Kołakowski realized, were no longer obliged to oppose the Church. Vatican II had shown they could do so within a Christian moral framework.

Yet most of those dreaming of a 'humanistic socialism' still stood a long way from the Church. For most East European citizens, the abstract musings of Catholic and Marxist intellectuals held little interest. In 1964, when two young Polish communists, Jacek Kuroń and Karol Modzelewski, circulated a Marxist critique of the current system's 'bureaucratic repressive apparatus', it was heard about only by a few fellow-academics. Both were thrown in jail. The Party had given its answer.

Against this background, it was hardly surprising that many questioned John XXIII's wisdom. Khrushchev had assured the American Norman Cousins that he was not against 'religion as such'. Soviet anti-religious repression, the Soviet leader insisted, had been the fault of the Tsarist Church, whose priests 'weren't men of God, but the Tsar's gendarmes'. Greater freedom could be granted if the Church's role was 'clarified'. 'I myself had a religious background, and even Stalin was educated in a seminary', Khrushchev continued. 'Now we have no more trouble with the Church and can even protect it if it keeps out of politics.'[7]

From Eastern Europe, it looked as if the Vatican had taken Khrushchev's claim at face-value. The Pope's much-quoted diary meditations about a 'return to unity' in the 'vast lands of Russia', and about 'spiritual conquests for the truth, the Gospel, the Holy Catholic Church',[8] could have various meanings. Did he hope for the reincorporation of a liberated Russia into the universal Church, the end prophesied by Vladimir Soloviev in the nineteenth century? Or did he have in mind the religious transformation of Soviet communism itself? Whatever John XXIII's intention, his words seemed to contradict the bitter realities of the communist-ruled East.

Karol Wojtyła had been canoeing in northern Poland with students from the Catholic University of Lublin (KUL) when, on 18 August 1958, he had received news of his nomination as auxiliary bishop of Kraków. Six weeks later, aged 38, he was consecrated in Wawel cathedral.

It was a surprising appointment. Among priests, Wojtyła was widely seen as independent-minded, even radical. He had taken a manuscript on the canoeing trip to discuss with his companions. It was a study of sexual ethics called *Love and Responsibility*; and it was, Wojtyła said, the fruit of his work among young people.

He had come up with a contradictory mixture of tradition and innovation. On the one hand, the book stuck to the orthodox line that sexual acts involved an 'active, giving' man, and a 'passive, receiving' woman. On the other, it attempted to justify sexual pleasure and the equality of marriage partners. 'Married sexual life is needed not only for procreation, but also for love', Wojtyła noted. 'The human body is an authentic part of the truth about the person, just as the sexual impulse is an authentic part of the truth about human love.'[9]

For a priest who had not yet proved his worth as a philosopher, this was a risky topic. And when *Love and Responsibility* was published in 1959, after Wojtyła's consecration, it caused near-outrage in the Church. Here was a Catholic bishop detailing everything from the construction of the genitals to masturbation and the menopause. Communist commentators lauded the book's 'secularizing potential' in questioning contemporary Polish Catholic attitudes. The Professor of Ethics at KUL accused Wojtyła of violating the Church's moral teachings.[10]

These were simplifications. In reality, *Love and Responsibility* was a competent lecture on human dignity which clearly contradicted the 'socialist morality' of Poland's 1956 family law. But although the book became a best-seller, Wojtyła never returned to the topic. Sexual ethics were an area where theological novelties were unwelcome.

Wojtyła was, however, ready to defend his position on social issues. A 'naive faith', he told the Polish Bishops' Conference, was characterized by 'avoidance of the hardest, deepest and most internal questions'. By contrast, a 'critical faith' tended to 'destroy secondary values'. But it 'concentrated on the most important issues'. Of course, this capacity to be critical should not be confused with the 'aggressive criticism' of communist propagandists. But while 'the human being trusts in God', Wojtyła wrote, 'a thinking person has a right to ask questions. Ethical attitudes anchored in conviction are what promote human maturity.'[11]

Wojtyła's vision of Catholicism was considered élitist by other Polish bishops. If forced to choose, most would have opted for a 'naive faith' which held Church and nation together, rather than a 'critical faith' which risked opening up divisions the Church's enemies could exploit. As head of the

132

Church's youth pastorate, Wojtyła remained (in a colleague's words) 'the only Polish hierarch you could say everything to'.[12] But his new duties also took him outside his familiar surroundings—to places like Nowa Huta, Kraków's vast steelworker suburb. Nowa Huta was a test-case. It was intended to be a socialist metropolis of work to counter Kraków's traditional cultural atmosphere. If the Church was to remain a social force, it also had to be present in 'modern' places like this.

A brick was sent from St Peter's in Rome as the foundation stone for a church at Nowa Huta; and in 1960, protests erupted when police removed a cross from its intended site. But the Gomułka regime could not prevent outdoor Masses being staged for workers at the complex—often staged under pressure in freezing conditions. They were Wojtyła's first encounter with industrial Christianity. Church leaders had traditionally feared the disruptive potential of mass gatherings. But it was at Nowa Huta that Wojtyła was able to sense the positive energy which emanated from sympathetic crowds, the power of the masses to champion good causes in the Church's service.

The experience taught Wojtyła the importance of patriotic symbols and brought him closer to the 'popular Catholicism' associated with Cardinal Wyszyński. But his public statements were not noted for any overtly political content. On 30 December 1963, Gomułka consented to his promotion as Kraków's new archbishop. The regime had rejected seven other candidates in the year since the death of Archbishop Eugeniusz Baziak. At 42, Wojtyła was judged by the Confessions Office to be pliant and inexperienced. There was speculation that it had waited specially for his name to come up.

The nomination found Wojtyła immersed in Vatican II. Most East European participants had had trouble here. The German bishops were said to have descended on Rome with a whole library and team of experts, whereas the Poles came alone after having to wrangle over their passports. They felt discriminated against by language barriers, and sensed that their Western counterparts saw them as backward. But Wojtyła had some advantages. He had studied in Rome, knew languages and had enough ideas of his own about Vatican II's objectives to play a prominent part.

Like Cardinal König and Archbishop Bengsch, Wojtyła opposed an explicit condemnation of communism in *Gaudium et Spes*, believing it would have no impact and merely impede John XXIII's conciliatory policy. This placed him with the Council majority. But he also worked alongside radical reformers like Yves Congar, Bernhard Häring and Dom Helder Câmara of Brazil. It was a formative experience.

Vatican II ended Wojtyła's isolation and made him noticed. Like other East Europeans, however, he saw the Council in a distinctive way. Its main purpose, Wojtyła believed, was to return the Church to its Gospel roots. 'The Council's progressiveness means a fuller approximation to the revealed truth', he wrote in a regular column in *Tygodnik Powszechny*. 'The lines of development lead not only to the future but also to the past, revealing new aspects of the truth. The Church is trying to present its teaching in a full light. It is living in tradition.'[13]

That was not quite how Western participants saw Vatican II. For many, it meant a revolution in Church thinking, a radical break with the past. But Wojtyła came from a region where a radical break had already been inflicted, and where the words 'revolution' and 'progress' conjured up images of destruction. For him, the Council made sense only in reaffirming the Church's continuity, in wisely adapting old truths and paradigms to new needs and conditions.

Wojtyła was well aware that the Council's conclusions had been defined in Western categories. Such phrases as 'openness to the modern world' illustrated this. In the West, it meant openness to modernity, to a liberal agenda shaped by contemporary society. In the East, where regime propagandists constantly harped about the Church's reactionary stance, 'openness to the world' appeared to imply acceptance of communism. Here too, the Church had to understand contemporary dilemmas and hardships. Yet it was called to be 'open' not through adaptation, but through testimony—through a return to truths and values the contemporary world had corrupted. For Karol Wojtyła, this had always been the Church's mission—what Vatican II was proposing was not new, only a rewording of old maxims. Far from bowing to the world's definitions, the Church had to work out its own answer to modernity.

This gave the terms 'liberal' and 'conservative' a different meaning in Eastern Europe. It also changed the sense of key concepts, such as ecumenism and collegiality. In the West, ecumenism meant dialogue between Churches, something presupposing a certain elasticity on points of doctrine. But for Wojtyła, it also meant dialogue between the Church and those outside. This required doctrinal firmness. 'The unity of Christians is not only an internal matter for the Church and Christianity, but a great issue for all humanity', he wrote in his column. 'For this external dialogue, the Church must have an even stronger, more fundamental sense of faith—a *sensus catholicus* more mature than if no such dialogue existed.'[14]

In the West, collegiality meant decentralization, especially in decision-making by national Bishops' Conferences. But for Wojtyła, the emphasis was on equal partnership between Eastern and Western bishops—a 'mutual service and exchange of gifts'. The Pope's primacy remained unchanged: he was 'not only the head, but the keystone of collegiality in the Church'.[15] The young archbishop returned to Poland a Council enthusiast. But he had his own views about what it portended for his own region.

Wojtyła's enthusiasm was not shared by other East European Church leaders. Most saw Vatican II, even more than Wojtyła did, as a Western-dominated affair, reflecting a Western diagnosis of contemporary Church issues. Others also had argued against a direct condemnation of communism. But many were suspicious that Vatican II had failed even to mention it by name. Talk of a 'new attitude' was widely derided. So were phrases in *Gaudium et spes* such as 'nations which favour a collective economy'. In its sections on atheism, the Pastoral Constitution had avoided the word *damnare* (condemn) in favour of the milder *reprobare* (reject). Far more attention had been devoted to population growth, hunger and inequality—North–South issues which had no claim to priority over East–West ones.

Despite Wojtyła's involvement, most Polish bishops had mixed feelings about the Council documents. The very issue of religious freedom had a starkness in Eastern Europe which seemed barely accounted for in *Dignitatis humanae*'s genteel references to 'civil society' and 'constitutional order'. The Decree reaffirmed that no one should be 'restrained from acting in accordance with his conviction', and stressed the State's duty to 'look with favour' on religious activity. But it made no more than a passing reference to 'forms of government under which ... public authorities strive to deter citizens from professing their religion'.[16] For those expecting moral support, this was hardly satisfactory.

John XXIII's own familiarity with Eastern Europe was well known. He had visited Kraków in 1912, and had got to know Polish and Soviet ambassadors during his decade in Bulgaria, a country with close ties to Russia. In 1935, his name had been put forward as a possible Nuncio to Poland. While en route to Rome, Cardinal Wyszyński had usually stopped off discreetly in Venice when Roncalli was Patriarch there.

Yet so much of what John XXIII had said and done seemed guided entirely by Western perspectives. *Pacem in terris* had deplored colonialism in the Third World but said nothing about colonialism in the heart of Europe. It had rejoiced that 'soon no nation will rule over another, and none be subject to an alien power', and that the inferiority and superiority of classes was 'rapidly becoming a thing of the past'.[17] But it had made no mention of Eastern Europe, where Soviet dominance and class hatred were institutionalized.

Cardinal Wyszyński had angered anti-communists at the 1958 Conclave for criticizing Pius XII's 'unrealistic' rigidity towards Eastern Europe in a memorandum to fellow-cardinals. But did John XXIII's *rapprochement* with Khrushchev not take 'realism' a bit far? Provocative condemnations were best avoided; but was it not premature to speak of co-operation?

The record spoke for itself. Romania's August 1965 constitution guaranteed 'liberty of conscience', while the Communist Party's new programme in East Germany pledged 'full respect for believers' religious feelings'. In practice, however, the communist regimes made no real concessions.

In the Soviet Union, Khrushchev's contacts with the Pope spurred a petition movement in the early 1960s. But the repression continued. Admissions to Lithuania's only seminary at Kaunas fell from 80 in 1958 to 28 in 1964.[18] Leonid Brezhnev's accession in 1964 brought cosmetic modifications. But in 1966, restrictions were tightened further under a new Soviet Penal Code.

When Cardinal Stepinac died in 1960, Vatican officials had worried that Yugoslavia's bishops could be lured into a damaging accommodation with Tito's regime. In 1964, however, the Holy See began its own talks without consulting them. This weakened the bishops' position. Although an April 1963 constitution guaranteed Church rights in areas like education and property ownership, the bishops still complained of a 'strange psychosis' in national life. Religious freedoms existed on paper, but Catholics were afraid to act on them. In 1966, when the Vatican signed its 'Protocol', allowing for an exchange of diplomats, Church leaders felt humiliated to see clauses threatening canonical sanctions against priests who engaged in 'acts of terrorism'.[19]

Czechoslovakia's July 1960 constitution had also enshrined 'freedom of confession'. But since all bishops were already in jail, there was no one to monitor its implementation. Although seven bishops were freed at the same time as Archbishop Beran in 1963, none were allowed to resume their functions.

In Hungary, an 'agreement' with the Vatican in 1964, reached after five rounds of negotiations, allowed the appointment of five new apostolic administrators, the first for fourteen years. This left all but one of Hungary's eleven dioceses with bishops. And in return the Church agreed to a loyalty oath. But the appointees were of questionable material; and within two years, five bishops had asked to retire. In 1965, a year after the agreement, long jail sentences were handed down on 30 more priests. Several were murdered in detention.[20]

While exploiting Vatican II's declarations, the communist regimes took action to keep its modernizing teachings at bay. The Council texts were not published in Czechoslovakia until 1968, while Hungary's seminaries were still ignoring them twenty years later. Even in Poland, the regime impeded their distribution.

Some Church leaders were not sorry to see Vatican II's arrival delayed.

Most disliked its liturgical reforms, seeing them as a threat to traditional Slavic devotions. Talk of collegiality was viewed, similarly, as a Western abstraction which threatened the Church's structure of authority. Putting the Council's decisions into effect would be 'very difficult', Wyszyński cautioned the Pope in late 1965. 'Therefore, we ask one favour—complete trust in the Episcopate and Church of our country . . . It is difficult to judge our situation from afar.'[21]

The Polish Church had good reason to feel apprehensive about Rome's diplomatic forays. Throughout the 1950s, its bishops had ensured the Church's survival through relentless petitions to regime officials, covering everything from religious education to the use of loudspeakers at Mass. After twenty years' steady rebuilding, it now had over 60 bishops in seventeen dioceses, served by 18,000 priests, 28,000 nuns and 4,000 students at 70 seminaries—twice the numbers of 1945. That made it a formidable force in Polish life, besides which the Vatican's efforts were unlikely to make much difference.

'As Primate, I have never received instructions—from Pius XII, John XXIII, Cardinal Tardini or anyone else in Rome', Wyszyński had assured Gomułka in 1960. 'In this respect, we are fully self-governing.'[22] The regime was aware, nevertheless, that Polish Church leaders relied on Rome's support. It also took an interest in preparations for Vatican II, sensing the Council could affect Polish interests. The German Church, for example, was believed to have a stronger presence in Rome. So the position adopted by Polish bishops could be important. John XXIII had named seventeen new Polish bishops in the first two years of his pontificate, in what communists saw as an attempt to strengthen the Church for a 'renewed struggle'. Having granted passports, the regime set out to gain whatever capital it could.

Wyszyński had teamed up with French and Latin American Cardinals to 'force through' John XXIII's compromise candidacy in 1958, noted a paper by the government's Confessions Office. The Pope's 'personal friendship' gave him considerable influence in Rome, and helped guarantee his 'total domination' of the Polish Bishops' Conference. But while the Primate's 'pro-capitalist and anti-socialist policy' had the support of other Polish Church 'reactionaries'—men like Archbishop Kominek of Wrocław and Bishop Antoni Baraniak of Kraków—it was opposed by moderate, realistic bishops who wished to avoid 'provoking the state power.'[23]

The Office believed the Vatican had given Wyszyński 'a largely free hand' in Poland, but was increasingly worried about his centralized power. Though seen as a man of the Right in Poland, he was viewed as a 'Leftist' in Rome—particularly by integrist cardinals who would not forgive him for 'talking to communists' in the 1950s. Could a wedge be driven between the Vatican and the Polish Church?

In 1963, the Polish regime followed the Soviet Union in acknowledging John XXIII's 'anti-war position', and sent a Central Committee member, Zenon Kliszko, to Rome to spread a good account of its religious policy. At a Polish Embassy press conference, Kliszko announced that his government was ready to open relations with the Vatican, if only the Polish Church would desist from its 'anti-communist campaign' and accept reality, as its Russian Orthodox counterpart had done.

The Vatican closed ranks behind the Polish Church and the anti-Wyszyński strategy came to nothing. But the incident poisoned relations between Wyszyński and Gomułka, whose personality clash was already obvious. 'I witnessed a sloganeering liar, full of narrowness and half-intelligent arrogance', the Cardinal noted after meeting the Party leader the same year.[24] Gomułka blamed Wyszyński for blocking attempts to bolster his regime's international image. It would have been a nice touch, achieved at the Church's expense.

Wyszyński explained the regime's 'motivations' in a long memorandum to the Vatican Secretary of State, Cardinal Amleto Cicognani. It had used the Western press to show the Polish bishops were blocking an improvement in relations, he said. In reality, the Polish Church would be pleased with any agreement, if it was negotiated by 'responsible people' and brought an end to repression. But it was far more likely the Party would merely exploit ties with Rome to weaken the Polish bishops, without keeping a single promise.

'There can be no real dialogue from a position of power', Wyszynski reminded Cicognani.

> Communists can give certain things, but only from a conqueror's position ...
> There is a danger of tricks and illusions if talks are conducted by regime people
> on one side, without Catholics, and by people on the other who lack
> experience of dealing with communists and can be manipulated in their
> methods.[25]

Despite their misgivings, the Polish bishops were too wise to be seen to question the Council's directives publicly. The Polish Church had organized special 'night vigils' before Vatican II's opening session. As it progressed, they tried to use the conciliatory atmosphere to support their demands. Wyszyński met the Russian Orthodox observer, Archpriest Borovoi, and agreed with him on the necessity of improving Polish–Russian relations. He invited Cardinal König of Vienna and Archbishop Bengsch of Berlin, both of whom were against a denunciation of communism, to visit Poland. König was refused a visa—Wyszyński had not obtained government consent, Gomułka said, for a visit with 'political implications'.[26]

The most sensational step, however, came in 1965. The Polish bishops had promised Gomułka they would oppose 'anti-Polish revisionist statements' from the German Church. But in summer 1965, the Polish and German Evangelical Churches drew up a programme for reconciliation. Archbishop Kominek of Wrocław urged a similar Catholic gesture. People on both sides would see any form of dialogue as a betrayal, he warned. But those wishing to build bridges between nations must risk 'personal sacrifices'.[27]

On 18 November, an Appeal was duly sent by the 34 Polish bishops and archbishops in Rome to their German counterparts, The time had come, twenty years after the war, it declared, to rebuild friendship and trust. The German-language text deplored Nazi wartime crimes. But it also acknowledged the post-war sufferings of German civilians. It contained the closing words 'We extend our hands to you, pledge forgiveness and ask for it'.[28]

The Appeal provoked a furious reaction. 'The text is political and has nothing to do with religion', declared the Communist Party Central Committee. 'This time, the bishops have gone too far, in openly declaring against the policy of People's Poland on issues fundamental to our nation's future.'[29] A short German reply three weeks later welcomed the Appeal as 'the very valuable fruit of our common Council work'. But the Polish bishops felt the German Church had failed to respond adequately. Even the Catholic Znak deputies criticized the bishops for failing to inform the Polish government. 'Bitter reactions' were understandable, the deputies added, at a time when the German Church was still demanding border revisions.[30]

The Polish Church was dissatisfied with the Vatican's stance too. In 1962, John XXIII had raised hopes that the Holy See would at last recognize Poland's 'Recovered Territories' by referring to 'Western lands repossessed after centuries'. But although Paul VI named four apostolic administrators for the Territories in 1967, plans for a meeting of the Conference of European Bishops in the region were called off by its secretary-general, Archbishop Roger Etchegaray, to avoid offending the German Church.[31]

By then, the Polish Church was feeling the effects of another big showdown with the government, this time over the 1966 millennium of the Poles' first Christian state. The Gomułka regime wanted to stress the anniversary's 'state' character and did its best to disrupt the Church's celebrations. Jasna Góra's Black Madonna icon was seized by police when it was taken on a tour of the country. Meanwhile Paul VI was twice refused authorization—in May and December—when he offered to visit the national shrine. It was, the Pope testified, a 'very painful' episode.[32]

The mass turnout did, however, indicate how much Polish society identified with the Church. The recriminations were protracted. In September 1967, Wyszyński was denied a passport for the first Synod of Bishops in Rome—a punishment for his 'cynical attempts' to 'secure the deep clericalization of society'. Other Church leaders refused to go without him, and the Pope deplored the Polish Church's absence. But the government was unrepentant. There would be no passport for the Primate, it stated, 'until he changes his disloyal attitude to the Polish People's Republic'.[33]

Ironically, when serious discontent erupted in Poland six months later, it had little to do with the Church. In March 1968, to appease Moscow, the Polish government decided to close a production of *Dziady* (Forefathers), a patriotic play by the nineteenth-century poet Adam Mickiewicz, which had been running to packed audiences in Warsaw's Great Theatre. The action provoked an outpouring of pent-up frustrations. Students took to the streets demanding cultural and intellectual freedoms. On 8 March, a 'workers militia' was sent in to disperse them. The wave of arrests and beatings was paralleled in Kraków, Gdańsk, Poznań and other towns.

Gomułka used the March events to purge his opponents. He blamed Party 'liberals' for whipping up the discontent, and did his best to inflame nationalist prejudices against 'Jews, Zionists and revisionists'. Up to 20,000 Jews were forced to leave the country during the ensuing anti-Semitic and anti-intellectual clampdown, which resembled the campaign against 'cosmopolitans' in the Soviet Union two decades earlier.

In most senses, 1968 in Eastern Europe was the opposite of 1968 in the West. While Western middle-class students raged about revolution, their impoverished Eastern counterparts demanded democracy. But there were common elements too. Both episodes symbolized the erosion of post-war hopes in a perfect society. Both ended in the apparent parallel triumphs of capitalist and communist establishments.

Most books on Poland have downplayed the 1968 events. But for the generation directly affected, they marked a turning point, by dismantling the myth that intellectuals were communism's standard-bearers and teaching a lesson to anyone who still believed—twelve years after the 'Polish October'—that the one-party system could be made open and accountable.

The March clampdown posed a test for the Church. But although Church leaders spoke against the repressions, their reaction was late in coming. It took till 21 March for the Bishops' Conference to deplore the 'painful events' in a pastoral letter. A letter was also sent to Poland's communist prime minister, Józef Cyrankiewicz, urging the freeing of detainees and an end to 'drastic, anachronistic methods' of interrogation and punishment. 'The rubber truncheon is no argument for a free society', the letter added. 'It merely awakens the worst associations and mobilizes opinion against the established order.'[34]

Yet these were cursory messages only, condemning violence and urging calm. No full assessment of the events came until 3 May, when another pastoral letter urged dialogue and accused the communist press of lying. Yet even this declined to condemn the clampdown's anti-Semitic and anti-intellectual dimensions. Instead, it deplored foreign Jewish accusations that Poles had been co-responsible for the Holocaust.[35]

The main Catholic reaction was left to the Znak deputies in the Sejm, who became the only public figures to question the regime's line unreservedly. The Communist Party's reaction was predictable. Jerzy Zawieyski was dismissed from Poland's State Council and replaced as 'Catholic representative' by the Pax chairman, Bolesław Piasecki. But the Znak intervention challenged Gomułka's claim to be rooting out a 'Zionist, cosmopolitan conspiracy'. It also suggested that, when the moment came, Catholics could find common values with other critics of the system.

Church leaders still remained wary. After the reactions to their 1965 letter to the German bishops, they were reluctant to throw their weight behind other politically sensitive causes. The protests and repressions were viewed anyway as a quarrel between rival communist and liberal groups, which had little if anything to do with the concerns of ordinary Catholics. The Polish government's Confessions Office reported that local priests had removed student posters and placards from their churches.[36] In October, Wyszyński was allowed to make his first visit to Rome for several years—a reward, perhaps, for staying aloof.

By then, the atmosphere in Eastern Europe had been changed dramatically by events in Czechoslovakia. The 'Prague Spring' reform movement touched off by Alexander Dubček's appointment as Communist Party leader on 5 January had offered hope to the Church. In March, 22,000 Catholics had sent Dubček a petition, describing the Catholic Church as the 'last enclave' for Stalinist repression.[37] The new regime responded quickly. Priests and lay Catholics were released from jail, restrictions were removed from seminaries, and the Prešov-based Greek Catholic Church was allowed to revive. The notorious 'Peace Priest' Fr Josef Plojhar was finally dropped from the government and talks initiated on the return from exile of 79-year-old Cardinal Beran.

The Prague Spring also brought an infusion of post-Vatican II ideas. Yet here too, the Church's hierarchy, or what remained of it, dragged its heels. In a March pastoral letter, the Prague archdiocese's administrator, Bishop František Tomášek, asserted that the Church was 'not wanting privileges', only to 'reclaim in good faith its rights in a democratic society'. But the Vatican appeared convinced that Czechoslovakia's 'reform communists' were moving on a separate track. Visiting Rome in April, Tomášek was reputedly advised to avoid formal contacts with the Dubček regime. Only in June did he finally send a telegram confirming Church support for the reforms.[38]

When Warsaw Pact tanks smashed their way into Prague on 21 August, the Vatican reaction was muted. Soviet troops were on every street corner. But Dubček was kept in office. In November, when Tomášek went to Rome to discuss possible negotiations, Paul VI told a group of Slovak pilgrims he still hoped to see 'a certain improvement' in the Church's situation. It was not until February 1969 that the Pope finally sent greetings to Dubček, acknowledging the religious liberalization which had occurred under his rule. Even this was indirect, delivered via another pilgrim group. Two months later, Dubček was out. But the new Party leader, Gustáv Husák, a former Stalinist-era prisoner, pledged to maintain the reforms. In a last letter to his homeland, Cardinal Beran spoke forlornly of his hopes for 'a new flowering in our land'.[39]

Throughout Eastern Europe, eyes had been fixed on the Prague Spring to see how much democracy and openness would be tolerated. Moscow had given its response—the time for experiments was over. In Hungary, the Kádár regime had pre-empted possible disorder with a 'New Economic Mechanism' which made a show of deference to would-be Party reformers. By 1969, however, this was under attack too. The country's Catholic Church had been unprepared for the year's events. The established Church–State pattern—protection for subservience—had produced weak, unconvincing leaders, and the Church had long since ceased to express solidarity with potential opposition forces. It deeply distrusted Hungary's Marxist revisionists. And it was shunned in turn as the regime's co-opted accessory by a generation raised without religion.

In Poland, a September 1968 Bishops' Conference pastoral letter marking the fiftieth anniversary of national independence stressed the Church's role in freedom struggles. Archbishop Kominek of Wrocław had spoken publicly of 'the Spring coming from Prague'—a place which had effused 'only evil and degeneration', he added, had become the source of 'hope in a new resurrection'.[40] But when the Confessions Office organized a nationwide enquiry into Church reactions to the August invasion, it drew a different conclusion. Local priests had been 'very interested' by events to the south, the report noted, while 'opposition elements' in the Church had defended the right of Czechs and Slovaks to decide their own fate. But the bishops had advised against public statements. Some said the Prague Spring had been misused by 'subversive elements', making a Soviet riposte inevitable.[41]

The period after 1968 was one of low morale in Eastern Europe. Borders were closed, independent activity curbed, hopes and expectations discredited. In Czechoslovakia, 5 million citizens were screened and 1.5 million sacked from their jobs. With orthodox views reimposed, half a million Party members were expelled too. 'What the powers that be call "consolidation and normalization" of our national life in fact brought about its utter stultification', wrote the Slovak communist philosopher Miroslav Kusý.

> Anyone who does not prove suitable becomes an outsider, a person without a future. This inevitably means that the vast majority resort to hypocrisy, a 'double face', the schizophrenic upbringing of their children; it leads to apathy and cynicism, the disintegration of the nation's moral fibre.[42]

It had already been sensed in Poland that the populist ideals of 1956 were dead, and that 'reform communist' ideas would not be tolerated. The 'Brezhnev Doctrine' heralded by the invasion of Czechoslovakia—giving communist states the right to intervene in each other's affairs—suggested fresh thinking was needed. Communist abuses of power could no longer be seen as merely a betrayal of the revolution—a revolution which nevertheless preserved its sense as the vehicle for human progress. Instead, it was becoming clear that the whole communist vision was wrong.

Of course, there were those who believed the regimes would rebuild their ideological coherency, and that it was worth staying in the Party in the hope of exerting an influence. But for many, co-operation and participation were no longer political options. They had become moral dilemmas too.

If Marxist revisionism was dead, so was Catholic neo-positivism—that old post-war dream that Christians could 'humanize communism' by accepting reality and working from within. 'We believed the path of socialism could develop in a way open to personal values', explained Tadeusz Mazowiecki, one of Poland's Znak parliamentarians. 'We are all to some extent a "mixture"—not because we betray the values we were brought up on, nor because we are doctrinally uneducated or vague in our ideas, but because this is the character of our century's culture.'[43] By the end of the 1960s, being a 'mixture' was no longer possible. The time had come for hard choices.

Even at the best of times, Znak had no claim to represent the Church. But the Church's position was certain to be affected by the course of events. In Poland and Czechoslovakia especially, as erstwhile communists turned their backs on the Party, many began to reconsider their once-dismissive attitude to it. For all the caution exhibited by its leaders, there was no doubt the Church's interests lay with democratic reform. At a time when many intellectuals felt isolated from society—much of which remained passive, even hostile, to their ideals—the Church's role as a repository of values appeared to grow in importance.

For their part, Marxists and liberals had shown a readiness to put their lives on the line in opposing communist injustices. Whatever its reservations, the Church could hardly be indifferent to the courage and conviction so many had exhibited.

The Polish Bishops' Conference sensed the change in atmosphere. A 'more objective attitude to religion' was emerging even among Marxists, the bishops had told Gomułka's regime in 1968. Why then did the government still cling to an 'anachronistic nineteenth-century philosophy', which held that the Church was intent on restoring capitalism? Vatican II had shown the Church was not tied to any political order. It was not wanting privileges, only the 'just rights belonging to it'. As long as the State promoted atheism and materialism, the bishops continued, it was inevitable that 'political tendencies' would be linked with the Church.[44]

In its 1968 report, the Polish government's Confessions Office claimed to have identified Catholic priests who were now 'in solidarity with the opposition'. It was a sign, the Office argued, that the Church was now no longer defending its own interests alone, but beginning a 'wider campaign' to promote Catholicism as a 'counter-programme to communism'.[45] Local Polish clergy were indeed showing signs of greater self-confidence. In 1960, 90 per cent had come from rural origins, just as two-thirds of all city industrial workers had themselves migrated from the countryside. But by the end of the decade, a new generation of priests had emerged, often drawn from urban intelligentsia origins during the social and economic changes of the 1950s and 1960s. Priests like this, educated under communism in atheist schools, had done military service and held secular jobs. Many had also studied Marxism and experienced the ideological conflicts of the 1960s.

In Czechoslovakia, similarly, a younger generation was emerging alongside the older veterans of Nazi occupation and Stalinist persecution. Many were converts, with roots in other traditions and a fresher approach to Christian life. The communist regime maintained a policy of negative selection. The most able candidates, particularly those with professional abilities, were barred from seminaries, so the best pastors had often trained secretly or been denied State licences. Since the Church had no independent funds, priests like this had to find paid work. As with the French and Belgian 'worker priests' of the 1940s and 1950s, this gave them exceptional exposure them to the problems of daily life.

The growing Church preoccupation with rights and freedoms even found its way to Soviet-ruled Lithuania. When a new wave of petitions began in the late 1960s, Lithuania's 772 surviving priests featured prominently among the signatories—a fact acknowledged and praised by the Soviet Union's secular dissidents.[46]

Although the documents of Vatican II were still little known in Eastern Europe, some of their notions of engagement were filtering through. The Dogmatic Constitution, *Lumen Gentium*, had urged priests to be ready 'to confess Christ before men and to follow him along the way of the cross amidst the persecutions the Church never lacks'.[47] That message had been spelled out further by the first Synod of Bishops in 1967. While priests must keep their distance from politics, they were also obliged 'to select a definite pattern of action when it is a question of defending fundamental human rights'.[48]

Church leaders in Eastern Europe had become more aware of the communist system's potential weaknesses. After the confrontations of 1968, those determined to resist communist abuses had opted for an evolutionary approach. This brought them closer to the Church's position, even if they had nothing else in common. If communist power could not be beaten, it could perhaps be ignored—at least enough to enable the semblance of a normal life.

In Poland, nevertheless, the language of Bishops' Conference statements became more forceful. In a bloody sequel to the events of 1968, December 1970 saw protesting workers machine-gunned by troops in the Polish Baltic ports after the announcement of pre-Christmas price rises. Gomułka—the man who in 1956 had commended the 'justified protest' of the Poznań strikers—angrily branded it a 'counter-revolution', and sent Zenon Kliszko, the man who had tried to undermine the Polish bishops at Vatican II, to quell the disturbances. But the Party tyrant's days were numbered. On 17 December, desperate to reassert control, the Central Committee dismissed Gomułka and handed power to Edward Gierek.

In a striking re-enactment of Gomułka's own declarations fourteen years earlier, Gierek acknowledged that Polish workers had been 'provoked beyond endurance' and promised a fresh start. Many scorned his declarations, sensing the Party could never regain public confidence. But many also believed his good intentions and agreed to exchange submissiveness for the promise of better living standards. Among many offers, Gierek included a 'full normalization' in Church–State relations. But the Church made clear it would hold him to his promises. The 'precondition for peace' must be freedom of conscience, social justice, truthful information, a dignified existence.[49]

As Archbishop of Kraków, Karol Wojtyła had been an architect of the Church's new outspoken stance. Despite his enthusiasm for Vatican II, he had shared Wyszyński's doubts about 'simplistic reform conceptions' in Eastern Europe. This did not dilute the importance of Vatican II's recommendations—liturgical reforms, for example, had a political significance since they affected the Church's communication with society. But Wojtyła urged his priests to read the Council texts and avoid 'one-sided, tendentious interpretations'. Vatican II's implementation could not be left to 'élite, specialist groups'. It needed 'authentic participation' and a 'proper interpretation' for Polish conditions.[50]

The triumph of folk Christianity at the 1966 millennium had forced the postponement of a 'proper, detailed study' of Vatican II. But it had also restored the Church's links with Polish society and revived national values and traditions. For Wojtyła too, it taught an important lesson about the political impact of mass devotions.

Wojtyła had helped draft the Polish bishops' controversial letter to Germany in 1965. It had been written for a religious event, he pointed out. It had also stressed the harm done by Germans. If a new Europe was to be constructed, it was important to distinguish forgiving from forgetting. Yet the reactions came as a shock. In a statement prompted by communist officials, Wojtyła's wartime co-workers at the Solvay factory in Krákow accused him of overstepping his authority. In his reply, Wojtyła regretted that the signatories had 'blindly repeated' distorted German and Polish press reports. But he admitted feeling 'hurt'.[51] Even among Kraków priests, while most praised the bishops for asserting the Church's co-responsibility for Poland's fate—something which had particularly enraged Gomułka—some also questioned the letter's wisdom.

The episode showed how easily people could be persuaded to distrust the motives of those seeking reconciliation with former enemies. But it also gave the word 'forgiveness' a symbolic meaning. All communist regimes depended on stoking resentments and prejudices. Overcoming them—even forgiving the Germans (and later the communists too)—was therefore a step towards freedom. 'The Church carries within itself not only the deposit of faith, hope and love, but also the deposit of human freedom', Wojtyła noted in *Tygodnik Powszechny*. 'We should know how to lose freedom in order to gain it.'[52]

Since Vatican II, Wojtyła's thinking had become more precise and self-confident. What he said was still rooted in Polish realities. But it was acquiring a more universal dimension too. For the first time, he was able to see clearly how his own Church stood in relation to the Catholic world.

Wojtyła became one of 27 new Cardinals on 28 June 1967, welcoming the new responsibility with 'apprehension'. His refusal to attend that autumn's Rome Synod in solidarity with Wyszyński was an important personal move.

The Gomułka regime had tried to play up differences between both men. 'As a teacher's pet of the Vatican, Karol Wojtyła does not act independently', the Confessions Office noted in its 1968 report. 'So if he engages himself on the side of Wyszyński, it is only because he has been directed to.'[53]

Talk of disagreements was an exaggeration, however. Wojtyła attracted controversy. In one case, he had agreed to officiate at a former priest's church wedding, and had only withdrawn after Kraków priests objected. Archbishop Kominek had welcomed him back from Rome with a hint of irony as 'our theologian of Church dialogue'.[54] But Wojtyła learned as much from Wyszyński as he questioned. Whatever his personal feelings, he too could see the vital importance of maintaining the strength in numbers that went with 'popular religiousness'. No less than Wyszyński, Wojtyła knew the Church needed the spectacle of fervent devotion.

In March 1968, it was Wojtyła who drafted the message and letter from the Bishop's Conference, deploring the regime clampdown.[55] Like other bishops, however, he chose to remain personally aloof during the March events. When police jostled priests and worshippers during June Corpus Christi processions in two local villages, he exploded with threats of excommunication. But despite pleas from associates at *Tygodnik Powszechny* he said nothing when they beat Kraków students outside his own window. Why was he so reticent?

Publicly at least, Wojtyła saw the disorders as an internal Party affair. He had known Jews as a child, and had supported Vatican II's condemnation of anti-Semitism in *Nostra aetate* (28 October 1965). But he had made no mention of Jews in a 1965 sermon commemorating the liberation of Auschwitz. Was the view that the March events were an 'internal Party affair' really just a Church alibi, an excuse for not intervening in an unpopular cause involving 'intellectuals and Jews'?

If it was, Wojtyła made amends by visiting a Kraków synagogue the following February. A likelier explanation for his silence in 1968 was that, amid rumours of plots and conspiracies, he could not be certain what was happening. He stayed silent that August too when Polish troops participated in the invasion of Czechoslovakia—an event mid-way between the national feasts of the Assumption and Our Lady of Jasna Góra. But the year's events had their effect. There was still a large section of society Wojtyła had to understand. Even among Marxists and communists, there were people who needed and deserved pastoral care.

In 1969, besides touring North America, Wojtyła published a new book. *The Acting Person* was intended as a further exposition of Vatican II. But it also came as a rebuff to a new work by Poland's foremost Marxist theorist, Adam Schaff.[56]

It was surprising that Wojtyła had time for a profound treatise at all, let alone one which set out to confront communist ideology head-on. But Marxism's economic and social failures, he had concluded, derived from its misunderstanding of human nature. *The Acting Person* had a philosophical aim: to explore the meaning of human subjectivity without becoming trapped in idealism. Marxism postulated that the 'acting person' could become master of history, but that he was also a product of social forces who needed a correct *praxis*. Wojtyła's task was to find a complete counter-proposition to this Marxist vision of mankind, which could finally fill the remaining gaps in his ethical explorations over the last twenty years.

The book had a pastoral purpose too. After the cataclysms of the twentieth century, it was essential to try to understand why so many people had succumbed to the siren's song of communist revolution. Communists saw activism as a duty, where personal interests were sacrificed for humanity's redemption. Wojtyła's challenge was to rediscover the link between this kind of activism and Christian faith. The human person 'fulfils himself by his actions', he acknowledged; and the actions performed shape the world and mark the course of history. But *good* and *bad* actions are determined by free choice, systematic effort, responsibility—not by the moral determinism found in Marxism.

The Acting Person was difficult to read—Kraków priests joked that it would be a task assigned to sinners in Purgatory. But it was a crucial book since it completed Wojtyła's Christian re-reading of Marxist values. Stage by stage, Wojtyła dissected and refuted the Marxist conception of the world. Then, he gradually reassembled it in a Christian form, using concepts Marxism had expropriated—such as alienation, injustice, exploitation. For those who had lost their ethical bearings, it explained the meaning of authentic values and absolute truths with a clarity going far beyond his youthful investigations of the 1950s.

The word *osoba* (person) has a special intensity in the book—the person in all his or her existential dimensions, bodily and emotional, biological and spiritual. For all his imperfections, the human person is destined to be a participant in events. What kind of participant? Once again, Wojtyła rejected both 'individualism' and 'totalism'. Instead, he offered a definition of what he had earlier called 'solidarity'.

> Solidarity means corporate integrity—the duties we expect from others and the rights we demand for others. And the attitude of solidarity goes together with the duty of opposition ... Far from cutting themselves adrift from the community, those who oppose do so to find their own constructive place within it.[57]

That notion of solidarity—of civil opposition as a form of social love—had found expression elsewhere in the world since Vatican II. In Wojtyła's hands, the correcting of injustices became a common task. Resignation or non-participation—the attitudes so often resorted to under communism—were no defence. It was wrong to allow oneself to be 'carried along with the anonymous majority'.

But error and sin were products of the mind, rather than the will—the result of mistaken thinking, rather than evil desires. So those who failed to discern what was morally righteous had the chance to be converted afresh. Like John XXIII, Wojtyła was certain the Church could not reject anyone. It had to be ready to talk—even with communists. Where the struggle for the person was concerned, the conscience was a universal value. Non-believers had consciences too. Both religious people and atheists could be guided by the same vision of an integrated humanity. 'The dangerous temptation of unbelief is coming to us from outside in a programme of atheization and laicization', Wojtyła had declared in 1968. 'But the same temptation also comes to us from inside, exploiting our character weaknesses.'[58]

By the end of the 1960s, the Gomułka regime had detected a change in Cardinal Wojtyła. His mild talk of coexistence had looked promising earlier in the decade—quite unlike the 'dangerous social influences' emanating from figures like Kominek. But there was something unsettling about *The Acting Person*. One Marxist reviewer detected the influence of a 'Marxist theory of alienation' in the book. Wojtyła had made the usual 'world-view errors', the writer added. He believed the world could be made better by human spirits, and failed to recognize the role of social and historical contexts. 'According to Wojtyła, man acts in a specific way because he thinks according to specific rules', the review noted. 'So it is enough to introduce an appropriate scheme into his psyche for his material activity to obtain the anticipated shape.' But Wojtyła's stress on the Church's role in society was new, the writer pointed out. This confirmed that, in Eastern Europe too, the Church was 'turning towards the world'.[59]

No one could accuse Wojtyła of 'fighting communism'. He had, after all, said virtually nothing about the Party's economic and social record. Nor had he spoken directly against communist institutions. What he *had* said was that Christians had a duty to be active in defending truths and values. The 'Person' went with the 'Act'—that was the real meaning of solidarity, and of the new kind of 'opposition' it engendered. For a regime whose legitimacy had come to be based increasingly on apathetic acceptance, this notion had dangerous overtones. To polemicize about values was one thing. But it was quite another to enter a realm of ideas and axioms expressly reserved for communists. Wojtyła had infringed a convention—Church leaders were not permitted to intrude on the structures of power and ideology.

A 'consistent line' was needed, Kraków officials warned, 'to force Cardinal Wojtyła to respect state power'. The 'elastic policy' shown towards him had not 'brought the expected results'. 'The four years since 1963, when this policy started, have not mobilized him to seek a modus vivendi with the authorities', the report continued. 'Just the opposite—our pliant attitude has encouraged him to adopt a more active stance, to acquire more political elements in his contacts with the Kraków youth and intelligentsia.'[60]

Notes

1. Roger Garaudy, *From Anathema to Dialogue* (London: Collins, 1967), pp. 72–9.
2. Rosanna Mulazzi-Giammanco, *The Catholic–Communist Dialogue in Italy* (New York: Praeger, 1989), p. 62. For the PCI's advice to the CPSU, see Giancarlo Zizola, *The Utopia of Pope John XXIII* (New York: Orbis Books, 1978), p. 118.
3. 'Referat Urzędu do Spraw Wyznań' (undated 1961); in Peter Raina (ed.), *Kościół w PRL—Dokumenty 1960–1974* (Poznań: W Drodze, 1995), p. 57.
4. Quoted in Christopher Read, 'The Soviet attitude to the Christian–Marxist dialogue', *Religion in Communist Lands*, vol. 1, no. 6 (November–December 1973), p. 9.
5. Secretariat for Unbelievers, *Humanae personae dignitatem* (28 August 1968), no. II, 2.
6. *Tygodnik Powszechny* (Kraków: 8 January 1967).
7. Zizola, op. cit., p. 137.
8. *Giovanni XXIII, Il Giornale Dell'Anima* (Rome: Edizioni di Storia e Letterature, 1964), pp. 452–4.
9. Ks. Biskup Karol Wojtyła, *Miłość i Odpowiedzialność: Studium Etyczne* (Kraków: Znak, 1962), pp. 41, 177–8; English edition: *Love and Responsibility* (San Francisco: Ignatius Press, 1993).
10. The book was specifically said to contradict Pius XI's 1930 encyclical *Casti connubii*; see Adam Michnik, Józef Tischner, Jacek Żakowski, *Między Panem i Plebanem* (Kraków: Znak, 1995), pp. 101–2. For communist comments, see Dionizy Tanalski, *Bóg, Człowiek i Polityka: człowiek w teorii Jana Pawła II* (Warsaw: Książka i Wiedza, 1986), pp. 61–6.
11. Address at KUL (1960); in Karol Wojtyła, *Aby Chrystus się nami posługiwał* (Kraków: Znak, 1979), pp. 445–6; *Miłość i Odpowiedzialność*, op. cit., p. 54.
12. Stefan Swieżawski, *Owoce życie 1966–1988* (Lublin: Wydawnictwo KUL, 1993), p. 173.
13. Letters to *Tygodnik Powszechny* (1965); in Wojtyła, *Aby Chrystus*, pp. 334, 345.
14. Letter (4 April 1970); ibid., p. 353.
15. Letters (1957 and 1965); ibid., pp. 131–56, 336–8.

16. *Dignitatis humanae* (7 December 1965), nos 2–3, 14.

17. *Pacem in terris* (11 April 1963), nos 42–43.

18. See Stanley Vardys, *The Catholic Church, Dissent and Nationality in Soviet Lithuania* (Boulder: East European Monographs, no. XLIII, 1978), p. 86.

19. Text in Stella Alexander, *Church and State in Yugoslavia Since 1945* (Cambridge: Cambridge University Press, 1979), pp. 313–15. The Protocol's wording was branded 'deeply offensive' by Vladimir Pavlinic, former editor of the weekly *Glas Koncila*; *Religion in Communist Lands*, vol. 4, no. 3 (Autumn 1976), p. 41.

20. The murdered priests are listed in Gyula Havasy (ed.), *Martyrs of the Catholics in Hungary* (Budapest: privately published, 1993), pp. 124–6.

21. Speech at an audience with 38 Polish bishops (13 November 1965); in Hansjakob Stehle, *Eastern Politics of the Vatican 1917–1979* (London: Ohio University Press, 1981), pp. 341–2. See also Stefan Wyszyński, *Un Évêque au service du peuple de Dieu* (Paris: Éditions Saint-Paul, 1970), pp. 51–2.

22. 'Zapiski Prymasa S. Wyszyńskiego z jego rozmów z I Sekretarzem KC PZPR' (11 January 1960); in Raina, op. cit., pp. 9–11.

23. 'Referat Urzędu'; ibid., pp. 48–9; 'Referat Dyrektora Departamentu IV Ministerstwa Spraw Wewnętrznych' (12 August 1963); ibid., p. 234.

24. 'Zapis Prymasa S. Wyszyńskiego z Jego rozmowy z W. Gomułką' (26 April 1963); ibid., pp. 215, 224–30.

25. 'Opracowanie Prymasa S. Wyszyńskiego dla Papieża Pawła VI' (22 November 1963); ibid., p. 254.

26. 'Zapis Prymasa'; ibid., p. 227.

27. Kominek outlined the Polish position in a separate letter to the German bishops in October 1965, 'Dialog Deutschland–Polen? Gedanken und Vorschlage'; in Raina, op. cit., pp. 348–55.

28. 'Orędzie biskupów polskich do ich niemieckich braci w Chrystusowym urzędzie pasterskim' (18 November 1965); ibid., p. 362.

29. 'Projekt II listu do organizacji Polskiej Zjednoczonej Partii Robotniczej' (January 1966); ibid., p. 371.

30. 'Pozdrowienie biskupów niemieckich dla polskich braci' (5 December 1965); ibid., pp. 362–4; 'Komunikat Sekretariatu Episkopatu' (15 December 1965); ibid., p. 365; *Tygodnik Powszechny* (19 December 1965); Andrzej Micewski, *Kościół-Państwo 1945–1989* (Warsaw: Wydawnictwo Szkolne Pedagogiczne, 1994), p. 45.

31. In a letter to the Confessions Office, Archbishop Kominek admitted he had hoped to stage the meeting in Wrocław 'for international propaganda'; Peter Raina (ed.), *Kościół-Państwa w świetle akt wydziału d/s wyznań* (Warsaw: Książka Polska, 1994), p. 246. See also Micewski, op. cit., p. 44.

32. Paul VI's statement in *Słowo-Dziennik Katolicki* (28 May 1996); Wanda Chudzik et al. (eds), *Uroczystości milenijne 1966 roku: sprawozdania urzędów spraw wewnętrznych* (Warsaw: Ministerstwo Spraw Wewnętrznych, 1996).

33. 'Odpowiedz szefa Urzędu Rady Ministrów' (6 October 1967); in Raina, *Kościół w PRL*, op. cit., p. 461. Paul VI sent telegrams to Wyszyński and Wojtyła which

never arrived, although the Polish government accused *L'Osservatore Romano* of inventing the story.

34. Jerzy Eisler, *Marzec 1968* (Warsaw: Państwowe Wydawnictwo Naukowe, 1991), pp. 325–6; 'Pismo konferencji plenarnej Episkopatu Polski do Premiera J. Cyrankiewicza' (21 March 1968); in Raina. *Kościół w PRL*, pp. 500–1.
35. Raina, *Kościół Państwa*, p. 268.
36. 'Sprawozdanie urzędnika Urzędu do Spraw Wyznań' (16 April 1968); in Raina, *Kościół w PRL*, p. 503.
37. Text in Dennis J. Dunn, *Detente in Papal–Communist Relations 1962–1978* (Boulder: Westview, 1979), pp. 158–60.
38. Mireille Macqua, *Rome–Moscou: L'Ostpolitik du Vatican* (Louvain-la-Neuve: Cabay, 1984), p. 161.
39. *L'Osservatore Romano* (26 January 1969).
40. 'Pismo kierownika Wydziału do Spraw Wyznań' (14 October 1968); in Raina, *Kościół w PRL*, pp. 527–8.
41. Raina, *Kościół-Państwa*, op. cit., pp. 273–336, for Office reports from various towns.
42. See Kusý's essay in *A Besieged Culture: Czechoslovakia Ten Years After Helsinki* (Stockholm: Charta 77 Foundation, 1985), pp. 95–6.
43. *Więź* (November–December 1968), pp. 27–8.
44. 'List biskupów polskich do Rządu' (28 June 1968); in Raina, *Kościół w PRL*, op. cit., p. 513.
45. 'Protokół a narady kierowników Wydziałów do Spraw Wyznań' (16 February 1968); ibid., p. 488.
46. Comparative statistics from Soviet and underground sources in Vardys, op. cit., pp. 212–18.
47. *Lumen gentium* (21 November 1964), no. 42.
48. Synod of Bishops, *Ultimis temporibus* (30 November 1967), no. 2b; *Christus Dominus* (28 October 1965), no. 13.
49. 'Przesłanie Rady Głównej Episkopatu Polski do wszystkich rodaków' (29 December 1970); in Raina, *Kościół w PRL*, op. cit., p. 561.
50. Wawel cathedral sermon (6 March 1964), and letter to *Tygodnik Powszechny* (4 April 1970); in Wojtyła, *Aby Chrystus*, pp. 200, 358–9.
51. Michnik et al., op. cit., pp. 128–30; text of Wojtyła's reply in Adam Boniecki, *Kalendarium życia Karola Wojtyły* (Kraków: Znak, 1983), p. 243.
52. Letter to *Tygodnik Powszechny* (1964); in Wojtyła, op. cit., pp. 344–5.
53. 'Protokół', op. cit., p. 489.
54. Boniecki, op. cit., p. 278.
55. According to Bishop Alojzy Orszulik: *Gazeta Wyborcza* (10 March 1998).
56. Looking back many years later, Wojtyła insisted the book had not arisen 'from the disputes with Marxism, or, at least, not as a direct response to these disputes'. He confirmed, however, that 'interest in man and in his dignity' had by then become 'the principal theme of the polemic against Marxism', since Marxists themselves had made 'the question of man the centre of their

arguments': see John Paul II, *Crossing the Threshold of Hope* (London: Jonathan Cape, 1994), pp. 197–9. The book could be compared to Schaff's *Marksizm a jednostka ludzka* (Warsaw: PWN, 1965).

57. Karol Wojtyła, *Osoba i Czyn oraz inne studia antropologiczne* (Lublin: Wydawnictwo KUL, 1994), pp. 316–17. An English-language edition, *The Acting Person* (Boston: D. Reidel, 1979), was authorized by Wojtyła but differs substantially from the Polish original, which is used for the title and quotations cited here.

58. Lenten pastoral letter (5 February 1968); in Karol Wojtyła, *Nauczyciel i Pasterz* (Rome: Ośrodek Dokumentacji, 1987), pp. 238–9.

59. Andrzej Papuziński, *Filozofia społeczna papieża Jana Pawła II* (Warsaw: Nauk Społecznych PZPR, 1988), p. 40. Wojtyła acknowledged later that Marxists had been the 'first to take notice' of the book, seeing it as 'an unsettling element in their polemic against religion and the Church': John Paul II, *Crossing the Threshold*, op. cit., p. 199.

60. 'Załącznik: notatka dotycząca sytuacji w kurii krakowskiej' (13 October 1967); in Raina, *Kościół-Państwa*, op. cit., p. 115.

8

✂✂✂✂✂

The small steps of Paul VI

The late 1960s had brought a reimposition of order in the Church as well. The encyclical *Humanae vitae* (25 July 1968) had reaffirmed traditional Catholic teachings on marriage and procreation. A year earlier, the first Synod of Bishops had spoken of a 'modern crisis of civilization and human culture', and condemned what it saw as an 'arbitrary and false interpretation of the Council's spirit'.[1] Many believed Vatican II had gone too far in its dialogue with modernity.

Pope Paul VI had injected a note of caution before the Council finished. His first encyclical *Ecclesiam Suam* (6 August 1964) readopted John XXIII's buzz-word *aggiornamento* as the 'aim and objective' of the new pontificate. But it had also given a foretaste of where the new Pope would differ from his predecessor.

Paul VI listed his priorities. The first would be deeper self-knowledge by the Church, and a recognition that it would never achieve the full 'perfection, beauty, holiness and splendour' intended by Christ. The second would be renewal—Church members must 'correct their faults'. The third would be deeper reflection on the modern world—a world offering the Church 'not one but a hundred forms of possible contacts'.[2]

That recognition of the complexity of the Church's tasks summed up Paul VI. When it came to 'atheistic communism', the new Pope's position was unchanged. He condemned the 'foolish and fatal belief' that 'ideologies denying God and oppressing the Church' could emancipate mankind. Any social system based on atheist propositions was doomed to destruction.

Yet even here, *Ecclesiam Suam* left open certain possibilities. 'Is it really so much we who condemn them?' it asked meekly of communists.

> Truth to tell, the voice we raise against them is more the complaint of a victim than the sentence of a judge ... In these circumstances, dialogue is very

difficult, not to say impossible, although we have no preconceived intention of cutting ourselves off from the adherents of these systems and these regimes. For the lover of truth, discussion is always possible.[3]

Coming just a year after John XXIII's *Pacem in terris*, the more cautious tone of *Ecclesiam Suam* disappointed the communist regimes. But Paul VI's circumspect style did not stop diplomatic approaches. On 30 January 1967, the president of the Supreme Soviet, Nikolai Podgorny, became the first senior Soviet leader to have a private audience.

There had been other direct contacts before. The Soviet Foreign Minister, Andrei Gromyko, had met Paul VI at the UN in 1965 and visited the Vatican the following spring. Meanwhile, Rome had used the thaw to rebuild links with Russia's Orthodox Church. The new Pope had sent a personal emissary for Patriarch Alexei I's 80th birthday in 1963, while a senior metropolitan, Nikodim of Leningrad, had visited Rome that September. The angry initial Orthodox reaction to Vatican II was politely passed over.

Several East European regimes also, bidding for international respect-ability, had re-started talks. An under-secretary from the Vatican, Agostino Casaroli, had travelled unofficially to Czechoslovakia in May 1963 to negotiate the amnesty for Archbishop Beran. The 78-year-old agreed to leave for Rome two years later to assist 'chances of progress' in Vatican–Czechoslovak relations. In 1968, Beran hinted that he had left expecting to be allowed back three weeks later. He never saw Prague again.[4]

Similar compromises were occurring elsewhere. Ties were re-established with Romania through a Rome visit by the Prime Minister and Foreign Minister in January 1968. The government of neighbouring Bulgaria consented in 1965 to the appointment of a Catholic apostolic administrator and Greek Catholic bishop—but only on condition that a more capable bishop, Mgr Bogdan Dobranov, clandestinely consecrated in 1959, was discarded. The price of official contacts would be paid by the underground Church.

Some diplomatic brick walls were inevitable. In China, the Mao regime had accused the Vatican of being a 'puppet of American imperialism'. It expelled all foreign bishops, leaving the 4 million-strong Catholic Church at its mercy. Not surprisingly, China's 'Patriotic Catholic Association' became the first Church organization to defy Rome openly, by consecrating 30 new bishops without canonical approval. In September 1958, Pius XII denounced the 'false shepherds' who had rebelled against his authority. But it made no difference. Three of the new bishops were installed on 9 October, the day the old Pope died.

Not even the Patriotic Association could avoid falling victim to Mao's 1966–67 Cultural Revolution. When Podgorny visited Rome, the Xinhua newsagency poured scorn on the 'Soviet revisionists' who hoped 'pilgrimages to the Vatican' would open the door to 'capitalism and its capital'. The Holy See was the only state in Europe still recognizing Taiwan. In 1966, the Vatican upgraded its Taipei representation to a full Nunciature.

Setbacks did not deter Casaroli. The 'Act with Annexed Protocol' signed with Hungary in 1964 had been the first formal deal with a communist government since the Vatican's famine relief accord with Moscow in 1922, Paul VI was said to have consented only 'with fear and trembling'.[5] Yet it was hardly suprising that he should give priority to rebuilding contacts with communist states. Aged 60 at his election, the new Pope had diplomatic experience going back 40 years to his months as a Warsaw Nunciature attaché in 1923. He believed in 'saving what could be saved'.

In Agostino Casaroli, Paul VI found a man who believed even more was possible. Casaroli had joined the Vatican's diplomatic service as a young priest in the 1940s. In April 1963, as under-secretary, he had been sent by John XXIII to a UN conference in Vienna, where he had met communist officials for the first time. Visits to Prague and Budapest followed a month later, marking what Casaroli believed was 'a historic turning-point, daring and unexpected, but decisive'.

> When I gave an account of these two missions to Pope John a few days before his death, he said 'It is not necessary to hurry or succumb to illusions: but we must continue, trusting in God'. The two motives which drove the Holy See to begin a dialogue with the communist world—to know the Church's problems, and to be active in a world searching for peace and progress—were already evident in these first contacts.[6]

The Monsignor made trips to Eastern Europe anonymously too, travelling on a passport made out in his mother's maiden-name—a method also used by Cardinal König of Vienna. But he approached his work as a diplomat, often paying scant regard for the impact his efforts would have on Catholic and international opinion.

Casaroli used a Latin analogy to explain his step-by-step approach. The Church's immediate objective, he argued, was simply to 'live' (*esse*). But it could also hope to go a stage further and 'live well' (*bene esse*). And in future, if things worked out, it might even 'live fully' (*plene esse*). Of course, written agreements had limited value—what counted was practical implementation. But Casaroli was convinced the Vatican had to work against any repeat of the 1962 war scare. Far from stopping communist expansionism, war had always boosted Soviet power. By contrast, peace allowed the Church to work and manoeuvre. The ideal was *pax in iustitia*—peace with justice. But until justice was achieved, peace should be preserved anyway. Even Pius XII had warned that 'everything can be lost by war'.[7]

Casaroli was finely attuned to geopolitics. By Paul VI's accession, the Soviet Union had assumed superpower status. Khrushchev's strategy of 'peaceful coexistence' had brought a nuclear stalemate with the US, which kept military confrontations in check while communist influence was extended in the Third World. The Vietnam War, in full swing by 1967, would end in a humiliating US defeat, while communist-backed movements reached for power in Angola, Mozambique and elsewhere. With Soviet military power building up in the Mediterranean and Indian Ocean, the balance of forces seemed to be shifting in Moscow's favour.

The division of Europe had therefore to be accepted. And while trade and cultural exchanges could modify its negative consequences, some kind of accommodation was needed if the Church was to survive. Survival meant an episcopal structure. And although bishops could be appointed covertly, it was much better to act with agreement.

Casaroli could place himself in the tradition of the great nineteenth-century Cardinal-diplomats Ercole Consalvi and Giacomo Antonelli. Like him, they had shown mole-like perseverance in tunnelling out discreet practical agreements with republican regimes, at a time when, on the surface, the Popes were publicly proclaiming their rejection of any accommodation. Of course, the East European regimes would only make concessions which contributed to communist objectives. But Casaroli believed they could be persuaded that a show of toleration was in their interests. Elements of that post-war optimism felt by the architects of 'Christian–communist collaboration' still lingered—that repression was a temporary stage which would be attenuated by social advances once communism was secure.

Some observers detected signs of evolution in the regimes' atheist ideology too. Western Eurocommunists had already concluded that the denial of Christianity was not essential. If official atheism was not abandoned altogether, it could at least be modified for *realpolitik* reasons. Hopes like this had provided the cue for some tentative intellectual approaches. A Bavarian Jesuit from Rome's Gregorian University, Professor Edward Huber, had worked on Marxism at Moscow University, while Professor Gustav Wetter, another Rome specialist, had been invited to lecture there. By the late 1960s, the view had grown that Christianity could remind Marxism of its humanistic premises, whereas Marxists could teach Christians something from their methods of analysis and vision of the future.[8]

It was to explore theories like this that 250 German-speaking philosophers and theologians met in 1965–67 under the auspices of the Munich-based St Paul's Society (Paulusgesellschaft). The Christian side, which included figures like Karl Rahner and Johannes Baptist Metz, attempted to see their Marxist interlocutors in a positive light. They invented a concept, the 'anonymous Christian', to describe those outside the Christian tradition who nevertheless lived by Christian values. The Marxist side did something similar, claiming to identify Christians who had incorporated Marxist deductions in their view of the world.

The Paulusgesellschaft meetings marked the first top-level acknowledgement that Christians and Marxists should take each other seriously. But the learned partners who gathered at Salzburg, the Chiemsee and Marienbad were not typical. The best East European Marxist philosophers were barred from attending, and directed instead to parallel symposia where the official line on religion was reaffirmed.

Meanwhile, the show of Catholic openness hardly reflected the Vatican's position either. In August 1968, the Secretariat for Unbelievers reiterated John XXIII's observation that 'undertakings originating in ideologies hostile to Christianity can arrive at a state which no longer corresponds with their beginnings'. However, dialogue should only be undertaken if place and time favoured a 'true dialogue'—it was better not to try at all 'if it is obvious that a faction is using it for its own purposes'.[9]

That could not really be said of the Paulusgesellschaft meetings; so there was room for some kind of movement. Paul VI had made clear there would be no change in the Church's attitude to communism. But he had personally supported the decision not to condemn it at Vatican II. *Ecclesiam Suam* noted that many communists believed they were 'serving a demanding and noble cause'. Many were 'men of great breadth of mind, impatient with the mediocrity and self-seeking which affects so much of modern society'. The fact that they used concepts from the Gospel—'brotherhood of man, mutual aid, human compassion'—suggested their impulses were similar to those of Christians, and might even 'bring them back to God'.[10]

Like John XXIII, Paul VI sensed there was more to communism than the dismissive condemnations of Pius XI and Pius XII had allowed for. Did he perhaps privately sympathize with some of its declared objectives? That question was asked with the appearance of his next encyclical.

Populorum progressio (2 March 1967) called on Christians to change the world. They could not accept systems based on an 'atheist or materialist philosophy'. But the imbalance between rich and poor nations was 'growing with each passing day', bringing social unrest and flagrant inequalities. The Pope's solution was a 'new humanism'—a 'solidarity in action' to tackle 'the material poverty of those who lack the bare necessities of life, and the moral poverty of those who are crushed under the weight of their own self-love'. As St Ambrose had written, 'You are not making a gift of what is yours to the poor man, but you are giving back to him what is his ... The Earth belongs to everyone, not to the rich.'[11]

Very similar things had been said by Leo XIII and Pius XI in their own day. But in the 1960s, against a background of anti-colonial movements and Western left-wing agitation, *Populorum progressio* sounded like a revolutionary trumpet-call. The *New York Times* called the encyclical 'strongly leftist, even Marxist in tone'.[12]

Paul VI had, in fact, gone a lot further than his predecessors. He 'gladly commended' trade unions, and noted that Third World debt and liberal market prices were 'open to serious question'. Free trade could be called just 'only when it conforms to the demands of social justice'. Governments were entitled to intervene when 'private gain and basic community needs conflict'. Meanwhile, landed estates could be expropriated when they 'impede the general prosperity'. The Pope condemned the 'hardships, unjust practices and fratricidal conflicts' caused by capitalism. But while acknowledging the possibility of revolution, he nevertheless counselled against it.

> Everyone knows that revolutionary uprisings—except where there is a manifest, long-standing tyranny which would do great damage to fundamental personal rights and dangerous harm to the common good of the country— engender new injustices, introduce new inequities and bring new disasters ... It is not just a question of eliminating hunger and reducing poverty, but of building a human community where men can live truly human lives, free from discrimination on account of race, religion or nationality, free from servitude to other men or to natural forces they cannot yet control ... where the needy Lazarus can sit down with the rich man at the same banquet table.[13]

For all its reservations, there was plenty in *Populorum progressio* which would be quoted out of context. Its talk of legitimate resistance was seized on by proponents of a new 'Liberation Theology' for the Third World.

Some Latin Americans saw the origins of Liberation Theology in the protests of early missionaries, such as the sixteenth-century Dominican Bartolomé de las Casas or Bishop Antonio de Valdivieso of Nicaragua, stabbed to death by a governor's henchmen for denouncing 'colonial Christendom'. The 1959 Cuban revolution, which many Catholic priests supported, highlighted Latin America's political, social and economic plight, and encouraged Marxist-led guerrilla movements elsewhere. The US Kennedy Administration responded with an 'Alliance for Progress', which combined development aid with counter-insurgency backing. Against this background, it was again argued that a deeper dialogue between Christianity and communism could be postponed in favour of a 'primacy of action'. Western Marxists such as Louis Althusser were already claiming to distinguish between Marxism as a science and as ideology. Many Catholics rejected the Church's traditional emphasis on charity and social harmony as a ruling class deception. They believed Marxist praxis could be used without its materialistic premises. Class struggle could be an act of Christian love, a means of redemption for rich and poor alike.

On 15 February 1966, radical Catholics gained a new symbol when a former Catholic priest, Camilo Torres, was killed in combat with Colombia's National Liberation Army (ELN) guerrillas. Torres had resigned his priesthood six months before.

> I was called by Christ to be a priest forever, because I was moved by the desire to dedicate myself full-time to the love of my fellow-men. But as a sociologist, I wished this love to be effective. I discovered that revolution was necessary to feed the hungry, to satisfy the thirsty ... I consider the revolutionary struggle to be a Christian and priestly struggle, since it is only through revolution that we can realize that love which men must extend to their neighbours.[14]

That summed up the spirit of Liberation Theology. In a declaration after *Populorum progressio*, eighteen Latin American bishops went as far as to describe 'authentic socialism' as 'Christianity lived to the full', at a time when violence was being inflicted by 'existing economic, political, social and cultural power structures'.[15] How to put radical tendencies like this in a proper context was in the mind of Paul VI when he warned Colombian *campesinos* in August 1968 not to place their trust in 'violence and revolution'. The Pope was speaking a day before the Second General Conference of Latin American bishops in Medellín began attempting to apply Vatican II to Latin American conditions. Two documents came out of the meeting, both proffering a concept of liberation which Church leaders could promote as their own.

The first, on justice, distanced the Church from both liberal capitalism and 'the temptation of the Marxist system', but acknowledged that Latin America was now caught between the two. It called for *concientización*—a concept borrowed from the Brazilian educationist Paulo Freire. And it urged the Church 'to lend support to the downtrodden of every social class, so they might come to know their rights and how to use them'. The second, on peace, condemned the 'international imperialism of money', and committed the Church to defend the rights of the poor.[16] Some Catholics dismissed the bishops' appeal as a charade—a smokescreen concealing a lack of real commitment. Many others saw them as signalling a shift away from the Church's traditional alignment with Latin America's wealthy classes—a change of emphasis from 'development' to 'liberation', from economics to politics.

Further milestones included the victory of Salvador Allende's socialist Popular Unity coalition in Chile's election two years later, and key expositions on Liberation Theology by the Brazilian Hugo Assman and

Peruvian Gustavo Gutiérrez. A reaction was not long in coming. Military coups in a dozen countries ended talk of Allende-style socialist reforms. Meanwhile, the November 1972 election of Bishop Alfonso López Trujillo, a conservative, as secretary-general of CELAM, the Latin American Conference of Episcopates, heralded a campaign against Liberation Theology in the Church as well.

The heated political climate did not prevent the Vatican from improving ties with Cuba, where John XXIII's death had been marked by three days of official mourning. In 1967, Fidel Castro himself took the unprecedented step of attending an Apostolic Delegature reception. In 1974, the Vatican's chargé d'affaires was raised to full Nuncio.

But where Catholic–communist co-operation was concerned, Paul VI soon tightened his definitions. *Octogesima adveniens* (14 May 1971) was not an encyclical, but a letter to Cardinal Maurice Roy, president of the Pontifical Justice and Peace Commission, marking the 80th anniversary of *Rerum novarum*. Coming four years after *Populorum progressio*, it reiterated the Church's condemnation of discrimination and exploitation. But as a 'personal letter', it did not require such a formal authoritative tone. For the first time, the Pope set out to analyse communism's various manifestations with objective rigour. He acknowledged 'the aspirations to equality and participation' which were growing stronger as people became better informed. In a sceptical world, it was no longer enough to 'recall principles, state intentions, point to crying injustices, utter prophetic denunciations'. What was needed was 'effective action'. But the diversity of situations Christians now found themselves in, the letter added, made it hard for the Church to offer a 'united message'. This was not its mission. Instead, it was up to local Christians to work out their own 'options and commitments'.[17]

Paul VI condemned totalitarianism. But he also denounced 'liberal ideology' and its exaltation of unlimited freedom. If the much-predicted 'retreat of ideologies' actually occurred, this might create an opening to Christianity. But for now, the historical movements which had emerged from these ideologies still continued.

Paul VI recognized that many Christians were attracted to socialism, seeing in it 'aspirations which they carry within themselves in the name of their faith'. He also accepted that, as a 'historical current', socialism had taken different forms. But socialism should not be viewed idealistically as just some vague pursuit of 'justice, solidarity and equality'. It still drew inspiration, as did communism, from 'ideologies incompatible with faith'. Competing interpretations of Marxism had pitted Eurocommunists, China and the Soviet Union against each other.

But it would be illusory and dangerous to reach a point of forgetting the intimate link which indirectly binds them together, to accept the elements of Marxist analysis without recognizing their relationships with ideology, and to enter into the practice of class struggle and its Marxist interpretations, while failing to note the kind of totalitarian and violent society to which this process leads.[18]

With the Third World forecast to provide 70 per cent of all Catholics by the year 2000, theological trends there were clearly important. It was open to question whether Liberation Theology was really an expression of Third World grievances at all, or rather the contemporary reapplication of a nineteenth-century Christian socialism firmly rooted in Europe. The Colombian priest-hero Camilo Torres had taught social and political science at Belgium's Catholic Leuven University. Western religious groups like the US-based Maryknoll order were conspicuous in the spread of left-wing ideas. But there were signs that Paul VI's genteel reminders in *Octogesima adveniens* had failed to deter a growing identity of views between communists and radical Catholics. When the Synod of Bishops met again in 1971, it proclaimed 'good news to the poor, freedom to the oppressed and joy to the afflicted'. This seemed to capture the mood of Church leaders internationally.

A 'new awareness' had been born, the Synod report proclaimed, among the world's downtrodden. It was shaking them out of their 'fatalistic resignation' and driving them to liberate themselves. At such a critical hour, the Church must stand with the poor, forsaking its place 'among the rich and powerful'. The text spoke of God as 'liberator of the oppressed'; of the intimate link between preaching the Gospel and 'participation in the world's transformation'. It demanded 'education for justice' and urged collaboration with non-Christians who 'in their esteem for human values seek justice sincerely and by honourable means'.[19]

This was as ringing an endorsement as any radical group could hope for. But there was more to come. In April 1973, Cardinal Roy published a four-page essay in *L'Osservatore Romano* to mark the tenth anniversary of *Pacem in terris*. It spoke of a 'cultural revolution' in the Church and described the doctrine of class warfare as 'the fruit of a lucid dialectic'. It even criticized John XXIII's encyclical for saying too little about justice and liberation. The Cardinal claimed to have written the essay at Paul VI's request.[20]

Where Liberation Theology was concerned, there was now a firm bridge between the First and Third Worlds. One movement, 'Christians for Socialism', launched in Chile in April 1972, staged its first major conference in Italy eighteen months later, putting forward a materialist reading of the Gospel which linked readers' understanding to their class status. By the early

1970s, communist parties had gained 15 per cent or more in national elections in at least a dozen countries, including Italy, France and Finland. Church involvement in the defeat of an attempted 1975 communist coup in Portugal showed Catholic forces could still hold their own. But the likelihood that communist-led governments would be voted into power suggested olive branches were needed.

The Italian Communist Party was again wooing Italy's Catholics. The idea of a 'historic compromise' with 'anti-bourgeois' Catholic and Christian Democrat elements, first advocated in 1966, became a formal communist policy under the party's new secretary-general, Enrico Berlinguer. In his view, Vatican II had achieved a 'great novelty', by recognizing the need for man's 'earthly emancipation' as well as 'supernatural salvation'.[21]

Despite the Italian bishops' opposition, 1976 elections gave the Communist Party over a third of votes, making its co-operation necessary for the minority Christian Democrat government. But in May 1978, the murder of the Christian Democrats' pro-compromise leader, Aldo Moro, by Italy's Red Brigades put talk of a broader alliance on ice.

Moro's killing was a reminder of the deep hostility still felt among communists towards any accommodation with the class enemy. In the 1960s, talk of 'convergence' between communist and liberal democratic systems had been derided by the best Western experts. But Moscow and its East European satellites had rejected it too. Realists on both sides saw it as likely to undermine their alliances. Something similar could be said of Eurocommunism's search for ideological partners.

Paul VI never confirmed his attitude to Cardinal Roy's controversial *L'Osservatore* essay of 1973. But in late 1975 he issued another warning about the naive expectations of Liberation Theology. *Evangelii nuntiandi* (8 December 1975), marking a decade since the end of Vatican II, reiterated that the Church wanted a system which would be 'more humane, more just, more solicitous for the rights of the individual'. But it had to find a way of ridding the concept of 'liberation' from its ideological and political ambiguities.

> The Church proclaims liberation and co-operates with all those who are working and suffering on its behalf ... But she reaffirms the primacy of her spiritual function and refuses to substitute for the preaching of the kingdom of God a proclamation of liberation of the merely human order.[22]

That summed up the Vatican's stance on Liberation Theology. In 1977, on the fortieth aniversary of *Divini Redemptoris*, which had denounced communism as 'intrinsically evil', *L'Osservatore Romano* noted that 'profound changes' had occurred in communism since 1917. But Pius XI's diagnosis still presented the 'exact criterion', the paper added. For those who had worked so hard to foster Catholic illusions, this was a slap in the face.

The Liberation Theology debate had been followed in the Soviet Union. In 1969, a Moscow conference, convened to normalize inter-party relations after the invasion of Czechoslovakia, had noted that communists were co-operating increasingly with 'broad democratic masses of Catholics'. 'Dialogue on such issues as war and peace, capitalism and socialism ... is very pressing', the resolution continued. 'Communists are of the opinion that on this path—the path of broad contacts and joint activities—the mass of believers is becoming an active force in the struggle against imperialism and for thorough social transformation.'[23]

Back in 1961, Khrushchev had officially prophesied that a communist society would 'mostly be built' in the Soviet Union by 1980. Whether this would be accompanied by a 'withering away of the State' was not specified and seemed somewhat unlikely. But on paper at least, the doctrinal priorities set out by Lenin remained established policy. The Vatican's 'small steps' had to be seen in this light.

Gromyko had talked peace and progress with Paul VI in 1965 and 1966, but had insisted he was 'not competent' to discuss the position of Catholics in his country. Talks on that theme took place when the Soviet Foreign Minister returned in November 1970, and then only in the context of wider issues such as the Vietnam War and arms control. But Casaroli came back from Moscow the following March full of enthusiasm. The Vatican and Soviet Union had 'put an end to monologue and opened a dialogue', he said. Both had a 'common interest in peace' and had found a 'common field of action'.[24]

In reality, Moscow's propaganda drive had already assumed new proportions. The Berlin Conference of 'progressive Catholics', initiated in the mid-1960s, and the Prague-based Christian Peace Conference, set up by Josef Hromádka, both attempted to rally Church support for Moscow's 'peace offensive' and urged the Vatican to back its declarations about disarmament and social progress. Moscow was aware of Rome's traditional disdain for abusive capitalism and liberal democracy, and sensed this could affect Western public opinion. It knew that Rome had crucial interests in Latin America, Africa and parts of Asia, which could be harnessed to improve the Soviet image there. When Catholic and Russian Orthodox theologians met at Zagorsk in 1973, the communiqué said they had 'recognized the strong tendency in many parts of the world towards certain forms of "socialism"', whose 'positive aspects' should be recognized by Christians. The communiqué was not authorized, but L'Osservatore Romano printed it anyway.[25]

If the Church was to be made use of as a social force, it could not be undermined outright. The gains and losses registered by each side had to look reasonably genuine. Soviet leaders knew Casaroli and his associates were cunning men—certainly a cut above the 'useful idiots' spoken of derisively by Lenin—and would not be fooled or intimidated by half-hearted ruses. But they calculated that they could exploit the Vatican's limited options. Casaroli had to keep his distance from Catholic nationalism in Lithuania and Ukraine, as well as from the anti-communist *émigrés* who clustered around figures like Slipyi and Mindszenty. And since relations with Russian Orthodoxy were a high priority, Rome was also restricted in how far it could go in supporting the Soviet Union's Greek Catholics.

Moscow believed it could demonstrate that, far from standing up for hard-pressed Catholic minorities, the Vatican was actually selling them out. The fact that even Rome was now talking to Moscow could be used to show up the pointlessness of further defiance.

Casaroli played along. He shared the view of Western governments that too vigorous a defence of rights and freedoms would bring worse repression. It was a bogus argument: there was overwhelming evidence that communists made concessions only under pressure in the face of loud protests. Casaroli believed a distinction could be made between the Party, which was ideologically hostile to religion, and the State, which merely organized society. This was bogus as well: in reality, Party and State were effectively one and the same under all communist constitutions.

But Casaroli had other arguments too. One was that meagre concessions were better than none and merited maintaining contacts. Another was that communism would evolve (as Eurocommunism had done) like all ideological movements. Another was that priority in dealings with 'bad states' had to be given to purely technical solutions; another that the Vatican had to contribute to peace and could never ostracize particular regimes. 'It would not be wise', the diplomat insisted in 1977, 'to refuse what is possible today on the pretext that it is still partial and imperfect—always on condition that this does not harm the achievement of the end.'[26]

But that was the whole point—did it actually 'harm the achievement of the end'?

Casaroli had begun talks with Poland in 1966, the year Paul VI was barred from attending the Polish Millennium celebrations. It was after his first fact-finding visit that the Vatican had appointed apostolic administrators for the 'Recovered Territories'. Vatican II's Decree on Bishops had called for a 'prudent revision' of diocesan boundaries. But it had also noted that the views of local bishops 'should always be taken especially into considera-tion'.[27] In December 1970, a long-awaited Polish–German treaty cleared the way for Vatican recognition of the new inter-state border. Under German Church pressure, Rome waited until the Bundestag had ratified the *Grenzvertrag* in June 1972. It then announced the creation of full Polish dioceses in the former German lands. But talks on diplomatic relations between the Vatican and Poland had already begun a year before. In July 1974, Casaroli and Józef Czyrek, the Foreign Minister, agreed to open 'permanent working contacts'. And in 1977, the Polish Party leader, Edward Gierek, visited the Vatican. 'We expressed the wish—and on our part the strong wish—for co-operation', Paul VI reported.[28]

Talks with Czechoslovakia's Husák regime had restarted in October 1970, when the real post-Prague Spring repression was just beginning. In December 1972, when only one of the country's thirteen Catholic sees was still occupied, Casaroli announced that four new bishops had been agreed to. But the new bishops were all associated with the pro-regime Pacem in Terris association. Even when Casaroli came in person to consecrate them the following March, that still left eight dioceses empty. During his visit, Casaroli informed the veteran Bishop Štěpán Trochta of Litoměřice that he was to be made a Cardinal. Trochta died after a police interrogation in April 1974. But in February 1975, Casaroli was back.

A similar 'breakthrough' followed in January 1978, when Bishop Tomášek, who had administered the Prague archdiocese since Cardinal Beran's death, was named Archbishop with regime consent. This too was billed as a communist concession. But Tomášek was seen as a weak old man, not one to take a stand on Church rights. When he was allowed to receive his Cardinal's hat in Rome (bestowed *in pectore* two years before), the Czechoslovak Embassy even laid on a special reception.

Casaroli's diplomatic forays had continued elsewhere too. In 1970, four years after the signing of a controversial protocol, Yugoslavia became the second communist state after Cuba to establish a formal presence at the Vatican. But Paul VI's formulation of what was being attempted—'liberty and co-operation in respect for mutual sovereign rights'—nicely suited the Belgrade regime. In March 1971, Tito became the first Communist Party leader to be received by the Pope on an official visit.

In 1972, the regime of Nicolae Ceauşescu allowed Bishop Antal Jákab to succeed Áron Márton as Romania's only Latin Catholic bishop, and even permitted a group of theology professors to travel to Rome for studies. In May 1973, Ceauşescu was similarly received at the Vatican as an 'illustrious visitor' by Paul VI. Casaroli's assistant, Mgr Luigi Poggi, opened official talks in 1975 in a 'loyal, comprehending and cordial atmosphere'.[29]

In Bulgaria, the Greek Catholic exarch, Kiril Kurtev, died in 1971, 45 years after being consecrated by Angelo Roncalli while Vatican Nuncio in the 1920s. He was succeeded by Metody Stratiev, a man deemed so 'reliable' by the Bulgarian regime that he was allowed to attend the Synods of 1971 and 1974. Zhivkov became the latest communist leader to visit the Pope in June 1975, in an atmosphere of 'mutual familiarity'.[30] Paul VI named two new Latin bishops with the regime's consent a month later, and Casaroli paid a ten-day official visit to Bulgaria that November.

Hopes of a *modus vivendi* even extended as far as China. When Mao died in 1976, Paul VI sent a telegram expressing his 'profound consideration' for the Chinese people—as well as 'an invitation, always more pressing', to dialogue and 'respectful coexistence'.[31]

By then, the most controversial case of all had been conveniently closed. After fifteen years' asylum at the US embassy in Budapest, maintained by annual US Church donations of a thousand dollars, Cardinal Mindszenty had finally walked out in 1971 with an unsolicited amnesty for his 'crimes'. It had taken the Vatican a decade to move him. Even now, the ways and means had a distinctively underhand look.

By Mindszenty's account, a Hungarian-born Vatican official, Mgr József Zágon, visited the embassy on 25 June, and bluntly informed him that the Nixon Administration wanted him out. The Pope had devised a solution, Zágon said, which would allow Mindszenty to contribute to the renewal of Hungarian Catholicism abroad. Like Cardinal Slipyi in 1963, Mindszenty insisted he must stay with his flock. The Kádár regime, he added, would gain a propaganda coup if he fled. But Zágon assured him the Vatican would not allow this. The Pope would 'fight tenaciously' to ensure his departure served as a bargaining counter for concessions.[32]

The Vatican official listed conditions which the Cardinal was expected to accept. He would remain Primate but give up his 'rights and duties' in Hungary to an apostolic administrator. He would leave 'altogether quietly', although he could write a letter for the Vatican to use as a draft press statement. And he would keep his memoirs secret until the Vatican saw fit to publish them. It was, however, a further condition which caused Mindszenty most concern.

> What was asked of me was nothing less than that once abroad I should make no statement that 'might disturb relations between the Holy See and Hungarian government, or the People's Republic'. I declared unequivocally ... that I could not let the communist regime of Hungary, which was causing the destruction of the Hungarian Church and nation, be the judge of what I could or could not say.[33]

In the end, after three days of talks, Mindszenty refused Zágon's conditions. What finally settled the matter was a letter from Nixon confirming that he was now an 'unwanted guest'. 'I knew quite well that I had become an undesirable guest in the embassy not because of my illness, but because I stood in the way of the policy of *détente*', the Cardinal reflected later. On 29 September, Mindszenty was escorted by Hungarian police cars to the Austrian border and met by Casaroli at Vienna airport. Welcoming the new exile later at a Mass in St Peter's, Paul VI called him a 'glorious symbol of the living thousand-year unity between the Hungarian Church and Apostolic See . . . a symbol of unshakeable strength rooted in faith and selfless devotion to the Church'.[34]

This was Mindszenty's version. There were, of course, different interpretations. The most widely shared was that the 79-year-old had made a fatal public relations blunder in obtaining US protection in the first place, and in allowing himself to be depicted as a barrier to even prudent Church–State contacts.

Yet many believed that, with this barrier now cleared, the exasperated Mindszenty should be allowed to give his vigorous views an airing. Instead, he stayed less than a month in Rome before taking up residence in Vienna, long enough to encounter a 'general indifference'. Pius XII's 1957 excommunication of three Hungarian 'peace priests', who still held senior regime positions, was lifted two weeks after his arrival. Meanwhile, Mindszenty found himself gagged—quite literally. The Hungarian writer Éva Saáry met him at a quiet Rome reception and asked why he had left.

> The Cardinal looked at me sadly for a long moment. Then, when he opened his mouth to say something, Mgr Zágon put a small parcel in front of Mindszenty's mouth. Stunned silence followed. Taking advantage of the general chaos, another Hungarian reporter from Radio Vienna hurried to Mindszenty and asked, 'Your Eminence, would you tell us how you are keeping and when are you coming to Vienna?' 'Thank you, I am in good health', he answered, 'and as far as Vienna is concerned . . .' But at that moment Zágon again held the parcel in front of the Cardinal's mouth.[35]

Moving into Vienna's Hungarian seminary, the Pazmaneum, Mindszenty was told he must submit everything he said publicly for prior Vatican approval. When he sent his memoirs to Paul VI in 1973, the Pope described them as 'truly valuable, fascinating, overwhelming'. But he warned Mindszenty the Kádár regime would 'punish the entire Church of Hungary' if they were published.

The worst was still to come. Mindszenty insisted the Pope had personally assured him he would remain Archbishop of Esztergom, and that his destiny 'would in no way be subordinated to other aims'. But on 1 November 1973, two years after leaving Budapest, he was asked to resign 'in consideration of pastoral necessities'. The Kádár regime welcomed the move and sent Hungary's Foreign Minister, János Péter, to visit Paul VI the same month. In February, the 25th anniversary of Mindszenty's trial, Esztergom was declared vacant. Mindszenty issued a statement, 'correcting suggestions' that he had retired voluntarily: the decision was the Holy See's alone.[36]

With Mindszenty out of the way, Vatican–Hungarian ties advanced by leaps and bounds. It took less than a year to agree on five new bishops and the reactivation of Hungary's Greek Catholic see at Hajdúdorog. The fiery Cardinal died in May 1975, and was buried at Mariazell in Austria. Six months later, Hungary's communist Prime Minister, György Lázár, was privately received by Paul VI. And in February 1976, Esztergom's apostolic administrator, László Lékai, was raised to full Archbishop. By April, all eleven dioceses had bishops. By June, Lékai had been named a Cardinal in record time.

When Kádár was received by Paul VI in June 1977, the Pope called it the result of a 'slow but uninterrupted' 40-year process which had brought the Holy See and Hungarian People's Republic closer. 'Many are following this initiative and its results with a vigilant, often critical eye', he added. 'But the last word will belong to history, after the judgement of our conscience.'[37] Religious observances were at their lowest in Hungary—and Church–State ties at their closest.

Critics would maintain that the Vatican was merely following the ebb and flow of East–West relations. Talk of *détente* was in the air. Even the hardline Nixon seemed to have concurred that figures like Mindszenty impeded necessary progress.

The identification with Western policy aims had its limits. Pius XII had closely followed the anti-communist policy of the United States towards China and Southeast Asia in the 1950s, speaking up for South Korea during its bloody 1950–53 war with the communist North and even allowing whole articles from the US Information Agency to be reprinted in *L'Osservatore Romano*. But Vietnam posed a different problem. With South Vietnam's 1.5 million Catholics making up a tenth of its population, the Vatican and US positions moved apart after the CIA's killing in 1963 of the Prime Minister, Ngo Dinh Diem. Diem, a Catholic, had been friendly with President Kennedy and Cardinal Spellman. In 1965, as American troops massed, Paul VI warned of a 'new and terrible war' and wrote to Chairman Mao urging peace. In 1966, he condemned 'the separations imposed upon citizens, the nefarious plots, the slaughter of innocent people'.[38]

But the Vatican's diplomatic moves were ignored. When President Johnson visited Rome at Christmas 1967 during the US bombing campaign, in the year of *Populorum progressio*, he was accused of entering a 'blind alley' and allowing Washington's 'moral and political position' to be undermined.[39] Defusing Catholic criticisms may have been in Nixon's mind when he met Paul VI in March 1970 and appointed Henry Cabot Lodge, a former ambassador to Vietnam, to the new office of US Permanent Representative at the Vatican, Sharp Church criticisms nevertheless continued. Xuan Thuy, a North Vietnamese diplomat, came to Rome in February 1973 and thanked the Pope for his 'peace efforts'. But Hanoi showed no interest in the Vatican's gestures either.

By the mid-1970s, Paul VI had modified his passion for North–South issues in favour of a greater concentration on Europe. The vision of a re-Christianized continent looked less convincing than ever. The Four Powers Agreement on Berlin of 1971 and the East–West German Basic Treaty of 1973 all symbolized final acceptance of geopolitical realities. Yet at the same time opportunities for co-operation were increasing. East–West trade had expanded 25-fold in a decade; Nixon had visited Moscow; and a US–Soviet SALT I agreement had been signed on strategic arms limitations.

Détente was not a word used in the Vatican. But Casaroli and his team concurred that, although Europe seemed irrevocably divided, East and West nevertheless shared certain common interests. All that was needed was to express those interests in such a way as to promote stability and prosperity. Communist regimes would keep agreements—even agreements involving human rights—if they saw advantages in doing so. They too had concluded that conflicts of interest and ideology could no longer be solved by force. The world's social and economic development had created a web of interdependencies.

That was, in essence, the theory behind *détente*. And it appeared to offer a chance for mediation—or at least for helping governments articulate their differences. The Church, Casaroli told Polish officials in 1974, had a special obligation to 'seek existing convergencies, explore and foster them, and create new convergent planes'.[40]

Gestures like this suited Moscow too. In 1945, the Vatican had been excluded by Stalin's puerile question, 'How many divisions . . .?' But by the 1970s, the presence of an institution 'favourably disposed towards peaceful coexistence and a relaxation of tensions'[41] could be made use of by both sides. Vatican backing was obtained for Nuclear Test Ban and Non-Proliferation treaties in 1969–70, as well as for Mutual and Balanced Force Reduction (MBFR) talks in Vienna.

In 1970, Gromyko had asked the Pope and Casaroli to support another project too—a conference which would formally sanction the continent's geopolitical order. Addressing the opening session of the Conference on Security and Co-operation in Europe (CSCE) in 1973, Casaroli warned that human rights violations would lead 'sooner or later, somewhere in Europe, to grave internal disturbances' which threatened international peace. But the Vatican maintained a 'respectful discretion', he added, in areas outside its competence. It would gladly support any venture which brought the sides closer.[42]

When the CSCE's 35 participating states signed a 'Final Act' at Helsinki in August 1975, it listed 'respect for human rights and fundamental freedoms, including the freedom of thought, conscience, religion or belief' as one of ten principles for interstate relations. But this merely repeated in cursory language commitments made under previous international agreements. While these had had treaty status, furthermore, the Final Act was 'politically binding' only. A following section, 'Basket Three', was said to have given Principle VII a detailed application, but it contained no mention of rights, only of 'humanitarian co-operation'. Even then, every single undertaking contained an escape-clause. The logic of the text was intended to reduce concrete commitments to the barest minimum.

Casaroli believed the Final Act had engaged 'all signatory states in a sovereign capacity' and was 'the first sign of European unity'; but this was wishful thinking. Compared to what Moscow and its East European allies had gained at Helsinki—including far-reaching commitments to economic and technological co-operation—the achievements for human rights were negligible. The communist regimes had not, in fact, made concessions on rights at all. They had only consented to certain technical possibilities. And these would remain subject to each country's 'socialist legality'.[43]

Cardinal Franz König of Vienna, a man who had spent a quarter of a century rebuilding Church links with Eastern Europe—as well as with Bruno Kreisky's Austrian socialists—deplored the 'confessional state of atheism' now reigning to the east a month after the Final Act's signature. That October, Paul VI himself spoke of Christians 'oppressed by systematic persecution'. 'The drama of fidelity to Christ and of freedom of religion continues', he warned, 'even if it is disguised by categorical declarations in favour of the rights of the person and life in society.'[44]

Ironically, when the CSCE reassembled in Belgrade two years later for its first 'review meeting', a redrafted Soviet constitution contained a new clause on the 'right to conduct religious worship'. But the same notorious imbalance was kept between this and the 'right to conduct atheist propaganda'. Whatever Soviet spokesmen might argue, the war against religion continued.

Addressing diplomats nine months before his death, Paul VI defended his approach to communism.

> Is the time not ripe, is the historical evolution not sufficiently advanced for certain restraints from the past to be surmounted, for the supplication of millions to be accepted, and for everyone ... to benefit from a just space of freedom for their faith in both its personal and communal expression?[45]

It was a worthy hope, but whatever Vatican figures like Casaroli might insist about recognizing realities, the record was at best a mixed one.

Certainly, the Church was safer now—other than in Albania, where all religion had been outlawed in 1967. Priests were no longer jailed or shot by administrative order. They were merely harassed and intimidated. Although no *modus vivendi* had been conceded, it was possible to speak (as Cardinal Villot did) of a *modus non moriendi*—or at least of Casaroli's *esse*, if not his *bene esse*. Contacts with the West were no longer so exceptional. The aggressive denunciations of the 1940s and 1950s had moderated too. Meanwhile, although the Vatican had attached high priority to official relations with communist regimes, it had never abandoned the region's unofficial Church communities. Vatican Radio continued to broadcast to Ukraine and the Baltic States. The annual register, *Annuario Pontificio*, still listed dioceses belonging to the banned Greek Catholic Church.

But the Vatican had failed to see what East Europeans knew instinctively. While diplomacy could produce results when conditions were right, it could also be seen as a sign of weakness—even a sign that the Church had lost its way and sacrificed principle to expediency. If the repression had slowly eased, it was only because it was no longer needed.

In 1973, Paul VI had set out his vision of the Vatican's role on the contemporary world stage. Its task, he said, was to provide 'direction and moral inspiration' by proclaiming principles, as well as by participating 'as a member with full rights' in the life of the international community'.[46] In reality, this vision had never been realized. Vatican officials could say, as Cardinal Maglione had said under Pius XII, that the Pope had already condemned human rights violations, making constant repetitions superfluous. Yet this was hardly satisfactory. Whereas Pius XII had been too confrontational, rejecting even sensible, precautionary approaches, Paul VI had gone to the other extreme. He had restated Christianity's incompatibility with communism. He had also accepted the need for negotiation and compromise with communists. But by turning negotiation and compromise into points of principle, he had dragged the Vatican into a maze of hypothetical diplomatic calculations, depriving it of the power to discriminate firmly between the policies and practices of its interlocutors.

The real problem with the 'small steps' strategy was its very one-sidedness. It raised vital issues for the Church which had only a notional importance for communist regimes, who could make tactical retreats when it suited them, but could just as quickly institute new repressions. This constant threat inevitably curtailed the Vatican's freedom of action. It had to reward regimes which made a show of respecting the Church's rights, but it had no leverage of its own to ensure the deals and bargains were kept.

'It may be that the Holy See has not yet arrived at a full realization of the force it possesses'—even the Soviet Foreign Minister, Andrei Gromyko, had admitted as much after his first Rome meeting with Paul VI in 1970.[47] Like Pius XII, Montini had ultimately misunderstood the nature of totalitarian regimes by believing the Vatican possessed enough authority and influence to persuade communist regimes to make lasting concessions. His methods had been more sophisticated; but the truth was that communists responded, now as before, only to pressure—the pressure of internal resistance and international isolation. For all the deftness and perservance, there was no real evidence that the era of diplomacy had produced dependable results.

Notes

1. Synod of Bishops, *Ratione habita* (28 October 1967), nos 1–2.
2. *Ecclesiam Suam* (6 August 1964), nos 10, 13.
3. Ibid., no. 102.
4. From a May 1968 interview in *Student* (Prague); cited in Hansjakob Stehle, *Eastern Politics of the Vatican 1917–1979* (London: Ohio University Press, 1981), pp. 333, 426. Stehle says Beran also acknowledged that he would not be returning in 1963.
5. Antoine Wenger, 'La politique orientale du Saint-Siège' in Joël-Benoît d'Onorio (ed.), *Le Saint-Siège dans les relations internationales* (Paris: Éditions du Cerf, 1989), p. 175.
6. Casaroli's address to the Council on Foreign Relations, New York (24 October 1973); ibid., pp. 173–4.
7. Radio message from Castelgandolfo (24 August 1939). Casaroli's arguments are summarized from various public statements during the 1970s.
8. Pierre Teilhard de Chardin, *The Phenomenon of Man* (London: Collins, 1983), pp. 281–2, etc.; Peter Hebblethwaite, *The Catholic–Marxist Dialogue and Beyond* (London: Darton, Longman and Todd, 1977).
9. *Humanae personae dignitatem* (28 August 1968), III, IV, 2.
10. *Ecclesiam Suam*, no. 103. Paul VI wrote the entire text himself, making it 'the most personal encyclical ever written': see Peter Hebblethwaite, *Paul VI: The First Modern Pope* (London: HarperCollins, 1993), pp. 380–3.

11. *Populorum progressio* (26 March 1967), nos 1, 21, 23.

12. *New York Times* editorial (29 March 1967). Although criticized by right-wing commentators, the encyclical was also widely praised as a synthesis of the Ten Commandments with modern human rights instruments.

13. *Populorum progressio*, nos 23–24, 31, 47, 59.

14. Quoted in François Houtart and André Rousseau, *L'Église et les mouvements révolutionnaires* (Brussels: Éditions Vie Ouvrière, 1972), pp. 59–60.

15. Philip Berryman, *Liberation Theology* (London: I. B. Tauris, 1987), p. 21.

16. Nos 10, 20–21, from the texts in David O'Brien and Thomas Shannon (eds), *Renewing the Earth: Catholic Documents on Justice and Liberation* (New York: Image Books, 1977), pp. 549–60, 561–79.

17. *Octogesima adveniens* (14 May 1971), nos 4, 29–31, 48:1.

18. Ibid., no. 34.

19. Synod of Bishops, *Convenientes ex universo* (30 November 1971), nos 5, 30, 47, 62.

20. *L'Osservatore Romano* (11 April 1973); Hervé Leclerc, *Marxism and the Church of Rome* (London: Institute for the Study of Conflict, 1974), pp. 9–10.

21. Rosanna Mulazzi-Giammanco, *The Catholic–Communist Dialogue in Italy* (New York: Praeger, 1989), p. 68.

22. *Evangelii nuntiandi* (8 December 1975), nos 36, 38.

23. Christopher Read, 'The Soviet attitude to the Christian–Marxist dialogue', *Religion in Communist Lands*, vol. 1, no. 6 (1973), pp. 9–10.

24. Stehle, op. cit., p. 362; Katholische Nachrichten-Agentur (16 March 1971).

25. *L'Osservatore Romano* (16 June 1973).

26. Address in Vienna (17 November 1977); in Wenger, op. cit., p. 170. See also A. Casaroli, 'Le Saint-Siège entre les tensions et la détente', *Documentation Catholique*, no. 1740 (1978), pp. 380–5.

27. *Christus Dominus* (28 October 1965), nos 22–24.

28. Text in Bogdan Szajkowski, *Next to God ... Poland* (London: Pinter, 1983), p. 52.

29. Mireille Macqua, *Rome–Moscou: L'Ostpolitik du Vatican* (Louvain-la-Neuve: Cabay, 1984), pp. 155, 179.

30. Ibid., p. 102.

31. Quoted in André Dupuy, *La Diplomatie du Saint-Siège* (Paris: Tequi, 1980), p. 224.

32. József Mindszenty, *Memoirs* (London: Weidenfeld and Nicolson, 1974), pp. 232–3.

33. Ibid., pp. 233–4.

34. Ibid., p. 237.

35. Gyula Havasy (ed.), *Martyrs of the Catholics in Hungary* (Budapest: privately published, 1993), pp. 63–4.

36. Mindszenty, op. cit., pp. 239, 247.

37. 'Allocution de bienvenue de Paul VI'; in József Ijjas et al., *Ensemble pour une bonne cause: L'État socialiste et les Églises en Hongrie* (Budapest: Corvina, 1978), pp. 230–2.

38. *Mense Maio* (29 April 1965); *Christi Matri* (15 September 1966), no. 1.
39. From *L'Osservatore Romano*, quoted in the *New York Times* (4–5 January 1968). See also Hebblethwaite, *Paul VI*, op. cit., pp. 505–6. Cardinal Spellman, who visited Vietnam a year earlier, called the conflict 'a war for the defense of civilization'; Houtart and Rousseau, op. cit., p. 90.
40. Casaroli's Warsaw speech in *Życie Warszawy* (3 February 1974).
41. The words are from a Soviet manual on 'religious organizations and problems of European security'; Dennis Dunn, *Détente in Papal–Communist Relations* (Boulder: Westview, 1979), p. 40.
42. Text in *Orientierung* (7 July 1973).
43. *The Conference on Security and Co-operation in Europe, Final Act* (Cmd 6198; London: Her Majesty's Stationery Office, 1975). See also Jonathan Luxmoore, *The Helsinki Agreement: Dialogue or Delusion?* (London: Institute for European Defence and Strategic Studies, 1986); and Christine de Montclos-Alix, *Les Voyages de Jean-Paul II* (Paris: Centurion, 1990), p. 150.
44. Dunn, op. cit., p. 73; *L'Osservatore Romano* (17 October 1975).
45. Text in Dupuy, op. cit., p. 236.
46. *L'Osservatore Romano* (27 June 1973).
47. Wenger, op. cit., p. 166.

9

❧❧❧❧❧

Eastern Europe comes of age

The Vatican under Paul VI had failed to see something else as well—that by the early 1970s a new situation was emerging in the communist-ruled East. If the failed 'revisionism' of 1956 had dashed hopes of reform from within, the 1968 repressions had also taught that it was impossible to confront the system head-on. But in Poland at least there were signs of movement. Edward Gierek's promised 'economic miracle' had begun to break down under the impact of indebtedness to the West. Talk among the would-be opposition had turned to the more modest goal of creating 'democratic spaces'—of persistent but peaceful pressure which took account of prevailing realities.

The most active Polish dissidents still felt a sense of distance from the Catholic Church.[1] But the Church was the only independent force in Poland which embraced all social groups. Its leaders were naturally constrained in what they could say and do. But for all his tactical manoeuvres, Cardinal Wyszyński had never compromised with communist ideology. To have the Church's moral support would be the opposition's greatest asset.

Some former Marxists had turned to psychoanalysis for an alternative explanation of human behaviour; but some had turned to Christianity. *Letters from Prison*, the work of the German Protestant Dietrich Bonhoeffer, executed by the Nazis at the end of the war, was published in Polish in 1970. His much-quoted advice to 'live as if God did not exist' seemed to bring an injunction to change reality without retreating into prayers. For former Marxists now in opposition, it suggested Christian principles could be deployed in a struggle for justice and rights without necessarily submitting to the Church's dogmas.

In his letter *Octogesima adveniens* of 1971 Paul VI predicted a 'retreat from ideologies' would create an opening to Christianity. In *Evangelii nuntiandi* he

176

called on the Church to adapt its message to 'intellectuals'. What was occurring in Poland was a promising sign.

In winter 1971 the editors of *Więź* celebrated the Catholic monthly's fifteenth anniversary by inviting dissident former communists to visit their office at Warsaw's Catholic Intelligentsia Club (KIK). Poland's communist regime had had high hopes for *Więź* in the 1960s, seeing its 'more rational Catholicism' as an 'ally in the struggle for laicization'.[2] But things had changed. None of the 100-odd people involved in the KIK encounter could claim to be genuinely representative of any particular group. But their talks helped break the ice between communism's various opponents. 'The Church does not speak and listen to her own members alone; her dialogue is with the whole world', Paul VI had written that January.[3] If justification were needed, the KIK meetings reflected the signs of the times.

They also coincided with what sociologists identified as a 'de-secularizing current', as the psychological and cultural impact of two decades' industrialization slackened, producing signs of a religious revival. Nine-tenths of Polish citizens were baptized Catholics anyway. The proportion calling themselves believers had dipped in some areas of society. But most who did practised their faith.[4]

In a 1967 book, written before his banishment from Poland, Leszek Kołakowski had set out a vision of a world 'full of holes' in which the vagaries of life and history defied absolute explanation. By the 1970s the one-time Stalinist was speaking of the need for God's grace.[5] The readiness to work with Christians distinguished Poland's ex-communists from their Russian counterparts, who restricted their own influence by avoiding religious groups. It also produced results. In 1975 the Gierek regime tried to buttress its crumbling social base by amending the constitution to declare Poland a permanent 'socialist state'. The resulting protests brought together a disparate coalition, ranging from Party members to Catholic priests. Seven years after 1968, they were an important step towards a united opposition.

By 1975, Karol Wojtyła had been Archbishop of Kraków for eleven years. Regime propagandists had dubbed him the 'Red Cardinal' to set him at odds with the 'Black Cardinal', Stefan Wyszyński. But as communist ideology declined, Wojtyła had become increasingly assertive.

In December 1970, when striking shipyard workers were massacred in Gdańsk and Gdynia, he had deplored the new 'bloody stain' on Poland's history, and urged citizens to preserve an 'atmosphere of internal freedom and liberation from fear'.[6] Wojtyła had failed to react to the anti-Semitic repressions two years before. But the shock of the 1970 events marked a change in him. Having previously left 'political' statements to the mighty

Catholic Primate in Warsaw, he now attacked the regime's injustices openly. A silent Church, Wojtyła had concluded, was also a dead Church.

The December events had taught important lessons. One was that even morally legitimate economic demands were seen as a political challenge by the communist regime and were likely to draw a violent response. Another was that people—very ordinary people—were ready to die defending dignity and sense in their work.

This set Wojtyła on the trail of a coherent 'theology of work'. In 1971, he returned from the Rome Synod full of ideas about the Church and justice. But under communist rule, he concluded, justice largely came down to problems of work. As the poet Cyprian Norwid had written, work could be a form of liberation linking man to creation. But the workplace could be a place of enslavement—the most basic 'human arena of justice and injustice'. It was therefore a place for the Church.[7]

The deduction was a timely one. Most communist regimes were attempting to bolster their legitimacy through pragmatic, technocratic achievements. But these were often conjured up through phoney statistics. Wojtyła saw this as a new form of exploitation, which destroyed the true value of work.

Vatican II had directed the Church to engage in the problems of contemporary society; and Wojtyła was still agonizing over how best to apply its teachings to Polish conditions. He came up with two answers. One, a synod of the Kraków archdiocese, opened on St Stanisław's Day in May 1972, with the aim of 'finding a path to the Council's authentic reception', which would be neither 'progressive' nor 'conservative'.[8] It lasted seven years and involved over 10,000 people, becoming a permanent workshop on the Church's priorities and objectives.

The second was a book, *Sources of Renewal*, published the same year. It attempted to balance the scepticism shown towards Vatican II by most Polish bishops with the eagerness of pro-reform circles like Kraków's Catholic weekly *Tygodnik Powszechny*. Wojtyła still differed markedly from Western Church commentators in his conception of the Council. In his book, Vatican II was only 'one historical stage in the Church's self-realization'.[9]

From the Gierek regime's vantage-point, *Sources of Renewal* posed none of the problems of *The Acting Person* three years before. On the contrary, 'Wojtyła represents the humanistic stream in contemporary Catholicism, which acknowledges the value of the anonymous, powerless human being', one Marxist reviewer wrote. 'This acknowledgement points to Catholicism's secularization and Protestantization.'[10] But the book disappointed Catholic readers. Certainly, its restrictive view of Vatican II suited the Polish Church's desire for stability. But Wojtyła had tried to mobilize Poland's Catholic laity without touching the authority of the Church's hierarchy. His language was élitist and abstract—something he himself had warned against in the 1960s. He hid behind long quotations, and failed to convey the dynamism of post-conciliar discussions.

This was uncharacteristic. When it came to new methods of evangelization, Wojtyła was well ahead of other Church leaders. The new Oasis youth movement run by Fr Franciszek Blachnicki offered a forum, he believed, in which young people 'with the courage to be free' could become 'apostles of their own milieux'. So did Sacrosong, an annual festival of Christian rock music for youngsters on the Church's fringes. Most bishops saw Sacrosong as a disruptive, disrespectful intrusion. But with Wojtyła's backing, it expanded. The aim of new initiatives like this, he told the Vatican Secretariat of State in 1972, was a 'Living Church' which would not be confined to sacral buildings but exist wherever people met to pray.[11]

By now Wojtyła had become a frequent visitor to Rome. He had helped draft *Humanae vitae* in 1968; and Paul VI still returned to sexual ethics 'at virtually every talk' with him, knowing his 'interest in the subject'.[12] He also had a chance to observe the Vatican's policy towards communism at first hand. Wojtyła was dismayed by what he saw. He told the 1971 Rome Synod it should give 'justice concerning freedom of conscience and religion' equal weight with 'reforms in poverty and social misery'. He also caused surprise by talking of justice in the Church itself: all regions had a right to be heard, not just Western Europe and Latin America.

Wojtyła returned to both themes at the 1974 Synod. There were tensions in the Polish Church, he warned. 'We feel we have a particular place in the Church and the world, particular achievements in the history of Christianity ... But we sometimes feel humbled, like being of lesser value, abandoned on the margins.'[13] Re-elected to the Synod council, he worked on its final report alongside vigorous Third World figures such as Cardinals Lorscheider of Brazil and D'Souza of India. He was aware of the contrasting priorities facing each continent.

But Wojtyła's disenchantment persisted. Most Synod statements still gave the impression there was no such place as Eastern Europe. 'There was talk in the past about a "Church of Silence"', Wojtyła noted, recalling Wyszyński's words at Vatican II. 'I asked myself many times if this "Church of Silence" is the one which is silent, or the one about which there is silence.' Returning to Poland, he told Kraków students he was sure East European Christians had 'a keener vision of the truth about Man'.[14]

Wojtyła was asked to give his reflections to the Bishops' Conference Pastoral Commission. The tone of the report written under his auspices was one of bitter frustration. The 1971 Synod's report on justice had referred to those 'suffering persecution for their faith'. But it had failed to show 'the right proportion', the report observed, 'between various manifestations of injustice in the contemporary world'. By comparison, the 1974 Synod had shown 'definite progress'. But it too had been 'guided by concern for the fate of "Ostpolitik" and fear of administrative repression'.

Many people in the Third World believed Marxism offered a 'vision of human liberty', the report pointed out. This had found an echo at the Synod, which had discussed Marxism 'with a kind of fear and distrust in the efficacy of struggling against it—like a fatalist force which must come'.

> They see in Marxism a positive programme of personal liberation from unjust social, economic and political structures. Even more, they conclude that Marxism is the only programme which can be used to bring about a conclusive transformation of these structures ... Such opinions and tendencies must be decisively confronted with the Church's experience in societies already living in a system based on Marxist doctrines, for whom Marxism is no longer a 'fascinating abstraction' but an everyday reality.[15]

The paper blamed Marxism's infiltration of the Church for a growing feeling of 'Christian ineffectiveness'—a sense that the Church was unable to respond to the contemporary world's problems. In Western societies too, enjoying civil and political freedom, priests and lay Catholics were often heard 'arguing for Marxism'. They failed to see an 'obvious fact': any Marxist system 'carries with it a new form of human captivity, which goes much deeper than captivity in the capitalist and liberal system since it deprives people of their freedom of spirit'.

This 'conformist attitude to Marxism' was evident in Vatican documents too. The 'conspiracy of silence' about crimes committed against the human conscience could only make communism more aggressive. Wojtyła's report concluded:

> With the Church struggling to maintain its identity, Polish society is deeply sensitive, for historically determined reasons, to the attitude of the Holy See. What is most painful is that the Catholic Church is silent about its persecuted brethren ... This is tantamount to fleeing in fright from a region where crimes are being perpetrated so as not to be their witness.[16]

Liberation Theology, the banner of left-wing Christians, posed a serious threat to the Church in Eastern Europe by undermining the sense of its struggle. But East European objections had been ignored as irrelevant to Third World experiences. This made Wojtyła's testimony potentially important. In his view, the new theology turned the social categories of exploiter and exploited into predetermined, collective groups, thus denying individual freedom and responsibility. This had been Marxism's mistake: it too had aimed to liberate the human person, but in reality had captivated and abused him.

By the mid-1970s, Wojtyła had begun to devise a 'liberation theology' of his own. He believed that the social, economic and political structures which held man captive were products of sin; and that by liberating himself from sin, man could overcome them. Pursuing justice alone, without mercy, merely resulted in new inequalities and divisions. Instead, true liberation would come through forgiveness and penance, since these were the very values which all structures of power and violence sought to destroy.[17]

In Eastern Europe, moral resistance must have three objectives: reawakening each nation's Christian spirit through culture and historical consciousness; conducting pastoral work among those indoctrinated by Marxism; identifying values and ideas which Christians and non-believers upheld in common. Thus, although communism's 'anti-evangelization' was unprecedented in its intensity, it should be seen 'more as a calling than as a threat'. Even atheists could see in Christianity a valuable cultural and ethical inheritance. Wojtyła urged his priests not to let the world defeat them. 'Our vocation is not to be of this world', he reminded them in 1976, 'but we are nevertheless *in* the world, in its very heart, the furnace of its disorders.'[18]

The mid-1970s had marked a watershed for Eastern Europe's small but determined dissident groups. In June 1976, a new round of price rises in Poland triggered strikes in Warsaw and Radom. The Gierek regime violently suppressed the protests. But it also postponed the increases, suggesting for the first time that industrial action could force a change of decision. The ensuing recriminations brought the birth of Eastern Europe's first open opposition group.

The Committee to Defend the Workers (KOR) introduced itself with a statement of solidarity with the imprisoned June strikers. It was intended to be a limited initiative to collect donations for the families. But in September the group issued a formal founding declaration. The fourteen signatories represented all shades of opinion, from a prominent Party economist, Edward Lipiński, to a former wartime Home Army chaplain, Fr Jan Zieja.

This capacity to unite people from different backgrounds made KOR significant. The adjective invented to describe the group—*społecznikowski*—meant something like 'social welfare-orientated'. It conjured up images of the self-help co-operatives associated with Poland's socialist tradition. But KOR embraced other political outlooks too. All agreed on at least three points: totalitarian rule was wrong, Marxist ideology had failed, and the social and moral degeneration caused by communism had to be answered by a return to absolute values. KOR's aim was not to 'win'—'winning' was impossible. It was to campaign openly for justice and human rights.

Of course, not everyone agreed on how this should be done. In a book published in 1977, a young ex-Marxist, Adam Michnik, coined the term 'lay Left' to describe Poland's non-communist left-wing tradition, and urged its surviving representatives to build tactical bridges with the Church. But the term was widely disputed. Was it not wrong to associate the Left by definition with a non-Christian outlook, just as it would be to speak of a 'Catholic Right'? Did not left-wing humanists, even non-believing ones, have more in common with Christianity than with communism?[19]

A more important contribution to the opposition's self-understanding was made by Bohdan Cywiński, a young historian. His book, published by *Więź*, was intended as a straightforward study of Poland's turn-of-the-century intelligentsia. But Cywiński unwittingly proved a revolutionary thesis: in opposing Tsarist rule, Catholic and secular members of the intelligentsia, far from being at odds, had been linked by a common 'ethical consciousness'.

As a KOR collaborator, Cywiński believed the same shared opposition ethos was at work against communist rule too. Its historical figureheads had advocated romantic ends—but pursued by realistic means. One, the writer Stefan Żeromski (1864–1925), had shown how the intelligentsia's mission was to rebuild hope in the national future. Another, the socialist Edward Abramowski (1868–1918), had linked national independence with moral and social renewal. The coming 'revolution', Abramowski contended, would consist of social and moral changes rather than political upheavals or violent rebellions.[20]

Of course, talk of a common mission presupposed that people could change, and that former communists could be trusted to have renounced their Party allegiances. That, in the end, was a question for individual consciences. It was an area where KOR's Christian members contributed decisively.

The Polish dialogue-in-opposition reflected the country's unique predicament. But something not altogether dissimilar was occurring to the south in Czechoslovakia. On 1 January 1977 a 5,000-word declaration, Charter 77, was handed out at an impromptu Prague press conference to mark Political Prisoners' Year. It highlighted discrimination in education, public life, access to information and religion. And it called on the communist government to honour the human rights pledges made in its international agreements.

Charter 77 was not an organization. But although only 247 people signed it at first, it had many more active sympathizers. As with KOR in Poland, they came from many backgrounds: veterans of the 'reform communism' which had briefly triumphed in the Prague Spring; representatives of the liberal tradition associated with Masaryk; Catholic and Protestant Christians, some with prison experience. This variety added to the Charter's importance. Although arrests began within days, its initiators succeeded in issuing more than a dozen written statements before the end of 1977.

Charter 77 appeared at a time when public apathy was at its height and the Husak regime's 'normalization' seemed to be gaining international acceptance. The friends and confidants who now met regularly could look to a Czech tradition, stretching from the sixteenth-century educationist Jan Amos Komenský (Comenius) to the Romantic-era circles of the early 1800s, which had also tried to preserve the national identity when open activities were impossible.

But the Charter's philosophical architect, Jan Patočka, insisted its signatories were not questioning State prerogatives or claiming to speak as 'society's conscience'. Their protest was founded, the blacklisted professor argued, on one simple conviction: the State should respect moral principles and observe its own laws.[21]

On 13 March, less than three months after Charter 77's release, Patočka died of a heart attack following an eleven-hour police interrogation. He was 69. But his contribution to the movement was assured. In his writings, long since banned by Czechoslovakia's communist rulers, Patočka had resurrected natural law as a unifying thread between contrasting ideologies. Christian and ex-communist dissidents could not wish away their differences, he pointed out. But they *could* learn to trust each other and engage in constructive moral thinking together.

'Ex-communists associated with Charter 77 no longer represent the ideological avant-garde and Moscow—they are being persecuted like others', observed Zdeněk Mlynář, a former theorist of 1960s reform communism who was stripped of his Czechoslovak citizenship while visiting Vienna.

> There is no question that Marxism has failed—communist politicians have discredited it as a value-based orientation … Everyone now faces three choices: to become emptiness itself; to become a cynic—or to struggle against both by looking for values outside the officially proposed path.[22]

In Hungary, a Politburo resolution of 1973 branded the reform communist followers of György Lukács dangerous subversives. Their dispersal deepened the crisis of confidence in Marxism and encouraged a search for alternatives. Yet there had still been no meeting of minds between ex-Marxist and Christian dissidents. In the 1960s Lukács had castigated foreign Marxists like Roger Garaudy and Ernst Bloch for their 'dialogue' with Christians, accusing them of sowing ideological confusion. The 'absolute crisis' in religion was still to come, Lukács decreed before his death in 1971. But a 'profound fermentation' was at work, particularly among Catholics, as futile efforts were made 'to resolve contradictions between religious dogmas and the daily life experiences of workers, peasants and intellectuals'.[23]

On the Christian side, the Catholic Church's monthly *Vigilia* was still the only officially tolerated forum where religious ideas could be explored at a high level, and where the 'silent literature' of non-establishment writers stood some chance of finding a readership. Although *Vigilia*'s influence remained limited, some Catholics were ready to take up the banner of direct opposition. The best known, Fr György Bulányi, a Piarist priest, had been trained underground in the 1940s by Tomislav Kolakovič, a Croatian Jesuit who had also set up secret Christian networks in Czechoslovakia and the Soviet Union. As a university chaplain, Bulányi preached total pacifism. The world's social structures, he taught his young followers, were based on violence and murder. Those who connived with the powerful—including Hungary's post-1950 Church hierarchy—betrayed Christianity.

Criticizing the Church's subservience was quite legitimate. But Bulányi's questioning of Church order raised more fundamental issues. By the late 1970s, his movement, Bokor (The Bush), had begun to look like a sect. In *Evangelii nuntiandi*, Paul VI praised the work of small groups which 'come together within the Church to unite themselves with it and cause it to grow'. If they avoided politicization and 'systematic protest' they offered hope. But he warned of 'charismatic communities' whose 'special purpose is to attack and reject the hierarchy'.[24] Though intended for Latin America, this could apply to the Bulanyists.

Bokor was only one of many renewal groups which had attempted since the 1950s and 1960s to break out of the official Church's straitjacket. Some might have provided the nucleus for a Catholic opposition; but group members avoided politics. Catholics distrusted the ex-Marxists who dominated Hungary's dissident circles, while ex-Marxists scorned the Catholics' passivity. The brutal suppression of the 1956 uprising had left deep scars. Like their Romantic-era predecessors of 1848, Hungarians had tried and failed to wrest their country from the grip of outside powers. This naturally bred scepticism about the potential of any new opposition. By the 1970s, Kádár had ensured that most Hungarians had something to lose.

Yugoslavia's showcase Praxis Group was thrown out of Belgrade University in 1975. The ruling League of Communists was afraid its 'critical Marxism' could incite unrest. Yugoslavia continued to produce a vast literature about its own 'road to socialism', but communist writers still routinely denounced the churches as enemies of the 'Yugoslav peoples'.

In some parts of the Soviet Union, the record was better. In Lithuania religious groups had begun sending petitions to Moscow in 1968, in response to a Supreme Soviet pledge to respond within 30 days. During President Nixon's visit to Moscow in 1972 a 19-year-old student, Romas Kalanta, burnt himself to death in a Kaunas park as a protest against Lithuania's captivity. Soviet paratroopers were sent in to suppress the mass youth demonstrations which followed. The year brought the appearance of the *Chronicle of the Catholic Church in Lithuania*—a detailed *samizdat*, or underground, record of events. It was modelled on an existing dissident journal in Moscow. But Lithuania's human rights movement was broader-based than Russia's. Not all secular dissidents agreed with the Church; but religious rights provided a catalyst. Almost half of all Catholic priests signed petitions against a draft Soviet constitution in 1977. 'We need to unite currents of thought which regard Catholicism as the key to national salvation, with those prepared to accept a nationalistically inclined atheism', commented another *samizdat* title in 1978. 'No other force in today's world can help Lithuanians remain Lithuanian as much as religion.'[25]

With signs multiplying that communism was unable to recharge itself with new recruits and ideas, Karol Wojtyła was not the only Church leader to conclude that the Vatican's diplomatic antics appeared to take accommodation a bit far. Eastern Europe's Church leaders expected to be consulted. Instead, they found themselves treated to occasional terse communiqués noting that, over their heads, regime and Vatican negotiators had discussed 'problems of mutual interest'.

Rumours spread about political pressures exerted on the Pope directly. Paul VI's first encyclical, *Ecclesiam Suam*, had restated the Church's condemnation of 'atheistic communism'. But while *Populorum progressio* in 1967 had gone much further in defining the Church's duty to combat human wretchedness, it had said absolutely nothing about communism. *Octogesima adveniens*, Paul VI's 1971 letter to Cardinal Roy, had adopted a different tone. It denounced both liberal and communist ideologies, and stressed contemporary mankind's twin aspirations to 'equality and participation'. It referred to Eastern Europe, condemning attempts to impose 'a dictatorship over minds, the worst kind of all', and noting that there were places where Christians were 'enclosed without freedom in a totalitarian system'.[26]

But some East Europeans detected a kind of half-heartedness. The letter assumed a parity between 'bureaucratic socialism, technocratic capitalism and authoritarian democracy'. It was high-brow and theoretical, and failed to explain its terms and concepts.

Much the same was true of *Evangelii nuntiandi*, issued at the highpoint of

East–West *détente*. This took up the themes of 'justice, liberation, development and peace'. It also recalled Henri de Lubac's warning about 'the drama of atheistic humanism'; but those looking for a comparable reflection on communism found no mention of it. When it came to suggesting how to 'nourish and support' those threatened by secularism and atheism, all Paul VI had to offer was 'catechetical instruction ... in language adapted to the times and the hearers'. The exhortation was full of questions the Pope seemed reluctant to answer.

> To proclaim the gospel. What meaning did Christ attach to this mandate which had been given to him? It is not possible to state in brief and precise terms what exactly this evangelization is, what elements it comprises, by what means it may be accomplished, how Christ understood it, and how he put it into effect. It is not possible to achieve an adequate synthesis.[27]

Was the Vatican misinformed? This might have been the case with Catholic communities further afield—in Moldavia or Georgia, Siberia or Kazakhstan. But it could hardly be said of Lithuania, Ukraine or the rest of Eastern Europe. As for Poland, there were grounds for doubting whether Paul VI harboured much sympathy for the country. After his short spell in Warsaw in 1923, the then Giovanni Battista Montini had written of a country 'plagued by conflicts, plots, power-struggles, abuses, betrayals', characterized by 'distorted patriotism' and 'excessive nationalism'. The Pope's abortive plans to visit Jasna Góra in 1966 had impressed Polish Catholics. During Casaroli's first fact-finding visit a year later, however, his Church hosts had found him impatient. 'I had the impression that the issues causing most concern, which I myself considered most fundamental, were of no concern to him', one of his Polish interlocutors testified.[28]

Bishop Ignacy Tokarczuk of Przemyśl was one Church leader who had opted not to yield to communist restrictions. In the 1960s, to meet popular needs, he had begun building simple 'framehouse' churches illegally around in his southeastern diocese. By 1978, the year of Paul VI's death, the Bishops' Conference found itself under Vatican pressure to curb Tokarczuk's activities. Twice summoned to Rome, the bishop was warned he was 'impeding Vatican policy towards the East'.

> If I had not known clearly what truth is, what belongs to God and what to the Pope's authority, I would have resigned. But I was certain I was acting rightly ... I emphasized that I was not looking for trouble or applause—in reality, it was all costing me dearly. If I was acting incorrectly, they could dismiss me and I would not complain. But I would not change my views, which resulted from deep reflection and a practical knowledge of communism, rather than theoretical considerations.[29]

A Vatican official later apologized to Tokarczuk. It was only one of many cases in which Rome's diplomats had been proved wrong.

It was in the Polish Church's vital interests to ensure its leaders were never sidelined. When bishops were finally nominated for the 'Recovered Territories' in 1972, Wyszyński made the most of his own role in the long-running saga, insisting the breakthrough proved the Vatican's trust in local Church decisions.[30] But if it came to it, Wyszyński knew he had to be able to block unfavourable Vatican–regime deals. In November 1973, after spending an hour discussing 'peace and disarmament' with Paul VI, the Polish Foreign Minister, Stefan Olszowski, invited Casaroli to reopen talks. Wyszyński and his bishops welcomed the move as a positive step towards Church–State 'normalization'. But it would only have 'full meaning', they made clear, if religious freedom was respected.[31]

That precondition—guaranteed Church rights before any Vatican–regime accord—was hammered home repeatedly. When Casaroli paid his visit in February 1974 Wyszyński clarified local misgivings in a long Warsaw cathedral homily. Rome had to engage in talks with the Polish State, he acknowledged. After all, the State had led the nation to great achievements, such as at the battles of Grunwald (1410) and Vienna (1685). But the Church's bonds with the nation were 'more permanent, like a family'. And today, it was important to identify which values the Church was giving to the nation: 'faith, love, justice, peace, a spirit of mutual service'. Wyszyński continued with a touch of irony:

> During 25 years as Primate, I have had the chance the talk with three Popes serving the Church—Pius XII, John XXIII and Paul VI. And I must say I always found full understanding and support. But not everything could be done immediately. It has required time, exceptional patience ... When a fisherman sails on a calm sea, he can see to the bottom and spot every fish. But when the sea is disturbed, he sees nothing. To see the issues and tasks facing nation, Church and State, to assess them properly and confront them, needs preliminary calm, balance and patience.[32]

The sermon was addressed to Casaroli and preached in Italian. A month later the position was stated bluntly by the full Bishops' Conference. The Polish Church supported Vatican–regime talks, it insisted; but there were conditions. One was that the talks should be 'correct, frank and systematic', another that 'no decisions will be taken without participation by the Episcopate of Poland'. The bishops appealed to Vatican II. 'Within the framework of Council collegiality, direct responsibility for the Church in Poland is held by the bishops who make up the Bishops' Conference under the Primate's leadership.'[33]

Undeterred, Casaroli went ahead and established 'permanent working contacts' with the government under a July protocol. Henceforth, Vatican negotiators would be free to visit 'at any appropriate time'.[34] The bishops were assured no deals would be cut without consultation, but their misgivings were not allowed to affect the continuation of talks.

Predictably, the year witnessed a new offensive by the regime. 'The main organized anti-socialist power in our country, a veritable centre uniting all anti-State currents while at the same time representing their last hope, is the reactionary wing of the Episcopate', a Politburo member, Jan Szydlak, declared at a Warsaw meeting.[35] At the Rome Synod in October 1974 Wyszyński made clear this was not a time for compromising with communism. The Vatican should imbue its work in Eastern Europe with an 'unambiguous Christian courage', he said; 'diplomacy must not obstruct the spreading of the Gospel'. In Poland at least, the Church was strong through its own resources. If diplomatic deals were needed, it was only as 'tiles on the roof of a building that grows from its own foundations'.[36]

None of this went down well in Rome. In August 1976, when Wyszyński was obliged to offer his resignation after turning 75, the Secretary of State, Cardinal Jean Villot, persuaded the Pope to extend his office by three years only. This was not because of any lack of confidence, Paul VI assured Wyszyński; it was only to assure the Polish Church's future, since the Primate would not always be there. 'I may not', was Wyszyński's retort, 'but Our Lady of Częstochowa always will be.'[37]

Villot's reasons for wanting Wyszyński out had the air of a pretext. 'Cardinal Wyszyński's theory is as follows: the situation in Poland is fragile and the regime is divided against itself', he explained three months later.

> The Holy See is aware of the Cardinal's immense services to the Church in Poland. But it believes there has also been an abuse of authority in the nomination of bishops (they have been named in Warsaw before Rome), as well as in the transfer and dismissal of religious superiors, etc. The situation is abnormal. If a national Church exists anywhere, it is there in Poland.[38]

Complaints about Vatican diplomacy were heard virtually everywhere. Cardinal Mindszenty had presented his arguments to Paul VI why the Church should never make 'conciliatory gestures' in expectation of regime concessions. Russia's Orthodox Church offered an example: it had been persecuted as much in periods of coexistence as in periods of subjugation. Hungary's communists had made propaganda capital out of the Vatican's 'spectacular negotiations'; but the 'sole result', Mindszenty insisted, had been the appointment of bishops selected by the State Office for Church Affairs. Their activities had been 'profoundly detrimental to ecclesiastical discipline'.[39]

Mindszenty had made his point. Other East European Church leaders had thrown doubt on Vatican assumptions too. In 1966, a visiting Vatican official, Mgr Giovanni Cheli, had struck a straight bargain with Romania's rulers: Joseph Schubert, an uncompromised prison veteran, to be named Archbishop of Bucharest, and a collaborator, Franz Augustin, to be appointed his vicar-general. Schubert, just amnestied from a 1951 death sentence, refused point-blank. The president of the Vatican's Secretariat for Unbelievers, Cardinal König, visited Bucharest a year later at the invitation of Patriarch Justinian. Anti-Orthodox excesses were continuing, and a large proportion of Justinian's 10,000 priests were in prison. So König stuck to diplomacy. No public mention was made of the banned Greek Catholics who had been in jails and camps for two decades.[40] When Ceauşescu visited Rome in 1973, five surviving Greek Catholic bishops demanded his regime lift the 1948 prohibition of their Church, citing the Universal Declaration on Human Rights and Romania's own constitution. But when Mgr Poggi reopened talks in 1975 the subject was again avoided. It took three years for Vatican and Romanian negotiators to agree on the appointment of a single Latin Catholic bishop.

In Czechoslovakia, the consecration of four Pacem in Terris collaborators under Casaroli's 1972 agreement was resented by many Catholics. Certainly, an episcopal structure was needed. But were bishops of such doubtful calibre not a liability rather than an asset? Did they not actually hasten the Church's dissolution by sowing scandal and confusion? One of the four, Josef Vrána of Olomouc, had been appointed only provisionally—*ad nutum Santae Sedis*—on condition that he renounce Pacem in Terris. Vrána ignored the proviso but was allowed to stay on anyway. There was no let-up in the Husák regime's anti-Catholic campaign. A mere quarter-century of communist rule had reduced Czechoslovakia's Catholic clergy by 60 per cent.[41] When Vatican–government negotiations reopened in 1975 no information was made available. Why, many asked, did the Vatican not extract a higher price—at least by publicly condemning acts of persecution?

The urge to protest against Vatican 'betrayals' had been a key motive for Lithuania's underground *Chronicle*. Its editors studied the situation in other Soviet republics too, and argued convincingly that the Church's best hope lay not in accommodation but in resistance. Soviet promises of dialogue were an illusion, the *Chronicle* warned; only loud shouts and recriminations would have any impact on Soviet actions. The Vatican's current solution—to appoint appeasing bishops—was a mistake. It would only hasten the Church's destruction from within. As the *Chronicle* insisted,

> The future of Catholicism in Lithuania depends not on the number of bishops or administrators, but on pastoral work by dedicated priests. No concessions

can be expected from the atheists through bargaining—Lithuania's Catholics will have just as much freedom as they win for themselves.[42]

The journal urged the Vatican to publish prospective bishops' names at least six months in advance to allow Church members to give their opinions. In the mid-1970s, with the Mindszenty precedent to hand, the Vatican came under Soviet pressure to replace Bishops Steponavičius and Sladkevičius, who had spent almost two decades in internal exile. The *Chronicle* reacted swiftly. Both bishops, it warned, were uncompromised and enjoyed public respect. For them to be 'pushed aside' would 'psychologically disarm' Lithuania's most devoted priests, and deal 'an irreparable blow to the Catholic Church and Vatican'.

Rome backed down, and Steponavičius and Sladkevičius remained canonically in office. But the *Chronicle*'s warnings continued. Many Catholics were convinced the Vatican was being fed false information. 'We believe the Apostolic See's diplomatic activity is based on a sincere desire to help the persecuted Church', one group wrote to Cardinal Bengsch in August 1975, 'yet because of ignorance of the true circumstances, it may in some instances be serving atheist interests.'[43]

Emigré Ukrainian Greek Catholics had urged the Pope since the early 1960s to raise the exiled Cardinal Slipyi to the dignity of 'Patriarch', and thus give him jurisdiction over Church members worldwide. Rome hung back. Giving Slipyi special status would be seen as a provocation by the Soviet government and Russian Orthodox Church. There were rumours that a deal had been struck against any such step when Slipyi had been released in 1963.

In 1969 Slipyi broke a self-imposed silence and sent a letter describing his Church's plight to Catholic bishops around the world. There was no reaction in Rome. In 1976 the Russian Orthodox Church celebrated the thirtieth anniversary of the Ukrainian Church's suppression. Again there was no response. 'The Holy See follows a very prudent line of action', the Pope told Slipyi that December, 'and this is—as you well know—in the Ukrainian Church's best interest.'[44] The exiled Cardinal claimed to have seen 'secret documentation' detailing Rome's contacts with the Moscow Patriarchate. They were, he added, 'a death sentence for our Ukrainian Church', and proof that 'our constant warnings and humble arguments' had been ignored.[45]

By the late 1970s, more Church leaders were making common cause with Eastern Europe's human rights groups. Poland's Catholic Bishops' Conference had implicitly backed protests against the amendments to the constitution in 1975. 'Let no one think the bishops embarked on a struggle against the system', Cardinal Wyszyński declared. 'No, they only recalled the rights of man, of the family and of citizens in their own country. These are the only objectives that guide us.'[46]

Many priests and bishops concurred with Poland's communist regime in distrusting the KOR opposition group. Besides former communists, its members were believed to include 'Jews and freemasons' who might, in the words of one bishop, prove 'much crueller towards the Church than those governing today'.[47] Publicly, however, the Bishops' Conference agreed with KOR's demand that strikers sacked and jailed after the Radom and Warsaw protests should be reinstated. Wyszyński raised no objection when a group of KOR activists went on hunger-strike at a Warsaw church in May 1977. A large Gospel text, displayed above the altar, ended with the Polish abbreviation for St Paul's Letter to the Corinthians—KOR.

The threat of some kind of Church–opposition alliance helped explain why Gierek's regime became more conciliatory. On his 75th birthday Wyszyński was sent roses by the premier, Piotr Jaroszewicz. Having for long been Public Enemy No. 1, the Cardinal found himself cast increasingly as social arbiter and elder statesman. Successive crises had strengthened the Church's role as an alternative system of authority. Its capacity to influence society also empowered it to make demands. This gave the Church its window of opportunity. In a September 1976 pastoral letter the bishops called on Poles to 'make sacrifices' for the good of the country. The following June, however, they marked Media Day by denouncing the 'godless ideology' disseminated in the communist-controlled press. A million people signed a petition demanding greater Church access to radio and TV.

When Gierek met Paul VI in December 1977 in a bid to boost his flagging rule, the Polish Church downplayed the occasion. Meeting Wyszyński two months earlier, the Party leader had come up with little more than a grudging offer of more permits for church-building. If the Rome visit was Gierek's latest attempt to outflank Wyszyński and his bishops, he was wasting his time. The era had passed when such gambits might have weakened the Church's home position.

In Czechoslovakia, the Church hierarchy's subservience was being countered by Christian grassroots opposition. Twelve Catholic priests and fifteen Protestant pastors signed Charter 77. 'It does not speak about God or God's kingdom', a group of clergy signatories explained, 'but Charter 77 is fighting for freedom in religious matters, and in this way serving God's purposes. In this we glimpse the future universality of Christ's kingdom.'[48]

That was not how the country's few surviving bishops saw the Charter. Tomášek in Prague was destined to spring some surprises in the years ahead.

But in a statement in January 1977, published in the Pacem in Terris weekly *Katolické noviny*, he distanced the bishops from it, citing biblical injunctions and warning its Catholic signatories against claiming to represent the Church. There were doubts about the statement's authenticity; but no one had expected the weak, confused 76-year-old to react any differently. In an act of petty vindictiveness, Tomášek even ordered the now-ageing reform communist Milan Machovec, purged from his university post after 1968, to be stripped of his job as a church organist. Under regime duress, other confessions issued similar declarations against the Charter.

Despite everything, Tomášek was the only bishop not seriously compromised by collaboration—and the only possible hope if the Church's authority was to be brought to be bear in defence of human rights. It was a Jesuit Charter 77 signatory, Josef Zvěřina, a veteran of Nazi and communist prisons, who took up the task of prodding Tomášek in the right direction. Zvěřina had spent 30 years working out his own theology of persecution and forgiveness. He made short work of Tomášek's half-baked biblical references.

> Your statement was not inspired by the Gospel, but by the needs of shameful propaganda, by a hysterical witch-hunt against those who dared demand that the laws be kept ... The Gospel spirit requires that the Church stand up for the despised and rejected, persecuted and defenceless, poor and slandered. So why are we taking sides with the powerful, those who despise and slander others? ... You have taken a position against the wishes of fellow-believers and others who long for justice. You have brought Pope Paul VI and Catholic opinion into disrepute and weakened world opinion ... How degrading it is that we have to defend religious freedom—irrespective of denomination—not only against the State but even against our own bishops![49]

In neighbouring Hungary, the Church at least had a passable infra-structure. Its eight dioceses had bishops most of the time while its six seminaries and eight schools were turning out recruits for a 4,000-strong priesthood. 'We respect the believer's feelings. We do not attack him since this is not necessary', Kádár explained in 1974. 'In return, we propagate our own conception of the world and do not permit it to be denigrated or attacked.'[50] That summed up the basic principle—protection for subser-vience—guiding Church–State relations since the 1950s.

Yet there was another side to the coin. Vatican diplomacy had failed to improve conditions for Hungarian Christians. Although priests were rarely arrested now, 90 per cent had been co-opted into the communist-controlled Opus Pacis association. Church attendance had fallen drastically and demoralization was rife. While accepting religion as a 'natural phenomenon' during the evolution to a communist society, the Hungarian government's

Church affairs director, Imre Miklós, insisted the regime had 'absolutely not abandoned' its struggle against it.[51]

Cardinal Lékai, who had taken over Mindszenty's see of Esztergom in 1976, nevertheless lauded the Vatican's policies.

> We fully agree with our Marxist compatriots that basic ideological differences cannot be the object of trading. But I cannot render sufficient thanks and praise for the realist policy of the Holy See, for the great efforts by which it has put an end to our severe internal disputes, brought calm to the soul of priests and faithful, and helped us serve our faith and homeland harmoniously.[52]

Lékai had set a questionable example. As Mindszenty's one-time secretary, he had seemed a natural choice as successor. But his weaknesses were known. 'Please don't report to us every detail of your life, where you go, who you meet, etc., as your predecessor did', the local Party boss had told the new priest at a Lake Balaton village when he replaced Lékai in 1956. A group of Catholics remembered visiting the Primate at Esztergom and asking him to speak up for a man who had been jailed for refusing military service. 'Lékai telephoned Casaroli at once. He was told force and violence are different, that armed forces are necessary': the group's request was politely declined.[53]

Vatican diplomacy failed to overcome the impasse in other countries too. In Bulgaria Todor Zhivkov's 1975 Rome visit helped secure two new bishops, but had no effect on the surveillance and harassment of religious activities. By 1978, Bulgaria was home to just 40 Catholic priests, compared to 127 in 1945.

A new constitution in Yugoslavia in 1974 reaffirmed Church–State separation, but Church leaders continued to complain of State interference. A Croatian law in 1978 said religious activities should not be 'in contradiction' with the State's 'ideology, constitution and laws'. Since the previous law of 1953 had required them to be 'in conformity', that was a step forward. But had such abstract refinements on paper really justified Casaroli's years of bargaining and compromising?

By 1978, Church life in Eastern Europe had acquired its own dynamic, as restraints on official Church structures were matched by a spread of unofficial activities. In Romania 500 Greek Catholic priests were dispensing the sacraments in secret, while Hungary's base communities and renewal groups had at least 50,000 members. It had taken determination to see that the Christian faith had many ways of reasserting itself. But underground Christian groups were expanding in the Soviet Union too. In Ukraine at least three Greek Catholic bishops and 350 priests were by 1978 working secretly for what Soviet propagandists branded the 'bourgeois national Church'. In

Lithuania several Catholic priests joined an unofficial Helsinki Monitoring Group in 1975. In 1978 at least a thousand Catholic nuns were believed secretly active. Despite their collaboration, Lithuania's bishops never actually condemned the *Chronicle of the Catholic Church*, which continued to provide a unique record of arrests and protests. The picture emerging from its pages— of highly active priests and lay Catholics defying Soviet restrictions—was quite unlike the image presented in Rome of a battered Church driven by persecution into bowing before communist diktats.

A decade later Soviet officials would call this the era of stagnation. All communist regimes had given priority to economic expansion; but from the mid-1970s growth was slowing, generating pressure for reform. Having been criticized by Rome in the 1950s for seeking 'agreements with communists', Poland's Cardinal Wyszyński had been criticized in the 1970s for impeding them. But in Poland at least agreements seemed unnecessary. Although the post-1968 Brezhnev Doctrine enshrined Poland's geopolitical position, the once-isolated opposition had proliferated and was showing tactical sophistication. Dissidents talked of a 'self-organizing society', of breaking the State's monopoly on information.

Meanwhile smuggled Western books provided the first comprehensive critique of communism. The most important, *Main Currents of Marxism*, was published in Paris in 1976. Its author, the former Stalinist Kołakowski, seemed to have resolved his generation's dilemmas with moral conviction and intellectual rigour. Kołakowski had attacked Marxism from within, just as he had once attacked Christianity from without. Possibly, this radical critique should have been provided by Christians themselves; but their voices would never have had the power of persuasion of an experienced internal witness. Purged of previous affiliations, Kołakowski now stood close to a metaphysical view of the world. But he also had the authority to show how religious people could benefit from an ex-Marxist's insights.

In *Evangelii nuntiandi*. Paul VI had warned against a 'well-intentioned but certainly misguided' tendency to 'love Christ but without the Church'.[54] Yet something like this had stirred among many former communists who had made efforts to overcome the atheism instilled into them in youth, without as yet crossing the threshold of the Church.

Research data in 1978 suggested religiousness was growing among Poland's traditionally secularized groups, as forms of identity and tradition with a stronger integrative capacity than communist culture were reasserted. As in all communist countries, the absence of mediating institutions between State and society had strengthened local group loyalties. However, in Poland, they were defined less by region and class than by ethos and religious belief. This was where the Polish Church's growing social power lay.

The time had come, argued *Więż*'s co-editor, Tadeusz Mazowiecki, for Christians to stand up for legitimate freedoms.

We cannot forget or fail to criticize the Church's relationship with the forces which generated the formula of human rights in modern times. At certain times in history, human freedom was asserted against Christianity, making the Church treat liberating tendencies as a sign of rebellion against religion and God ... But today, a crucial change appears to be occurring: a shift from the defence of Church and religion to the defence of human rights.[55]

The case of Kołakowski had attracted the interest of Karol Wojtyła, now Cardinal Archbishop of Kraków. In 1976 Wojtyła's closeness to Paul VI had been rewarded by an invitation to lead the Vatican's Holy Week meditations. He now had a unique opportunity to explain how Christianity had withstood communist pressures.

Theorists of atheism, both East and West, maintained that God had died in human thinking, Wojtyła explained, thanks to the triumph of 'horizontal' sources of knowledge over the 'vertical'. But God was still present. He remembered talking to a Red Army soldier who had knocked on the door of the Kraków seminary in 1945 and asked to join. The soldier knew nothing about the Church, and had come purely on instinct. This spiritual instinct was what the communist system tried to destroy, Wojtyła said. Even the Devil, the father of lies, acknowledged God's power; but Marxism denied God's very existence and offered a 'full affirmation of man' instead. Therein lay the temptation of believing man was capable of building a perfect world. Communism had helped the modern world rediscover a sense of sin and evil. In this way, it had inadvertently strengthened Christianity by making it more aware of what threatened it.

Kołakowski's odyssey was particularly instructive here. The former ideologist had shown it was possible to liberate oneself from a false philosophy. He had come to see Christ as the source of an 'authentic radicalism'. 'Kołakowski bases his position on the notion that, regardless of religion and the Church, certain values and ideas exist independently within universal culture solely and exclusively thanks to Christ', Wojtyła explained. 'This is why he calls for Christ's return to culture.'[56]

What were these 'values and ideas'? Dialogue was needed to identify them definitively, but they certainly included personal conscience—the 'spiritual centre of humanity'.

The references to Kołakowski caused surprise. Most Church leaders distrusted communists who claimed to have seen the light; but Wojtyła had acknowledged Kołakowski's reasoning that it was possible to embrace Christianity without accepting the Church's dogmas.

Wojtyła claimed to be 'very satisfied' with his Rome meditations.[57] The experience had strengthened his self-confidence in Poland. When a Student Solidarity Committee (SKS) was formed in 1977 after the murder of a philosophy student, Wojtyła allowed Kraków's Catholic youth pastorate to support it. The killing of Stanisław Pijas, a KOR co-operator, was blamed on Kraków's secret police. Besides saying a special Mass for him, Wojtyła assigned the SKS a special chaplain. He also allowed it to meet in local churches, thereby guaranteeing its safety. That response—'planting a row of trees for each tree cut down'—had become characteristic.

In the winter of 1974–75 Wojtyła had held a long meeting with KOR's co-founder, Jacek Kuroń, the former activist expelled from the Party for his 1964 'Open Letter'. Though they had talked about intellectuals and the 'new ideas' they were bringing to the Church, Wojtyła had been particularly interested in the situation of Polish workers. The Church, he told Kuroń, was 'not only teaching, but being taught'. A 'great personalist revolution' was occurring daily in its ranks, thanks to the workers who were 'reclaiming it for themselves' and 'leading it with them into a struggle for social justice'.[58]

Kuroń says he came away 'illuminated' and reassured by Wojtyła's promise that the Church would never put regime concessions before the defence of human rights. This was Kuroń's version, but it squared with the facts. Opposition discussions in Kraków concentrated on counter-culture, and were less overtly political than Warsaw's, but Wojtyła was seen as a link between Christian and ex-Marxist dissidents. He was 'very well informed' about underground *samizdat* publishing. At some point, he met most of KOR's leading members.

The Gierek regime was aware of this. It was notified when the Cardinal travelled to Warsaw in plain clothes at the end of 1976 to meet Kuroń, the nationalist Antoni Macierewicz and KOR's socialist mastermind, Jan Józef Lipski. The meeting, hosted by the historian Bohdan Cywiński, covered 'moral and political issues'. Another KOR ex-Marxist, Adam Michnik, was arrested before he could follow up an invitation to meet Wojtyła; but he remembered him as 'warm and sympathetic' at a time when KOR was still avoided by most Polish clergy. Unlike the imperious Wyszyński, he 'used our language and talked clearly about human rights', Michnik recalled. 'He never actually declared himself for KOR, but we knew we could count on his sympathy ... In these years, Cardinal Wojtyła became a factor which brought us close to the Church.'[59]

When in Warsaw, Wojtyła often visited the Franciscan centre at Laski, which doubled as an unofficial retreat centre for the capital's dissidents. This was where Michnik had written his book about Poland's 'lay Left'. Wojtyła's personal confessor, Fr Tadeusz Fedorowicz, was Laski's chaplain. KOR's priest-signatory, Fr Jan Zieja, was also linked to the centre.

Wojtyła's openness to dialogue attracted like-minded Church leaders from abroad. Rare visitors to Kraków in the 1970s included Cardinal Gabriel-Marie Garrone of Toulouse, a man who had called Marxism 'a philosophical system needing far-reaching interpretation' at Vatican II. Another was the Croatian Cardinal Šeper, now Prefect of the Vatican's Congregation for the Doctrine of Faith, who had blamed communism and socialism on the 'egotism of Christians'.

Wojtyła had begun to reach out to Eastern Europe too. Like Bishop Tokarczuk of Przemyśl he was suspected of helping underground priests from neighbouring countries. The Czech regime made him sit with the congregation during Cardinal Trochta's funeral at Litoměřice in 1974. Wojtyła met Bishop Tomášek again that October, this time over dinner with Paul VI in Rome. The timid Prague bishop was put between Wojtyła and Wyszyński: for three hours he was grilled by the two Poles about his lack of firmness.

A Rome Synod on Catechization in 1977 gave Wojtyła more contacts. His diary included discussion meetings with bishops from the Baltic republics and Croatia, as well as a lunch with Casaroli, his Nuncio for Eastern Europe, Archbishop Luigi Poggi, and Bulgaria's Greek Catholic exarch, Metody Stratiev.

The 1974 paper for the Polish Pastoral Commission, written under Wojtyła's auspices, had assessed the view, common among Western and Third World Church leaders, that the Marxist system eradicated exploitation by destroying capitalism. In reality, through its 'totalitarian bureaucracy', communism itself became 'a kind of State capitalism', the paper pointed out. The position of the working man was dominated by the same 'capitalist spirit of exploitation'. As sole property owner, the State followed the same 'methods of capitalist production'. Leo XIII's remark in *Rerum novarum* about the medicine being more dangerous than the disease was still the best riposte to the naivety of Western Marxists. The report continued:

> It seems that the illusions surrounding Marxism are still stronger than sober consciousness of its reality. If it is right that the Church should participate in liberating the human person from unjust social and economic structures linked to the capitalist system, it is no less a necessity to liberate the person from the structures of the Marxist system. In these structures, the person is caught even more severely.[60]

By the late 1970s, Wojtyła's exchanges with ex-Marxists from Poland's 'democratic opposition' had given him a clearer grasp of how the Church could accomplish this. But it was important to make prudent distinctions. On the one hand, there was atheism as a programme, the official 'State religion'. It denied the human person's dignity and freedom, and was thus a human rights issue, a totally unacceptable violation of personal conscience. On the other, there were atheists as people. They were open to salvation, a challenging field of mission.

In several homilies, Wojtyła recounted his conversation with a top Polish communist.

> He talked about the desire which exists in a person to prolong life beyond the limits of mortality, and the feeling of unfulfilment that life exists only between the frontiers of birth and death. This desire, he said, is an internal truth about Man. Thus, we spoke with great mutual respect for our world-views and confessions.[61]

Being an unbeliever did not mean being an enemy of God, Wojtyła emphasized. Belief could be supremely difficult, the cause of great personal drama. The Church was sometimes 'powerless' to persuade the unbeliever to change his mind.

This was why Wojtyła had gone on studying the idea of dialogue and writing about Marxist philosophy.

The concept of 'alienation' was particularly important. It did not originate with Marxism. St John of the Cross, Wojtyła's one-time spiritual mentor, had spoken of the 'dark night of the soul' needed to overcome the person's alienation from God, whereas Marx had talked about the person's alienation from his labour. But both concurred that some form of conflict was a legitimate human response. In 1974, Wojtyła acted as assessor for a doctoral thesis on 'The theory of alienation in Polish Marxism'. A year later, he gave the title 'Participation and alienation' to his paper for a conference in Fribourg.

The paper defined alienation as 'everything which deprives a person of the possibility of fulfilment'. It detailed how the concept had developed in nineteenth-century Marxism, but it also showed how alienation was rooted in 'individualism'. Although linked with imperfections in the social, economic, political system, Wojtyła wrote, alienation could only be overcome fully with 'personalistic' criteria—in particular, by 'discovering an authentic sense of participation'.

In *The Acting Person* Wojtyła had attacked the work of Poland's foremost Marxist thinker, Adam Schaff. But he now admitted Schaff was right about one thing: in communist societies too 'some forms of alienation have not been overcome, and new ones may even be emerging'.[62]

Wojtyła took his reapplication of Marxist concepts a stage further at

Genoa in 1976. His title this time was 'Theory-praxis: a human and Christian topic'. The paper was weighty and jargonistic. But it revealed an extensive knowledge of contemporary Marxist writers from Roger Garaudy onwards.

In Marxism the human being becomes a person through praxis, or revolutionary action, Wojtyła pointed out. Since this made praxis the 'fundamental factor in changing the world', it also made it 'an issue predominantly of anthropology and ethics'. So it could be used by Christians too, in the form of a 'praxis of the Cross'. The 'openness of human praxis towards God' allowed each person to find himself 'within the full dimension of transcendence, existing at a deep level of the person's personal structure'.[63]

The paper made clear that Wojtyła was still building his own philosophy in the form of a polemic with Marxism—reinterpreting its concepts for a new Christian vision. What kind of vision would it be? Wojtyła had stressed the importance of culture in his speech to the 1971 Rome Synod. By 1978, he had begun to speak more dramatically of 'freedom through culture'. The Polish Church was confronted with an ideology whose 'sources and inspirations' were deeply atheistic, Wojtyła told a bishops' commission. Polish cultural traditions were predominantly Christian; so the 'official model' claimed the right to revise the heritage of Polish culture. But it faced growing resistance from a 'cultural underground', which had come to revolve increasingly around 'religious questions'. It was the Church's mission to provide patronage for this cultural underground, which had become 'the only means by which society can protect its authentic heritage'.[64]

The Church's mission, however, could not be conducted only 'in a confessional way', Wojtyła added. It had to provide a meeting-point between Christianity and other 'humanistic forms of inspiration' which were similarly denied an official outlet.[65]

As the nineteenth-century Polish poet Cyprian Norwid had written, to foster patriotism it was necessary to begin at a personal level—not only with the great evocations of Catholic nationhood associated with Wyszyński, but also by working through individual people as the myriad building blocks of a future society. This was not a political programme. It was merely a question of clarifying values, reasserting truths, creating an alternative sense of community. But it contained within it, just the same, the seeds of liberation.

By 1978, Wojtyła had become the main theorist of Poland's Bishops' Conference, the one who drafted its statements on all complex subjects. He was working on two—sovereignty and ecology—when he was summoned to Rome to elect a new Pope.

Notes

1. See Jonathan Luxmoore and Jolanta Babiuch, 'The search of faith: the metaphysical dialogue between Poland's opposition intellectuals in the 1970s', *Religion, State and Society*, vol. 23, no. 1 (1996), p. 77.
2. 'Referat Urzędu do Spraw Wyznań' (undated 1961); in Peter Raina (ed.), *Kościół w PRL—Dokumenty 1960–1974* (Poznań: W Drodze, 1995), pp. 62–4.
3. *Communio et progressio* (29 January 1971), no. 122.
4. Social research put the overall proportion of practising Christians at 80–90 per cent, while the figure for students was to rise again to 72 per cent in the 1970s. Figures from Zdzisława Walaszek, 'Religion and politics: the Roman Catholic Church in Communist Poland', unpublished University of Chicago paper (1986).
5. Leszek Kołakowski, *Kultura i fetysze* (Warsaw: Państwowe Wydawnictwo Naukowe, 1967).
6. Kraków homily (31 December 1970); in Adam Boniecki (ed.), *Kalendarium życia Karola Wojtyły* (Kraków: Znak, 1983), p. 393.
7. Poznań homily (18 November 1971); ibid., p. 432.
8. 'Przemówienie' (29 September 1972); in *Duszpasterski Synod Archidiecezji Krakowskiej*, vol. 2 (Kraków: Kuria Metropolitalna, 1985), p. 63.
9. Karol Wojtyła, *U podstaw odnowy: studium o realizacji Vaticanum II* (Kraków: Polskie Towarzystwo Teologiczne, 1972), p. 7.
10. Dionizy Tanalski, *Bóg, człowiek i polityka: Człowiek w teorii Jana Pawła II* (Warsaw: Książka i Wiedza, 1986), p. 32.
11. Tadeusz Pieronek and Roman Zawadzki (eds), *Karol Wojtyła jako Biskup Krakowski* (Kraków: Papieska Akademia Teologiczna, 1988), pp. 318–19, 340.
12. Address to Curia symposium (6 December 1972); in Boniecki, op. cit., p. 472.
13. Address at Dominican church (16 May 1974); ibid., pp. 582–3.
14. Conference at Papal Institute, Rome (23 October 1974); ibid., p. 606; homily in St Anna's church (10 December 1974); ibid., p. 614.
15. 'Pro Memoria Episkopatu Polski o sytuacji Kościoła'; in Raina, op. cit., p. 683.
16. Ibid., pp. 686–7.
17. Pieronek and Zawadzki, op. cit., p. 282; Karol Wojtyła, *Aby Chrystus się nami posługiwał* (Kraków: Znak, 1979), p. 125.
18. Address to priests (7 June 1976); in Boniecki, op. cit., p. 702.
19. Adam Michnik, *Kościół, Lewica, Dialog* (Paris: Instytut Literacki, 1977), pp. 13–16.
20. Bohdan Cywiński, *Rodowody niepokornych* (Warsaw: Biblioteka Więzi, 1971), pp. 8–11, 53–6.
21. Jan Patočka, 'La Charte 77: ce qu'elle est et ce qu'elle n'est pas', *Cahiers de l'Est*, nos 9–10 (1977), p. 167; E. Kozak, *Jan Patočka: Philosophy and Selected Writings* (Chicago: University of Chicago Press, 1989).
22. Zdeněk Mlynář, 'Exkomunisté a křestané v Chartě 77', *Studie*, vol. 6, no. 60 (1978), pp. 420–1; Jonathan Luxmoore and Jolanta Babiuch, 'In search of faith,

Part 2: Charter 77 and the return to spiritual values in the Czech Republic', *Religion, State and Society*, vol. 23, no. 3 (1995), pp. 291–304.

23. György Lukács, interview in József Ijjas et al., *Ensemble pour une bonne cause: L'État socialiste et les Églises en Hongrie* (Budapest: Corvina, 1978); Ferenc Fehér, 'The language of resistance' in Raymond Taras (ed.), *The Road to Disillusion* (New York: M. E. Sharpe Inc., 1992), p. 43.

24. *Evangelii nuntiandi* (8 December 1975), no. 58.

25. *Aušrele*, no. 1 (*samizdat*: 16 February 1978).

26. *Octogesima adveniens* (14 May 1971), nos 3, 25.

27. *Evangelii nuntiandi*, no. 7.

28. Stefan Swieżawski, *Owoce życia 1966–1988* (Lublin: Redakcja Wydawnictw KUL, 1993), pp. 19–20; Peter Hebblethwaite, *Paul VI: The First Modern Pope* (London: HarperCollins, 1993), pp. 77–8.

29. *Gazeta Wyborcza* (4 May 1996).

30. 'Komunikat konferencji plenarnej Episkopatu Polski' (28 June 1972); in Raina, op. cit., pp. 594–6.

31. 'Komunikat o sytuacji Kościoła' (25 January 1974); ibid., pp. 640–1; *Trybuna Ludu* (13 November 1973).

32. 'Przemówienie Prymasa Kard. S. Wyszyńskiego' (7 February 1974); in Raina, op. cit., p. 649.

33. 'Komunikat konferencji plenarnej' (29 March 1974), ibid., p. 653.

34. 'Protokół podpisany przez abp. A. Casarolego' (6 July 1974); ibid., p. 663.

35. Quoted in Dennis Dunn, *Détente in Papal–Communist Relations* (Boulder: Westview, 1979), p. 115.

36. Hansjakob Stehle, *Eastern Politics of the Vatican 1917–1979* (London: Ohio University Press, 1981), pp. 352, 354.

37. Antoine Wenger, 'La Politique Orientale du Saint-Siège' in Joël-Benoît d'Onorio (ed.), *Le Saint-Siège dans les relations internationales* (Paris: Éditions du Cerf, 1989), p. 182.

38. Ibid., p. 183.

39. József Mindszenty, *Memoirs* (London: Weidenfeld and Nicolson, 1974), p. 245.

40. Mireille Macqua, *Rome–Moscou: L'Ostpolitik du Vatican* (Louvain-la-Neuve: Cabay, 1984), p. 153. At least 5,000 Romanian Orthodox priests, including Patriarch Justinian himself, spent time in prison or under arrest during communist rule, with the most intensive wave of repressions occurring in the six years preceding a 1964 amnesty for 'political prisoners'; *Ecumenical News International* (11 April 1996).

41. Macqua, op. cit., p. 163. Pacem in Terris was set up in November 1971 from the remnants of Fr Josef Plojhar's 'peace movement', the MHKD, taking its name from John XXIII's encyclical.

42. From *Lietuvos Katalikų Bažnyčios kronika*, no. 10 (1974); in Stanley Vardys, *The Catholic Church, Dissent and Nationality in Soviet Lithuania* (Boulder: East European Monographs, 1978), p. 156.

43. From *Chronicle*, no. 19 (1975); Vardys, p. 165.

44. Quoted in Stehle, op. cit., p. 368.

45. Wasyl Lenczyk, 'Iosyf Slipyi—patriarch and martyr', *The Ukrainian Quarterly*, vol. 45, no. 3 (Fall 1989), p. 256.
46. Text in *Dissent in Poland 1976–1977* (London: Association of Polish Students in Exile, 1977), p. 150.
47. Adam Michnik, Józef Tischner and Jacek Żakowski, *Między Panem i Plebanem* (Kraków: Znak, 1995); p. 245.
48. 'Our attitude to the statements of Charter 77' (January 1977); in *Religion in Communist Lands*, vol. 5, no. 3 (1977), pp. 161–2.
49. Text in *Religion in Communist Lands*, vol. 8, no. 1 (1980), pp. 48–51.
50. Ijjas et al., op. cit., p. 9.
51. Macqua, op. cit., p. 12.
52. *Magyar Hírlap* (15 February 1976).
53. Gyula Havasy (ed.), *Martyrs of the Catholics in Hungary* (Budapest: privately printed, 1993), pp. 133–4, 136.
54. *Evangelii nuntiandi*, no. 16; Leszek Kołakowski, *Main Currents of Marxism* (New York: Oxford University Press, 1981).
55. Tadeusz Mazowiecki, *Druga Twarz Europy* (Warsaw: Biblioteka Więzi, 1990), pp. 79, 88–9.
56. Karol Wojtyła, *Znak któremu sprzeciwiać się będą* (Warsaw: Pallottinum, 1976), p. 103. Wojtyła referred to Kołakowski's 1965 article, 'Jesus Chrystus: prorok i reformator', published in the anti-Church journal *Argumenty*.
57. Speech in Kraków Curia (17 April 1976); in Boniecki, op. cit., p. 691.
58. Jacek Kuroń, *Wiara i wina: do i od komunizmu* (Warsaw: Nowa, 1990), p. 345.
59. Michnik et al., op. cit., pp. 259–60; Andrzej Drawicz's account in Wiesław Niewęgłowski (ed.), *Moje spotkania z Janem Pawłem II* (Warsaw: Wydawnictwo Rok, 1991), p. 27.
60. The meeting took place on 31 October 1977; Boniecki, op. cit., p. 785.
61. 'Pro Memoria', p. 684.
62. Wawel cathedral homily (18 April 1976); in Boniecki, op. cit., pp. 692–3.
63. Karol Wojtyła, 'Uczestnictwo czy alienacja?' in *Osoba i czyn* (Kraków: Polskie Towarzystwo Teologiczne, 1969), pp. 460–1.
64. Karol Wojtyła, 'Teoria-*praxis*: temat ogólnoludzki i chrześcijański', ibid., pp. 465–75.
65. 'Kościół i sprawy kultury w Polsce' (undated 1977 typescript); in Pieronek and Zawadzki, op. cit., p. 385.

10

രാധാധാധാ

The Slav prophet

There were no serious expectations that Cardinal Wojtyła might be a candidate for Pope himself, however much he might have impressed other influential Church leaders. In a commemorative note, the Polish bishops recalled Paul VI's brief stay in their country at the start of his diplomatic career in the 1920s. It had 'made it easier for him to understand Polish affairs', they said. His death on 6 August had robbed Poland of a 'proven friend'.[1] If that was all they had come to expect from Rome, the bishops were in for a shock.

Paul VI's successor, Albino Luciani, lived just 33 days as Pope John Paul I. It was long enough for Wyszyński to dissuade him from posting a permanent representative to Warsaw and lecture him on the need for closer co-operation between the Vatican and his Bishops' Conference. Much-vexed questions like this paled into the background however, when, on 16 October, dramatically and unexpectedly, Karol Wojtyła was elected to follow him as head of the Catholic Church. He was the first non-Italian Pope for 457 years and the first Polish Pope in history.

Wojtyła's election was the final *dénouement* in Polish Catholicism's 30-year struggle with communist rulers. Less than a month before the Conclave he and other bishops had issued their strongest statement yet, accusing Gierek's regime of 'paralysing' national life and demanding that the 'voices of millions' be heard.[2] Cardinal Wyszyński had led a Bishops' Conference delegation to Germany for reconciliatory talks. The Polish Church was robust and self-confident. Now, every assumption about the strengths and weaknesses of Church and State was suddenly overturned.

'There would be no Polish Pope on the throne of Peter if not for your faith, heroic hope, limitless confidence in the Mother of God', the new John Paul II told Wyszyński the day after his election. The compliment was seriously intended. For those who knew him, Wojtyła's approachable style contrasted clearly with the Primate's regal stature. But without Wyszyński's populist vigour, the Polish Church would undoubtedly have been a weaker institution. 'There is no longer a Church of Silence', John Paul II declared later, recalling Pius XII's controversial epithet. 'She now speaks with the voice of the Pope.'[3] On 22 October Poland's State TV carried John Paul II's four-hour enthronement live from St Peter's Square. It was the first Catholic ceremony broadcast since communist rule began.

The new Pope was known in Rome, at least by those who remembered Vatican II and his 1976 Lenten Lectures. Cardinal Poupard's Secretariat for Unbelievers had published a survey in March 1978 confirming Poland's place as by far the most religious society in Eastern Europe. After three decades of communism, 92 per cent of country people and 81 per cent of town-dwellers still declared themselves religious believers. That relatively small town–country differential was important: in comparison with other countries it suggested that urbanization and industrialization had not succeeded in secularizing Polish citizens. Poland's Marian tradition was known in the West—a national patriotic sentiment evoking the traditional Slavic reverence for mothers. But little had ever been heard about Polish theological and philosophical discussions. The impression was of an inscrutable though hard-pressed institution, combining stoical conservatism with romantic resistance.

It was an image captured by Wyszyński's Vatican Radio description of the new Pope—a man 'for whom prayer is a form of power, absorbed on bended knees with the full grasp of a childhood faith'. For Western Catholics who had worked hard defending Vatican II it was vaguely humiliating that the Cardinals had gone outside the pre-eminent Christian culture of Western Europe to the wilderness of the communist-ruled East for a new leader. Would a Pope from the backwater of Poland not find himself out of depth when he tried to balance out the competing pressures and strains of the modern Church?

Questions like that were for the future. In his Vatican Radio broadcast, Wyszyński recalled his own words in 1970 on the fiftieth anniversary of the 'Miracle on the Vistula'. The election of 'our mountaineer from Wadowice', he said, revealed the Gospel's power to create 'a spirit of universal brotherhood and unity among all languages, peoples and nations'. After centuries of Western dominance, the Church would have to get used to having a Slavic core as well.[4]

'Don't go!' a Kraków woman had told Wojtyła as he left for the Conclave in October, 'a Slav Pope will be the sign that the end of the world is at hand.'[5] The image conveyed Wojtyła's own mystical sense of his own destiny—a distant, little-noticed figure, called down, like the tax collector Zaccheus from his sycamore, to follow Christ and do his work. In that very paradox lay his sense of mission—since it was a paradox only explicable by the workings of the Holy Spirit.

'His election makes the problems of nations living in this second world the centre of attention for Christianity. It can be seen as a kind of compensation for history', was the reaction of Tadeusz Mazowiecki, editor of *Więź*.

> In Wojtyła's statements we find a constant stress on peace and justice. There is something very important in this, and its impact will modify the Vatican's so-called eastern policy. Should diplomacy have primacy over testimony? Or should diplomacy and testimony be inseparable? The Church under John Paul II will not abandon diplomacy. But there has been an awareness from the very outset that progress will not come through armchair politics, but through strengthening the spiritual energy of nations and awakening their life processes.[6]

It was a Catholic view. Non-Catholics also expected Wojtyła's Church to take a vigorous stand on human rights. 'The Church has offered opposition forces not only wise guidance, but also understanding and support', noted the ex-Marxist Adam Michnik.

> The Poles, Catholics and non-Catholics, are known to share their most treasured possessions with the world. Now it is the Archbishop of Kraków. What do they expect in return? They do not want ambrosia from the heavens or military intervention—nor do they expect the Yalta accords to be invalidated overnight. They do not expect miracles. For them, Cardinal Wojtyła's elevation to the Church's highest office is itself a miracle.[7]

That captured the hope and disbelief which greeted John Paul II's election in his home country. It had come as a bolt from the blue—the greatest single boost to national morale since Polish independence in 1918. After decades of negative memories, the bleak continuity of life was suddenly disrupted. Events had gained a tempo. There was something to look forward to: the new Pope's first statements, perhaps even a visit home. In the meantime Rome would have to be counted as a centre of gravity for Polish interests. Being from Poland had become a reason for pride rather than embarrassment.

The sense of euphoria—that the Slavic world was being reintegrated into the modern body politic of Western Christendom—was something the Gierek regime tried to tap into. Its very existence was premised on hostility to the Western capitalist world. But how could this ideological position be maintained now, when the Catholic Church, that arch-agent of Western capital, was itself headed by a Polish anti-communist?

That was Wojtyła's image among Polish Party leaders. Wyszyński was an 'anti-communist' too; but he was also viewed as a judicious man who put State interests first. By contrast Wojtyła was seen as a wild card, a figure in whom priestliness and subversion were fused indistinguishably. His appointment as Pope was interpreted as a political act by the Catholic Church. On 16 October the Politburo member responsible for Church–State relations, Kazimierz Barcikowski, had travelled to Kraków for a pre-arranged meeting of the Party's county committee. The topic, decided earlier, was 'How to resist the anti-socialist activity of Karol Wojtyła'. As the talks progressed a receptionist knocked on the door and relayed the radio news of Wojtyła's election. 'I must close the meeting then, and bring everyone a litre of vodka', the local First Secretary responded. 'From today, we are all going to have to kiss the Catholics' bums instead.'[8]

The Interior Ministry's Church-monitoring department, which had worked to discredit Wojtyła in Kraków, now came under intense pressure. It was anticipated that Catholic priests would be less susceptible to intimidation. Urgent orders were issued to find new informers who would know about likely links between the Polish Church and the Vatican. 'The authorities were scared—they sensed Wojtyła would light a bonfire for us', one operative recalled. 'From the centre through all regional departments, a great clamour went up: how had our operational channels failed to prevent this? . . . We were all ordered to throw everything down and concentrate on finding new contacts against him.'[9]

Publicly, Gierek's regime gritted its teeth and despatched 'hearty congratulations' to Rome. In his reply the Pope pledged to continue the 'spirit of dialogue' initiated by his predecessors. But he gave notice that he would also work to ensure a life 'more worthy of man' and to 'serve the great cause of peace and justice'.[10]

Gierek had quickly to come up with a realistic strategy. The Party's propagandists could set to work highlighting the common aims of communism and Catholicism—peace, humanism, détente. Talk of a reawakened 'Slavic Christian culture' could coexist with the basic realities of communist power. Added to that, the new Pope would be restricted by structures and conventions anyway. 'The Church's doctrine is not a private matter', noted a Party-commissioned report. 'Every Pope has to take account of the reality he operates in, and of the Church's overriding interest.'[11]

Observations like this were also designed to reassure Poland's Warsaw Pact allies. It was essential to show the situation was under control—there would be no spiral of confrontation. Eastern neighbours were not quite so sanguine. Moscow had learned to score propaganda points from Archbishop Casaroli's timid diplomatic forays. In October 1977, however, the fifth Synod of Bishops had called for 'more active catechization' in the Soviet

Union. This had been rather more ominous. From the Kremlin's vantage-point, the conflict between 'reactionaries' and 'progressives' at Vatican II had never really been resolved: with the election of a Polish Pope, the 'reactionaries' seemed to have made a comeback.

Officially at least, the prognosis was calmer. The Soviet ambassador to Italy, Nikita Ryzhov, was sent to the enthronement on 22 October and afterwards had a lengthy talk with the new Pope. *Pravda* reported that Brezhnev had sent a telegram congratulating the Pope and received one in reply. Soviet press commentaries dismissed claims that John Paul II had been chosen because he 'knew how to fight communism', and urged him to continue the 'political line' of John XXIII and Paul VI.

But Moscow was on its guard. Of course, Wojtyła was too smart to attack communism head-on, but his election was rumoured to have had a lot to do with pressure from the US Cardinals. Experts at the Soviet Academy of Sciences predicted criticism of the communist regimes would be stepped up, and recommended that a 'warning' be given that this would lead to harsher restrictions. But they also recommended steps to conciliate the Soviet Union's Catholic minorities. 'The Polish comrades characterize John Paul II as more dangerous at the ideological level than his predecessors', the director of the Soviet Religious Affairs Council, Vladimir Kuroyedov, told the Central Committee.[12]

The Soviet experts were right to anticipate that Wojtyła's election would trigger a wave of expectations. The *Chronicle of the Catholic Church in Lithuania* had begged God after Paul VI's death for 'a courageous, determined and holy Pope ... in whose heart our struggle against our country's forced atheization will find an echo'. The response was quick. By mid-November a new Committee to Defend Believers' Rights had been announced in Vilnius. John Paul II's election, the five priest-founders certified, had brought a relaxation in official pressure and encouraged a religious revival. A similar 'Initiative Group' was formed by dissenting Greek Catholics in Ukraine. 'This is a major event for us', concurred a Czech historian, Radomír Malý. 'A Pope from Poland can help Czechs understand that the Church is not limited to one part of the world. In its eyes, all nations, including the Czechs, have equal rights.'[13]

Paradoxically, John Paul had travelled more in the West than the East, getting to know the outside world through the medium of the Vatican and local Bishops' Conferences. But he knew Eastern Europe well enough to evoke the Christian culture Poland shared with other nations. This lyrical grasp of histories and identities owed something to the Romantic poets. But it gave him a language for summoning forth the region's untapped spiritual resources. In the 1960s and 1970s, Kraków had been a Mecca for inquisitive intellectuals from neighbouring countries. Some had learned Polish just to read the *Tygodnik Powszechny*, which was now crammed with proud reminiscences about the man who had lauded the work of 'worker priests' in its columns three decades before.

Wojtyła had chosen his name, as had his ill-fated predecessor, John Paul I, to stress continuity with John XXIII and Paul VI. Unlike them, however, he came from a land where the Church had withstood the entire machinery of a hostile State—a land which backed out on to a long-forbidden world of Orthodox holy men, ransacked churches, forests and cities, prisons and gulags. It had to mean a new beginning, a return to roots and sources.

There were signs that John Paul II had his own ideas about how to deploy the power of the Vatican—at least where communism was concerned. The Church remained 'open to every country and regime, according to the proven means of diplomacy and negotiation', he told Vatican-accredited diplomats. But the Holy See welcomed *all* representatives—not only spokesmen for 'governments, regimes and political structures' but also 'authentic representatives of peoples and nations'. The Church was seeking no privileges, only 'living space' to pursue its mission. If essential rights were respected, the Church could coexist with any political, social or economic system without 'inherent contradiction'.[14]

That was the message impressed on East Germany's Foreign Minister, Oskar Fischer, who arrived for formal talks less than a week after the inauguration. Other communist officials followed. Andrei Gromyko claims he warned the Pope against 'cock-and-bull stories' which portrayed 'lawbreaking criminals as great martyrs', and insisted Soviet treatment of religious believers was 'quite normal'. 'Do you consider it normal that more than a million Catholics in Byelorussia have no bishop and only 20 mostly elderly priests?', John Paul II reputedly hit back. Vatican sources said Gromyko had talked about peace while the Pope demanded assurances about Catholic rights.[15] In any event, the sounding-out encounter on 24 February got relations off to a bad start.

'Speaking of the Vatican's so-called eastern policy ... this policy, formulated under Paul VI, remains in force, confirmation being the naming of its creator Mgr Casaroli as the Vatican's Secretary of State', a Lithuanian priest, Fr Pranas Račiūnas, told Soviet officials after visiting Rome. 'But John Paul II intends to, and will in future, implement this policy more actively; and if, in the development of relations with any socialist state, this policy does not bring tangible results, the present Pope will without hesitation choose his own line.'[16]

Casaroli's promotion to pro-Secretary of State in April 1979 did indeed confirm that a high-powered diplomat—who had, in the Pope's words, accomplished 'important and difficult tasks'—remained available when diplomacy was needed. But new appointments also brought fresh talent into the Vatican's upper ranks. In the 1970s Rome's position had been premised on the view that the Church was up against an insuperable power, and must, to keep the faith alive, avoid confrontation at all costs. But a Pope who knew communism from inside could see that Christians had power too. It was only necessary to find out how to use it in a way which made them strong and the regimes weak.

Lithuania's underground *Chronicle* offered the new Pope some advice.

1. Atheist governments should not be granted concessions which harm pastoral work.
2. The affairs of religious believers in Eastern Europe should be entrusted to those in the Vatican best aware of their living conditions.
3. Both the official and unofficial Church should receive all possible support, with hierarchies appointed for the 'Church of the Catacombs'.
4. No person inclined to make concessions to the government should be appointed bishop.
5. Exiled bishops should be consulted about episcopal candidates and greater discipline imposed on clergy.
6. More energetic action should be taken to organize global support for persecuted believers'.[17]

That just about summed up John Paul II's plan of action. The Vatican's 'small steps' diplomacy would continue, but this time it would be run from a position of strength, in conjunction with local Bishops' Conferences. There would be no more talk of 'going over heads' or negotiating on separate tracks.

The Vatican's roving envoy, Mgr Poggi, made Hungary his first port of call in December. By April, four new diocesan appointments had brought Hungary's Bishops' Conference back to full strength. A papal letter reminded Catholics that religious teaching was permitted in schools under Hungary's constitution. It was rumoured the Pope had criticized Cardinal Lékai on his first Vatican visit for 'misinterpreting' the conciliatory stance of John XXIII and Paul VI.

Six months into his pontificate John Paul II celebrated a Croatian-language Mass for 10,000 pilgrims in St Peter's Square. In May he wrote to Archbishop Tomášek of Prague urging Czechoslovakia's Catholics to show 'courage and hope'. The same month, two bishops were named for Bulgaria as part of a Church reorganization. The Pope told the country's Foreign Minister, Petur Mladenov, he expected a 'common, not sterile, search for solutions'.[18]

In the meantime, John Paul II had ventured further on to the world stage. He made his first in-depth pronouncement on Liberation Theology at a meeting with Latin American bishops in January 1979, while an April visit to the European Parliament allowed him to caution Western MEPs against thinking they 'constitute Europe by themselves'. For the Church, John Paul II told an East–West meeting of bishops, Europe would always be 'the cradle of creative thought'. It was in Europe, rooted in Christianity but torn apart by ideological conflicts, that the coming restoration of human values must begin.[19]

By then, the Pope had issued his first encyclical. It was said he had personally drafted *Redemptor hominis* (4 March 1979) just after his election, making it the first major papal text to have its original in Polish. The encyclical reaffirmed Vatican II's teachings on human rights, social justice and economic development. But it presented its arguments dynamically, as if in conscious response to atheist propositions. It read like a personal manifesto—a clear, reasoned exposition of the new Pope's approach to the world.

In his own first encyclical, *Ecclesiam Suam*, Paul VI had repeated the Church's condemnation of 'atheistic communism', but had left open the possibility of cautious dialogue. *Redemptor hominis* took this as its starting point too, but in contrast to Montini's tormented uncertainties its tone was consistent and self-confident. It clearly reflected the evolution in the Polish Church's stance during the 1970s.

Vatican II had highlighted the unprecedented dangers posed by contemporary atheism, the Pope recalled, 'beginning with the atheism that is programmed, organized and structured as a political system'.[20] Against this, Christians should be like the 'violent people of God' spoken of in St Matthew's Gospel. The Church approached all cultures and ideologies with a deep esteem for human capabilities. But it also had to be a guardian of freedom, faithful to Christ's words: 'You will know the truth, and the truth will make you free.' This meant distinguishing between authentic and illusory freedoms. The Church was not to be identified with any political system. But it had to be aware of what threatened man's dignity. 'We are not dealing with the "abstract" man, but the real, "concrete", "historical" man', the Pope emphasized. 'Man is the primary route the Church must travel in fulfilling her mission.'

This struggle for the soul of contemporary mankind was an innovation in *Redemptor hominis*; but the encyclical took up the concern with structures and patterns of thinking which had also preoccupied papal texts from *Mater et magistra* to *Octogesima adveniens*. The Church still believed the mechanisms supporting the world economy were incapable of remedying the 'unjust social situations' inherited from the past. What was needed was an 'indispensable transformation of the structures of economic life'. All ideological outlooks needed 'continual revision', *Redemptor hominis* continued, to ensure they stayed true to their 'humanistic premises'. History showed the ignoring of human needs led to 'domination, totalitarianism, neo-colonialism and imperialism'.[21]

On this point at least *Redemptor hominis* stuck to the position of Paul VI, who had shown the dangers when social and political emancipation came up against authoritarian and totalitarian forms of government. But it went further. For the first time it highlighted the contradiction between human rights in letter and in spirit. It was a problem particularly marked under communism, which made citizens unsure of their rights and called in question the legitimacy of power.

> The essential sense of the State, as a political community, consists in that the society and people composing it are master and sovereign of their own destiny. This sense remains unrealised if, instead of the exercise of power with the moral participation of the society or people, what we see is the imposition of power by a certain group upon all the other members of society ... The Church has always taught ... that the fundamental duty of power is solicitude for the common good of society; this is what gives power its fundamental rights. Precisely in the name of these premises of the objective ethical order, the rights of power can only be understood on the basis of respect for the objective and inviolable rights of man.[22]

This, of course, required a vigorous defence of religious freedom, in the view of the Pope the most important of all human rights. Vatican II's Declaration on Religious Freedom, John Paul said, had shown that the violation of this freedom was a 'radical injustice' in that it offended both civil rights and man's inner nature. 'Even the phenomenon of unbelief, a-religiousness and atheism, as a human phenomenon, is understood only in relation to the phenomenon of religion and faith', John Paul II continued. 'It is therefore difficult, even from a "purely human" point of view, to accept a position that gives only atheism the right of citizenship.'[23]

In this way, *Redemptor hominis* posed an ideological challenge. Far from denouncing communism *tout court*, it showed how communist ideology had departed from its own claims and objectives, and destroyed its own legitimacy by violating the principles of power and authority. Instead, it presented a Church which had made these claims and objectives its own by reinterpreting them in a Christian way. It was the Church, not communism, which now stood firmly on the side of man. The true 'new man' had been born not through Lenin's revolution but through God's Redemption.

Redemptor hominis touched a chord in Eastern Europe—at least among those who had a chance to read it. In Poland, where the encyclical was published uncensored by *Tygodnik Powszechny*, Catholicism acquired new colour and vibrancy. In a Gdańsk University survey of 1979, 51 per cent of officially atheist Communist Party members described themselves as practising Catholics, compared to 75 per cent of the rest of society, while a further 22 per cent claimed to be non-practising religious believers. Social research suggested the passive values of egalitarianism, a secure job and housing were rooted in Polish society; but they were the only values communism had succeeded in implanting. By contrast, the moral and religious impulses associated with the Church's slogan *Bóg, honor, ojczyzna*—'God, honour, homeland'—appealed more deeply to the social consciousness.[24]

Redemptor hominis also impressed non-Christians. In a letter to the Pope, the KOR opposition group quoted it on the link between human rights and peace, State–society relations and the Church's condemnation of totalitarianism. 'We see in Your Holiness a spokesman for the best values of Polish culture', the letter declared, 'a culture free of narrow nationalism, based on tolerance and pluralism, linked to the Christian world of values.'[25]

KOR's letter was sent in May. By then John Paul's first homecoming was just a month away. He had wanted to come in May to mark the 900th anniversary of St Stanisław's martyrdom, for which in 1972 he had launched a seven-year prayer cycle. The eleventh-century Bishop of Kraków had been murdered by soldiers of King Bolesław the Bold while saying Mass, like the English St Thomas Becket. Communist writers considered him an 'anti-people conspirator' acting at the behest of a theocratic Pope Gregory VII. The Church saw him as a symbol of civic courage and moral resistance, and the obvious contemporary parallels irritated the Gierek regime. Only after a March visit by Casaroli did it consent to a pilgrimage in June. As a trade-off, the visit was extended to nine days instead of the original two.

The quarrel over St Stanisław had already erupted at Christmas when a message from the Pope to his former see of Kraków proved too much for the regime's censors. The offending, excised, passage called the saint a 'patron of moral order' in Poland.

> St Stanisław defended his contemporary society from the evil which threatened it, and did not hesitate to confront the ruler when defence of the moral order demanded it. In this way, he became a magnificent example of concern for the people, which we have to compare with our indifference, our negligence, our despondency ... Using modern language, we can see in St Stanisław an advocate of the most essential human rights, on which man's dignity, morality and true freedom depend.[26]

Enraged by the deletion, Wyszyński postponed his first meeting with Gierek since October 1977—not even the Russian Tsars, he thundered, had dared tamper with messages from the Pope. The message was read uncut in Kraków churches anyway. The government, plainly embarrassed, pinned the blame on an over-eager local censor.

This was hardly a crisis. But Gierek claims he received an agitated telephone call from Brezhnev early in 1979. 'Gomułka was a better communist because he would not receive Paul VI in Poland, and nothing terrible has happened', the Soviet ruler supposedly barked at the apologetic Polish Party boss. He eventually hung up, muttering threats that the Polish regime could do what it wanted so long as it did not 'regret it later'.[27]

Gierek flew to Moscow, Prague and Budapest to explain why the Pope's visit had been agreed to. His foreign comrades were not reassured. Vladimir Kuroyedov was told the Polish government had 'taken measures' to dissuade the Pope from coming. 'However, there has been a certain inconsistency', Kuroyedov reported home: Polish officials had separately assured the Western press that John Paul II would be 'received with all honours'. 'In our view, the measures taken against the Pope's visit to Poland were insufficient', the Soviet envoy noted ominously.

> We told our Polish friends that, according to our information, the Pope already has a worked out strategic plan for the Vatican's wide penetration in socialist countries ... According to John Paul II's plans, the 'bridgehead' for the offensive of Catholicism must be such countries as Poland, Hungary and Czechoslovakia ... We tactfully tried to give our friends to understand that it is necessary to study more deeply the course of world events connected with the new Pope's activity; not to sit and wait for things to happen, but to take concrete, practical measures.[28]

These were secret in-house discussions. Albania's communist rulers, at the other extreme, were convinced both the Soviets and Eurocommunists were themselves plotting with the Pope. 'The revolution which brought down all gods and angels from their thrones, emptied all places of worship, and chased out the clergy will be defended', a Party newspaper proclaimed.[29] The papal election of October 1978 had fluttered plenty of ideological dovecotes.

Did the Pope really have a 'strategic plan' when he arrived in Poland on 2 June? He was well aware of the dramatic expectations. In an underground statement, the head of the nationalist Confederation for an Independent Poland (KPN), Leszek Moczulski, had talked of 'catastrophic visions'. A top Party leader had warned the Central Committee of a 'very great anger' building up in society, Moczulski pointed out, while KOR's Jacek Kuroń also had intimations of a coming earthquake. 'The opinion is widespread that

Poland stands before a great social explosion', Moczulski continued, 'stronger by far than the events of 1956, December 1970 and June 1976 put together.'[30]

Yet these were intellectual voices. A better gauge of the national mood was offered by a group of agricultural workers, writing to the Pope from Zbrosza Duża, a 'peasant self-defence community' south of Warsaw. 'At this dramatic moment we sense the Holy Spirit guiding our common fate', the letter noted.

> In the hard work we are now beginning we need your fatherly, good, wise words ... You do not expect empty, obsequious greetings: you expect the truth from us ... We do not want war, military revolution, a bloody political coup. All of this leads to evil, criminality, destruction, death. We want a revolution in our hearts, minds and characters, out of which will come truth, life and justice. We want to raise our heads, respect each other and respect ourselves, live a dignified and honest life ... We will go on demanding that after this revolution within us the social situation will evolve, bringing just and trusted laws.[31]

This notion—that the visit would be a kind of psychotherapy for a society already prepared for some coming transformation—seemed to reflect the Pope's thinking too. John Paul II knew the atmosphere in Poland was potentially explosive and that responsibility for avoiding a violent confrontation lay with him. If he had a 'strategy' at all, it was simply to speak naturally, without inhibitions. This was a pastoral visit. Its aim was not to overthrow communism, but to strengthen Christian life and culture. If he did this it would be enough. The Poles would draw the conclusions themselves.

The Gierek regime had plenty of worries. A survey of religious attitudes among soldiers was said to have been commissioned to test the Army's loyalty. Detailed instructions were issued to journalists and teachers. It was felt necessary to remind the communist rank and file that they must stand firmly behind the Party. If the Pope merely talked vacuously about 'culture' and 'religion' the regime was sure it could handle things. The official press advised citizens against any 'illusions'. Stress was placed on the visit's potential to further the 'common goal' of a strong Poland.[32]

In the course of a week John Paul II preached 32 sermons in six cities before 13 million people. He talked about the right of Eastern Europe's 'often forgotten nations and peoples' to reclaim their place 'at the heart of the Church'. The Second World War had left Europe divided between rival regimes and ideologies; it must now rediscover its 'fundamental unity' by returning to the rich Christian heritage of Czechs and Slovaks, Croats and Slovenes, Bulgarians and Lithuanians—by 'opening the frontiers' to the Holy Spirit. 'Is it not Christ's will, is it not what the Holy Spirit disposes', the Pope declared at Gniezno, Poland's oldest Catholic see, 'that this Polish Pope, this Slav Pope, should at this very moment manifest the spiritual unity of Christian Europe?'[33]

What was it that stood against this? The main danger, the Pope made clear, came not from Marxist ideology, which was fast losing coherency, but from the 'programmed atheism' which was the destructive element common to all forms of communism. How could it be resisted? Gierek had evoked 35 years of communist Poland in his speeches; the Pope appealed to a Polish identity which was infinitely richer. Peace could only be assured, he told Gierek, when the nation was able to remain true to its culture and civilization.

> The whole historical process of a person's knowledge and choices is closely bound up with the living tradition of his or her own country, where, through all generations, Christ's words echo and resound with the witness of the Gospel and Christian culture ... By which rational argument, by which value close to the will and heart, could one stand before oneself, one's neighbour, one's fellow-citizens, one's country, and cast off all we have witnessed for 1,000 years, all that has constituted the basis of our identity?[34]

Vatican II had talked about the 'right to culture' and about Christianity's 'acculturation' in various contexts. But in the Pope's hands 'culture' became a word for identity, history and spirituality put together—the common good and soul of the nation, something more decisive than material power and boundaries.[35]

The Pope stressed the Church's temporal tasks in helping safeguard this national inheritance. As *Redemptor hominis* had reiterated, it only wanted what was essential for its mission. The Polish bishops had done a great deal 'in close collaboration with the Apostolic See' to establish conditions for normal Church–State relations. But 'true normalization' would become possible only when rights and freedoms were duly respected. The bishops had shown readiness for dialogue; but 'authentic dialogue' must respect believers' convictions and follow clear 'rules of procedure'. 'We are aware that this dialogue cannot be easy, since it takes place between two concepts of the world which are diametrically opposed', the Pope conceded; 'but it must be possible and effective if the good of individuals and the nation demands it.'[36]

In short, the Church and the Vatican were ready for good working relations with communist regimes; but they would be unbending when it came to the conditions. Agreements could be only the means to an end.

Visiting the former Nazi concentration camp of Auschwitz, the 'Golgotha of our times', the Pope warned against ideologies under which 'the rights of man are submitted to the exigencies of the system, so that in fact they do not exist'. No one, he urged, should remain indifferent to the fate of Jews who comprised 90 per cent of Auschwitz's victims. Meanwhile, he acknowledged that Russians had also died at Auschwitz and contributed to the 'freedom of people' during the war.

The pilgrimage gave the Pope a chance to develop his 'theology of work'. Today's Church was no longer afraid of worker movements, he declared in Kraków's Nowa Huta suburb. It recognized that the key issue facing human labour was one not of economics but of dignity. The Church was also thankful that industrialization in Poland had been matched by the spread of churches and parishes—it had not implied 'de-Christianization, a rupture of the alliance in the human soul between work and prayer'.

The Pope's forceful words revealed a powerful talent for evangelization. His invocation in Warsaw's Victory Square—'Let Your Spirit come down and renew the face of this land, *this* land!'—could hardly fail to touch hearts and minds. Yet what made them important was less the words themselves than how the Pope pronounced them. He said publicly what many had long wanted to cry from the rooftops; but he said it in a way which exactly captured and articulated the national mood.

Wojtyła had returned to Poland from the 'other world' beyond the western border with a language of human rights which formed part of an established international discourse. He had come with the full force of a universal Christian civilization behind him, and had presented the vision of an 'authentic' Poland, a Polish homeland to work for. He had also shown that the stultifying structures of communism would be changed not through violent rebellion but through a liberation built from free spaces—conscience, morality, culture, identity. He had opened up fertile, unexpected horizons, for a nation 'going forward towards the future'.[37]

The Gierek regime had long since ruled out fundamental reforms in Poland. Instead, it had tried to give priority to pragmatic economic solutions. Like its Hungarian counterpart it had relied on a *mała stabilizacja*, or 'small stabilization', to hold things in place—to legitimize the system by letting it generate a web of interests, contracts and loyalties, while ordinary people remained preoccupied with daily problems and uncertainties. The Pope's visit had shaken this to its foundations. He had spoken of a 'moral order', the order of St Stanisław, and of a 'moral disorder' which came from falsehood and shallow public subservience. He had shown it was legitimate to demand that this disorder be corrected; and he had talked about social engagement, that duty of 'solidarity' outlined ten years before in *The Acting Person*. 'Any man who chooses his ideology honestly and with conviction deserves respect', the Pope told students from his old Catholic University of Lublin. 'The real danger for both sides comes from the man who does not take risks and accept challenges ... who only wants to float in conformity, moving from left to right as the wind blows.'[38]

The Pope had instilled a sense of the possible. Over the previous decade, as the failures of Gierek's technocratic regime dulled any sense of hope, the Polish Church had risen to the challenge by speaking out for rights and principles; yet the Church by itself had been unable to offer clear perspectives for the future. This was what John Paul II now seemed to have provided. The Poles—the Church included—had not been waiting for a national Messiah: the impulses of rebellion were already at work. What they *had* needed was a true, ungainsayable authority who would confirm and strengthen their will for self-determination; who would show they were no longer isolated, no longer dreaming impossible dreams. In the Pope's hands forgiveness, trust and truthfulness had become tantamount to political acts, by defying the anti-values of the communist system.

John Paul II declared in his departure speech 'We must have courage to go the way no one has followed before'.[39] The message of optimism and endurance had been relayed to other East European countries through the images of Christian legend. It had also reached non-Christians who were searching for spiritual values. The week had shown that Polish society was able to organize itself freely and peacefully. To the surprise of the country's dissidents, something had after all been simmering silently, unnoticed behind communism's facade. After years of failure and disappointment Poland had become a *good* country again, revealing its inner character and shaking off its vices and weaknesses. The visit had de-mystified communism.

That was not how the Gierek regime interpreted the Pope's seven-day tour. It was pleasantly surprised that he had avoided overtly political statements. It was said he had toned down his sermons in response to a government request. Meanwhile, pro-regime Catholic parliamentarians had been invited to meet him at a Warsaw Church reception, but not Catholics linked to the KOR opposition. Those who had feared an anti-communist jamboree felt a sense of relief. Of course, there *had* been political accents—but not what Party alarmists had anticipated. All the Pope seemed to have done was ramble on about culture and morality. 'The Pope's ideas have much in common with ours', a Foreign Ministry spokesman confidently proclaimed. 'We are glad the Pope emphasized several times the Polish nation's unity on the basis of the family and labour. He also mentioned religion, but that is a personal matter we shall not go into.'[40]

The regime would have been wise to have studied John Paul II's words and gestures more closely, but it lacked the imagination to grasp the visit's potential social impact. The Pope had restated his readiness to go on working for a Church–State 'normalization'. The logic behind this, however, was clear. Paul VI had felt it necessary to conduct negotiations over the heads of national Church leaders. John Paul II was in a stronger position to ensure the Vatican and local Churches acted in harmony. That was what he had meant about ensuring 'clarity of procedures'. No Church–State deals could be struck until the states in question truly represented their citizens.

If it seriously believed the communist system would absorb this Catholic challenge the Polish regime was being dangerously complacent. 'Gierek even liked the new breath which had been given to the Polish language—perhaps it was thanks to his Catholic mother that he coped quite well', recalled a Politburo member. 'After the Pope's visit, half-jokingly but not entirely, we began to ask each other who'd been an altar-boy, who'd been baptized, whose parents were believers.'[41]

Neighbouring communist regimes seem to have pinpointed the dangers more astutely. Whatever the Polish assurances, it was clear that the Pope had openly defied the communist ascendancy—at least to those who still took their ideology seriously. Every East European government felt it had been personally targeted.

The Czechoslovak government had at the last minute allowed Cardinal Tomášek to travel to Poland, but it had prevented pilgrims from crossing the border. The Vatican was attempting to make up for its past hostility to the working classes, the propagandists noted, but a glance at Czech history showed it had always been 'on the side of our enemies'. The Pope's appeal to Europe's spiritual roots was 'an audacious challenge to communism'. So were his references to figures like St Stanisław, who embodied the medieval Papacy's attempts to rule the world.[42]

Tito's regime in Yugoslavia allowed extensive press coverage of the pilgrimage, and tried to portray it as confirming the possibility of 'normal' Church–State relations. For Albania's rulers, however, it was another sign of the 'ideological degeneration' sweeping Eastern Europe. The courteous welcome given to the Pope was the natural consequence of Khrushchev's 'bowing his neck' to John XXIII in the 1960s. The Polish Pope's aim was obviously to drive wedges between Eastern Europe's 'revisionists' and Moscow.[43]

The Soviet government also suspected the Pope was trying to drive wedges, but it was sure his 'strategy' went further. Ukraine's Soviet strongman, Vladimir Shcherbitsky, demanded stronger atheist propaganda against 'ideological diversions'. The republic's media set to work highlighting the Pope's nostalgia for wartime Ukrainian fascism. In Lithuania the Communist Party prepared its cadres for questions: why had the Polish government invited the Pope, given his 'reactionary character'? what 'advantage' had the Polish People's Republic gained from the visit? Priests and bishops were called in for talks and told concessions could be expected if they asserted their authority against would-be dissidents. Three-quarters of all clergy nonetheless signed petitions during the year against Lithuania's new religious regulations. It was rumoured—falsely—that the long-exiled Bishop Steponavičius had secretly been named a Cardinal.

In Moscow the Religious Affairs Council chairman, Kuroyedov, who had criticized Polish unpreparedness, arranged to meet his East European opposite numbers in September. In the meantime, he urgently instructed colleagues to keep a special watch on Catholic activities. The Soviet government claimed to be worried that Catholic assertiveness might coincide with Islamic fundamentalism in its southern republics. Gromyko made snide remarks comparing the Pope's Polish pilgrimage to the Ayatollah Khomeini's triumphant return to Iran in early 1979. He felt it necessary to remind *Pravda* readers that 'Poland was and remains an inalienable part of the socialist community'.[44]

This was public sabre-rattling. The Soviet Communist Party Central Committee, however, had analysed John Paul II's statements more seriously. Its reports contained the usual obligatory invective about 'increasing religious fanaticism'; but they also talked about the Pope's 'new policy' and 'new methods', and advised extreme caution. Moscow knew it had been caught off-guard by Catholicism's sudden rush of energy. Attempts would now intensify to transform the Church into a 'political opposition', Kuroyedov predicted. 'Active support' would be given to dissidents, and approaches made to communist society's two most vulnerable sectors: the young and the intelligentsia. A provocative, heavy-handed response, however, could merely strengthen the Vatican's hand.

Central Committee guidelines were issued in November. All organs and departments were to be deployed to highlight 'dangerous tendencies' in the Pope's behaviour, showing how Vatican policies jeopardized the Catholic Church's delicate position in Eastern Europe. The Council for Religious Affairs would recommend special measures for Catholic regions of Lithuania, Latvia, Byelorussia, Ukraine and Kazakhstan. The Russian Orthodox Church would be urged to 'define more concretely' its attitude to the Vatican and exert a counter-influence through the Geneva-based World Council of Churches.

A month later Kuroyedov conceded that all religious groups had become more active; but whereas Orthodox and Muslim clergy generally showed a 'loyal attitude to the Soviet state', extremism was growing among Catholics. The Vatican was 'openly expressing distrust of diocesan leaders who express loyal positions towards Soviet power'.[45]

In June 1979, *L'Osservatore Romano* had published a letter from the Pope to Metropolitan Slipyi, the exasperated leader of Ukraine's outlawed Greek

Catholics, reaffirming the right of believers to belong to the Church of their choice. The Pope had disagreed, like Paul VI, with Slipyi's demands to be raised to Patriarch; but his letter had made a 'major contribution', Kuroyedov was sure, to revived activism among Ukraine's 'disloyal priests'. The Russian Orthodox leader, Patriarch Pimen, accused John Paul II of 'cancelling' Vatican II's 'ecumenical policy' by supporting the Greek Catholics. A visiting Italian priest was expelled from Lviv after signing a confession that he had come 'as a blind instrument in the hands of anti-Soviet clergy'.[46]

The idea of pressuring East European Church leaders to resist John Paul II's 'aggression' made sense. Lithuania's exiled bishops, Steponavičius and Sladkevičius, taking advantage of their relative uninhibitedness, had sent a telegram inviting the Pope warmly, if rather futilely, to visit their country too. From the safety of Rome Cardinal Slipyi had also declared his certainty that John Paul II would 'reach out a helping hand to the oppressed, and not limit himself to words of consolation and patience, as his predecessors did'.[47]

Other Church leaders, however, were keen to stress the uniqueness of Polish conditions. Cardinal Lékai of Hungary had made a submissive trip to Lithuania in the month of Wojtyła's election, and left for another Soviet tour at Pimen's invitation in October 1979. He was in Poland for the Pope's visit, and praised its 'magic climate'. Western media had emphasized 'confrontational elements', Lékai complained. In reality, John Paul II would stick to the line of John XXIII and Paul VI: 'The situation of churches in socialist countries is very diversified, as are the stages of historical development. No single pattern of ecclesiastical polity can be transposed to all countries.'[48]

As it turned out the Pope's visit had speeded up the momentum of events. In Poland Gierek believed he still held the initiative, but his over-confidence was being challenged. In September local authorities began building a highway through the centre of Częstochowa which would have cut off the Jasna Góra shrine. Cardinal Wyszyński denounced the surprise project as an 'indescribable act of barbarity' and it was abandoned early in 1980. It bore the hallmarks of an attempt by Party hardliners to disrupt the icy stand-off in Church–State relations.

Undeterred, Wyszyński in an Epiphany sermon deplored the 'mendacious propaganda' disseminated by the official media, and called for an end to 'beggarly queues which are destroying human life'. The reference to queues was important. The bishops were talking more now about social and economic failures—the communist Achilles' heel. The regime was counting on Church help in securing a reasonable turnout to March elections for the Sejm; but it had few inducements to trade. It promised to increase by four the seats assigned to the pro-regime Pax Association and its 'Catholic' allies; but that amounted to a derisive 17 out of 460. In April it cleared the way for an uncensored Polish edition of *L'Osservatore Romano*, and in May it agreed to exempt seminarians from military service. These cosmetic changes had no impact on deeper tensions.

The Pope's visit had also given greater self-confidence to Poland's once-isolated 'democratic opposition'. Having been distrusted by much of society as irresponsible rebels with hopeless ideas, KOR's members sensed they were being taken seriously. Their moral postulates were close to the Pope's, who had simply expressed them in Christian language. 'It is obvious that we have experienced an event whose impact will continue to grow', KOR enthused in a July 1979 statement. 'For many people in Poland and beyond its borders, listening to the Pope has posed a moral obligation to start and intensify a struggle in defence of rights.'[49]

That 'struggle' had only affected a narrow band of Polish society. A 'Flying University' was staging unofficial lectures, while underground publishers had issued *samizdat* editions of Western writers—including, for the first time, the liberal critique of communism associated with such figures as Hannah Arendt and Raymond Aron. Meanwhile, 'revisionism' had made a comeback, with a much-quoted report by the Party's 'Experience and Future' group on the need for change 'within the system'. Human rights groups, whether Catholic or not, were given use of church premises, raising the prospect of a wider campaign.

Polish dissidents were looking further afield. At Gniezno the Pope had caught sight of a Czech banner in the crowd and read it out loud: 'Father, remember your Czech children.' Supporters of KOR and Charter 77 had met secretly on the Polish–Czechoslovak border for the first time in 1978. A hunger-strike was staged in a Warsaw church to protest against repression in Czechoslovakia, while in July 300 Catholic intellectuals sent a letter to Cardinal Tomášek, urging him to intervene on behalf of arrested members of VONS, the Committee for the Unjustly Persecuted. VONS, a Charter offshoot, was acting 'in agreement with Church teaching', the Poles reminded the frail Czech Primate.[50] The same month a Catholic priest, Fr Milan Grono, died after being tortured. In September the Jesuit who had pushed Tomášek towards a firmer stance, Fr Josef Zvěřina, was arrested for 'hindering State supervision of churches'.

Despite a religious revival among Czech and Slovak students, there had been no mass return to the Catholic Church. But the Polish Pope's clear alignment with human rights was changing attitudes. Catholic *samizdat* titles, circulated at great risk, were increasingly prominent in the country's 'parallel culture'. Pastoral work by unlicensed priests met the need for strong, coherent personalities acting outside the official constraints of communist society.

In neighbouring Hungary research data suggested the decline in religion, which had reached rock-bottom in the mid-1970s, had gone into reverse by 1980. The centre of gravity in Church life had moved from the traditional religiosity of the countryside to the city renewal movements. The Kádár regime made some concessions. A new edition of the Bible was made available for literature classes in Hungarian schools, while the country's top theologian, Tamás Nyíri, was allowed to start a correspondence course for laypeople at Budapest's half-derelict Catholic Theology Academy. The trend suggested a reconstruction was under way in Hungarian religious life.

The Polish Pope seemed to have given the Church a lease of life in other countries too. In November 1979 Romania's communist *Conducator*, Nicolae Ceauşescu, warned Party members that religious beliefs still persisted in their ranks.[51] The Pope had received 5,000 Catholics from Slovenia a month earlier for their Church's twelfth centenary. In Yugoslavia's biggest ever religious rally, 100,000 Catholics gathered at Nin, to mark the 1,100th anniversary of the Papacy's recognition of Croatian statehood. At Easter 1980, two months before Tito's death, Cardinal Franjo Kuharić of Zagreb denounced the 'atheist propaganda' forced on schools and newspapers.

Yugoslavia's Catholic weekly, *Glas Koncila*, talked about a 'Polish example'—an 'awakening and redefinition of modern Catholicism between the Baltic and Adriatic'. Nobody should be ashamed, the paper added, to 'learn from Poland'.[52] In the months ahead, Poland would be teaching some unexpected lessons.

Notes

1. 'Komunikat Episkopatu Polski' (7 August 1978); in Peter Raina (ed.), *Kościół w PRL—Dokumenty*, 3: *1975–1989* (Poznań: W Drodze, 1996), pp. 105–6.
2. 'Przesłanie biskupów polskich do wiernych' (17 September 1978); ibid., pp. 109–11.
3. John Paul II's statement to Wyszyński; in Antoine Wenger, 'La Politique Orientale du Saint-Siège' in Joël-Benoît d'Onorio (ed.), *Le Saint-Siège dans les relations internationales* (Paris: Éditions du Cerf, 1989), p. 183.
4. 'Przemówienie Prymasa Kard. S. Wyszyńskiego w radiu watykańskim' (17 October 1978); in Raina, op. cit., pp. 122–3.
5. Stefan Swieżawski, *Owoce życia 1966–1988* (Lublin: Redakcja Wydawnictw KUL, 1993), pp. 238–9. Comparative figures for country and town religiousness in Bulgaria and Yugoslavia were 26–10 per cent and 50–29 per cent respectively, in the Soviet Union 16–8 per cent; *Ateismo e Dialogo*, vol. 13, no. 1 (March 1978), pp. 20–7.

6. Tadeusz Mazowiecki, 'Zadania inteligencji katolickiej w Polsce wobec wyboru Jana Pawła II' (1 April 1979); in Zygmunt Hemmerling and Marek Nadolski (eds), *Opozycja demokratyczna w Polsce 1976–1980* (Warsaw: Wydawnictwa Uniwersytetu Warszawskiego, 1994), p. 345.

7. *Der Spiegel* (23 October 1978).

8. Adam Michnik, Józef Tischner and Jacek Żakowski, *Między Panem i Plebanem* (Kraków: Znak, 1995), p. 280.

9. The testimony is from Grzegorz Piotrowski, who was convicted seven years later for the murder of Fr Jerzy Popiełuszko: Tadeusz Fredro-Boniecki, *Zwycięstwo ksiedza Jerzego* (Warsaw: Nowa, 1990), pp. 49–50.

10. 'Depesza gratulacyjna władz polskich' (17 October 1978); in Raina, op. cit., pp. 123–4; 'Podziękowanie Papieża Jana Pawła II' (19 October 1978); ibid., p. 124.

11. From *Człowiek i swiatopogląd*, no. 3 (1980); in Patrick Michel, *Politics and Religion in Eastern Europe* (London: Polity Press, 1991), p. 142.

12. Quoted in Felix Corley, 'Soviet reaction to the election of Pope John Paul II', *Religion, State and Society*, vol. 22, no. 1 (1994), pp. 40–1; Soviet press reactions in *Le Monde* (10 November 1978); *Radio Liberty Research Bulletin* (19 October 1981).

13. Michel, op. cit., p. 134.

14. *L'Osservatore Romano* (19 October and 15 December 1978; 13 January 1979).

15. Corley, op. cit., p. 56; Wenger, op. cit., p. 186.

16. Račiūnas was reporting on a discussion with Mgr Ivan Dias, a member of Casaroli's Council for Public Affairs; Felix Corley, *Religion in the Soviet Union: An Archival Reader* (London: Macmillan, 1996), pp. 280–3.

17. *Lietuvos Katalikų Bažnyčios kronika*, no. 36 (January 1979).

18. French-language address in *L'Osservatore Romano* (15 December 1978).

19. Christine de Montclos-Alix, 'Le Saint-Siège et l'Europe' in D'Onorio, op. cit., pp. 154, 160.

20. *Redemptor hominis* (4 March 1979), no. 11.

21. Ibid., no. 17.

22. Ibid.

23. Ibid.

24. The survey concluded that Party membership had no 'significant influence' on attitudes to religion; *Kultura i społeczeństwo*, vol. 28. no. 3 (1984), pp. 202–3, 212–13.

25. Text in Jan Józef Lipski, *KOR* (Warsaw: CDN *samizdat*, 1983), vol. 2, p. 286.

26. Radio Free Europe, *Situation Report* (26 January 1979).

27. 'List Prymasa Kard. S. Wyszyńskiego do Premiera P. Jaroszewicza' (31 March 1979); in Raina, op. cit., pp. 131–2; Tad Szulc, *Pope John Paul II: The Biography* (New York: Scribner, 1995), p. 299.

28. Corley, 'Soviet reaction', op. cit., p. 42.

29. From *Ruga e Partise*, no. 2; *Radio Free Europe Background Report* (14 March 1979).

30. Leszek Moczulski, 'Rewolucja bez rewolucji' (June 1979); in Hemmerling and Nadolski, op. cit., pp. 518–88.

31. 'List KSCh Ziemi Grójeckiej do Jana Pawła II' (20 May 1979); ibid., pp. 499–502.
32. Lipski, op. cit., p. 287; Michel, op. cit., p. 142.
33. Pontifical Mass homily, Gniezno (3 June 1979).
34. Pontifical Mass homily, Kraków (10 June 1979).
35. Address to young people, Gniezno (3 June 1979).
36. Address to the 169th plenary session of the Polish Bishops' Conference, Częstochowa (6 June 1979).
37. Pontifical Mass homily, Kraków, op. cit.
38. Address to students, Częstochowa (6 June 1979).
39. Speech at Okęcie Airport (10 June 1979).
40. Michel, op. cit., p. 135. The Church hierarchy's apparent cold-shouldering of KOR collaborators, such as the devout Catholic Halina Mikołajska, was deplored by the group; Lipski, op. cit., p. 291.
41. Jozef Tejchma, *Pożegnanie z władza* (Warsaw: Wydawnictwo Projekt, 1991), pp. 97, 100. Tejchma was a former Minister of Culture.
42. Jan Milota in *Ateizmus*, no. 3 (1979); Michel, op. cit., pp. 136–7.
43. *Zeri i Popullit* (8 June 1979).
44. Corley, 'Soviet Reaction', op. cit., p. 43.
45. Ibid., pp. 48–9.
46. *Le Monde* (4 November 1979); *L'Osservatore Romano* (16 June 1979); Iwan Hwat, 'Ukraiński Kościół Katolicki, Watykan i Związek Radziecki', *Spotkania*, nos 33–34 (1987), pp. 79–92.
47. Declaration (3 November 1978); text in *Radio Liberty Research Bulletin* (18 June 1979).
48. *Vigilia* interview in Michel, op. cit., pp. 138–41.
49. 'Oświadczenie KSS KOR w związku z pielgrzymką Jana Pawła II' (1 July 1979); in Hemmerling and Nadolski, op. cit., pp. 592–4; Andrzej Micewski, *Kościół-Państwo* (Warsaw: Wydawnictwa Szkolne i Pedagogiczne, 1994), p. 65.
50. Bogdan Szajkowski, *Next to God . . . Poland* (London: Pinter, 1983), p. 74.
51. *Scinteia* (20 November 1979).
52. *Glas Koncila* (24 June and 5 August 1979).

11

❧❧❧❧❧

On the Polish barricade

By the summer of 1980, dramatic changes had occurred on the international stage. East–West *détente* had collapsed with the Soviet invasion of Afghanistan the previous December. The US Carter Administration had imposed sanctions on Moscow and suspended ratification of the SALT II arms treaty. Convinced the nuclear balance was tilting against it, NATO had unveiled plans for the deployment of Cruise and Pershing missiles in Europe. After the national failures of Vietnam and Watergate, and the humiliation of the 1979–80 Iranian hostage crisis, Americans looked set to elect the tough-talking Republican Ronald Reagan in an autumn presidential election. In the West too, the self-confident Polish Pope seemed to be recalling values modern societies had forgotten about.

From his Rome vantage-point, John Paul II could hardly fail to be moved when he saw the first pictures of a large-scale occupation protest at the Lenin Shipyard in Gdańsk that August. Visiting Poland in 1979, he had conjured up images of a nation defiantly reasserting its identity against the external forces of power and coercion. He had shown how a kind of freedom could be achieved, even against impossible odds, through upholding the values of trust and forgiveness which communism denied. Today, in the place where workers had been shot down in that bleak, far-off winter of 1970, the word 'Solidarity' appeared on the banners of 17,000 Gdańsk strikers. The Pope's picture was everywhere. His words were being repeated.

Solidarity had needed a spark; and as with previous revolts, it had been price rises. But although the Baltic strikers acted spontaneously, they showed tactical sophistication—enough to stay united and avoid being provoked into violence. It turned out to be their crucial asset: peaceful moral protests were a form of resistance to which communist regimes had no answer.

Academics argued over Solidarity's motives, usually portraying it as a political revolt driven by economic grievances. The truth was a lot more complex. Workers in Poland's strategic industries had been treated in a way calculated to ensure loyalty by sowing rivalries. Solidarity successfully countered these methods by creating a network of mutual support. The 9.48 million members it amassed in its first months called themselves a trade union; but Solidarity was really a social movement, motivated by civil and national demands as much as by economic and social ones. If it had one overriding aim, it could be summed up thus: to restore dignity to life and work, and to demand the justice and truthfulness which went with it. The August strikes were an industrial action, but they were also a spiritual experience.

Solidarity owed a great deal to the persistent efforts of Poland's 'democratic opposition', but the Pope's 1979 pilgrimage had also been a kind of dress rehearsal. The movement needed a new form of moral authority to replace the political and economic formulations of communism. This was one reason why it turned to the Church, and why religious symbols were used to express its aims and ideals. Tension between Solidarity's 'liberal-secular' and 'Catholic-national' wings was evident from the beginning. But it was the conviction that bridges could now be built between a rebellious social reformism and the values of Christian tradition—across the age-old fault line of the past two centuries—which enabled Solidarity to grow in strength.

The Polish Church had kept the rights of workers (in Cardinal Wyszyński's words) 'under study for a long time'. When controversy erupted in 1974 over planned changes to the Labour Code in Poland, the Bishops' Conference warned that workers' rights were the key to an efficient, productive economy. Wyszyński had called for Christian morality to be reflected in Poland's economy. 'At present, there is less and less hope of solving the proletarian problem with Marxism', the Primate warned in 1977. 'In the final analysis it is becoming clear that Marxism brings about the rebirth of capitalism by making man an appendage of the productive system and condemning him once more to slavery.' But Wyszyński had also reminded workers they were working 'for the whole nation'. Their tools and machines were not their own: they belonged 'to the whole working people'.[1]

In summer 1980 Wyszyński was sure about the causes of the labour protests. Output per worker in Poland, he pointed out, was only 25–30 per cent of that in the West. Because of wastage and inefficiency, living standards were well below what society was capable of achieving. Meanwhile, the Party monopolized economic life, depriving workers of 'freedom of opinion and the means of standing up for their rights'.[2]

The Pope pledged to be with his country throughout its 'ordeal'. Vatican II's Pastoral Constitution had enshrined the rights of workers to form unions and go on strike. It had called for 'human solidarity', and had listed 'degrading working conditions' alongside slavery and prostitution as 'offences against human dignity'.[3] Here at last was the kind of movement Pius XI had dreamed about in *Quadragesimo anno*: a movement defending workers' rights but also steered by Christian principles. Solidarity derived its strength from workers raised in supposedly godless urban developments. As time went on, however, it also drew in people from the Church's rural heartlands as well as city intellectuals and cultural personalities. From the Church's standpoint there could be no doubting Solidarity's demands were legitimate.

Yet Polish Church leaders responded cautiously to the prospect of social unrest. Remembering the bloody events of 1970, Bishop Lech Kaczmarek of Gdańsk urged the strikers to act 'wisely and prudently', and sent a team of priests to say regular Masses. Solidarity's sudden emergence clearly carried profound implications. In the 1970s, when workers' voices had been weak and inarticulate, the Church's tactic had been to rely on discreet behind-the-scenes bargaining. Ironically, preoccupation with practical issues had diverted the Church away from a comprehensive critique of communism, as well as from a clear vision for the society of the future. The result had been permanent deadlock, but the kind of deadlock in which manoeuvring was still possible, accompanied by slow, intermittent advances.

All established procedures now appeared to have been thrown in doubt. Poland's bishops had no idea how to handle an 'independent self-governing trade union', one which had emerged meteorically in the complex geopolitical conditions of the communist-ruled East. Dissidents from KOR and disgruntled Party members had also appeared at Solidarity's helm. So had nationalists and militant anti-communists. Was the movement really open to Christian inspiration? Would it stand up for Church rights too? Never before had the Church found itself depending on the initiatives of industrial workers; never before had it had to coexist with a mass social movement which looked set to gain more in days than the Church's bull-like negotiators had achieved in decades.

Wyszyński was said to have answered an urgent summons to Edward Gierek's country residence at Klarysew on 24 August 1980, and to have found the Party leader on the edge of breakdown. For an hour, Gierek begged the Cardinal to help calm the situation, rambling on distractedly about Soviet invasions and impossible demands.[4] Some of the story may well have been imagined; nonetheless it illustrated the importance attached to the Church by both sides. Barely a fortnight later Gierek was out, taking his 'Silesian Mafia' with him. A decade before he had pledged a new start after the excesses of Władysław Gomułka. Now,

Stanisław Kania, the new Party boss, promised Poland a new beginning after the failures of Edward Gierek.

Wyszyński had spent half his life building coexistence between the Church and communism. He hardly needed Gierek's panic-stricken splutterings to realize that Solidarity posed grave dangers as much as it created dramatic opportunities. Preaching before tens of thousands at Jasna Góra on 26 August, the feast of Our Lady of Częstochowa, he urged Poles to remember one thing: 'No one is without sin, no one without guilt.'

The new situation required a sense of responsibility, the Cardinal continued. Not even 'correct demands' could be fulfilled immediately.

> Let's think! How are *we* performing our own jobs? What contribution are *we* making to social life and the national economy? ... Sometimes we have the right, when there's no other way, to state our position even by stopping work. But we know this argument is expensive—the costs run into billions. They burden the national economy and ricochet back, piercing the life of the whole nation ... First, let's fulfil our duties; and then, when we have fulfilled them, we will be more entitled to demand our rights.[5]

The Polish regime seized on the homily as an appeal to end the strikes. Extracts were carried on newspaper front pages and broadcast repeatedly by the radio. Wyszyński had also condemned 'propagandist atheization'; but this was passed over. So was a Bishops' Conference communiqué the same day, defending worker, union and family rights with copious quotations from *Gaudium et spes*.

The Primate did indeed intend his words to have a calming influence. He had had the best part of a month to work out his reaction to the Baltic disturbances. He knew Solidarity's demands were justified—no one could reasonably doubt it. But how best to press those demands—that was a question of political wisdom. The Poles could be thankful for the relative freedoms they already enjoyed and could hardly be blamed for trying to extend them while an opportunity existed. An escalating conflict, however, could provoke outside intervention and sweep away everything. Patience and moderation would be required if Solidarity were to avoid falling into the trap of the honourable, but quixotic, rebellions of the past.

Wyszyński had offered to mediate. He was anxious to be seen as a Catholic mentor for all Poles, above the divisions between State and society. Like others, he was unaware that a new situation now existed in Poland. Solidarity's shipyard strikers were not the same as the angry protesters of 1970. They had been made wiser by a decade's experiences—as well as by the words of the Pope. They had learned the arts of democratic procedure within the confines of an authoritarian state. They had also learned how to feel free. This knowledge came not from books and theories but through encounters with other free people. It was a kind of freedom which was irrevocable, whatever Solidarity's fate might be.

This was one reason why the Primate's mediation attempt never quite materialized. Although a team of Church observers was despatched to Gdańsk they played little part in negotiations. The Gdańsk Agreement, signed on 31 August 1980, nevertheless promised 'protection of religious feelings', as well as radio broadcasting of Sunday Mass and Church access to the media. A week later, on the day of Gierek's ouster, Wyszyński received Lech Wałęsa, Solidarity's leader. He commended the Polish workers' struggle for 'social justice and freedom' in a pastoral letter.

Church leaders counted on their political sagacity to influence Solidarity, ensuring its demands did not escalate too quickly and provoke a communist over-reaction. Some were worried that more overtly political intellectuals from KOR could steer the movement in a confrontational direction. KOR had played a vital role in publicizing the strikes; but when Michnik, Kuroń and other activists were detained, the Church did nothing to help them. Instead, surviving KOR members were discouraged from coming to Gdańsk to offer advice.

Wyszyński himself was not against intellectual 'experts'; but he, like most Polish bishops, saw them as potential competitors for national leadership, whose commitments and loyalties were unpredictable. If Solidarity needed 'experts' at all, he wanted them to be people he knew and trusted. 'Remember that the heart, though very important, is lower than the head', Wyszyński told Solidarity representatives in December. 'Achieving even reasonable rights demands a hierarchy of values, and patience. What is most important is to safeguard the nation and family, to save the legal, social, cultural, moral, religious and economic order within the present system.'[6]

The Cardinal was speaking in exceptional circumstances. A Moscow summit meeting of Warsaw Pact leaders two days before had raised fears of a Soviet invasion. The US State Department had reported naval movements in the Baltic and an army alert in neighbouring countries. The Pope mentioned the 'alarming news' from Poland on 8 December and appealed to the Virgin Mary's intercession. Now was the time to give reassurances that communism was not about to be overthrown.

The Church's stance would, however, be subject to persistent disinformation. Wałęsa said he had wanted the movement to be more 'Christian', but had been advised by the Church itself against tabling too many religious demands. Yet the minutes of a Church–State mixed commission, revived after thirteen years' inactivity, reveal how the Bishops' Conference team used Solidarity's advances to obtain more and more concessions. In November it listed 30 demands, from recognition of the Church's legal personhood to the relaunching of Catholic publishing houses. The tone was sometimes agitated. Yet the impression conveyed by the minutes is mostly one of amicable familiarity. Both sides respected each other's concerns. They were free to take arbitrary decisions without any recourse to the will of Polish citizens. Only occasionally did the Church side say anything about the injustices of communist power.[7]

The Pope's position was quite different. He fully concurred with Wyszyński that Wałęsa and his colleagues should allow their heads to rule their hearts. But whereas the Polish Church was compelled to respond with day-to-day judgements and decisions, he could watch events from a distance, taking a wider panoramic view. John Paul had established that the Church was on the side of human rights. He had demonstrated how it could amass power, by acting as a conduit for suppressed cultures and identities. And he had shown where communism was weak. Successive acts of compromise and brutality had broken the back of Marxist ideology, leaving communism's structures intact but under pressure. What remained now was to work out how to dismantle these structures peacefully and irrevocably. It meant thinking in a long-term perspective, gaining and holding the moral high ground.

Heading a delegation to the Vatican in January 1981, Wałęsa assured the Pope Solidarity's aims were non-political. It was only interested, he added, in 'the rights of Man, of humanity, to faith and its proclamation'. It had learned from the Pope, Wałęsa said, that 'people must help their neighbours and fellow-men'.

Union rights were essential, the Pope responded, for human labour and working people. He had two wishes for Solidarity: that it should continue its search for justice 'calmly, persistently and fruitfully'; and that it should always show 'the same courage'—combined with 'the same circumspection and moderation'.

'Throughout this difficult period, I have been with you in a special way', the Pope continued, 'above all through prayer, but also by letting the fact that I am with you be known from time to time—in the most discreet way, and yet in a manner adequately understandable to you and to all the world's people.'[8] The encounter coincided with a Vatican document reaffirming the Church's duty to promote justice in work and defending the involvement of members of religious orders in trade unions.[9]

The Pope's forthright backing for Solidarity was only a symptom of deep changes in the Vatican's attitude to Eastern Europe. In 1974, Archbishop Casaroli had visited Poland as a guest of the regime. Today, by contrast, Vatican diplomats played down official contacts. 'Peace priests' were no longer made bishops: sees were filled by candidates 'supporting a central position'. Public diplomacy had gained the edge over the private contacts of the past.

The Soviet government was growing agitated. At the Ukrainian Catholic bishops' Rome synod in March 1980, the Pope had designated a US-based archbishop, Miroslav Lubachivsky, to succeed the ageing Metropolitan Slipyi—a sign that Greek Catholic resistance would outlive its contemporary figurehead. Slipyi had promised to 'devote himself entirely to God', the Soviet authorities pointed out, when he was released at John XXIII's request in 1963. Instead, he had gone on trying to revive Pius XII's 'crusade against the Soviet Union'. He was one of many 'revanchists and enemies of democracy' who looked hopefully upon the new Pope.[10]

Beyond the rhetoric, Kiev ideologists saw real dangers in the new Pope's talk of a part-Catholic Ukrainian identity. They hit back, stressing the Greek Catholic Church's historic association with foreign occupiers.[11] But the uneasiness mounted. The 'Polish contagion' of religiously-inspired dissent had to be contained.

The view was growing that the survival of religion owed something to alienation in communist society. Scientific achievements, some Party analysts pointed out, rarely reached the level of mass consciousness. Religion would persist as long as human ideals were unrealized.

I. R. Grigulevich, a member of the Soviet Academy of Sciences, diagnosed the problem this way: having been separated from it by modernity, the bourgeoisie was seeking a new alliance with the Church; meanwhile, the Church, thrust into crisis by the twentieth century's social and scientific revolutions, had turned to nationalism and political extremism to maintain its position. Hence, Grigulevich argued, the 'gigantic, well-developed machine of anti-communism' which had grown up around the Catholic Church. Yet the academician stuck to the orthodox view: the only real answer was 'improved Party work'.[12]

That was a crude euphemism. The only Catholic priest in Soviet Moldavia, Fr Vladislav Zavalnyuk, was expelled in May 1980 for venturing outside the boundaries of the Chişinău administrative region. Catholic documents submitted to the Conference on Security and Co-operation in Europe provided evidence that at least five priests had been murdered in Lithuania and Latvia in 1980–81. Several were said to have been KGB informers attempting to escape secret police clutches. These were only symptoms of the worsening situation facing religious believers throughout the Soviet Union.

Lithuania's Soviet regime restricted all contacts with Poland, warning citizens that 'bandits' were operating again in forested border regions. In early

1981 the Baltic republic's Church affairs commissioner, Petras Anilionis, put the number of 'extremist priests' at 150, a quarter of Lithuania's total. All priests were 'well-fed blood-suckers', Anilionis added. Their subversive acts were supported by the Vatican as a 'diversion' from events in Poland. Steps were taken to disrupt pilgrimages to Lithuania's new shrine at Šiluva to prevent 'something similar to the Polish situation'. In December 1981, Vilnius Radio denounced the 'ardent anti-communists' who sat 'at the microphones of Vatican Radio'. They were driving law-abiding Lithuanian Catholics, the radio added, into a confrontation with the Soviet regime.[13]

Catholic dissidents were not intimidated. Lithuania's unofficial Catholic Committee praised the Pope for 'reminding the forgetful West that Lithuania is a European country'.[14] There were rumours that Moscow had proposed to allow Bishops Steponavičius and Sladkevičius to be reinstated in exchange for the appointment of three 'reliable' prelates. But the Church's acting head, Bishop Liudas Povilonis, returned empty-handed from a Soviet-approved mission to Rome in 1981. The Lithuanian *Chronicle* showed solidarity with human rights groups in other Soviet republics. In February 1980 it asked the Pope to support Andrei Sakharov, the Soviet physicist just banished to the city of Gorky. A month later it wrote to Brezhnev demanding the release of three Orthodox dissidents: Gleb Yakunin, Dmitri Dudko and Alexander Ogorodnikov.

Concern over the Pope's role was growing in Eastern Europe too. East Germany's secret police archives suggest an agent inside the Vatican had given Erich Honecker's regime regular information under Paul VI. The material, passed on to the Soviet KGB, supposedly provided the Stasi with 'exact details' of the 1978 Conclave, enabling it to analyse Wojtyła's background and profile his immediate entourage. Evidence suggests the trail ran dry after John Paul II's election.[15]

In Hungary, Kádár played down the impact of Polish events, and was even said to have put in a word for the country at a February 1981 Soviet Party Congress. Czechoslovakia, on the other hand, closed its border and turned up its propaganda barrage. Solidarity's leaders were quite open about their Church links, declared the Slovak *Pravda*. The Catholic Church had supported the Hungarian and Czechoslovak 'counter-revolutions' of 1956 and 1968. It was now enforcing an anti-communist campaign in Poland as well.[16]

Yugoslavia was one of just two communist states with official Vatican ties. The other, to the bemusement of East European communists, was Cuba. But even in Yugoslavia there was no ideological let-up. Srdjan Vrčan, a Zagreb University researcher, conceded that religiousness expressed 'genuine problems'. What *were* the problems? Vrčan listed labour hardships, inadequate wealth distribution, repressive measures, lack of identity. When discontent was suppressed it sought refuge in religion as a 'traditional consciousness' which contrasted with the 'revolutionary consciousness' of modernity. But Marxism, Vrčan believed, still offered the only effective counter-analysis.[17]

Party hardliners sensed the best hope of dealing with the Polish crisis lay in provoking violence, or at least making the threat of violence credible enough to force Solidarity to back down. Fears of Soviet intervention had been played up by the Polish regime from the beginning. When strikers had blocked the Polish–Soviet rail link at Lublin in July, the Soviets were said to have warned that they would come and reopen it themselves. 1956 and 1968 had shown Moscow had the will to defend its interests.

That was one of the areas where Poland's shadowy Church–State commission found common ground. Worries were exchanged about neighbouring states, as well as about Solidarity's impact on trade and economic links. The Church side listened sympathetically when regime representatives asked for homilies preached during radio Masses to be censored because they could also be heard abroad.

The Pope had referred to the dangers of outside intervention in an October 1980 letter to Wyszyński. Putting the Gdańsk Agreement into practice, he told the Primate, required 'understanding, dialogue, patience and perseverance'; but Poles had a right to 'solve their own problems by their own means'.[18]

In December, the Pope was reported to have warned a visiting Soviet Communist Party official, Vadim Zagladin, against a Soviet invasion. The December scare subsided; but in January the Warsaw Pact's commander-in-chief, Marshal Viktor Kulikov, was in Warsaw on the day of Wałęsa's Vatican visit. Within two months, the tension again came to a head.

With Solidarity calling a general strike for 31 March, the Warsaw Pact 'indefinitely extended' its latest military manoeuvres. Cardinal Wyszyński described the situation as 'desperate', warning Solidarity that its demands endangered Poland's 'territorial integrity'. This time, the Pope acted directly. He sent a message to Brezhnev via the Soviet Union's embassy in Rome, promising the general strike would be called off. The Soviet leader sent his agreement back 'within an hour'—no strike: no intervention—and the Pope informed Wyszyński, who persuaded Wałęsa to cancel the general strike call without consulting other Solidarity leaders.[19]

When the Church–State commission met in April government negotiators thanked the Pope and Wyszyński for helping to 'preserve calm'. Church representatives were informed that Soviet troop movements had increased to and from the German Democratic Republic, but were assured that their deployment in Poland's southern forests was no more than a 'dangerous rumour'.[20]

The March showdown failed to halt a growing radicalization on both sides. On the afternoon of 13 May 1981, a Turkish assassin, Mehmet Ali Agca, shot the Pope through the abdomen in the middle of a crowd of 20,000 pilgrims in St Peter's Square. If the 9mm Browning Parabellum bullet had hit his central aorta, it would have killed him instantly. As it was, surgeons fought for more than five hours to save his life. He was in hospital for three months.

The finger of suspicion pointed at Moscow and the Soviet Union's allies in Bulgaria. Cardinal Wyszyński, now 79, had been confirmed dangerously ill with cancer the previous month. When he died on 28 May, after 32 years as Primate, the Polish press called him a 'spokesman for sound judgement' who had enjoyed 'society's full confidence'[21]—a nice irony in view of what had been said about Wyszyński two decades before. Had John Paul II died too, Poland's Catholic Church would have lost its two towering leaders in a fortnight. The Pope's death might have deflated Polish resistance; it might just as easily have fanned the flames of open rebellion.

'There are no words severe enough to condemn the criminal minds which conceived this plan', the Polish Communist Party's daily, *Trybuna Ludu*, declared, perhaps sensing a provocation. All public entertainment was cancelled: Kazimierz Barcikowski, a Politburo member, confided to Church negotiators two days later how he had wandered forlornly around Warsaw trying to buy cigarettes.[22]

Having blamed the Pope for events in Poland, communist leaders would have shed few tears for him; but evidence of Soviet and Bulgarian responsibility was sketchy. It was said that Yuri Andropov, the KGB chief, had investigated the possibility of killing the Pope, but even when the KGB's archives were opened in the 1990s, no firm clues were found. If communist agents were involved at all, they had uncharacteristically botched the job. Agca was a convicted terrorist. He was known to Western intelligence. He had fired at the Pope at close range, yet one of his two bullets had missed completely. He had left a trail of easily traceable contacts from Ankara and Sofia via Frankfurt to Rome. He had been certain to be caught, ending up in a high-security jail where, for years to come, he could spill the beans on everyone involved.

The Soviet press followed the case closely. As more details came to light it accused the Italian secret services and the American CIA of plotting the assassination to provoke an uprising in Poland.[23] On 5 June, three weeks after the St Peter's Square outrage, the Soviet Communist Party wrote to the Polish Party, accusing Kania and his Prime Minister, Wojciech Jaruzelski, of failing to control 'counter-revolutionary forces'. This time there was no voice in Rome to counsel prudence and restraint.

Viewed from the West, there could be no doubting the validity of John Paul II's campaign for human rights. It was unclear, however, what the impact of a crusading bridge-builder could be on the bipolar post-war order which had been rubber-stamped at Yalta. Europe had achieved peace and stability at the cost of the freedom and prosperity of three Eastern generations. It was the peace of the cemetery, the stability of gulags. But it was peace and stability all the same. How could there be a valid alternative?

That was how some Western officials looked at Solidarity and the Pope. The Church saw the priorities differently. Gathering with John Paul at St Benedict's birthplace, Subiaco, in September 1980, Europe's Catholic bishops had warned that the 1975 Helsinki Final Act would remain a 'dead letter' until 'peace with justice' was achieved. This required 'concrete solidarity' between Eastern and Western Christians.[24] The Pope had given the dream of a reunited Europe a new boost on 31 December, by declaring the Eastern saints, Cyril and Methodius, co-patrons of the continent with St Benedict. Meanwhile, he had repeatedly defended the rights and dignity demanded by Solidarity.

He now went a step further. *Laborem exercens* (14 September 1981) was delayed by his stay in hospital. It now coincided with Solidarity's national congress in Gdańsk, and was believed by Poland's communist regime to be directly addressed to it. The encyclical was intended to update Catholic social teaching on the 90th anniversary of Leo XIII's *Rerum novarum*. The world was living through a new phase of development comparable to the Industrial Revolution, the Pope said. It was bringing a reordering of economic structures which required the Church to restate the rights of workers.

As in *Redemptor hominis*, the Pope paid tribute to his immediate predecessors. John XXIII's *Pacem in terris* had set out the Church's 'key position', he said; and this had been taken further by Paul VI in *Populorum progressio*. Although these encyclicals had differed from earlier documents by dealing with worldwide issues rather than with nations and classes, pre-war teachings remained relevant for the light they threw on social injustices.

Yet *Laborem exercens* took the Church's analysis much further. It placed human work first—as 'a key, probably the essential key, to the whole social question'.[25] Marx had also considered work as central to the 'social question'. He believed the key to understanding it lay in the conflict between labour and capital—a conflict at the root of the human person's alienation, and to be resolved by proletarian revolutions which would abolish private property and exploitation. In *Laborem exercens*, the Pope took up these Marxist concepts and turned them in a Christian direction, just as, in a theoretical way, he had done in *The Acting Person* twelve years before. Both communism and capitalism, he pointed out, had treated work as a 'merchandise' sold by the worker to the employer. Work was today evaluated in 'more human ways'; but dangers still existed of a 'capitalist' reversal of order.

> Everybody knows that capitalism has a definite historical meaning as a system, an economic and social system, opposed to 'socialism' or 'communism'. But in the light of the analysis of the fundamental reality of the whole economic process—first and foremost of the production structure that work is—it should be recognized that the error of early capitalism can be repeated wherever man is in a way treated on the same level as the whole complex of the material means of production, as an instrument not in accordance with the true dignity of his work ...[26]

The human person was 'a subjective being, capable of acting in a planned and rational way'. All types of work, however high and low, were to be judged by how far they reflected this subjectivity.

The Pope looked back to the nineteenth century. The 'liberal socio-political system', he said, had fostered economic initiative by the possessors of capital alone, without paying attention to workers' rights. The resulting injustice and harm had 'cried out to heaven for vengeance'. They had given rise to a 'just social reaction', a 'great burst of solidarity' especially among industrial workers. Of course, this 'worker solidarity' had since brought great changes. But injustices were still being perpetuated worldwide. Some were 'much more extensive' than the nineteenth century's.[27]

What was needed now, *Laborem exercens* said, were 'movements of solidarity' which united all those facing poverty and exploitation. John Paul II did not deny that the 'great conflict' of labour and capital still existed, and that it had found expression in an ideological conflict between liberalism ('understood as the ideology of capitalism') and Marxism ('the ideology of scientific socialism and communism'); but he was against Marxist attempts to accentuate it with ideological and political weapons. He also differed from his predecessors when it came to offering a Christian answer. Popes from Leo XIII to Pius XII had talked complacently about Christian charity, while John XXIII and Paul VI had gone to the other extreme and demanded a transformation in the world's 'structures'. Instead, John Paul II saw the problem primarily in anthropological terms. The conflict of labour and capital had not resulted from structures at all: the economic process showed labour and capital as 'inseparably linked'. Rather, it had been caused by the 'error of economism', which had placed the spiritual and personal 'in subordination to material reality'.

The 'error of economism', produced by primitive capitalism and liberalism, had led to Marx's dialectical materialism. Its origins could be found in eighteenth-century theories which had laid the philosophical foundations for industrialization. But the 'error' was still occurring whenever efficiency and wealth creation were given priority over social justice and the primacy of labour. It had to be 'radically overcome' through adequate changes in 'theory and practice'.[28]

Which 'adequate changes' did the Pope have in mind? The key, as before, was to be found in the ownership of property. He pointed out that the Church had never regarded this as an 'absolute and untouchable' right. It was subordinate to the right of common use and the 'universal destination of goods'. In Catholic teaching, ownership had to reflect a harmony between capital and labour. Owning capital had no 'legitimacy' unless it served the interests of labour.

The Church's position obviously differed from 'rigid capitalism', the kind of capitalism which defended private ownership as an 'untouchable dogma of economic life'. It also 'diverged radically', however, from Marxist collectivism: converting the means of production into State property merely placed power in the hands of particular groups. What the Church had in mind instead was 'socialization'.[29]

This concept was not new. John XXIII had advocated something similar, and had been unable to prevent communist propagandists from portraying it as an endorsement of 'socialism'. This time, however, *Laborem exercens* provided it with protective packaging. Instead of demonizing communism, as previous Popes had done, John Paul II provided a rational, well-argued case against Marxist propositions. He also showed a capacity to think in the same terms, and brought Catholic social teaching up to date with contemporary economic thought.

The Pope concurred with Marxism that work helped clarify the attributes and potentialities of the human person. But whereas Marx had viewed the person as no more than a minor extra in the historic drama of competing forces, *Laborem exercens* placed him centre-stage. Marx had not respected work. He had seen it only as a tool for liberating human beings from the world of nature, something which would become unnecessary when the 'kingdom of freedom' was constructed. For the Pope, on the other hand, work was something positive, a participation in God's creation. It was the working person, linked to God by conscience and will, who was history's prime mover, not the external forces of wealth and power.

The most important right of workers, *Laborem exercens* continued, was a just wage. But close on its heels came the right to form trade unions and make them 'a mouthpiece of the struggle for social justice'. Unions formed part of the 'system of interconnected vessels' which made up social and economic life. Their activity entered the field of politics, but they could not be used for one-sided political ends.[30]

The encyclical drew an important distinction between the direct employer (the company) and the indirect employer (the State). Since unemployment was 'in all cases an evil', preventing it required planning and organizing by the State. It was still possible to ensure 'universal and proportionate progress by all', as *Populorum progressio* had suggested, by discovering the 'right proportions' between each branch of the economy; but this meant a 'just and rational co-ordination' which safeguarded initiative, not 'one-sided centralization'.

What *Laborem exercens* seemed to have sketched out was a 'humanistic' market economy, checked and balanced by moral principles—a harmonious social order not far removed from what Leo XIII had imagined or from Pius XI's 'community of communities'. But there was a key difference. Although previous Popes had similarly stressed labour's priority over capital, the anthropological focus of *Laborem exercens* was something new. John Paul had not wasted time condemning communism and urging Catholics to shun it. Instead, he had given a positive affirmation of what the modern Church had to offer. Human beings possessed dignity not only because of their likeness to God, but also because of work. They had a worldly dignity as well as a transcendent one; and it was possible to speak of justice only when these twin forms of dignity were upheld—when the organization of life and work allowed the human spirit to develop. This new philosophy of work was the fruit of the Pope's Polish reflections. Work lay at the heart of the social question. It was a key to understanding human beings. So it had to be the first point of departure for human liberation. God had given men and women the will to disobey worldly powers, while at the same time obeying values. It was through work that they recognized and served these values. This was how they became free and gained control of their destiny.

Poland's Catholic bishops reacted cautiously to *Laborem exercens*. Besides condemning injustices, they pointed out, it warned unions not to 'play politics'. This was an 'important lesson' for both Solidarity and the regime.[31]

The Pope's forthright defence of human rights, however, could hardly fail to have an effect in other countries too. In Czechoslovakia, Cardinal Tomášek had complained about being too old and isolated. But he now had a team of advisers, headed by his one-time critic, the Jesuit Fr Zvěřina, and was showing unexpected assertiveness. Czech and Slovak Catholics were plainly dissatisfied with their Church's 'minimization' strategy. More signatures had been added to Charter 77. Unofficial Church activities were on the increase. In December 1980, the Slovakia paper *Pravda* had publicly attacked the 'underground Church'. It had been active since the 1950s,

Pravda disclosed, and was perpetuating 'the action by reactionary forces in 1968'. Seen ideologically, this was something of a shot in the foot.

A clampdown duly ensued. But in mid-1981 the country's main Catholic *samizdat* publication, *Informace o církvi*, was adamant that the Church's rediscovery, especially by young people, was continuing undeterred. In late 1981, the government itself admitted that at least a third of citizens still saw themselves as Catholics.[32]

In Hungary the quarrel had intensified over religious base communities and renewal movements. Most dated from the 1950s and 1960s; but one, Regnum Marianum, had been launched at the turn of the century by the social reformer, Ottokár Prohászka. With at least 50,000 members nationwide no one could deny that they formed an integral part of Hungarian Catholic life.

But they also highlighted the official Church's passivity. This was what Hungary's bishops found hard to accept. Citing *Evangelii nuntiandi*, Cardinal Lékai had warned them against forming a 'church within the Church'. In summer 1981 he suspended two priests from Fr Bulányi's Bokor group for challenging the hierarchy's position on conscientious objection. The Primate ignored the protests. Conscientious objection was barred under Hungary's constitution, he insisted, and the Church would not sanction violation of laws. In early 1982 the Bishops' Conference branded Bokor a 'grave subversive movement' which had spread 'mistaken teachings' by 'guileful manipulation'. Bulányi was barred from ministering publicly the following June, accused of 'erring' from Catholic doctrine on religious revelation and Church order.[33]

If the Bulányi case highlighted the hierarchy's subservience, it also showed the dangers of going too far too fast when dissenting against it. That was a view the Pope seemed to share; but he could see the Bulányists' point. The situation was plainly intolerable for any Catholic with energy and initiative. Something needed to be done to shake Hungary's Church leaders out of their torpor.

When he met the bishops that October, the Pope reiterated that base communities must stay in unity with their bishops. Those who did so deserved to be 'supported and openly helped', he stressed. The implication was clear: Bokor could go to the wall, but the bishops should be doing more to support other groups.

Cardinal Lékai defended his policy. Hungary's communists had implemented the social and ethical principles set out in 1931 by *Quadragesimo anno*, the Primate brazenly asserted. This was why the Church would not attack them, and why it believed in negotiating 'small steps' behind the scenes rather than acting in a 'theatrical fashion'. The bishops were not against communities and movements in principle, Lékai conceded. On the contrary, small groups—with the exception of a minority—were 'the hope of our Hungarian Church'.[34]

Of course, every Church leader in Eastern Europe had his local situation to consider. In most countries, there were signs of restlessness. In a rare show of open criticism after Cardinal Bengsch's death in December 1979, East Germany's Catholic bishops attacked educational indoctrination in a pastoral letter. In neo-Stalinist Romania, Bishop Áron Márton of Alba Iulia protested against the forced assimilation of ethnic Hungarians. In Ukraine, the leader of an unofficial Greek Catholic 'Action Group', Iosif Terelya, who had unsuccessfully petitioned Paul VI to speak out, was arrested in 1982. Aged only 39, Terelya had already spent eighteen years in Soviet prisons and camps.

Observant East Europeans could sense the lessons to be learned from the Polish campaign of peaceful resistance. If Wałęsa's workers had gone out into the streets in August 1980, the regime would again have sent in its tanks. Communist hegemony would have been forcibly restated—accompanied, as before, by ostentatious breast-beating about 'listening to the people'.

This time, however, the workers had been smarter. They had grasped the dynamics of communist power and challenged it where it was weakest—with the kind of moral campaign it was unable to confront head-on. 'Solidarity was the first workers' revolution in history; the Bolshevist coup of 1917 has no claim to this title', Leszek Kołakowski wrote from exile in Oxford. 'It follows that the first workers' revolution in history was directed against a socialist state, and has proceeded under the sign of the cross with the blessing of the Pope. So much for the irresistible laws of history discovered scientifically by Marxists.'[35]

What brought the Polish experiment to a halt was, in the end, simple incompatibility—between a free trade union and a one-party State. In theory, Solidarity had faced a choice between consolidating its gains or advancing further. In practice there had been no such choice, for when rights and principles were at stake, how could a revolution agree to limit itself? Wyszyński had counselled moderation, but he also understood that freedom had a dynamic of its own. 'There is no doubt about Solidarity: it is what the Church has been struggling for over 30 years', Wyszyński wrote in his notebook.

Solidarity has broken the back of a monopolistic dictatorship—a monopolistic wrong interpretation of socialism. Socialism is not monopolistic, whatever doctrinal reservations we may have about historical materialism. Nor is it dictatorial, even if it talks about dictatorship of the proletariat.[36]

Not everyone shared Wyszyński's rosy view of socialism. At the Church–State commission in April 1981 the head of Poland's Bishops' Conference, Archbishop Bronisław Dąbrowski, had praised Wałęsa for following a 'rational policy' despite constant provocations. But by autumn it was clear a confrontation was coming. At Solidarity's Gdańsk congress, staged against a backdrop of Warsaw Pact naval manoeuvres in the nearby Baltic, there was talk of a 'self-governing republic'. An appeal was sent to fellow-workers around Eastern Europe, encouraging them to fight for 'free trade unions'. The Soviet Communist Party branded the appeal a 'repulsive provocation'.[37] Solidarity had crossed the Rubicon. Since Gierek's dismissal the year before, the Polish Party's membership had declined by a quarter, opening up bitter divisions. Power was slipping from the Party's hands. For neighbouring communist regimes, that was the decisive issue.

Church leaders believed hotheads from KOR, immune to the Church's moderating influence, had radicalized Solidarity. That was a point on which the State's new ruler, General Wojciech Jaruzelski, claimed to be in full agreement with the Church's new leader, Archbishop Józef Glemp.[38] When KOR dissolved itself in summer 1981 the move was merely interpreted as proof that it had successfully infiltrated the movement. The Bishops' Conference spokesman, Fr Alojzy Orszulik, was given a copy of Jacek Kuroń's 'political programme' by Barcikowski that November. He shared the view that Solidarity had made 'many mistakes', and that Wałęsa had lost control to 'radical activists'. Poland's bishops, Orszulik told regime negotiators, had a 'critical attitude' to Solidarity's activities too.[39]

With polarization intensifying, Glemp was adamant the Church would stay 'politically neutral' and not let itself be a 'tool in the hands of Solidarity or the State'. It would support Solidarity if it stayed 'faithful to its ideal of helping the workers'; but it would also support the State if it 'worked for the common good'. 'The Church will stand where the truth is', Archbishop Jerzy Stroba of Poznań assured regime officials. When Barcikowski suggested sharing information about an approach to the Pope, Cardinal Macharski of Kraków promised 'total discretion'.[40]

Church leaders made one final attempt that November to broker a solution by supporting proposals for a Front of National Unity. This would have recognized the Party's leading role but allowed independent figures to hold government positions. But by then Solidarity had fragmented. Jaruzelski's regime was under pressure to take decisive action.

It was in the small hours of 13 December 1981 that the tanks finally rolled. The imposition of martial law caught Poland unawares. But if General Jaruzelski had expected to quell resistance overnight, he was mistaken. Some

Solidarity members—Wałęsa included—argued that immediate protests could force the regime to back down. Others favoured underground resistance, steady pressure over a longer term.

The regime monitored Church reactions. Informers were posted at every Mass, local bishops called in to have martial law explained to them. Church leaders faced a grave dilemma. Torn between social unrest and State power, they had somehow to defend Solidarity's legitimate demands while also encouraging a prudent realism. And they had to respond quickly, at a moment when key factors—popular reactions, Army loyalties, Soviet attitudes, Western responses—were uncertain. In a fateful early-morning broadcast, Jaruzelski insisted his sole aim was to protect public order within the 'normal mechanisms of socialist democracy'. When the internal situation was stable, the General promised, the restrictions would be lifted. But Poland now stood 'on the brink of the abyss'. Failure to act would condemn the nation 'to catastrophe, chaos, poverty, famine'.[41]

The first Church response was quick in coming. In a hastily prepared sermon at Warsaw's Jesuit church, Archbishop Glemp gave Jaruzelski the benefit of the doubt.

> The authorities consider the exceptional state of martial law is dictated by higher necessity, the choice of a lesser rather than greater evil. Assuming the correctness of this reasoning, the man in the street will subordinate himself to the new situation ... There is nothing of greater value than human life. That is why I myself will call for reason, even if I become the target of insults. I shall plead, even on my knees: do not start a fight of Pole against Pole.[42]

The Primate preached a second sermon that day. The front line, he told young people, was 'not between Solidarity and government, but good and evil'. The best response was a 'realism of the Cross'.[43] It was his first sermon, however, that was seized on by Jaruzelski's Military Council and broadcast repeatedly by State radio, just as Wyszyński's Jasna Góra caution had been in August 1980.

Glemp's words were widely resented. Draconian measures were now in force: civil rights were suspended, thousands of civilians interned. Surely, many Poles demanded, there *were* more important things than human life. This was not the moment to try to be even-handed.

The Primate could hardly be blamed. He had accepted a Military Council explanation early that morning—that the immediate priority had been to prevent Party hardliners from staging a coup. Like other Church leaders, Glemp was sure the reforms were too far advanced to be turned back. Poland would be ungovernable without a national agreement. So far at least, this was a Polish quarrel. It could still be resolved by Poles; but if popular resistance proved too strong, Glemp seemed to reason, Jaruzelski would call in the Soviets. That would sweep away everything, just as it had done in Hungary and Czechoslovakia.

Even if open resistance seemed pointless, Church leaders still had to tread carefully. The Church itself faced fewer restrictions. If it gave the impression of tempering its response merely to safeguard its own interests, it risked alienating society. If, on the other hand, it rejected the regime's approaches outright, it could jeopardize whatever leverage it possessed. On balance, the Bishops' Conference endorsed Glemp's circumspection. The Church was convinced the nation 'will not retreat', its Main Council declared five days later.

Even the Vatican seemed ready to give Jaruzelski a chance. The Pope had been formally notified of martial law by the Polish Embassy in Rome. 'There must be a return to the path of renewal', he declared on 16 December, the day communist riot police opened fire on striking miners at the Wujek colliery in Katowice, killing nine and wounding 21. 'The strength and dignity of the authorities is expressed through dialogue, not force.'[44]

The Pope shared the view of Helmut Schmidt's government in West Germany that the outside world should not react precipitately. Later, the Vatican even called a press conference to deny Reagan Administration claims that the Pope favoured sanctions.

On 20 December the Vatican's Nuncio for 'special missions', Archbishop Poggi, arrived in Warsaw on a fact-finding visit. He brought a message from the Pope, urging Jaruzelski to repeal martial law, with a copy and covering letter for the interned Wałęsa. Regime officials said his Christmas Eve meeting with the General passed off in a 'spirit of mutual understanding'.[45]

But the Pope's reaction soon hardened. 'Working people have the right to create independent unions', he reiterated on 1 January 1982. 'Solidarity belongs to the modern heritage of working people in my homeland—and, I would go so far as to say, in other nations too.'[46]

By then it was clear that martial law had been well planned. As the immediate threat of violence receded, the Polish Church spoke more forcefully too— though Archbishop Glemp still believed nothing should be done to undermine Jaruzelski, and risk handing the initiative to 'hardliners' supposedly lurking in the wings. Glemp was living in Wyszyński's shadow. 'No handcuffs, no regulations, no exiles' could destroy Solidarity's ideals, he assured Mass-goers; but the late great Wyszyński had always warned that 'Rome was not built in a day'. Living and working could sometimes be a 'greater heroism' than giving one's life on the field of battle.[47]

Glemp's uncertainties were shared by the Bishops' Conference. Every passing day diminished the likelihood that Solidarity would be reactivated. It also brought fresh confirmation of society's determination to go on resisting. It took till late February for the bishops to come up with an authoritative collective statement, demanding a swift end to martial law and negotiations with 'credible representatives' of society, Solidarity included. It appealed to each side's sense of responsibility.

> Social accord makes demands not only on the authorities, but also on the whole of society. It is society's duty to adhere to a sense of realism in assessing our country's geopolitical situation. This does not mean either conformism to, or abandonment of supreme national values ... It requires us to define our individual and social demands wisely, taking a long-term view of our national future.[48]

When the Church–State commission met on 18 January both sides agreed in their basic reading of the situation. Perhaps, in the murky conditions of martial law, a firm stand on principle was impossible, but the commission's minutes refute the tidy image often painted of Church defiance under martial law. 'We think some of martial law's achievements can be to some extent accepted, although we think its very proclamation signifies a failure', Archbishop Stroba told regime officials. 'We don't deny that political methods were used on Solidarity's side, and that extremist forces dominated it. This is why we are suffering, although we also see something positive in Solidarity.'[49]

Jaruzelski's Military Council was keen to keep the Church's acquiescence. 'There are now two forces in public life which will determine the solutions: the Party-State on one side, and the Church and lay Catholics on the other', Barcikowski told the commission. 'We propose to construct a polygon from this axis, engaging other forces. But we cannot return to the triangle with Solidarity, since this has failed.'[50]

Church leaders knew this was a bluff: once social resistance was suppressed, the Church would be the regime's next target. The bluff could work both ways: the Church could also tempt the regime with gestures of support. 'Introducing martial law wouldn't have been so easy if not for the Church's attitude', Archbishop Macharski of Kraków reminded the commission.[51] There were moments, however, when Church negotiators seemed to succumb to the regime's blandishments. They proposed setting up a 'permanent contact' with Poland's Interior Ministry to co-ordinate the release of Solidarity leaders. They agreed that Wałęsa 'lacks intelligence to formulate anything himself'. 'We are close to each other', Stroba told regime officials. He was talking about young people. 'We are terrified that not only you, but we too cannot control them.'[52]

Both sides also shared misgivings about the role of John Paul II. When the regime protested against the Pope's appointment of an apostolic visitor for Wrocław's German-speaking Catholics, Stroba assured Barcikowski the Pope's decision was 'also very unpleasant for us'. Church representatives insisted the Pope took account of 'all forces' in his statements—not just the Church and Solidarity. Like Casaroli and his colleagues, they said, John Paul II was 'sympathetic to Polish realities'.[53]

Jaruzelski's regime viewed the Vatican differently. The Pope was believed to be under the thumb of Solidarity exiles in the West. 'We're worried the Church in Poland will find itself too strongly pressured by the Vatican, and start formulating Western-style demands', Barcikowski explained. 'You bishops know how the Vatican machine works. There are various interests at work there.'[54]

Whatever their negotiating stance, the Polish bishops' practical track-record was sound. They gave pastoral care to internees and opposed the sacking of Solidarity members who refused to renounce their loyalties. They also provided a venue for talks and intervened in hundreds of humanitarian cases. But the dilemmas mounted. How could the Church go on urging dialogue when Jaruzelski showed no sign of honouring his pledges? Many Poles believed the Church's authority was being exploited. 'Who has the right to speak on behalf of the victims about reconciliation?' one KOR activist wrote to Archbishop Glemp from an internment camp. 'Any concessions granted will merely mean returning part of our inalienable rights. But nobody knows for how long, for what price.'[55]

Perhaps the bishops' appeasement policy was the only option available; but it contributed to breaking the backbone of social enthusiasm for Solidarity's objectives. Had Church leaders really believed—or wanted to believe—in what Solidarity seemed to be offering? They had accepted Solidarity; but in practice this meant the part of Solidarity which embodied their own priorities. Solidarity, like Polish society, was a pluralistic mixture of good and bad. This was why their attitude to martial law was ambivalent. It would have been more forceful if Solidarity had been just as the Church wanted it to be.

There were no such doubts when it came to the Pope. Soviet propagandists continued to portray him as the main inspirer of events in Poland—part of a worldwide anti-communist conspiracy involving KOR, the CIA and the Reagan Administration. Solidarity had been born, the TASS news agency declared, 'in the bosom of the Catholic Church'. If Gierek's indebtedness to the West was largely to blame for Poland's crisis, his policy of Church–State co-operation had also demoralized and humiliated the ruling Party.[56]

When Reagan visited the Vatican in June 1982, just two months before John Paul was scheduled to make his second Polish pilgrimage, *Pravda* in

Moscow announced authoritatively that the US President had offered to send money to the Polish underground via Church channels, and had urged the Pope to go to Poland 'under the pretext of attending religious ceremonies'. The Vatican denied that the pilgrimage had even been mentioned, but the claim was used as one of several pretexts for cancelling the August visit.[57]

Rumours about secret Vatican–US contacts also persisted in the West. One press report said the Vatican had sent $50 million to Solidarity via the American AFL-CIO unions, another that the same $50 million had been sent by the CIA via the Church.[58] It was undeniable that the Vatican and the Reagan Administration shared an interest in keeping the human rights struggle alive in Poland, but they were working on different wavelengths and agendas. Reagan's envoy, Vernon Walters, and his Vice-President, George Bush, were said to have urged the Pope to back the US position at meetings in November 1982 and February 1983. But allegations of intelligence-sharing and secret accords are unlikely and unproved. In reality, John Paul endorsed the Polish bishops' statements while adding his own emphasis, thus bringing them into line with everything he had said in 1979. No Church–State deals could be cut without prior concessions to society. Like the bishops, he continued to oppose economic sanctions—the nub of US policy.

Czechoslovakia's regime nevertheless saw martial law as a defeat for the line laid down in *Redemptor hominis*. The 1979 encyclical had been deliberately titled, it said, to recall Pius XI's *Divini redemptoris*, the 1937 'anti-communist pamphlet' which had led to 'bloody terror'. The Slovak *Pravda* compared the position taken by Polish Church leaders to Cardinal Mindszenty's appeal for 'morality and patriotism' in 1956. The Church had exploited the Polish Communist Party's pragmatism and self-satisfaction, the paper added, as well as its lack of respect for 'socialist moral principles'. It had 'skilfully manipulated' all Polish social groups.[59]

The truth was that martial law had widened the division in world communism. In 1981, when Lithuanian Catholics appealed to Euro-communist parties on behalf of political prisoners, they showed sound instincts. In its 1979 programme the Italian Communist Party had confirmed that the heritage of Marx, Engels and Lenin had been 'enriched' by Gramsci and Togliatti. 'In the reality of the contemporary world', the Party added, 'the Christian conscience can stimulate commitment to the struggle towards society's socialist transformation.' The Party's leader, Enrico Berlinguer, insisted in an exchange of letters with Bishop Luigi Bettazzi of Bologna that aiming at a 'lay state' was not the same as being atheist. In December 1981, the Party daily *L'Unità* dismissed as 'false and devious' Soviet claims that Poland's 'counter-revolution' had been caused by the Catholic Church.[60]

Eurocommunist revisionism drew enraged reactions. Czechoslovakia's communists accused Western parties of 'playing into the hands of the class enemy'. Even in relatively moderate Hungary the idea that Marxism had become 'pluralized' was vigorously rejected. Of course, objective truth had to be 'critically and precisely verified', Party writers acknowledged. But not even György Lukács had wavered from the conviction that Marxism recognized only 'one correct answer to every question'.[61]

Martial law had, however, also dealt a death blow to Eurocommunism. Cardinal Roger Etchegaray, who headed the papal Council on Justice and Peace, acknowledged that he had 'generous and sincere' communist friends. But the Communist Party of France had unsuccessfully offered an 'extended hand' to Catholics for 40 years, Etchegaray said. Most still saw this as no more than a 'tactical gesture'. It was a sad tragedy that, wherever it was attempted, the liberation proclaimed by communists had led only to 'more crushing forms of alienation'.[62]

The rebuilding of communist power had deepened the rift between State and society in Poland. In October 1982, when Solidarity was banned under an arbitrary Union Act, it became clear that the Church had been double-crossed. It had urged calm on the promise that union rights would be restored. But the regime had gambled that its power was now secure. In casting aside the 1980 agreements it had rejected the Church's mediation, and forfeited the confidence of anyone who still believed a national accord was possible.

The new situation placed additional burdens on the Church's shoulders. It was now the only tolerated institution outside the State's direct control. With Solidarity's underground leadership unable to propose anything but further demonstrations, it seemed inevitable that the mantle of opposition must pass increasingly to the Church.

The bishops responded by retreating to a kind of strategic high ground. The idea of resurrecting Solidarity should be abandoned: this was clearly impossible. Instead, efforts should be made to preserve the Christian values Solidarity had embodied. The union's prohibition, Glemp told Warsaw Catholics, had initiated a 'third period' after those of August 1980 and December 1981. Authentic dialogue had been eliminated, along with Solidarity. 'But a Christian always starts again', the Primate added. 'We have great human solidarity, solidarity in work and national self-perception. It does not have to take the form of an organization.'[63]

This was hardly convincing. On 31 December, the Jaruzelski regime felt its 'normalization' was advanced enough to suspend martial law, after institutionalizing its restrictions through new laws. Some Poles believed the

Bishops' Conference had compromised itself. A year before, it had persuaded society to acquiesce, on the implicit understanding that, if it did, the Church would ensure concessions. So much for the regime's promises! So much for the Church's promises!

In reality, the bishops were simply making the best of a bad situation. Their priority now was to ensure nothing disrupted plans for a papal visit, now set for June. Jaruzelski was confident he could use the pilgrimage to drive a further wedge between the Church and Solidarity. But Solidarity's national commission, the TKK, also concurred that the best hope of re-establishing the movement's presence now lay with the Pope. In a letter to Rome, the TKK recalled Solidarity's role as a 'spiritual revolution'. But nothing should be done, they acknowledged, to jeopardize the visit in advance.[64]

To allay the regime's fears, Church negotiators denied any link between John Paul's 1979 pilgrimage and the rise of Solidarity. The Pope would not 'try to reawaken Solidarity', Archbishop Stroba assured his interlocutors. The latest visit, coming during a Holy Year, would have an 'approving' character.[65]

The regime had drawn its own conclusions. In two secret reports, the Party's Central Committee warned that the Pope's appearance could reactivate Solidarity, as well as strengthening the Church. That was not all: his 'messianic ambitions' could also undermine stability in neighbouring countries.

But the situation was more complex, the department pointed out. Some bishops were afraid the Pope's unpredictable behaviour could 'complicate future conditions for the Church's work'. Even in Rome there were worries that his 'one-sided political involvement' was endangering the Vatican's 'Eastern policy'. Church and government representatives had signed an agreement on the pilgrimage's main themes; but the Pope was not bound by this: he might well completely ignore it.

Yet the reports were upbeat. Church leaders had accepted Solidarity since it had boosted their influence in 'worker and peasant circles'. They were now co-operating with the State, however, fearing extremist acts would jeopardize Church 'achievements'. Most bishops—Glemp, now a Cardinal, was the best example—were decisively against opposition attempts to use the Church as a base. Out of 85 bishops, only three or four gave their preaching a 'negative content'. Out of 21,000 priests, only 390 were 'sporadically', 'frequently', or 'systematically negative'. The priority now should be to cut remaining Church links with the 'anti-socialist opposition'.[66]

The director of the government's Confessions Office, Adam Łopatka, was less optimistic about the proportion of 'anti-communist' clergy. But Łopatka had high hopes for Cardinal Glemp too. The Church had its own Central Committee and Politburo, he told Party lecturers. Notwithstanding Wyszyński's 1950 agreement and Vatican II, it had always sided with 'reactionary forces' and in 1980 it had merely renewed its reactionary stance. But the year 1982 had marked a 'political turning point', Łopatka argued. This was thanks to Glemp. Everything should be done to strengthen his position.[67]

The regime bargained long and hard over the Pope's itinerary. It rejected his request for a prior amnesty and demanded advance copies of his sermons 'according to custom'.[68] Even then, a series of provocations in the spring suggested hardline communists were adamantly against it. So were some Solidarity members, believing it would give legitimacy to Jaruzelski's regime.

On 16 June 1983, however, John Paul stepped into the Polish cauldron. By that evening, he had spoken of the 'bitter taste of deception, humiliation and suffering, of freedom denied and human dignity trampled upon'.[69] There was no single theme to the Pope's second Polish pilgrimage—other than maintaining the momentum of aspirations and reassuring Poles their struggle was not in vain. He fine-tuned the social teaching he had elaborated in 1979. A nation was genuinely free, he said, when it could 'mould itself as a community'. A State was truly sovereign when it served the common good, and allowed the nation to 'realize the subjectivity and identity peculiar to it'. The State's sovereignty was linked with its capacity to promote the nation's freedom—'to create conditions which enable the nation to express the whole of its historical and cultural identity, to be sovereign *through* the State'.[70]

Obviously, none of this could apply to a one-party State under martial law. But Jaruzelski's regime did its best to benefit from the pilgrimage, stressing the closeness of Church–State ties and reasserting its commitment to reform. It played its trump card repeatedly: 'when the State weakens and falls into anarchy', the General reminded the Pope, 'it is the people who suffer.' To support his case, Jaruzelski recalled the words of the hero of Poland's 1781 uprising, Tadeusz Kościuszko: 'The time has come when much must be sacrificed to save everything.' 'Poland is said to be suffering, the General told the Pope, 'but who will place in the balance the infinite sufferings, torments and tears we have been able to avoid?'[71]

The Pope made short work of the regime's claims that Solidarity was now just history. During a 'brutally frank' meeting with Jaruzelski in Warsaw's Belweder Palace, he said his image of Poland was of a 'vast concentration camp', full of 'hungry, shoeless, ill-clothed people'. Jaruzelski travelled to Wawel Castle in Kraków for a second meeting five days later. He told an aide he was worried Party colleagues would see it as an act of contrition.[72]

The pill was made more bitter still by John Paul's insistence on meeting Wałęsa. The Solidarity leader was flown to the Tatra Mountains aboard a Polish Army helicopter. It was a symbolic but crucial encounter—an acknowledgement that Polish conditions were not solely as the regime had defined them. Some Church and Vatican figures shared the regime's view that the meeting should not have taken place. Unnamed Church officials assured Western journalists the Pope had changed his 'negative view' of General Jaruzelski and saw him now as 'a sensible man with a great sense of responsibility'.[73] L'Osservatore Romano's deputy editor, Virgilio Levi, was persuaded to write that he had urged Wałęsa to give up Solidarity. This was pure disinformation. Even when the Vatican publicly disowned the article and demanded Levi's resignation, not everyone was convinced. But it was obvious too that the accommodationist stance of Polish Church leaders was not shared by the Pope.

At Jasna Góra the Pope offered a prayer for 'the difficult task of those who wield power on Polish soil'. But nothing 'real or just', he added, should be lost from the achievements of August 1980. Three Christians who were beatified during the visit all personified the triumph of the will over human frailty—whether in the courage of militant resistance or in the selflessness of aiding the poor. One was Adam Chmielowski, Brother Albert, whose 'righteous anger' had inspired the Pope all those years ago in his play *Brat Naszego Boga*.

In Warsaw, the Pope again urged Poles to work for a moral victory—a victory which came from 'living in truth, uprightness of conscience, love of neighbour, ability to forgive'. Poles should not want a homeland 'which costs nothing', he added.[74]

The Church–State commission expressed 'mutual satisfaction' with the pilgrimage. But this was for public consumption. An internal Party memo confirmed that the government had protested about the Pope's 'most aggressive' statements in Częstochowa, branding them a 'call to open rebellion and religious war', and threatening to curtail the visit. The Pope had presented a programme for 'Poland's total Catholicization', the memo noted. And he had incited listeners to pay a 'high price' for it.[75]

The truth was that the visit had cleared the air in Poland. The Pope had reaffirmed the legitimacy of the struggle for justice and dignity. He had given Polish Church leaders, after their hesitancy and indecision, a chance to start afresh. He had also set the Solidarity experience in a religious light, giving a Christ-like dimension to the suffering and bestowing a righteous sense that the suffering had its purpose.

The pilgrimage had highlighted the gulf separating the State's structures of power from the expectations of society. John Paul had again convinced his listeners that non-violence was essential. He had shown how liberation could be achieved by overcoming the desire for revenge. 'We experienced how much we can do when unified, and saw that things were not so bad for us', was Cardinal Glemp's reaction. 'In the final analysis, it is not structures that shape the spirit but the nation's spirit that gives the structures content.'[76]

The Jaruzelski regime followed up the pilgrimage with an amnesty. This, of course, had nothing to do with the Pope, government spokesmen quickly stressed. Nor did it cover KOR members or the Solidarity leadership. Martial law was finally lifted on 22 July, though the regime reserved 'special powers'. By now, Poland's communist rulers had irrevocably alienated the best and brightest citizens.

Notes

1. Quoted in Patrick Michel, *Politics and Religion in Eastern Europe* (London: Polity Press, 1991), pp. 89, 93; 'Memoriał Episkopatu Polski do Rządu' (1 April 1974); in Peter Raina (ed.), *Kościół w PRL—Dokumenty 1960–1974* (Poznań: W Drodze, 1995), pp. 653–4.
2. Speech at September 1980 pastoral conference; in Michel, op. cit., p. 92.
3. *Gaudium et spes*, nos 26, 74; Bogdan Szajkowski, *Next to God ... Poland* (London: Pinter, 1983), p. 92.
4. Wojciech Jaruzelski, *Stan Wojenny—dlaczego* (Warsaw: BGW, 1992), p. 89. Gierek gave a highly coloured account of his meeting with Wyszyński: Tad Szulc, *Pope John Paul II: The Biography* (New York: Scribner, 1995), pp. 346–7.
5. Text in Zygmunt Hemmerling and Marek Nadolski (eds), *Opozycja demokratyczna w Polsce 1976–1980* (Warsaw: Wydawnictwa Uniwersytetu Warszawskiego, 1994), pp. 725–33; Andrzej Micewski, *Kościół-Państwo 1945–1989* (Warsaw: Wydawnictwo Szkolne Pedagogiczne, 1994), p. 65.
6. Vatican Radio broadcast (5 December 1980).
7. 'Propozycje porządku dziennego obrad Komisji Wspólnej, Dokument nr 5' (13 November 1980); in *Tajne dokumenty Państwo-Kościół 1980–1989* (Warsaw: Aneks and Polityka, 1993), pp. 12–14ff.
8. Vatican Radio broadcast (15 January 1981); 'Przemówienie Papieża Jana Pawła II'; in Peter Raina (ed.), *Kościół w PRL—Dokumenty 1975–1989* (Poznań: W. Drodze, 1996), p. 199.
9. Sacred Congregation for Religious and Secular Institutes, *Le scelte evangeliche* (January 1981), nos 11–12.
10. For example, TASS (9 November 1981); N. O. Safronova in *Radio Liberty Research Bulletin* (16 March 1983).
11. Ibid. (3 December 1980).
12. *Literaturnaya gazeta* (23 December 1981).

13. *Lietuvos Katalikų Bažnyčios kronika*, no. 50 (8 December 1981); *Literatūra ir menas* (1 May 1982).
14. From the Committee's Document no. 21; *Lietuvos Katalikų Bažnyčios kronika*, no. 47 (19 March 1981).
15. *Der Tagesspiegel* (21 September 1996); *Rzeczpospolita* and Catholic News Service (29 September 1996).
16. *Népszabadság* (20 February 1981); *Pravda* (Bratislava: 23 May 1981).
17. Jure Krišto, 'Catholicism among Croats and its critique by Marxists' in Dennis Dunn (ed.), *Religion and Nationalism in Eastern Europe and the Soviet Union* (London: Rienner, 1987), pp. 79–82.
18. 'List Papieża Jana Pawła II do Prymasa Kard. S. Wyszyńskiego' (October 1980); in Raina, *1975–1989*, op. cit., p. 187; 'Relacja z posiedzenia Komisji Wspólnej, Dokument nr 6' (2 March 1981); in *Tajne dokumenty*, op. cit., pp. 16–20.
19. The messages and Wyszyński's role were documented in East German Stasi archive material; *Rzeczpospolita* (6 October 1984). Zagladin's meeting was reported in *La Stampa* (16 December 1980).
20. 'Dokument nr 7' (1 April 1981) and 'Dokument nr 8' (15 May 1981); in *Tajne dokumenty*, op. cit., pp. 46–8, 56; Micewski, op. cit., p. 69.
21. Polish Press Agency (28 May 1981).
22. *Trybuna Ludu* (14 May 1981); 'Dokument nr 8' (15 May 1981); in *Tajne dokumenty*, op. cit., p. 51.
23. For Andropov's alleged involvement, see Felix Corley, 'Soviet reaction to the election of Pope John Paul II', *Religion, State and Society*, vol. 22, no. 1 (1994), p. 58.
24. 'Deklaracja biskupów Europy' (28 September 1980); in Raina, *1975–1989*, op. cit., p. 171.
25. *Laborem exercens* (14 September 1981), nos 2–3.
26. Ibid., no. 7.
27. Ibid., no. 8.
28. Ibid., no. 13.
29. Ibid., no. 14.
30. Ibid., no. 20.
31. 'Komunikat konferencji plenarnej Episkopatu Polski' (16 September 1981); in Raina, *1975–1989*, op. cit., pp. 240–1; 'Dokument nr 12' (9 October 1981); in *Tajne dokumenty*, op. cit., p. 121.
32. *New York Times* (4 October 1981).
33. *Új Ember* (4 April 1982); *Népszabadság* (20 February 1982).
34. *The Tablet* (30 October 1982).
35. Quoted in Michel, op. cit., p. 3. See also Kołakowski's introduction to 'Poland under Jaruzelski', *Survey: A Journal of East and West Studies*, vol. 26, no. 3, part I (Summer 1982), pp. 3–5.
36. 'Notatki ze spotkania Prymasa Kard. S. Wyszyńskiego z przedstawicielami NSZZ Solidarność' (4 January 1981); in Raina, *1975–1989*, op. cit., p. 197.
37. Szajkowski, op. cit., p. 135; 'Dokument nr 7' (1 April 1981); in *Tajne dokumenty*, op. cit., p. 48.

38. Jaruzelski, op. cit., p. 193.
39. 'Dokument nr 14' (18 January 1982); in *Tajne dokumenty*, op. cit., p. 168.
40. 'Dokument nr 12' (9 October 1981); ibid., pp. 116, 124. Glemp's interview in *Le Figaro* (15 September 1981).
41. Quoted in Jonathan Luxmoore, 'The Polish Church under martial law', *Religion in Communist Lands*, vol. 15, no. 2 (Summer 1987), p. 126.
42. Ibid., p. 127.
43. 'Kazanie Prymasa abp. J. Glempa' (13 December 1981); in Raina, *1975–1989*, op. cit., p. 249.
44. Vatican Radio broadcast (16 December 1981).
45. Agence France Presse (27 December 1981).
46. Szajkowski, op. cit., p. 207.
47. Luxmoore, op. cit., p. 133.
48. Ibid., p. 137.
49. 'Dokument nr 14' (18 January 1982); in *Tajne dokumenty*, op. cit., p. 165.
50. Ibid., p. 163.
51. Ibid., p. 164.
52. Ibid., p. 174; 'Dokument nr 15' (5 May 1982); ibid., p. 184.
53. 'Dokument nr 19' (22 February 1983), ibid., p. 237; 'Dokument nr 12'; ibid., p. 119.
54. 'Dokument nr 14'; ibid., p. 172.
55. Letter from Anna Kowalska in *Communist Affairs: Documents and Analysis*, vol. 2, no. 1 (January 1983), pp. 105–6.
56. *Pravda* (Moscow: 19 June 1982). The full English-language exchange between Reagan and the Pope was published in *L'Osservatore Romano* (24 June 1982).
57. TASS (29 December 1982).
58. For example, *The Guardian* (8 January 1982). See also Carl Bernstein and Marco Politi, *His Holiness: John Paul II and the Hidden History of Our Time* (New York: Doubleday, 1996), pp. 235ff. No documentary evidence is provided in this book to substantiate its authors' claims that the Vatican and the Reagan Administration shared 'intelligence' on a regular basis.
59. *Pravda* (Bratislava: 5 March 1982).
60. *International Herald Tribune* (31 December 1981). The 1979 programme and Berlinguer's letter in Rosanne Mulazza-Giammanco, *The Catholic–Communist Dialogue in Italy* (New York: Praeger, 1989), pp. 70–1.
61. *Népszabadság* (13 May 1983).
62. *Le Figaro*, interview (3 January 1983).
63. Quoted in Luxmoore, op. cit., pp. 146–7.
64. Ibid., p. 155.
65. 'Dokument nr 16' (8 June 1982); in *Tajne dokumenty*, op. cit., p. 203.
66. 'Notatka Wydziału Administracyjnego KC PZPR, Dokument nr 20' (30 March 1983); ibid., pp. 208, 245–7.
67. 'Wystąpienie kierownika Urzędu do Spraw Wyznań A. Łopatki na spotkaniu z lektorami KC PZPR' (15 December 1982); in Raina, *1975–1989,* op. cit., p. 369.

68. 'Dokument nr 18' (21 February 1983); in *Tajne dokumenty*, op. cit., pp. 217–33.
69. Warsaw cathedral homily (16 June 1983); in Luxmoore, op. cit., p. 158.
70. Jubilee Mass at Jasna Góra (19 June 1983); in Jonathan Luxmoore, 'Polish Catholicism under fire', *Ethics and International Affairs*, vol. 1 (1987), pp. 172–3.
71. Belweder Palace address in *Dziennik Ludowy* (18–19 June 1983).
72. Jaruzelski spoke of 'going to Canossa', in a reference to the medieval Emperor Henry IV's humiliation by Pope Gregory VII; Mieczysław Rakowski, *Jak to się stało* (Warsaw: BGW, 1991), p. 56.
73. For example, a report in *Le Figaro*; in *Tajne Dokumenty*, op. cit., p. 322.
74. Warsaw Stadium Mass (16 June 1983); in Luxmoore, 'The Polish Church', op. cit., p. 160.
75. 'Opracowanie władz partyjnych' (20 June 1983); in Raina, *1975–1989*, op. cit., pp. 405–7. Łopatka's letter to Macharski; in *Tajne dokumenty*, op. cit., p. 294.
76. Vatican Radio broadcast (10 July 1983).

12

⌘⌘⌘⌘⌘

The long march of hope

'After the slavery of capitalism was overthrown, the workers found themselves in a totalitarian-collective slavery. Now they are threatened as much, like all humanity, by the slavery of technocracy.' The words of Cardinal Wyszyński's last will were written in 1969, but they could just as easily be applied to the Poland of 1983. A Warsaw University survey summed up the paradox. Asked who deserved public trust, 82 per cent cited the Church and 37 per cent the ruling Party. These figures needed interpreting. Fewer than half wanted the Church to increase its presence in public life. Religious and social sympathies did not necessarily translate into political loyalties.[1]

Jaruzelski's regime realized this. It saw its task as one of containment: keeping power despite losing support. So it fell back on a revised ideology—Polish *raison d'état*. Only the Communist Party, the regime insisted, could ensure the type of State acceptable to Moscow.

From the Party's perspective, this was a scenario in which a co-opted Church had a key role to play. It tempted Poland's bishops with attractive talk about 'socialism with the Church'. 'The Church must become part of the establishment in a new State, and feel responsible for it', the Confessions Office director, Adam Łopatka, told Bishops' Conference officials that December.[2]

The regime knew it faced a hard task. Church leaders could exploit its need for moral approval. But whatever their reservations, they also had to identify with popular grievances. The Solidarity experience had shown that a social movement needed binding values—values which provided a way of thinking and communication, which motivated acts of self-sacrifice and mutual support. It had also shown that these values could originate outside the Church—in traditions of civil disobedience and industrial unrest. The Bishops' Conference never quite accepted this. It knew, however, that all

255

advances in Church–State relations had to be linked to gains by society. The Pope had enshrined that principle. The Polish Church could hardly discard it.

John Paul's Thomist grounding had helped him. So had his studies of Marxism. From his Rome vantage-point he could see that power, in the end, could only be defeated by superior power. The Warsaw Pact's tanks, fighters and missiles could overrun Europe in days, but without people to drive, fly and fire them, there were only scraps of metal. It was in the hearts and minds of people, then, that this countervailing power lay. What the Church had to do was find a way of harnessing it.

The Jaruzelski regime had evaluated the Pope's 1983 visit guardedly. The Pope had given the impression of making 'concessions', a Party report noted. He had criticized 'socialism as a system', but had not tried to undermine it directly. Meanwhile the public reaction had been calmer than in 1979. Seven million people had attended John Paul's Masses, suggesting the Church's 'mobilization potential' was 'very big but not insuperable'.[3] But his talk of 'peaceful evolution' was more than it seemed, the report continued. It implied a shift from 'temporary political confrontation' to 'ideological-level conflict'. This was a novel and serious challenge.

The visit had also shown up differences in the Communist Party. A Central Committee member was under investigation for installing a papal shrine in his window. Local Party activists were complaining that the visit had 'morally strengthened the underground'. The Pope appeared to be suggesting Solidarity could be revived under the Church's umbrella. This was certain to encourage 'anti-communist clergy' and threaten the 'moderate line' of Cardinal Glemp. 'The Church is in a triumphalist mood', the report added. 'We must make the clergy aware the Church obtained this "triumph" not *against* the State, but thanks to far-reaching co-operation with the State.'[4]

The Party report noted 'big interest' in the visit among neighbouring communist regimes. As in 1979, the Soviet Union was concerned about the wider impact. Although the Vatican's 'principal interest' was in Poland, Hungary and Yugoslavia, one KGB directive claimed, it also calculated its new tactics would 'lead to political destabilisation ... in some parts of the Soviet Union'.[5]

Church leaders in Lithuania and Latvia had been refused passports for the Polish visit. They were now denied permits to attend a Rome Synod in October 1983. In East Germany an SED Politburo dispatch, compiled by agents in Poland, echoed the standard view that the Pope's visit formed part of the Reagan Administration's 'crusade against communism'. It was, however, upbeat. 'The Pope's confrontational political line is encouraging polarization within the Polish Party', the report noted. 'It should strengthen Party forces pressing for a more offensive Marxist-Leninist course.'[6]

The regimes had taken careful note of one thing: the Pope's defence of trade unions. The communist media recalled how Leo XIII had tried a similar strategy to block the advance of socialism. The 'theology of work' outlined in *Laborem exercens* posed new political dangers.

So did the technological advances which were making it harder to keep 'hostile ideas' at bay. In 1984, besides raising priests' salaries the Czechoslovak government printed 400,000 hymnbooks, 70,000 catechisms and 200,000 Bibles in a bid to deflate religious frustrations. At the same time, with at least 500 priests ministering secretly, complete with their own seminaries and convents, it also entered a new phase in its anti-religious strategy, drawing a distinction between the 'underground' and 'illegal' Church. Catholic spokesmen saw behind this. The 'underground Church', they insisted, was a communist invention, intended to provide a police target. In reality, those working in secret were merely doing what was necessary to keep the Church alive. They were acting with the Church's authority and were not anti-State.

But the 'illegal Church' was something different. Pius XII had granted the Church emergency 'special powers' to appoint clergy during the Stalinist persecutions. But unauthorized ordinations and consecrations had continued beyond that, among Catholic groups who had taken resistance rather far. At least 250 priests and sixteen bishops had started this way. Many were married; most had no documentation. The State knew all about them, and calculated that it could use them to undermine the Church's canonical order. This posed grave dangers—graver by far than ham-fisted acts of persecution.[7]

The veteran Eastern Europe-watcher, Cardinal König of Vienna, saw no change in communist policies. The 'joint line' was still defined by Moscow, König pointed out, which was still 'fighting religion as a matter of principle'. Of course, each government conducted policy according to local circumstances, but State atheism still asserted a 'total claim' on the human person.[8]

The Cardinal's interview was broadcast by Vatican Radio shortly before the Pope's September visit to Austria, during which John Paul prayed at Cardinal Mindszenty's tomb in Mariazell. Coming from a man who had helped engineer the conciliatory approaches of John XXIII and Paul VI, they were a significant indicator of how attitudes had hardened. König's remarks still betrayed a nostalgia for that era of 'long-term dialogue', observed the Slovak *Pravda*. But the lap-dog had followed his master. Now, even König had surrendered to John Paul II's 'vulgar anti-communism'.[9]

There was, in reality, a great deal more to John Paul II's outlook than that—as all communist regimes knew well. The Pope's conception of a reunited Europe presupposed some kind of reconciliation with other Churches, especially Russian Orthodoxy. The contacts initiated by Kotliarov and Borovoi at Vatican II had hardly progressed. The Soviet government had always been wary. Rome's rejection of a Ukrainian Greek Catholic patriarchate was seen as proof of the priority attached to relations with Orthodoxy. Discouraging Catholic–Orthodox links remained a key constituent of Kremlin policy.

In September 1978 the Russian Church's youthful foreign relations director, Metropolitan Nikodim of Leningrad, had collapsed and died, spectacularly, in the arms of John Paul I. Though the tragic heart attack had robbed Orthodoxy of a leading ecumenist, the Moscow Patriarchate had sent a delegation to John Paul II's inauguration a month later. Vatican and Orthodox delegations had also met at Bari and Odessa, continuing the theological debates begun at Zagorsk in 1973.

As a price for these encounters, the Vatican was ready to dabble in the peace slogans foisted on Orthodox leaders by the Soviet government. In December 1981, two days after the imposition of martial law in Poland, Brezhnev, with professors from the Pontifical Academy of Sciences, had denounced nuclear war. The following May, the Pope sent representatives to Patriarch Pimen's 'World Conference of Religious Workers' in Moscow.

John Paul II was, however, painting his ecumenical policy on a broader canvass. When he had declared Sts Cyril and Methodius co-patrons of Europe in 1980, he had called them symbols of 'the union of two currents of Christian tradition'.[10] In *Slavorum apostoli* (2 June 1985), he explained why. As creators of the Old Slavonic liturgy and Cyrillic alphabet, the encyclical noted, the Salonika-born saints had defended the Slavic identity against the Roman–German Empire. Having ministered as subjects of the Eastern Empire, while seeking approval from the Roman Pope, they were also 'models of acculturation', of a rediscovered Christian universality. 'Cyril and Methodius made a decisive contribution to the building of Europe not only in Christian religious communion but also to its civil and cultural union', *Slavorum apostoli* continued. 'Not even today does there exist any other way of overcoming tensions and repairing the divisions and antagonisms in Europe and the world.'[11]

Talk of a reunified Christian Europe spurred communist resistance. Paul VI had declared St Benedict Europe's first patron in 1964. Benedict's monasteries had been 'seedbeds of obscurantism' and had resisted the brothers' work, a Czech paper declared. Far from being 'mere acolytes', Cyril and Methodius had refused to allow the Pope to 'order them about'.[12] The Soviet press insisted that the Cyrillic script had long predated St Cyril himself. 'Christian Europe' was just a ploy by Western powers to provoke political opposition.

In Poland, the concessions won during the Solidarity era when the Party was weak were gradually being neutralized; but the opposition was deeply entrenched, backed up with an underground network of hundreds of publishers with even their own banks and insurance schemes.

While safeguarding its bonds with society, the Church had to maintain relations with the State. This meant looking in two directions, a mixture of testimony and diplomacy. The result, since Cardinal Wyszyński's death, had been a devolution of authority, giving local priests greater leeway in responding to the needs of their communities.

Under martial law many had let their churches be used as meeting places and shown a forceful lead. The bishops criticized the regime when it harassed them. The regime blamed the bishops for failing to control them. By 1984 both sides were accusing each other of becoming more combative.

In 1979 the Pope had commended the martyred St Stanisław as a model for bishops. But some 'radical priests' enjoyed tense relations with their superiors. In December 1982 Cardinal Glemp had sat in his Warsaw Curia for three hours, stony-faced, while 200 local priests threw epithets at him about 'acting against the nation'. He hit back, accusing them of behaving like 'journalists and politicians'.[13]

Only in a handful of cases, however, did Glemp or his bishops ever attempt to silence outspoken pastors. Society expected leadership through concrete words and deeds, most Church leaders insisted. No one would tolerate mealy-mouthed distinctions between the 'language of politics' and 'language of morality'. The priests in question were not linked to political factions and did not intend their words to have political effects. As Vatican II had ruled, the Church did not interfere in temporal government.

> It should, however, always and everywhere, have true freedom to proclaim the faith and its teachings about society, to fulfil its tasks among people without hindrance, and to make moral judgements even on political issues, if fundamental human rights or the saving of souls require it. So a moral evaluation not only of the behaviour of individuals but of all institutions comes within the Church's mission and is of a religious nature. The Church, fulfilling its mission of love, always has the duty to combat evil. It has a particular duty to do this when evil appears in public life.[14]

The regime saw things differently. In 1983 it denied compiling a blacklist of 69 'extremist priests', but confirmed that legal assessors had checked dozens of sermons. In a classified memorandum, the Confessions Office spoke of 'an illegal nationwide counter-revolutionary organization of clergy and laity'. Its 'main base', the Office noted, was Warsaw's church of St Stanisław Kostka. Its leader was a 36-year-old from near Białystok—Fr Jerzy Popiełuszko.[15]

Popiełuszko was well known in Poland. His powerful homilies drew on the simple exhortation from St Paul's Letter to the Romans: 'Overcome evil with good.' In February 1984 the Pope sent Popiełuszko a personal rosary: nine months later it was placed on his coffin. Church leaders in Poland treated the priest more cautiously. Under government pressure, Cardinal Glemp claimed to have given him 'paternal reprimands'; but regime officials believed his sermons were approved in advance by his seminary supervisor, Bishop Władysław Miziołek.[16]

There was, in retrospect, a kind of inevitability about Fr Popiełuszko's fate. A huge security apparatus had been built up under martial law, but the Jaruzelski regime had opted to combat opposition with administrative measures, rather than by outright repression. This had created many frustrations. Unexplained deaths in 1983–84 had fuelled fears that communist agents could resort to violence. Popiełuszko's murder on 19 October 1984 was precisely that—a classic act of terror intended to intimidate others.

It backfired disastrously. By the time the priest's body was dredged from Włocławek Reservoir, the whole story was in the world's press.

Jaruzelski condemned the killing and came up with a quick answer: it was a 'political provocation' by communist hardliners opposed to his policies of reconciliation. The regime was in the middle, Jaruzelski maintained, surrounded on all sides by forces of confrontation. This was the court's version, too, when four Interior Ministry agents were convicted in February 1985. The extremist Popiełuszko had been killed by extremists on the other side. The Church was largely to blame—it had failed to rein him when it had the chance.

In reality, communist responsibility for the priest's death certainly extended higher—some said to the Interior Minister, General Czesław Kiszczak, himself. A month before, Jaruzelski's spokesman, Jerzy Urban, had denounced Popiełuszko as the 'Savonarola of anti-communism', a practitioner of 'black Masses' and 'seances of hatred'.[17] There was no paper trail to prove the killing had been inspired and directed at top level. The evidence was overwhelming, but only circumstantial. Over 400,000 people attended Fr Popiełuszko's funeral in Warsaw on 3 November, in a massive show of support for the Church and Solidarity. In his sermon Cardinal Glemp called the priest a martyr and admitted his teachings had been theologically sound. 'It may be that this offering of life was necessary', Glemp told mourners, 'in order that the hidden mechanisms of evil would reveal themselves, and that the aspirations for good, honesty and trust might be liberated more forcefully.'[18]

The Popiełuszko case did, indeed, force the regime to place its apparatus of repression in the spotlight. This was not only humiliating: it was also the first of what would become a series of decisive political blows. 'All the material proves', a distraught Bishops' Conference secretary, Archbishop Dąbrowski, told Łopatka after the Toruń trial, 'that Church issues aren't dealt with by the administrative organs at all, but by the secret police.'[19] The Party Central Committee had been due to discuss measures against other radical priests. After Popiełuszko's murder, however, violent, arbitrary actions became much harder. The whole world was watching. The young priest's death had, in this way, saved the lives of others.

A pastoral letter from the Bishops' Conference told Polish citizens that Popiełuszko had died a 'heroic death'. Archbishop Stroba of Poznań tried to reassure regime negotiators: the priest was widely seen as a 'saint *against* the Bishops' Conference', he told them that April. But even Stroba had hardened. 'There's no doubt some priests' statements present us with a task', he told Łopatka, 'but you should calm down your own people. We have a common interest in avoiding conflicts and emotions.'[20]

The slaying deepened the sense that a moral struggle was under way in Poland. For a nation attached to its symbols, the figures of the vulnerable priest and his murderer, Grzegorz Piotrowski, personifying a godless, alien creed, driven mad by the goodness of his victim, conveyed powerful images. They raised the psychological barriers separating regime and citizens.

By the mid-1980s Jaruzelski's regime had been reduced to little more than a holding operation. It lacked the economic means to buy support, and was unable to make democratic concessions. In short, it was failing on both counts. Its only priority was to prevent a new social movement and hang on to power by ruses and stratagems. Poland was left with a relatively free civil society, existing within a shell of communist institutions. But society was too fragmented to be mobilized in opposition. Even if it had been, 'geopolitical realities' ruled out deeper changes. Thus, neither side could make headway against the other, as Poland slowly slumped into debt-burdened insolvency.

The regime needed the Church's pacifying influence as badly as ever, but was still trying to drive wedges by tempting Church leaders with privileges. The bishops had been promised $28 million in Western aid for a pilot agricultural foundation, to raise food production by boosting private farming. The Church-administered foundation would have circumvented foreign sanctions and could have attracted $2 billion in foreign donations. But it would have given the Church economic influence, and this was why the government blocked it. In the end, whatever the circumstances, the regime had to give precedence to its own power.

Bishops' Conference negotiators continued to protest their loyalty. 'I react with pain when it's said I am an oppositionist', Cardinal Macharski of Kraków told the Church–State commission. 'Tell it in the right places that I hold a different view.'[21] The mid-1980s, however, brought many other seemingly senseless Church–State disputes. 'There is a regress in Church–State relations now', Barcikowski told Church partners in April 1985. 'Poland has the greatest margin of freedom; and yet it is still isolated. Has its image been made any better by having a countryman in the Holy See?'[22]

The Pope had consistently demanded a return to the principles of the 1980 Gdańsk Agreement. 'The real problem is not between Church and State', he told Poland's Foreign Minister, Józef Czyrek, during a stormy meeting that June. Czyrek had come to renew Gierek's proposal for Polish–Vatican diplomatic relations, 'The real problem is between the State and Polish civil society.'[23] Seen in these terms, the deadlock was obvious. When Cardinal Glemp met Jaruzelski in April 1986, both reluctantly agreed that Vatican ties would be feasible only when 'essential Church–State problems' had been sorted out. The Polish bishops had a precondition—full settlement of the Church's legal status. The government wanted the Church to sign a declaration first, recognizing the immutability of Poland's socialist order. But how could the Church agree to this, when the government might then renege on the settlement? The regime wanted the commitments left vague. The Church wanted them precise and dependable. This was why there was no movement.

Presenting the Party's programme in December 1985, Jaruzelski gamefully warned members they faced a long struggle against 'internal enemies'. High priority would be given, he said, to countering 'political clericalism and intolerance'.[24] There were rumours of a new campaign to purge religious believers from the Party.

That was rather a sick joke for the Party's 'principled atheists'. An internal report by the Party's social scientists said that 49.2 per cent of PZPR members had admitted to being practising Catholics in 1981, while 69.9 per cent claimed to believe in God. The proportions had fallen by 1985 to 33.5 per cent and 59.5 per cent, the report added, confirming the Party was still 'more laicized' than the rest of society; but 17 per cent of Party members had accepted Church aid parcels while 92 per cent supported religious lessons and believed only the Church could guarantee of the nation's moral education.

The Party blamed Gierek. 'We are harvesting the fruits of his policy of ideological capitulation for the sake of the temporary political benefit of limited support from the Church hierarchy', the report concluded.[25]

The apparent fall in 'religious' Party activists after 1981 had a simple explanation. Most members with genuine ideals had left in protest under martial law, leaving the Party's ranks open to valueless careerists. Poland's ruling body had long since lost the capacity to recruit new talent. By contrast, Polish Catholicism's moral and intellectual standing was at a historic high. Catholics now generally won their arguments with Marxists. The cherished theories of materialism and class struggle had faded from serious discourse.

The regime still persisted in its efforts to divide and rule the population. In September 1986 it amnestied political prisoners and announced plans for a civil rights ombudsman and consultative council of public figures. Church leaders liked the council idea. They discussed possible candidates with regime representatives and summoned them for talks in a bid to persuade them.[26] Few respected figures agreed to join. In any case, the US lifted sanctions the following February, while plans for a new papal visit were set in motion when Jaruzelski visited the Vatican in January. But there was still no sign of compromise. The scheming and manipulating continued.

The Polish government could at least plead geopolitics. No other communist regime had shown signs of serious reform either. In March 1985, after gerontocratic interludes under Andropov and Chernenko, the Soviet Communist Party had acquired a robust new General Secretary. Mikhail Gorbachev was consolidating his power. At the twenty-seventh Party Congress, he declared war on 'reactionary nationalist and religious survivals'. *Pravda* celebrated the 40th anniversary of the Ukrainian Greek Catholic Church's suppression by demanding reinforced atheist propaganda.[27] Gorbachev had yet to utter the words which would become household terms world-wide: *glasnost* and *perestroika*.

The Pope had, however, thrown down a few gauntlets in the rest of Eastern Europe. In March 1982 a decree from the Vatican's Congregation for Clergy had barred priests from organizations 'undermining the authority of bishops'. It mentioned two types: those 'orientated towards trade unions', and those 'apparently supporting humanist ideals, such as peace and progress, but in reality pursuing political goals'. The decree applied to Pacem in Terris in Czechoslovakia. 'We all know about the activities of this association', the Congregation's prefect, Cardinal Silvio Oddi, told an Italian paper, 'and how brutally it interferes in the religious sphere.' In a Vatican Radio commentary, Pacem in Terris members were given a choice: obey Rome or give up the priesthood. Those who defied the decree, the Radio said, would have 'excommunicated themselves'.[28]

The timing was intentional. Cardinal Tomášek was in Rome with his four surviving bishops on 11 March, three days after the decree. The ageing Czech Church leader was being primed for action.

The Czechoslovak regime denounced the document and barred its publication. It was actually no different, the press proclaimed, from Pius XII's 1949 Holy Office decree which had forbidden Catholics to co-operate with communists. This time too priests would ignore it, thus exposing the weakness of 'political Catholicism'.[29]

The Pope was not mocked so easily. On his return, Tomášek branded Pacem in Terris guilty of a 'gross infraction of ecclesiastical discipline' and instructed the Czech and Slovak bishops to make the prohibition known. By August several dozen priests had resigned from the association. When its weekly, Katolické noviny, still refused to publish the Vatican decree, Tomášek withdrew its right to call itself 'Catholic'.

The regime instructed Katolické noviny to ignore the Cardinal's ruling. It warned that it was considering retiring all priests over 60, a move which would cripple the Church. It leaked rumours that Pacem in Terris would convoke a Lviv-style synod and proclaim the Czech Church independent from Rome. But samizdat journals supported the Vatican. 'God's work is conceived, strengthened and bears fruit on the basis of obedience', Vatican Radio emphasized. 'As Peter's successor, John Paul II is pastor of the whole Church. He does not need advice or guidance from Western or Eastern politicians. He does not yield to threats, or succumb to flattery from Left or Right.'[30]

The next Czechoslovak flashpoint came in 1985. Catholics had petitioned the Pope to visit Velehrad for the 1,100th anniversary of the death of St Methodius. The government refused to 'guarantee his safety'; so a papal pilgrimage was impossible. Meanwhile visas were refused to foreign Church leaders, including Cardinal König of Vienna, though the Pope succeeded in sending Casaroli. Over 150,000 Catholics descended on Velehrad to hear the Vatican Secretary of State say Mass. It was the largest religious gathering since 1945.

Supporters of Charter 77, which now had over a thousand signatories, welcomed the new Catholic assertiveness. The regime was used to Czechoslovakia's much-harassed political dissidents—'irksome weeds', one Politburo member called them in 1986.[31] It was not accustomed, however, to tense, large-scale religious events. After the Velehrad anniversary, Catholic shrines began attracting as many as 50,000 pilgrims on feast days. Tomášek gave up thoughts of retiring and started briefing Western journalists. 'The Pope is certain to come eventually', the 87-year-old declared in 1986. 'Our Church is not only working and praying, but also suffering for Christ and being crucified for Him.'[32]

Czechoslovakia's communists had worked hard playing up anti-Catholic traditions. Instead, they had placed the Church alongside the downtrodden, allowing it to rebuild its social bonds. Like Masaryk before them, they had also alienated Catholic Slovaks. Every act of repression was now challenged by human rights groups abroad.

John Paul II faced problems elsewhere. In Romania only one of the legal Latin Catholic Church's five dioceses had a bishop. Facing economic insolvency, Ceauşescu had taken drastic action. Food and heating were rationed, and those beyond working age refused medical treatment. A third of Romania's population was scheduled to be relocated, and half its 13,000 traditional villages demolished, to make way for 'agro-industrial centres'. Though Ceauşescu's mad-cap schemes were making even communist allies edgy, internal protests were rare. One in five Romanians had links with the secret police.

Something more could have been expected in Hungary, but without some spark of official Church dissent there was little the Pope could do. Cardinal Lékai still believed his Church's record was in line with Vatican II. *Gaudium et spes* had established that the Church was ready to co-operate with any political order if its mission was assured, the Primate pointed out. Today, as Kádár's Hungary continued its 'second stage of socialism', the Church's survival proved that antithetical value systems could meet on key points.[33]

By Lékai's death in June 1986 more than half Hungary's eleven dioceses were in the hands of sick old men. Half the country's 2,700 priests were past retirement age.

The 1982 decree had drawn angry Soviet reactions too, but there were cracks in the atheist façade. Being religious had become semi-respectable, even patriotic, by the mid-1980s. The Soviet Party's youth paper, *Komsomolskaya pravda*, admitted that many members attended church. Of course, the 'absolute majority' were really non-believers, the paper joked: they were forced to go by relatives. But many communists seemed unaware of the 'social hazards' of a 'modernized religion', Lithuania's chief atheist acknowledged.[34]

In Lithuania at least it was too late to dream up a new atheist offensive. The Soviet government had finally allowed the deposed Bishop Sladkevičius back to his Kaišiadorys see in 1982. When Lithuania's best-known dissident priests, Alfonsas Svarinskas and Sigitas Tamkevičius, were sent to the labour camps a year later, there were rumours of some kind of trade-off. If so, it had no deterrent value. Over 450 priests, three-quarters of the total, signed a Catholic Committee petition in 1982. 'History will forgive no one who has helped the atheist government's efforts to destroy the Church', noted the *samizdat* journal *Auŝra*. 'Whatever one's view of religion, everybody who considers himself Lithuanian should realize that contributing to atheist propaganda amounts to a betrayal of Lithuania.'[35]

The Pope received a new invitation from Lithuania's bishops for the 500th anniversary of the death of St Casimir, the Kraków-born national patron, in August 1984. Though the Soviets vetoed the idea the episode was given unexpected publicity by the Vatican. It was not John Paul's style to be fatalistic about a Soviet refusal. He was particularly offended that he was not even allowed to send Casaroli.

Fresh talk of a visit came round three years later, for the 600th anniversary of Lithuania's conversion. It was vetoed again, but this time Moscow felt obliged to give its reasons. They included Vatican Radio's 'anti-Soviet propaganda' and the Pope's 'support' for Lithuanian émigrés. By then, nationalist feeling was running high in all three Baltic republics. A month afterwards the anniversary of the 1939 Molotov–Ribbentrop Pact was marked by big demonstrations.

There were no regular *samizdat* journals in Latvia and Estonia to publicize Church problems. The Church was alive nonetheless. Cardinal Vaivods of Riga was given a Soviet award in 1985 for 'patriotic activities in defence of peace', but the honour was disingenuous. Even at 90, Vaivods was not a pliant figure.

Before dying in exile in September 1984, Cardinal Slipyi had spoken of three underground Greek Catholic bishops in Ukraine. When his successor, Archbishop Miroslav Lubachivsky, addressed the Rome Synod in 1985 he put the figure at ten. Ukraine was reported that year to be the home of 50 per cent of all new religious groups in the Soviet Union. 'You should know how difficult it is for atheists here', one Party teacher told a Soviet journal. 'I have been engaged in grass-roots propaganda of Soviet rites for many years; I have turned over mountains of literature ... How far the official figures diverge from reality!'[36]

The leader of Ukraine's Church 'Action Group', Iosif Terelya, who was sent back to jail for seven more years in 1985, claimed some local Catholics had considered launching a guerrilla war after the Popiełuszko killing in Poland. Wiser counsels prevailed. That March, the Pope received the Soviet Foreign Minister for the first time since 1979. Gromyko had met Paul VI five times in a decade; but now, he had little to say other than complaining about the Vatican's 'intolerance'.[37] The next Russian visitor John Paul received was the wife of the dissident physicist, Andrei Sakharov.

'We were looking at men who had lost some of their assurance', the Jesuit Jean-Yves Calvez remarked after a 'Christian–Marxist' dialogue in October 1986. The 30-strong Budapest meeting, co-organized by Cardinal Paul

Poupard's Secretariat for Unbelievers, was the first attended by Vatican representatives. 'Nowadays, there is not the slightest misunderstanding about the nature and development of Marxism and Christianity.'[38]

Even in 1986, that was an exaggeration. In Latin America especially the Pope had inherited a major challenge in Liberation Theology. Paul VI had warned Catholics against the myth of violent revolution. He had effectively discarded John XXIII's famous theory–practice distinction by reminding Christians that Marxist activity led to a 'totalitarian and violent society'.[39] But offering an alternative 'liberation' had been left to his Polish successor.

The Latin American Church faced the same problem as Eastern Europe's: how to combine diplomacy towards the powerful with testimony towards the powerless. The conditions, however, were utterly different. The wretched of South and East were like victims of fire and flood. Both had suffered pain—but in ways which made it impossible to comprehend each other's experiences.

In most of Eastern Europe the Catholic Church had been purged of its historic associations with wealth and power. In much of Latin America, those associations were as strong as ever.

Another contrast concerned Marxism. Even in Latin America, most radical theologians might well have concurred with the Brazilian Juan Luis Segundo that choosing between communism and capitalism meant 'choosing between two oppressions'. Yet from their Third World perspective they would also have agreed that 'the history of Marxism, even oppressive, offers greater hope than the history of existing capitalism'.[40] Ironically, similar things had been said in post-war Eastern Europe.

Liberation Theology was never a uniform movement, but certain emotions were shared. One was that theology must take account of real conditions and stop 'mystifying' injustices. Another was that the Church's view of itself as a model community, a *societas perfecta*, had been found wanting.

Gaudium et spes had begun to change things. Its very first sentence had acknowledged 'the grief and anguish of the men of our time, especially of those who are poor or afflicted'. Championing the 'Church of the poor', therefore, meant responding to the Council's challenge. That was what the 1968 Medellín conference of Latin American bishops had tried to do. By the time of the election of John Paul II some priests had taken this to further lengths.

Christian socialists had warned against attempting to construct a just order by 'vague denunciations and appeals to goodwill'. What was needed was 'an analysis highlighting the mechanisms that drive society', and a commitment to political action. Latin America's liberation from Spain, some argued, had merely opened the door to Anglo-Saxon colonialism. The Cuban revolution had established a fundamental alternative. The Church was duty-bound to respond with new forms of prophecy:

> A free press, free trade, education, politics—all the 'achievements' of liberalism—were the privilege of the élite. For the growing Latin American masses, under-nourishment, slavery and illiteracy, and later forced migration, unemployment, exploitation and crowding, and finally repression when they claim their rights—these are the harvest of the century of liberal democracy … The ideological appropriation of the Christian doctrine of reconciliation by the liberal capitalist system in order to conceal the brutal face of class and imperialist exploitation and conflict is the major heresy of our time.[41]

For some, revolutionary violence was justified against the violence of an unjust order which, in the name of 'peace' and 'reason', prevented human beings from perceiving and achieving righteousness. It was, as the *Communist Manifesto* said, 'the midwife of all old societies pregnant with the new'. Christ had commanded his followers to love their enemies, but he had not said they should not have enemies. Nor had he said all enemies should be loved in the same way. A Christian could love the oppressed by defending them. But radicals could also love their oppressors by combating them. In this way, both poor and rich could be 'liberated' at the same time.

These were some of the ideas which had spread among Christians in Latin America. The Peruvian Gustavo Gutiérrez had spoken of 'theology from the underside of history', of a Church ready to 'descend into the hell of this world' and be reborn from its 'complicity with oppression'. For some, Third World liberation required universal changes in Church thinking. The Brazilian Hugo Assmann wrote:

> If the historical situation of dependence and domination of two-thirds of humanity, with its 30 million deaths per year from hunger and malnutrition, does not now become the starting point for any Christian theology, in the rich and dominant countries too, theology will no longer be able to locate and give specific historical expression to its basic themes.[42]

Only a small proportion of Latin American priests had become involved with Marxist movements, but many sympathized with them. Opinions within the Church were sharply divided. Some had scorned Paul VI's cautious reminders and urged the Vatican to set the record straight. It was time to update Pius XI's denunciations in *Divini Redemptoris*, they argued, by reaffirming that communism was 'intrinsically evil'. Yet Rome's policy of 'dialogue' had given the impression that communism was acceptable—to be debated with rather than shunned. In this way, the Church itself had helped communism's expansion. Had not Lenin predicted as much when he called religion a 'most fertile field of infiltration'?

Liberation Theology's critics rejected the claim that Marxism's methods of social analysis could be distinguished from its atheist philosophy. Such concepts as 'class struggle' and 'superstructure' were only comprehensible in the light of Marx's proposition that consciousness was determined by one's social being. So also was proletarian revolution, the ultimate expression of historical dialectics.

Wojtyła's first major encounter with Liberation Theology as Pope came just three months after his election at Puebla in Mexico. Paul VI had promised to meet Latin American bishops here for the tenth anniversary of Medellín. He had left his successor a complex task: how to curb Marxist influences in the Church without reducing its commitment to social justice.

John Paul II praised the Medellín initiatives to foster 'an integral liberation of men and peoples'. But some 'interpretations' of the 1968 discussion, he added, had been 'not always favourable to the Church'.

That phrase, 'integral liberation', indicated the thrust of his critique. Liberation could never be merely a question of altering structures, the Pope made clear. It had to begin with a moral revolution—a revolution of consciences. Meanwhile, the idea that the Gospels could be 're-read from the viewpoint of the oppressed' was a dangerous fallacy too. So was the image of a 'new Church springing up from the people'—an *iglesia popular*.

> The Church has a duty to declare the liberation of millions of human beings, and a duty to aid them in consolidating this liberation. But she also has the duty to proclaim liberation in the integral, profound sense Jesus announced and realized ... a liberation which, in the mission appropriate to the Church, cannot be reduced to some pure and simple economic, political, social or cultural dimension, and cannot be sacrificed to the exigencies of strategy ... Man is not a being subordinated to economic and political processes: these very processes are ordered by man and subordinate to him. So the Church has no need to resort to systems and ideologies to love and defend man, and to collaborate in his liberation.[43]

There could be no doubting the new Pope's commitment to human rights. At Puebla he defended trade unions—an explosive issue in Latin America—and reminded listeners that private property could be 'expropriated without hesitation' if the common good required it.

John Paul saw his aim, however, as being to correct the 'mistakes' of Medellín. The imperfect liberation proclaimed by Marxism, he made clear, would always contrast with the 'true liberation' which came from a personal relationship with Christ. This would not be achieved by turning Christ into 'the subversive agitator of Nazareth'. Christ's image as a man who 'fought

Roman domination' and 'engaged in class struggle' violated Church teaching. The Gospels showed 'political attitudes' had been a temptation to Christ, not a vocation.[44] 'Remember: you are priests and monks, not social and political leaders', the Pope urged Mexico's Catholic clergy. Human rights were being 'trampled on as never before', but political action was a task for laypeople. They were called to struggle for social reform. They were not required to support Marxist ideology—or any other ideology.

The Puebla conference's concluding 'Message to the Peoples of Latin America' echoed the Pope's standpoint. It spoke of a growing gap 'between the many who have little and the few who have much', and warned that cultural values were being endangered by foreign exploitation and military rule. It also reaffirmed the prophetic responsibility of bishops as 'interpreters for our peoples'. But as *Octogesima adveniens* had noted, it would be 'foolish and dangerous' to forget the close link between Marxist theory and practice. 'We must note the risk of ideologization run by theological reflection when it is based on a praxis which has recourse to Marxist analysis', the Message cautioned. 'The consequences are the total politicization of Christian existence, disintegration of the language of faith into that of the social sciences, the draining away of the transcendental dimension of Christian salvation.'[45]

Had Latin American theologians actually gone this far? Some Church members thought John Paul had been fed a distorted picture of their teachings by critics like the secretary-general of the Latin American Bishops' Council (CELAM), Archbishop Alfonso López Trujillo. The Pope had not questioned the 'option for the poor'; but he had said little about the regime violence to which many priests had fallen victim. He seemed to have left the burning issues open, deflating rather than redirecting the Latin American Church's new-found dynamism.

What sort of counter-proposition was John Paul II really offering? In *Dives in misericordia* (30 November 1980) he returned to the Old Testament, as proponents of Liberation Theology had done. Christ had used the words of Isaiah to describe his own mission: 'to preach good news to the poor ... proclaim release to the captives and recovering sight to the blind, to set at liberty those who are oppressed'. But its full dimensions had been revealed by the Resurrection, with its promise of a 'new heaven and new earth'. Today, in a world 'entangled in contradictions', uneasiness was felt by rich and poor alike. Wealthy societies lived in plenty, while others died of hunger. This had created a 'gigantic remorse'.

> Man rightly fears falling victim to an oppression that will deprive him of his interior freedom ... This is why moral uneasiness is destined to become even more acute. It is obvious that a fundamental defect, or rather series of defects,

indeed a defective machinery is at the root of contemporary economics and materialistic civilization, which does not allow the human family to break free from radically unjust situations.[46]

The encyclical, the Pope's second, was optimistic. The reawakening of demands for 'decisive solutions', it argued, was proof that current tensions had an 'ethical character'. The Church shared these demands. It too wanted greater 'education and formation of human consciences in the spirit of justice'; but it also believed it necessary to restore the correct relationship between justice, love and mercy.

This was the point. Many programmes had been motivated by the idea of justice, but they had been distorted in practice, allowing hatred and cruelty to take over. 'Historical' and 'class' justice were good examples. They showed justice by itself was not enough if the 'deeper power' of love was absent.

To talk of love was not sentimentality. Marxism had done much to reveal the mechanisms of social injustice. If it had reminded the Church of something, it was that Christians could not confine themselves to personal sufferings alone: they had to be concerned with collective sufferings too, taking social and economic dynamics into account. Yet Marxism had given a collective class liberation precedence over personal liberation. Its 'programme' of justice, in the end, was more important than the individual's freedom. This was why love had to be the moral priority.

John Paul had talked about love's primacy over justice at the 1974 Rome Synod. Today he believed the Church also needed to rediscover the 'God of mercy'. His study of Scheler had taught him early on that resentments and hatreds, however understandable, were ultimately self-defeating. Personal strength lay in forgiveness, not in revenge. No acts of revolutionary violence would match the strength conferred by forgiveness. 'A world from which forgiveness was eliminated would be nothing but a world of cold, unfeeling justice, in the name of which each person would claim his or her own rights vis-à-vis others.'[47]

That was sound teaching, but it was hardly a practical alternative to Liberation Theology. Even when the Pope condemned the 'error of economism' and commended 'socialization' in *Laborem exercens*, many reformist priests were certain he had gone nowhere far enough.

Steps were already being taken, however, to reimpose order. Under Paul VI, the Jesuit order had been accused by critics of being over-tolerant towards Marxist influences. In 1978, its Basque Father-General, Pedro Arrupe, had warned that some Jesuits' 'commitment to Marxism' was causing 'scandal and confusion', particularly for those already 'suffering oppression and persecution under Marxist regimes'. But Arrupe had said other things too. For one, Jesuits should not 'close themselves' to the 'good that can be found in Marxism'. For another, they should not exclude 'a certain critical collaboration with groups and movements of Marxist inspiration'.[48]

The Father-General commissioned a survey on Marxism among members of the Society of Jesus in 25 countries. Some argued that elements of Marxist analysis—as opposed to 'vulgar Marxism'—could be used critically with other methods. Others cautioned against this: an atheist conception of the person, they insisted, was central to Marxist analysis. Most agreed that Marxism should be studied, in recognition of its influence on modern thinking. After all, St Thomas Aquinas had Christianized Aristotle's thought at a time when it too was seen as pagan and materialistic, and when many believed accepting a part meant accepting the whole. Marxism was waiting for its Aquinas, for someone to reinterpret it in a Christian direction.[49]

In a follow-up letter in December 1980, the Father-General listed the useable elements of Marxist analysis: 'an attention to economic factors, to property structures, to economic interests . . . a sensitivity to the exploitation that victimizes entire classes, attention to the role of class struggle in history'. He warned that 'everything must be verified, nothing can be presupposed'. He also advised against adopting Marxist analysis in its entirety, and against 'strategies which threaten Christian values'.

Jesuits should nonetheless remain 'fraternally open to dialogue' with Marxists, Arrupe reiterated, as well as to 'practical co-operation in concrete cases where the common good seems to call for it'. Although the existence of class struggles should not be 'generalized', it should be 'realistically and fully recognized'. Liberal methods of social analysis were also affected by anti-Christian ideological assumptions.

'I hope this letter will help all Jesuits who feel the need to analyse society', Arrupe concluded.

> We should also firmly oppose the efforts of anyone wishing to take advantage of our reservations about Marxist analysis in order to condemn as Marxist or communist, or at least minimize esteem for, a commitment to justice and the cause of the poor . . . Have we not often seen forms of anti-communism that are nothing but means for concealing injustice?[50]

Jesuit attitudes were important. With 25,000 members, the Society was the world's largest religious order. It ran Rome's Gregorian University, Vatican Radio and other major institutions. Politicization here, real or imagined, would have knock-on effects. In October 1981, when Arrupe was ill, the Pope suspended the Jesuits' constitution and put an 80-year-old Italian, Fr Paolo Dezza, in charge as his personal representative. In September

1983, when the order was allowed to hold a long-delayed congress, a Dutch conservative, Hans-Peter Kolvenbach, took over as Father-General.

That did not stop the feuding in Latin America. When Nicaragua's Somoza dictatorship was overthrown by Sandinista revolutionaries in 1979 the country's Catholic bishops had proclaimed it a 'sign of the Kingdom'. One of three priests given Cabinet positions, Ernesto Cardenal, had seen his Christian island community at Solentiname devastated by Somoza's troops. Cardenal called himself a 'Marxist who believes in God'. He had been converted to Marxism, he said, by reading the Gospel.

But Liberation Theology had acquired an even more powerful symbol in strife-torn El Salvador. When Paul VI had named Oscar Romero Archbishop there in February 1978 he had been viewed as a quiet, middle-of-the-road figure. Romero, however, had been radicalized—not least by the murder of Catholic priests. With most Salvadorean bishops fearing communist infiltration from Nicaragua and Cuba, Romero's forceful testimony divided the local Church.

At meetings in May 1979 and January 1980, the Pope warned Romero against becoming associated with the political Left. Regime extremists went further—they accused the Archbishop of encouraging El Salvador's Marxist guerrilla army, the Farabundo Martí Liberation Front (FMLF). On 24 March 1980, Romero was shot dead while saying Mass. Up to 50 mourners were massacred at his funeral a few days later.

The outrage was intended to deter radical priests. Instead, like the later Popiełuszko killing in Poland, it fuelled their fervour. The Vatican's March 1982 decree, barring priests from political organizations, was intended for Latin America too. At least two groups named by Cardinal Oddi—Sacerdoti Solidarios in Peru and Golconda in Colombia—were banned by their Bishops' Conferences. But it was in Central America that the deepest, most dangerous quagmire lay. How could the Pope counter alleged Marxist influences in the Church without at the same time identifying himself with the region's military-backed regimes and their US sponsors?

That was the question of the hour in March 1983, when the Pope paid his first visit. Over 35,000 Salvadoreans had died in four years of civil war. While most of the country's bishops opposed negotiations with the FMLF, Romero's successor, Arturo Rivera y Damas, had offered to mediate. He agreed with the Pope that the violence was 'deeply rooted in social injustice'.[51] But John Paul had demanded Church unity. That was certain to be his key concern.

Central America's bishops were said to have declined the Pope's request for a joint regional report on the grounds that local conditions were too varied. A CELAM delegation had been dispatched instead. Its findings, drawn up under López Trujillo's auspices, revealed deep differences—over Marxism, Romero's martyrdom and the 'option for the poor'.

The retired Mexican Bishop Sergio Méndez Arceo of Cuernavaca told Cuba's Communist Party daily in February how he believed 'clear-thinking Christians' should support the Nicaraguan revolution and work alongside Marxists and communists.[52] Voices like this were becoming rarer. The Pope had reiterated his position before reaching Central America. In a combative letter to Nicaragua's bishops he described the *iglesia popular* as 'a church born from the supposed values of a particular stratum of society rather than the free, unsolicited initiative of God'. It was being 'easily infiltrated', the Pope added, by 'strongly held ideological ideas linked with class struggle and acceptance of violence for the pursuit of determined ends'.[53] The hand of the anti-communist lobby was clearly evident.

The Pope was not even off the tarmac of Managua airport when he publicly reprimanded Fr Cardenal for 'acting outside or against the will of the bishops'. The Sandinistas hit back. The Pope's main Mass in the capital, celebrated before 250,000, was disrupted by hecklers. At one point, visibly enraged, he was reduced to shouting 'Silence!'

In El Salvador, FMLF guerrillas rejected Church calls for a truce and blacked out half the country on the eve of the Pope's arrival. John Paul paid homage to the assassinated Romero by praying at his tomb; but the Archbishop's sacrifice should not be 'instrumentalized', he added, by 'ideological interests', even though the current violence found its 'true, deep cause' in social injustice.

> The Gospel proclaims that the rich man who lives calmly and unjustly in egoistic possession of his goods can and must change; that the person trapped by terrorism can and must change; that the person who holds hatred in his heart must free himself from servitude; that love must reign where the language of armed conflict holds sway.[54]

In Guatemala, where five priests had lost their lives helping local Indians, the Pope said the Church knew the 'suffering, deprivation and injustice' many inhabitants faced. He urged Guatemalans, however, not to let themselves be used by 'ideologies which incite violence and death', or persuaded to 'take up arms of hatred and struggle'.[55]

The Pope gave his impressions of Central America when he returned to Rome. Arms were being supplied, he said, against the will of a majority which wanted 'peace and democracy'. The region's conflicts resulted from 'socio-economic structures' which had allowed a 'small élite' to accumulate goods while most of society lived in abject poverty. 'This unjust system must be changed by appropriate reforms', the Pope said, 'by observing the principles of social democracy.'[56]

The stormy pilgrimage was over, but it had not exorcized the spectre of Liberation Theology. In June 1984, editors of the Dutch-based *Concilium*, including the doyen of Vatican II theologians, Karl Rahner, made a 'strong and vigorous protest' against the charges levelled at it. Church leaders had 'stifled the Spirit', they added, with 'suspicious and unjust criticisms'. 'We firmly believe the Church's future, the coming of the Kingdom and God's judgement are tied up with these movements', the protest continued.

> These are tensions necessary to the Church's life. But today they are exacerbated by integrist and neo-conservative groups. Resisting all social change and holding that religion has nothing to do with politics, they fight against movements of liberation and make choices that are an offence to the poor and oppressed.[57]

John Paul II made two other Latin American trips in the next half-year. In October he told a Church conference at Santo Domingo that Catholic social teaching offered enough conceptual tools for fighting hunger and poverty; it did not need 'ideologies foreign to the faith'. Three months later he again denounced the 'intolerable abyss' between rich and poor in Venezuela, Ecuador and Peru. It was time, however, for Church leaders to 'correct with charity and firmness those who have erred'.[58]

'Charity and firmness' had been made easier thanks to the Vatican's Sacred Congregation for the Doctrine of Faith (formerly the Holy Office), which had just issued its first formal response to the Latin American challenge. The *Instruction on Certain Aspects of the Theology of Liberation* (3 September 1984) re-committed the Church to respond to the cry for justice 'with all her might'. It recognized the need for a scientific analysis of poverty's causes, and forbade those 'contributing to wretchedness' to exploit its reservations.

But it also criticized 'deviations brought about by certain forms of liberation theology'. Among others, it listed an 'exclusively political' reading of Bible texts; the view that sin was 'rooted in social structures'; and a notion of the Eucharist as a celebration of struggle rather than sacrament of unity.[59] Even the Church's Magisterium, the Instruction said, had been assigned to the 'class of oppressors'. Its teachings were being ignored as the false reflections of class interests.

In reality, the document continued, Marxism was 'epistemologically unique'. Its concepts could not be separated. To see things otherwise merely led to 'terrible contradictions'.

> The overthrow by revolutionary violence of structures which generate violence is not *ipso facto* the beginning of a just regime ... Millions of our contemporaries legitimately yearn to recover those basic freedoms of which

they were deprived by totalitarian and atheistic regimes ... which came to power precisely in the name of the people.[60]

The Instruction drew heated reactions. Brazil's powerful 360-member Bishops' Conference warned that its denunciations would provoke 'alarm'. When a leading Franciscan, Fr Leonardo Boff, was summoned to Rome that month to have his writings examined, Cardinals Aloisio Lorscheider and Paulo Arns went with him. The Instruction had failed to find a balance, Lorscheider explained, between Marxism and capitalism. It would have worked a lot better if it had highlighted the uselessness of violence without singling out Marxism.[61]

Other critics accused the Vatican of ignoring Latin America's needs and caricaturing the key issues. It spoke authoritatively of 'theologies of liberation', they pointed out, but then denounced them all generically. In effect it accused them of heresy, of reducing the Gospel to an earthly programme. This was unjust since no exponents of Liberation Theology had accepted Marxism uncritically. They *had* used Marxist categories, but so also had the Pope—most recently in *Laborem exercens*. The kind of undiluted political Marxism demonized by the Instruction was a tool of populists, not theologians. The latter were turning more and more now towards 'Third World' categories in their thinking. The Vatican had attacked an 'enemy' who was already in retreat.

The document was widely seen as part of a more general assault on the Church's post-Vatican II direction. When the Pope convened an Extraordinary Synod in 1985 to review the Council's teachings, that perception gathered strength.

The Congregation prefect who had drafted the Instruction, Cardinal Josef Ratzinger, was sure the Church had 'opened itself indiscriminately to an atheist and agnostic world'. 'We expected a new unity among Catholics', said Ratzinger, who had advised the German bishops at Vatican II. 'Instead, we have met with dissent, which seems to have gone from self-criticism to self-destruction. Paradoxically, the faith seems safe only in countries where it is officially persecuted.'[62]

Opinions varied as to how far Ratzinger's views coincided with the Pope's; but the latter clearly shared some deep reservations. Vatican II had never meant the same from a Polish perspective as it did in the West. 'The crisis is important and profound', John Paul concurred during a Belgian visit in May 1985. He was speaking not far from Leuven, where Camilo Torres, Gustavo Gutiérrez and other Third World theologians had studied.

> The Second Vatican Council determined the basic principles and means for the Church to carry out an appropriate spiritual renewal. But some have

studied, interpreted or applied it badly. Here and there, the renewal has been a cause of disarray and division. It has been unable to prevent a religious decline.[63]

Liberation Theology was not on the agenda at the Extraordinary Synod, but it was discussed enough to reveal deep splits in the Latin American Church. In the end the Final Report upheld the Pope's strictures against 'false sociological or political interpretations' of Vatican II; but it also drew a striking contrast between First World 'disaffection' towards the Church and Christian dynamism in Eastern Europe and Latin America. As Ratzinger had said, the Church was being accepted more where it was 'oppressed by totalitarian ideology'. It was also winning followers where it had 'raised its voice against social injustice'.

Meanwhile, the document corrected the naive optimism of *Gaudium et spes*—the 'signs of the times' looked different twenty years later. Hunger, oppression, injustice and war were spreading everywhere, demanding 'new and deeper theological reflection'. But there were true and false forms of *aggiornamento*, John XXIII's slogan. The Church would 'not only accept but fiercely defend' all truly human values. It recognized, however, that 'integral salvation' was possible only when these were purified by God's grace.

The Report invited Church members to debate what the 'option for the poor' really meant, as well as how the Church's social doctrine could be brought up to date. It also called for a more balanced concern between the Third World and Eastern Europe, where Christians were also 'suffering persecution for their faith and their support for justice'. Since Vatican II, the Church had become more aware of 'her mission to serve the poor, oppressed and marginalized'. Yet poverty took many forms. It meant a lack of material goods, but also the absence of spiritual goods. This kind of poverty was 'especially serious' when religious freedom was forcibly suppressed.[64]

Seen from Rome, the writing was on the wall for Liberation Theology. Gutiérrez's books were being checked by Vatican assessors. The Nicaraguan Ernesto Cardenal had been suspended from the priesthood. His brother, Fernando, had left the Jesuits. But did the Church have an alternative to offer? That question was still open.

An answer finally came in the shape of a new *Instruction on Christian Freedom and Liberation* (22 March 1986). Ratzinger's Congregation intended this to be more 'positive'. It acknowledged the 'powerful aspirations to liberation' at work in the contemporary world, and again recognized that it was up to local Church leaders to apply Church teachings directly.

From the French Revolution onwards, the Instruction said, the call to freedom had achieved many things: the abolition of slavery, equality under the law, the rejection of racism, human rights. But it had also generated confusion about the very meaning of freedom. The Enlightenment's 'individualistic ideology' had unleashed liberation movements, often Church-backed, against the poverty caused by industrialization. But these had often given rise to injustices just as grave as the ones they were meant to eliminate. 'Contaminated by deadly errors about man's condition and freedom, the deeply-rooted modern liberation movement remains ambiguous', the Instruction stressed. 'It is laden both with promises of true freedom and threats of deadly forms of bondage.'[65]

Christians had been guilty over the centuries of 'errors of judgement and serious omissions', the document admitted; but the Church's warnings had also been misunderstood. It had been accused of impeding liberation when in reality it sought to remind the world that the most fundamental liberation was from the 'radical bondage of evil and sin'. Some world-views saw atheism as a form of emancipation—and religion and moral law as forms of captivity. These were mere delusions. They left people to decide the meaning of good and evil for themselves. In this way, they helped create the very structures of 'slavery and exploitation' which they claimed to condemn.[66]

The Instruction took up Liberation Theology's familiar biblical themes: the delivery from the house of bondage in Exodus; the struggle of the poor of Yahweh in the Prophets; the passionate words of temporal salvation contained in Mary's Magnificat. Building the Kingdom and pursuing earthly progress, the text noted, were 'distinct but not separate'. Human beings belonged to different communities; so their liberation could be helped or hindered by just and unjust social orders. But the 'radical reason' for the loss of freedom always lay in sin—man's alienation from himself through his attempts to place his will above God's. This alienation lay at the root of all other forms of alienation.

This was why the 'option for the poor' could not be reduced to sociological and ideological categories. It was not a 'partisan choice'. It could not exclude anyone.

Catholic social teaching, the Instruction said, developed with the changing circumstances of history. It offered 'principles for reflection and criteria for judgement', as well as 'directives for action'. What kind of action? At this point, the Instruction seemed to reiterate traditional Church injunctions that the poor should accept their lot. The Church helped liberate the poor, it said, through 'numberless works of charity'. But it was concerned that its mission should not be 'absorbed by preoccupations concerning the temporal order'. The Church recognized the right of the oppressed to secure structures and institutions which ensured their rights. Structures could not, however, guarantee good results: moral integrity was also needed. It was necessary to work simultaneously for 'conversion of hearts and improvement of structures'. The Church condemned the violence of the powerful against the poor, but it also condemned 'systematic recourse to violence' as a means of liberation. Liberation was incompatible with hatred—even hatred of enemies.

> Situations of grave injustice require the courage to make far-reaching reforms and to suppress unjustifiable privileges. But those who discredit the path of reform and favour the myth of revolution not only foster the illusion that the abolition of an evil situation is in itself sufficient to create a more humane society; they also encourage the setting up of totalitarian regimes.[67]

The Instruction went on to modify *Populorum progressio*'s justification of violence. Armed struggle could be used, as Paul VI had ruled, as a 'last resort' against an 'obvious and prolonged tyranny'. This was accepted by the Church's Magisterium. Nonetheless, passive resistance offered a way 'more conformable to moral principles and having no less prospects for success'.[68]

The document acknowledged that salvation was inseparably linked to 'improving and raising conditions of human life in the world', and that 'ambitious programmes' were needed to liberate millions from oppression. It then relapsed, however, into the idealism of the pre-war Popes—the idealism which John Paul himself had once so effectively challenged. What was needed to cure the world's injustices, it said, was a 'just civilization of work', based on fair wages, participation and dialogue, the rich in solidarity with the poor.

> It would be criminal to take the energies of popular piety and misdirect them towards a purely earthly plan of liberation, which would very soon be revealed as nothing more than an illusion and a cause of new forms of slavery. Those who in this way surrender to the ideologies of the world and to the alleged necessity of violence are no longer being faithful to hope, to hope's boldness and courage.[69]

The Pope had 'approved' the Instruction. Yet there was something in it, as in the 1984 document, which jarred with his thinking. For one thing, both texts had generalized—about Liberation Theology and Marxism—polarizing their claims in order to undermine them. This had not been Wojtyła's approach. For another, both had highlighted the false reality conjured up by Marxism. Wojtyła, however, would have placed equal stress on the 'just anger' caused by abusive capitalism. Both documents had also ignored Marxism's 'social' dimension—its followers were usually motivated less by theories than by group affiliations, which appealed to the mentality of an exploited worker class and offered a sense of dignity. By simply condemning any truck with Marxism, the Vatican had failed to make sensible distinctions. It had not talked about social instincts at all: the word 'democracy' did not appear.

Clearly, Ratzinger's aim had been to harness Liberation Theology, and redirect it in a way acceptable to the Magisterium. On that point at least, the Pope must have concurred. But it was one thing to tender pious formulations, and quite another to offer practical guidance, a Christian praxis against Third World injustice. The Vatican had, in effect, stifled Liberation Theology, but had found nothing to put in its place. It had terminated dialogue with one of the twentieth century's most dynamic ethical initiatives.

The Pope met Nicaragua's Church leaders again at the Vatican in August 1988. The role of bishops, he told them, was to build unity under papal authority. He called for peace and dialogue, more vocations and improved catechesis. There was no mention of 'liberation'.[70]

The Pope spoke more strikingly in southern Africa a month later. There was nothing cowardly or passive in non-violence, he told his audience. Structures could be changed by changing human hearts. If that was the message from Eastern Europe, could it have worked in the Third World? In Poland the Church had been confronted with a mass revolt against the established power. It had succeeded in identifying with it, absorbing its energy. In Latin America, however, the Church had shrunk away from the proponents of radical change.

Of course, the situation was different; yet in both Eastern Europe and Latin America the conflict had similar features. Unjust ruling establishments were opposed by social movements from below. One was mostly hostile to Marxism, the other generally sympathetic; but both demanded much the same: human rights and dignity, democratic freedoms, a worthy existence. Why had the Pope disappointed Latin America, after so vibrantly answering the call from Eastern Europe?

One reason was that the Latin American Church, unlike Eastern Europe's, was not threatened by the established power. This was why it was divided over the aims of opposition. In the end, John Paul had to decide which side to come down on. He chose the *status quo*, the side which believed in change from within.

Another reason concerned the local regimes. The innate weakness of Eastern Europe's had been exposed, even with Soviet backing. But Latin America's, with US support, were not yet ripe for collapse. Even if they had been, what then? Was Liberation Theology an authentic response to local conditions, with thought-out, practicable objectives. Or was it just an abstraction, a projection of Leftist idealism? The aims of Eastern Europe's dissidents were achievable because they were mostly political and cultural. They were also cautious and carefully graduated: no one talked about seizing power or proclaiming revolution. The aims of Latin America's were less achievable because they were emotional and far-reaching. Revolution might bring a fairer regime, new laws, improved procedures, but it would not bring wealth and prosperity—at least not in the foreseeable future.

This had been the major problem with Liberation Theology. It had threatened to entangle the Church in a web of impossible commitments and responsibilities. Was it not better simply to nurture the faith, and allow individuals to act for themselves, rather than offer programmes, strategies, theologies which raised utopian hopes and expectations? In the end the Church's spiritual and social roles were both essential; but they could not be placed in conflict or allowed to endanger each other.

'It is the poor, the object of God's special love, who understand best', noted the 1986 Instruction, 'that the most radical liberation ... is the liberation accomplished by the Death and Resurrection of Christ.'[71] On that point at least, Ratzinger was right. But the long, bitter struggle over Liberation Theology had marked a change in John Paul II. For the first time, he had witnessed a human tragedy the Church seemed powerless to confront, which had brought him face to face with his own limitations and inadequacies. It had revealed a sullen, imperious Pope—a Pope who dampened rather than ignited enthusiasm for the cause of humanity, whose counsel was one of resignation rather than resistance. That was not an image Wojtyła had wanted for himself.

The Pope's handling of Liberation Theology drew scornful jeers from Eastern Europe. John Paul's calls for 'the pauper's reconciliation with the rich' were obviously phoney, noted the Czechoslovak daily Tribuna: he himself had taken a clear stand alongside 'reactionary, anti-popular forces'. He had reduced Marxism to 'primitive collectivism', agreed a Polish propagandist. Marxism and socialism had been anathematized to assist 'anti-dialogue forces' in the Catholic Church.[72]

Church opinions were divided. The Hungarian Bishop József Cserháti of Pécs believed the Vatican had condemned Liberation Theology too hastily. Others backed Ratzinger. 'It is one thing when the Antichrist acts in devious ways—through social exploitation and misery', a Lithuanian samizdat noted. 'It is something entirely different when the Antichrist seizes the helm of the State.'[73]

The latest blow inflicted on Catholic–Marxist links had an effect in Western Europe too. In Italy, the Communist Party's electoral support was fading anyway. There was no more talk of a 'historic compromise'. By contrast, hopes of 'moral reconstruction' were being harnessed by Church-backed renewal movements. One, Comunione e Liberazione, claimed 100,000 members by the mid-1980s, and had acquired features reminiscent of Luigi Gedda's Comitato Civico in the 1940s. It was widely criticized for its clan-like 'neo-integrism'; but it also showed that the Church could mobilize spiritual energies in a political direction. Comunione e Liberazione and movements like it were closest to Europe's Christian Democrats. They claimed to have the Pope's enthusiastic backing.

His latest encyclical set out to reaffirm the Church's rock-like permanence amid current uncertainties. *Dominum et vivificantem* (18 May 1986) evoked the Holy Spirit's constant presence in history, guiding the Church but also acting outside the Church's 'visible body' in the hearts of people. In the 'monumental struggle against powers of darkness', the encyclical noted, the conscience spoke as the voice of God. Ideologists who proclaimed the death of God were in reality proclaiming the death of man.[74]

The message of the coming Millennium, according to *Dominum et vivificantem*, was one of liberation by the power of this Spirit. The human person's freedom and dignity had acquired a special force in the case of persecuted Christians. They could be confident in the future, as well as in the power of prayer—the 'voice of those who apparently have no voice'.[75]

This was the year Mikhail Gorbachev pledged a 'resolute and uncompromising struggle' against religion. But it was a half-hearted statement. Gorbachev's book *Perestroika*, published in 1987, spoke of a 'democratized' communist order, purged of its failures by 'new thinking'. Of course, socialism would still triumph, the Soviet leader insisted; but it would triumph peacefully, as capitalism was forced to accommodate the righteous demands of the world's downtrodden. As for Moscow's client-states in Eastern Europe, each ruling party had 'sovereign rights'. 'Drawing on the Soviet experience, some countries failed duly to consider their own specifics', Gorbachev noted. 'A stereotyped approach was given an ideological tint by some of our own theoreticians and especially by practical leaders who acted as almost sole guardians of truth.'[76]

'Freedom within communism' was not quite a reversal of the 1968 Brezhnev Doctrine. Nor did it come anywhere near satisfying demands for change. The real aim of *glasnost* and *perestroika*, East Europeans felt sure, was to strengthen communism rather than dismantle it. Yet the strange noises coming out of Moscow *did* put in question a key premise of East European communism—that attempts at reform would always founder on the rock of Soviet refusals.

Western governments had begun a dialogue of sorts with East European dissidents. That was a significant departure from the cold *realpolitik* of *détente*:

it suggested communism's downtrodden critics were being seen as potential co-rulers. It also reflected a changing East–West equation. NATO had defied Western peace movements and deployed its Cruise and Pershing missiles. Scientists and engineers were at work on the US President's Strategic Defence Initiative (SDI), a calculated escalation intended to place intolerable strains on the Soviet defence budget; but a 1987 Reagan–Gorbachev summit in Rejkjavík had heralded a moderation in US policy. The high-tension confrontation of the early 1980s was easing.

John Paul II was working hard to maintain the momentum. In May 1987 he told French Catholics of his vision of a 'Europe united from the Atlantic to the Urals'.[77] This was a Marian Year and the Pope was speaking a month before his third visit to Poland. This time, however, he would be coming to a tired, despondent country. There was freedom of a kind in Poland—citizens spoke openly; the official media faced stiff competition from a 'second circulation' of underground books and newspapers; small-scale entrepreneurs could buy their way through the State bureaucracy. But the atmosphere was one of stasis, a directionless mix of frustration and deadlock.

As in 1983 there was uncertainty over what John Paul's homecoming would actually achieve. Rumours of Church–State deals had persisted through the 1980s. Church leaders had insisted there was no point waving Solidarity banners at the Pope's Masses. Would the pilgrimage not merely give a propaganda boost to Jaruzelski's regime?

Once again, events turned out differently. The Pope's meeting with Jaruzelski on the day of his arrival was devoted to human rights. A massive thunderstorm hit Warsaw soon after—a portent of what was to come. At his old Catholic University of Lublin the Pope spoke up for academic freedom. In the southern city of Tarnów he defended rural workers. In Kraków he urged listeners to combat prejudice and untruthfulness. In coastal Szczecin and Gdynia he championed the rights of families, young people and women.

There was no going back, John Paul made clear: the values and ideals of Solidarity were safe. Polish society still retained the coherence and wholeness given back to it in 1979–80. Its hopes and aspirations were legitimate—nothing had happened to invalidate them. All that was needed was to go on thinking in a 'long-term perspective', aided by the patient self-confidence supplied by Christianity.

Praying at Fr Popiełuszko's grave, the Pope appeared to endorse the mission of Poland's 'radical priests'. Meanwhile, at a special Mass for workers outside Gdańsk the Pope evoked the 'prospects of freedom' opened up by the nearby Baltic. The true meaning of Solidarity, he said, was bearing each other's burdens. No social or political theories could be invoked against it.

The world's workers were grateful for the August 1980 agreement, and for what it taught about the relationship between work and human dignity. The Church was grateful, too, that Poles had done their 'work on work' in a Christian spirit. 'Man has a right to share in decisions about his workplace', the Pope added. 'He has a right to self-management—including trade unions, independent and self-governing, as was stressed right here in Gdańsk.'[78]

The Pope also had special words for intellectuals, especially for the majority who had turned to the Church under the shock of events in the 1980s. 'People of culture and creativity, often coming from afar, have rediscovered their bond with the Church to an unprecedented degree', he told writers and artists in Warsaw. 'They have found in the Church a dimension of freedom they could not find elsewhere, discovering also its spiritual essence and reality, which they once saw only from outside. The Polish Church must respond to their trust, and find a language which reaches into their hearts and minds.'[79]

On several occasions the Pope welcomed pilgrims from other East European countries. In Kraków's Wawel cathedral he petitioned the revered Queen Jadwiga (1374–99) to embrace their 'destinies, aspirations and struggles', and reveal God's designs 'for Poland, Lithuania, the Russian lands'. And he called on Polish Catholics to show a 'missionary enthusiasm' in preaching the Gospel. Above all, the Pope challenged the assumption that change was impossible—the assumption which killed the civic spirit. Work and faith, he assured listeners, would produce a better future.

The Jaruzelski regime had hoped to show Polish citizens had accepted 'normalization', and that the Church, the object of their loyalties, was co-operating closely with the State. This cosy image now lay shattered. It was clear that society had *not* accepted its lot. Nor would the Church ever be co-opted while a Polish Pope remained at its helm.

Addressing Poland's 97-strong Bishops' Conference he scotched suggestions of any imminent move to establish Polish–Vatican diplomatic relations. It was a welcome prospect, he noted, but ultimately a decision for local bishops. Church–State relations must always reflect State–society relations. They could never amount to an administrative relationship between two self-interested entities.

Cardinal Glemp's advisers believed the Pope had given a 'great and new dimension' to the word 'Solidarity'. That was something even Jaruzelski tried to tap into. Millions of Poles, he told John Paul in a closing speech, believed religion could coexist with the values of socialism.

May the word solidarity flow from our land—with all people suffering from racism and neo-colonialism, exploitation and unemployment, persecution and intolerance. Your Holiness will shortly bid farewell to the homeland. You will take her image in your heart, but you cannot take her real problems with you. The nation remains here between the Bug and the Odra. It has to cope with the challenges on its own.[80]

Jaruzelski had looked angry when he walked out of his final meeting with the Pope. His half-baked appropriation of 'solidarity' broke the bounds of good taste. In any case, it made little difference. In his speech to the Polish bishops the Pope had assessed some of the lessons learned from the confrontation with communism. He spoke as if the challenge was over—a historical challenge sent by providence 'to purify and mobilize Christians for new tasks'. 'The Church has taken up this challenge', the Pope said, 'identifying it as a providential "sign of the times". Through this "sign" it has given witness to the truth about God, Christ and Man with new depth and force.'[81]

The Pope returned to this theme at the end of the year. *Sollicitudo rei socialis* (30 December 1987) marked the twentieth anniversary of *Populorum progressio*, the encyclical which had urged Christians to change the world through 'solidarity in action', and had condemned the 'hardships, unjust practices and fratricidal conflicts' caused by capitalism. John Paul II's aim was to apply Paul VI's insights to the 1980s, using a 'fuller and more nuanced conception of development'.

Populorum progressio had been highly original, he said, for linking development with justice and peace, but the hopes it had raised in the optimistic 1960s had not been met. Instead, the North–South divide had widened, while the frontier of development and under-development now ran through rich countries too. The human race's unity was 'seriously compromised'.[82]

Sollicitudo rei socialis attacked communism for suppressing the right of economic initiative. This had led to a 'levelling down', to passivity and submissiveness to a bureaucratic apparatus which placed everyone 'in a position of absolute dependence similar to the traditional dependence of the worker-proletarian in capitalism'. Communist parties had assaulted the 'creative subjectivity' of citizens by 'usurping the role of sole leader'. As for the claim that communism had overcome poverty, this was not true either. Denial of rights impoverished the human person just as much as material deprivation.[83]

The encyclical condemned terrorism, the arms race, the proliferation of refugees. It listed some positive signs: a growing concern for human rights and ecology; a sense of interdependence and common destiny; an awareness that peace and justice were indivisible. But it was particularly concerned to show the 'true nature' of development. The Pope criticized the 'naive mechanistic optimism' which held that development was automatic: such a view had more in common, he said, with Enlightenment 'progress' than modern realities. The ever greater availability of material goods met human needs and opened horizons; but true economic development needed what Paul VI had called a 'civilization of love'.

To understand development properly, the encyclical added, meant returning to the idea of sin. Unjust political and economic structures, far from being fixed and inevitable, were subject to the concrete acts of individuals. They had their roots in personal sins. What kind of personal sins? The encyclical listed selfishness, shortsightedness, 'mistaken political calculations', 'imprudent economic decisions'. But the most important was the 'absolutizing of human attitudes'—whether through an all-consuming desire for profit or through a thirst for power. And it was not only individuals who fell victim to this sin:

> Nations and blocs can do so too ... If certain forms of modern 'imperialism' were considered in the light of these moral criteria, we would see that hidden behind certain decisions, apparently inspired only by economics or politics, are real forms of idolatry: of money, ideology, class, technology ... It is a question of a moral evil, the fruit of many sins which lead to 'structures of sin'.[84]

What could be done? The answer lay once more in the concept of solidarity. Solidarity was not a 'feeling of vague compassion or shallow distress' at the misfortunes of others. It meant a determined, persevering social commitment. The strong had to feel responsible for the weak; and the weak had to make their contribution too. The Church's evangelical duty was to 'stand beside the poor', but without losing sight of the good of other groups.

The solidarity principle needed applying to international relations as well, the encyclical continued. Pius XII had made *opus iustitiae pax* the 'motto of his pontificate'. Paul VI had used the same slogan. Yet a better contemporary catchphrase was *opus solidaritatis pax*. World peace was inconceivable unless national leaders recognized that 'interdependence demands ... the sacrifice of all forms of economic, military and political imperialism'.[85]

Sollicitudo rei socialis was marred by vagueness and repetitiveness, but its widening of the concepts of development and solidarity broke new ground. So did its parallel treatment of East and West. The failure of Paul VI's hopes for development, the encyclical pointed out, was also linked to the East–West conflict. Both sides upheld different visions of humanity, antithetical attitudes to labour and ownership. Both backed them up with 'propaganda and indoctrination', as well as military power.

This 'logic of blocs' had gravely harmed developing countries, the encyclical argued, by denying them 'effective and impartial aid' and embroiling them in ideological conflicts. In reality, both rival concepts of development—the West's and the East's—needed 'radical correction'.

> This is one of the reasons why the Church's social doctrine adopts a critical attitude towards both liberal capitalism and Marxist collectivism. ... Each of the two blocs harbours in its own way a tendency towards imperialism, or towards some form of neo-colonialism: an easy temptation to which they frequently succumb.[86]

In apparent references to the US and Soviet Union, the encyclical deplored an 'unacceptably exaggerated concern for security which deadens the impulse towards united co-operation', as well as 'an economy stifled by military expenditure and by bureaucracy and intrinsic inefficiency'. It repeated *Populorum progressio*'s claim that resources devoted to arms production could be used to alleviate Third World misery, and accused East and West together of betraying 'humanity's legitimate expectations'.

This moral equivalence was the most controversial aspect of *Sollicitudo rei socialis*. It represented a vigorous attempt to reassert the Church's independence from rival powers.

> The Church's social doctrine is *not* a 'third way' between liberal capitalism and Marxist collectivism, nor even a possible alternative to other solutions less radically opposed to one another: rather, it constitutes a category of its own ...
> Its aim is to interpret realities, determining their conformity with or divergence from the lines of the Gospel.[87]

By highlighting human responsibility for injustices, the encyclical had restored some kind of balance between utopian preoccupations with structural change and a disembodied anthropocentrism. It had fine-tuned the Church's definition of poverty, showing it to be an East–West issue as well as a North–South one. It had also globalized the challenge of solidarity: what was needed was not a redistribution of resources so much as a 'sharing of burdens'.

In its closing sections, the encyclical reflected again on what it meant to 'love the poor'. Certainly, action against poverty must include reforms in the world's trading, monetary and financial systems; but it must also have a political dimension. 'Corrupt, dictatorial and authoritarian forms of government' had to be replaced by 'democratic and participatory ones'. Rule of law and respect for human rights were 'necessary conditions' for the human person's development. The struggle for them formed another aspect of that same 'love of the poor'. The private sins which underpinned the 'structures of sin' also included 'fear, indecision and cowardice'. Christians were called to action.[88]

Sollicitudo rei socialis was the least incisive of John Paul II's encyclicals. Perhaps its reluctance to offer firm answers reflected the breakdown over Liberation Theology. It nevertheless tightened the Church's arguments in the struggle against communist injustices. A top-secret report to the Polish regime had seen some positive features in the Pope's visit in the summer of 1987. This time there had been less 'political emotion, mass fanaticism and religious exaltation'. The Pope's talk of work ethics might even be socially useful.

The negative features, however, were a lot more numerous. The whole pilgrimage had been dominated by a 'confrontational tone', the report said. It was not that the Pope had taken issue with dialectical materialism—this was only to be expected. What was more alarming was that he had spoken in the name of workers—and been ecstatically applauded for it. He had given to understand that only Solidarity embodied 'humanistic social ideals', a notion which cut across vital communist interests.[89] He had also 'publicly glorified' the murdered Fr Popiełuszko, and beatified Karolina Kozka (1898–1914), a peasant girl killed by a Russian soldier. Politburo members had protested to Casaroli about the Pope's 'teaching, moralizing' attitude towards them. 'The Church will not leave the ideas worked out by Solidarity in the hands of political adventurists. It is trying to take over the opposition', the document concluded. 'This is how it will strengthen its influence on strategic processes within the Polish nation.'[90]

The Church had become increasingly assertive in other countries too. It took barely a year for *glasnost* and *perestroika* to unleash a war of invective between reformists and conservatives throughout Eastern Europe. By 1988 'geopolitical realities' were no longer the decisive factor. Each country's domestic balance of power counted as much.

In Poland the regime tried and failed with a referendum in November 1987 to trade tough economic reforms for a vague promise of freedoms. It publicly permitted a few unofficial journals, promised to review its law on associations, and marked the anniversary of the student clampdown of March 1968 by acknowledging past 'mistakes'. Meanwhile, it tried to harness lay Catholic support through a discreet dialogue with Warsaw's Catholic Intelligentsia Club.

Its moves inspired no confidence. Strikes in April and May 1988 spread to the Lenin Shipyard in Gdańsk, and restarted that summer after a visit by Gorbachev in July. On 26 August, eight years after the Gdańsk Agreement and desperate to restart production, the government again bowed to demands for free trade unions. Negotiations opened that autumn for government–opposition Round Table talks.

With the Communist Party still deeply divided over whether to negotiate at all, the regime encouraged Church leaders to view themselves as powerbrokers. 'We don't see it as a "black–red" or "throne–altar" alliance, as some have called it', a Politburo member reassured the Church–State commission. 'But we believe Church–State ties have provided the foundation for changes.'[91]

In February 1989 the Bishops' Conference sent two observers to the Round Table talks. When a power-sharing agreement was initialled that April, the Pope told Glemp he had finally agreed to diplomatic relations. The changes in Poland, he said, had brought a 'moment of credibility'—for 'stressing the State's sovereign rights, based on the full sovereign rights of society'.[92]

Conditions still diverged sharply around Eastern Europe. When Gorbachev visited Prague in April 1987, Charter 77 signatories urged his help in overcoming two decades of 'political, economic and moral crisis'. The Husák regime made a stab at reforms. It announced plans to modify central economic planning, and abolish 'pointless restraints and prejudices'. It even hinted that some Prague Spring reform communists could be 'rehabilitated'.[93] But communist control remained as rigid as ever. The Party was gambling, dissidents sensed, that Gorbachev would not survive. It was merely paying him lip-service with promises and half-measures.

The Chartists had seen the importance of Church support. In 1987, a sixteen-point 'Charter of Believers' was circulated with Tomášek's approval and a decade of prayer inaugurated. A year later, a 31-point Catholic petition drew half a million signatures, the largest protest in communist history. The regime's response was double-edged. A March 1988 Catholic demonstration in Bratislava was brutally dispersed with dogs and tear-gas, while in May the regime consented to three new bishops, the first for fifteen years. But that still left most sees empty and 75 per cent of Czech parishes without pastors. There was no discussion of a change in Church–State relations. Arrests and harassments went on.

In neighbouring Hungary the Pope had spent nine months finding a successor to Cardinal Lékai. He finally settled in March 1987 on László Paskai. Theoretically a compromise candidate, Paskai had toed Lékai's line. But political pressure was building up. In 1986 the anniversaries of Hungary's war of independence in 1848 and of the Soviet invasion in 1956 had been marked by large demonstrations. Reform voices were growing louder within the ruling Party, as Kádár's 'retirement' beckoned in May 1988. In a bid for nationalist support the government engaged in a war of words with Romania over Hungarian minority rights in Transylvania. Over a hundred Hungarian newspapers were banned by the Ceauşescu regime, including several communist dailies.

Archbishop Paskai showed no change in his attitude to the Bulányists, but the suspended Bulányi had become marginal to the growing web of dissent. In 1987, the Vatican again condemned his 'false, dangerous and misleading views'. At the same time, steps were taken to improve the Bishops' Conference's ties with other movements and communities.[94]

In the Soviet Union, signs of popular revolt centered on Lithuania. When the republic's bishops visited the Vatican in April 1988, the Pope assured them of his 'universal, fraternal solidarity'. 'Your Church is confidently entering its seventh century of Christianity', he added. 'Fresh breezes of renewal are beginning to blow among you, arousing new, strong hopes among millions.'[95] The former exile, Bishop Sladkevičius, was raised to Cardinal a month later, becoming the Soviet Union's second after Vaivods of Latvia and Lithuania's first since the seventeeth century. By then agitation was growing against the Soviet Army presence. Church leaders attended unofficial national commemorations. Similar events were occurring in Georgia, Armenia and other republics.

A State commission in Moscow was reviewing the Soviet Union's religious laws. In April 1988 Gorbachev told the Russian Orthodox leader, Patriarch Pimen, that the new regulations would respect religion by 'restoring Leninist principles'. It was the first top-level Church–State encounter since Stalin's overnight Kremlin meeting in 1943.

The Soviet leader had good reason for courting Russia's Orthodox Christians. The millennium of Christianity in Russia fell that June—an event Soviet propagandists had prepared for since the early 1980s. Gorbachev saw religious people as natural supporters of his 'new thinking'. For the first time in many decades the prospects for change had begun to seem genuine.

In 1985 the Pope had looked ahead to the Russian millennium in *Slavorum apostoli*. The baptism of Prince Vladimir of Kievan Rus' in 988, he now told Catholics, had initiated the 'totally original form of European culture' embodied in Eastern Christianity. Like Cyril and Methodius, Vladimir had maintained ties with both Rome and Constantinople; so the anniversary offered a chance to re-stress the common Christian roots of Europe, in which the Church's Eastern and Western traditions 'complement each other like two "lungs" of a single body'.[96]

The Pope sent a separate letter about the millennium to the banned Greek Catholic Church of Ukraine. 'The Ukrainian, Russian and Byelorussian peoples find in this event not only their Christian identity', he reminded Archbishop Miroslav Lubachivsky, 'but also their cultural identity and, in consequence, their history.' The 1596 Union of Brest, under which Ukrainian Christians were allowed to keep their Eastern liturgy while reverting to Roman jurisdiction, had been intended to build a Church in which East and West enjoyed 'full and visible unity'.[97] Members of the still-outlawed Ukrainian Church were barred from the Moscow celebrations in June 1988, but a Ukrainian delegation met Casaroli in a Moscow hotel. By then the Soviet press was questioning the hostility shown to Greek Catholics by the Kremlin and the Orthodox Patriarchate. In September the Polish government allowed Lubachivsky to attend an 'alternative commemoration' at Jasna Góra. Over 15,000 Byelorussians mobbed Cardinal Glemp when he crossed the border into their republic that month. The return of Bishop Steponavičius to Vilnius after 27 years' exile was greeted by 500,000 Lithuanians.

The Pope had received his first conciliatory message from Gorbachev during General Jaruzelski's Vatican visit in January 1987. He sent a letter back via Casaroli during the millennium; but it was left to the Pope's old antagonist Gromyko, now President of the Soviet Union, to assure him that the Kremlin would not 'stand in the way of the Catholic Church's expansion'.[98]

Speaking in October 1988 to the European Court in Strasbourg, John Paul said the concept of human rights was a common good of all humanity. But human rights depended on the rule of law as well as on institutional safeguards. By defending them, the Church had become the ally of authentic human freedom.

> The Church vigorously defends human rights because it considers them a necessary part of the recognition that must be given to the human person's dignity ... Human rights draw vigour and effectiveness from a framework of values, whose roots lie deep within the Christian heritage which has contributed so much to European culture. These founding values precede the positive law which gives them expression, as well as the philosophical rationale that various schools of thought are able to give them.[99]

At some stage in 1989 all communist regimes had to choose between fighting and capitulating. Communists fought and lost in Romania where Nicolae Ceauşescu was shot by a firing squad after a kangaroo trial on Christmas Day. They fought and won in China where hundreds of students paid with their lives in Beijing's Tiananmen Square. It was said that East Germany's Honecker regime had equipped Leipzig's main theatre with body-bags and operating tables, and that Czechoslovakia's riot police had readied themselves for massacres in Prague and Bratislava.

But in the end, most backed down. The ice had been broken in Poland where opposition leaders were already sitting in parliament and running ministries. The will to reimpose communist power evaporated with the autumn winds.

'Human history is in continual movement; times change with the various generations', the Pope told Czech and Polish pilgrims in Rome in November 1989. They had come for the canonization of Brother Albert, Karol Wojtyła's one-time spiritual mentor, and a thirteenth-century princess, Agnes of Bohemia. The 'Velvet Revolution' began five days later, and the Pope's text was from St John the Divine's Revelation: 'I saw an immense multitude, which no one could count, from every nation, race, people and tongue. They were standing in front of the throne ... And they shouted aloud, Amen!'[100]

Notes

1. Figures in Patrick Michel, *Politics and Religion in Eastern Europe* (London: Polity Press, 1991), pp. 63–4. Wyszyński's will was dated 15 August 1969: Bronisław Piasecki, *Ostatnie dni Prymasa Tysiąclecia* (Rome: Dom Polski, 1982), pp. 169–73.

2. 'Relacja z posiedzenia Komisji Wspólnej, Dokument nr 26' (20 December 1983); in *Tajne dokumenty, Państwo-Kościół 1980–1989* (Warsaw: Aneks and Polityka, 1993), p. 340.

3. 'Ocena wizyty papieża w Polsce, Dokument nr 23' (24 June 1983); ibid., pp. 276–8.

4. Ibid., p. 289; 'Ocena wizyty papieża Jana Pawła II, Dokument nr 25' (8 July 1983); ibid., p. 330.

5. Felix Corley, 'Soviet reaction to the election of Pope John Paul II', *Religion, State and Society*, vol. 22, no. 1 (1994), pp. 53–4.

6. SED archive extracts in *Tygodnik Powszechny* (10 June 1994).

7. The regime's policy was described by Fr Josef Zvěřina in a letter to *L'Avvenire* (9 March 1984).

8. *Herder-Korrespondenz*, interview (18 July 1983).

9. *Pravda* (Bratislava: 6 October 1983).

10. From *Egregiae virtutis* (31 December 1980); in *La Documentation Catholique* (January 1981), pp. 110–11.

11. *Slavorum apostoli* (2 June 1985), no. 27.

12. *Tribuna* (3 January 1985). The paper also attacked the Czech–Polish patron St Adalbert (956–997) as 'a servant of the German Emperor and angel of death for Baltic Prussians'.

13. Jonathan Luxmoore, 'The Polish Church under martial law', *Religion in Communist Lands*, vol. 15, no. 2 (Summer 1987), p. 149; 'Relacja z posiedzenia', op. cit., p. 339.

14. 'Komunikat konferencji plenarnej Episkopatu Polski' (14 February 1985); in Peter Raina, *Kościół w PRL—Dokumenty 1975–1989* (Poznań: W Drodze, 1996), p. 458.

15. 'Pro memoria Urzędu do Spraw Wyznań' (17 September 1984); ibid., p. 437.

16. 'Dokument nr 26', op. cit., pp. 341–4; Piotr Nitecki, *Znak Zwycięstwa* (Wrocław: Wrocławskiej Księgarni Archidiecezjalnej, 1991), pp. 151–64.

17. *Tu i teraz* (19 September 1984). Urban penned the attack under his pseudonym 'Jan Rem'.

18. Homily (3 November 1984); from Jonathan Luxmoore, 'The Polish Church: strength and weakness', *The Month* (July–August 1986), p. 245.

19. 'Pismo Sekretarza Generalnego Konferencji Episkopatu Polski, Dokument nr 28' (4 March 1984); in *Tajne dokumenty*, op. cit., pp. 381–2.

20. 'Dokument nr 30' (24 April 1985); ibid., pp. 398, 401.

21. 'Dokument nr 34' (23 December 1985); ibid., p. 464.

22. Ibid., p. 461. Among other disputes, the regime cut its newsprint allocation to Catholic periodicals in 1985 by 20 per cent, when Poland already had only 33 Church-approved titles compared to 2,766 Party titles. The 33 periodicals accounted for 43 per cent of all censorship deletions. A March 1985 Ministry of Culture questionnaire confirmed that virtually all known cultural figures in Poland maintained close ties with the Church: 'List wiceprezydenta m.st. Warszawy' (4 March 1985); in Raina, op. cit., pp. 459–66.

23. Jonathan Luxmoore, 'The Pope takes up the cross of Poland', *The Wall Street Journal* (9 June 1987).

24. Luxmoore, 'The Polish Church: strength and weakness', op. cit., p. 244.

25. 'Analiza postaw członków PZPR wobec religii, Dokument nr 32' (18 July 1985); in *Tajne dokumenty*, 430–5; 'Uwagi w sprawie stosunku kierownictwa, Dokument nr 33' (22 October 1985); ibid., pp. 439–42.

26. 'Dokument nr 35'; ibid., pp. 476–80.

27. *Pravda* (28 September 1986).

28. *La Repubblica* (11 March 1982); *The Tablet* (20 March 1982). Oddi confirmed this in a letter to Tomášek, dated 18 March 1982.

29. *Rudé právo* (27 April 1982); *Pravda* (Bratislava: 14 March 1983).

30. Vatican Radio broadcast (8 May 1982).

31. Alois Indra in *Rudé právo* (16 June 1986).

32. *Neue Kronen-Zeitung*, interview (9 February 1986). Around 36 per cent of Czechoslovakia's adult citizens, and 30 per cent of Communist Party members, were described as 'religious' in a 1984 Academy of Sciences survey: *Sociologie*, no. 1 (Prague: 1984).

33. *Catholic Herald*, interview (7 June 1983).

34. *Komsomolskaya pravda* (12 March 1982); statement by the head of the Znanie atheist association in *Sovietskaya litva* (13 April 1982).

35. *Aušra* (samizdat), no. 28 (September 1981).

36. *Nauka i religiya*, no. 10 (1984), p. 11.

37. Corley, op. cit., p. 57; Terelya's claim in *Radio Liberty Research Bulletin* (18 September 1985).

38. *Le Monde* (15 October 1986).

39. *Octogesima adveniens* (14 May 1971), no. 34.

40. Quoted in Michael Novak, 'Liberation Theology and the Pope', *Commentary* (June 1979), p. 62.

41. José Miguez Bonino, *Doing Theology in a Revolutionary Situation* (New York: Fortress Press, 1975); Christians for Socialism, *Final Document* (Santiago: April 1972).

42. Hugo Assmann, *Theology for a Nomad Church* (New York: Orbis Books, 1976), p. 37; Gustavo Gutiérrez, *The Power of the Poor in History* (London: SCM Press, 1983), p. 211.

43. 'Discours pour l'ouverture des travaux de la IIIe conférence de l'Episcopat Latino-Américain', *La Documentation Catholique* (February 1979), pp. 164–72.

44. Ibid., p. 165.

45. 'Le Message de l'Assemblée de Puebla aux peuples d'Amérique Latine', *La Documentation Catholique* (4 March 1979), pp. 220–1.

46. *Dives in misericordia* (30 November 1980), no. 11.

47. Ibid., nos 12, 14.

48. From *Acta Romana*, no. XVII, pp. 456–7.

49. The survey results were summarized in 'Marxist analysis: a consultation', undated manuscript circulated to Jesuit offices (1981), pp. 5–13.

50. Letter to Latin American Provincials (8 December 1980); in 'Marxist analysis', op. cit., p. 19.

51. *International Herald Tribune* (23 February 1983).

52. *Granma* (27 February 1983).

53. Quoted in *The Tablet* (26 February 1983).

54. *Le Figaro* (7 March 1983); *Le Monde* (8 March 1983).

55. *Le Monde*, ibid.

56. *Le Monde* (18 March 1983); *The Tablet* (26 March 1983).

57. Text in *The Tablet* (30 June 1984). Before his death in March 1984 Rahner defended Gutiérrez's 'entirely orthodox' teachings in a letter to Cardinal Juan Ricketts of Lima.

58. *The Times* (28 January, 11 February 1985).

59. *Instruction on Certain Aspects of the Theology of Liberation* (6 August 1983), nos XI, 1–2, VIII, 5.

60. Ibid., no. IX, 10.

61. Rosino Gibellini, *The Liberation Theology Debate* (London: SCM Press, 1987), pp. 49–50.

62. From Ratzinger's interview in *Jesus* (November 1984); in Peter Hebblethwaite, *Synod Extraordinary* (London: Darton, Longman & Todd, 1986), p. 50.

63. Homily at Malines (18 May 1985); ibid., p. 49.

64. *The Final Report and Message to the People of God* (7 December 1985), nos D, 1–7.

65. *Instruction on Christian Freedom and Liberation* (22 March 1986), no. 19.

66. Ibid., nos 22–24.

67. Ibid., no. 78.

68. Ibid., no. 79.

69. Ibid., no. 98.

70. Address to the bishops of Nicaragua (22 August 1988); in *The Pope Teaches*, no. 19 (London: Catholic Truth Society, 1988), pp. 311–16.

71. *Instruction on Christian Freedom*, op. cit., no. 22.

72. *Tribuna* (20 July 1983); 'Dokument nr 30'; in *Tajne dokumenty*, op. cit., p. 396.

73. *Lietuvos ateitis (samizdat)*, no. 6 (November 1984).

74. *Dominum et vivificantem* (18 May 1986), nos 38, 54.

75. Ibid., no. 65.

76. Mikhail Gorbachev, *Perestroika: New Thinking for Our Country and the World* (London: Collins, 1987), pp. 162–3, 165.

77. Homily at Spire (4 May 1987); in Christine de Montclos-Alix, 'Le Saint-Siège et l'Europe' in Joël-Benoît d'Onorio (ed.), *Le Saint-Siège dans les relations internationales* (Paris: Éditions du Cerf, 1989), p. 159.

78. Homily at Mass for Working People, Zaspa (12 June 1987).

79. Address to Representatives of Creative Milieux, Warsaw (13 June 1987).

80. Speech by President of the Council of State, Warsaw (14 June 1987).

81. Address to the Conference of the Polish Episcopate (14 June 1987).

82. *Sollicitudo rei socialis* (30 December 1987), no. 14.

83. Ibid., no. 15.

84. Ibid., no. 37.

85. Ibid., nos 38–39.

86. Ibid., no. 22.

87. Ibid., no. 41.

88. Ibid., no. 47.

89. 'Ocena wizyty papieża w Polsce, Dokument nr 36' (19 June 1987); in *Tajne dokumenty*, op. cit., pp. 508–13.

90. Ibid., p. 511.

91. 'Dokument nr 40' (23 January 1989); ibid., p. 558. The speaker was Stanisław Ciosek.

92. 'List Papieża Jana Pawła II do Prymasa Kard. J. Glempa' (11 April 1989); in Raina, op. cit., pp. 610–12.

93. For example, statement by Prime Minister Lubomir Strougal; AFP report (14 April 1987).

94. *Új Ember* (14 June 1987). The Vatican condemnation applied to Bulányi's book, *Church Order*.

95. Address to the bishops of Lithuania; in Lithuanian Information Centre bulletin (New York: 27 April 1988).

96. Apostolic Letter *Euntes in mundum* (25 January 1988), nos 3, 5.

97. Letter to Ukrainian Catholics *Magnum baptismi donum* (14 February 1988).

98. *National Catholic Register* (20 November 1988).

99. Papal address to the Court of Human Rights (8 October 1988).

100. Homily (12 November 1989); in *The Pope Teaches*, op. cit., pp. 357–61.

13

☙☙☙☙

The burden of history

'The painful trials so many citizens were subjected to because of their faith are widely known', the Pope told Mikhail Gorbachev on 1 December 1989. 'Our meeting today can hardly fail to have a powerful impact on world opinion. It will be seen as singularly meaningful, a sign of the times that have slowly matured.' The last Soviet leader to sit in the same chair, Nikolai Podgorny, had been so tense he had asked Paul VI for a cigarette. Gorbachev was of calmer breed. The Soviet Union recognized the right of believers to satisfy their spiritual needs, he assured the Pope. Moscow was learning the 'difficult but indispensable art' of co-operation.[1]

Diplomacy aside, serious problems lay ahead. The Pope reminded Gorbachev that the Soviet Union's scattered Catholic communities still awaited recognition. The Supreme Soviet had yet to enact laws making this possible.

Russian Orthodox leaders complained bitterly that Gorbachev had promised to make Ukraine's outlawed Greek Catholic Church legal again. Party officials accused him of 'destroying the Soviet Union', pursuing 'policies our enemies would bless'.

But the communist leader had made a lasting friend. In 1992 he admitted that the end of communism would have been 'impossible' without John Paul II and insisted he now agreed with 'many elements' of the Pope's teachings. 'I believe he is the world's most left-wing leader', the former Soviet General-Secretary mused again in 1997. 'No one else reacts with such pain to poverty, injustice and human misery, to the tarnishing of human life even though it is a gift from God. I can see how he contributed to our understanding of communism.'[2]

Gorbachev was not the only former communist leader to sing the Pope's praises as he beat a path to Rome, hoping to steal a few rays of John Paul II's limelight. But his remarks had a ring of truth. There were many factors which helped explain why communism had collapsed: economic crisis, ideological breakdown, nationalist revolt, Western pressure; yet none could account for its suddenness, or for its near-total peacefulness.

The Pope had seen from the outset that violence would never be the answer. History had shown totalitarian regimes emerged stronger when challenged by force. They had, however, no answer to moral resistance. He could be thankful that East Europeans had learned this from experience and instinct, and that his Church's growing self-confidence had coincided with a loss of will by communist governments.

East Europeans had ousted their oppressors by their own efforts. The Pope had, however, given the movement a spark of certainty. Using simple notions from Catholic tradition, he had reminded confused and demoralized people of truths they knew but had forgotten. What made them decisive was how they were spoken—not in the sedate settings of churches and convents, but in the full blare of industrial plants, housing developments and city squares.

John Paul II had been a catalyst for the pent-up dynamics of revolt. His luck lay in appearing at a particular moment of opportunity, his greatness lay in the force of a personality which enabled him to exploit this opportunity to the full. If this had been the work of the Holy Spirit, then the Spirit had been unusually assertive: it had given him a gift of prophecy and made him an instrument in the hands of providence. The Pope had proved that dreams come true, that ideas shape realities.

Four months after his historic meeting with Gorbachev, John Paul found himself before the high altar of St Vitus cathedral in Prague, where the ill-fated Cardinal Beran had once been shouted down by communist agents. 'Today, we stand before the ruins of one of the many towers of Babel in human history', he told the Czechs. The posters in the streets outside pictured the banner held up during the new Pope's first Polish pilgrimage—'Father, remember your Czech children'. They were captioned 'Gniezno 1979—Prague 1990'. 'You were called the Church of Silence', the Pope continued. 'But your silence was not the silence of sleep or death. In the spiritual order, it is in silence that the most precious values are born.'[3]

In the years ahead, the Pope would make other visits to Eastern Europe too, but the challenge set out in his Prague address would remain as fresh as ever. He knew the years of repression had forced the Church to reflect deeply about the meaning of faith and suffering, about God's designs and interventions. The return to sources and foundations had created a spiritual richness.

April 1990 was a time of lofty visions. Classical Greek and Judaic thinkers were in vogue, from Plato and Aristotle to Buber and Lévinas.

Czechoslovakia's new playwright-President, Václav Havel, had revived a Hussite concept—the 'power of truth'. Poland's Catholic premier, Tadeusz Mazowiecki, had vowed to breathe a 'spiritual dimension' back into politics. Efforts were underway to rekindle public trust in the State and rid words like 'party' and 'programme' of their negative associations. There was talk of 'returning to Europe', of 'reclaiming the public sphere'.[4]

Amid the optimism, however, questions needed answering. Twentieth-century Europe had fallen victim to totalitarian ideologies, before which both the rationalist humanism of the Enlightenment with its optimistic faith in human progress, and Christian ethics founded on human dignity, had been made to stand like bewildered onlookers. Why had the Church proved so weak? What had it learned from its experiences of the communist era?

Communism had come to Eastern Europe with Stalin's victorious Red Army; but it would be a serious mistake to see it as no more than a heresy imposed by force of arms. Its propagandists had successfully exploited capitalism's vices. They had talked alluringly of neutralizing inequalities, bringing suffering and exploitation to an end.

In retrospect, pre-war disorders had demanded a new kind of Christian sensitivity, capable of understanding and moderating the emotions behind contemporary political protests. But for all the paternalistic efforts of Catholic philanthropists, the Church had stayed dangerously weak on social issues, especially when it came to demanding precautionary restraints on wealth and privilege.

This was why its theologians and philosophers had been unable to make themselves heard above the siren song of communism's ideologues. It took many years of disillusionment for the Church to move out of its self-defensive bastion and lay down an effective counter-challenge, ultimately identifying itself with the social movements which brought communist rule to an end.

One of the lessons from the communist period concerned the Church's place in society. Communism would not have been overthrown at all without solidarity—a readiness by diverse people to co-operate in opposition. Experience showed this kind of active solidarity constituted a form of power—a power which became invincible when applied to the struggle of individuals and societies to rediscover and reassert their will. Christians could not achieve this by themselves. They needed the help of others; and this presupposed tolerance and respect, a readiness to defend the rights of non-Christians too, and to accept the validity of views of mankind and the world which were born outside the Church.

Another lesson was about the dangers of compromise—of leaning on diplomacy at the cost of testimony, and sacrificing the Church's independence for institutional protection. Corruption from within had done more damage than ham-fisted persecution.

The Church had learned it was not enough to pay lip-service to values. Totalitarian failures had shown the futility of attempting to adjust the world to utopian models. Just because reality could not be made perfect, however, did not mean there was no duty to change it. Just because social justice required moral methods did not mean it could be ignored in practice.

Besides recognizing individual dramas, the Church also had to concern itself with injustices suffered by groups and communities. Whether the solutions came from Left or Right, they had to be authentic, not used as instruments for furthering ideological interests. Sooner or later, coercion would always fail: people would never forget they were created to be free, to decide for themselves and be guided by truth.

These, at any rate, were some of the lessons highlighted by the communist period. It was another question whether the Church would take them to heart—or had merely acknowledged them as temporary necessity.

The collapse of communism had overturned the international system born at Yalta in 1945. Pius XII had condemned it from the beginning. He had warned that stability would never be achieved by the arbitrary decisions of an oligarchy of states at the cost of the rights and aspirations of nations. The wiry Italian had been ignored by the architects of post-war *realpolitik*. Their successors in the 1980s, however, had not been able to ignore John Paul II. He had been the first Pope to pinpoint correctly the strengths and weaknesses of rulers and ruled, to take his cause direct to the common man over the heads of the wielders of power.

This had owed a lot to the temporal insights born in the Church at Vatican II. Yet John Paul had also seen more clearly than his predecessors how spiritual loyalties could have political consequences. The world, he knew, functioned not through governments but through people. The Church's power was as a social force, mobilized by evangelism. Nineteenth-century Popes, mesmerized by images of destruction from the French Revolution to the Paris Commune, had feared the potential of spontaneous social movements. John Paul II had seen them as allies, a creative energy which the Church could harness and direct for godly purposes. The 'movements of solidarity' he had spoken of in *Laborem exercens* were not foes, but friends, of Christianity.

John Paul II had also understood communism. His predecessors had seen it as a misguided response to the iniquities of industrial society. To curb its influence, they had demanded measures to protect the new working class. They had failed to see that communism was a response not only to poverty, but also to indignity, which had successfully exploited rising social consciousness and demands for political emancipation.

Pius XI and Pius XII had tried to counter communism by confronting it—the first branding it 'intrinsically evil', the second excommunicating its collaborators. John XXIII had modified this policy and applied the 'medicine of mercy rather than severity'. Paul VI had tried to 'save what could be saved' by showing communists what they could gain from concessions.

John Paul II's approach had been different. He saw communism less as an enemy than as a misunderstanding—a wrong turn towards a false conception of humanity and the world. After the chaos of war, communism had proved attractive for people of social and moral sensitivity. To correct any error, one had first to understand it.

By the time of John Paul II's election in 1978, communism's rock-like façade had been softened up by economic failures and political pressures, and its humanitarian claims discredited. The ideals which had motivated its earliest followers were nevertheless still very much alive. Shorn of their totalitarian and ideological distortions, they could now be reapplied in a Christian way. The task was to transform illusory values into genuine ones.

That was what John Paul tried to do—to rekindle the moral impulses of social reformism in an encounter with Christian tradition, and to help 'people of goodwill' meet on the common ground of a true consensus. The radical sympathies of his youth helped him understand the angry frustration which had encouraged the search for revolutionary answers. History had taught, however, that efforts to change the world had to begin with people, not with programmes. They had to serve people too, not amorphous classes or abstract aggregates. This had been communism's mistake. It had elevated its own praxis above the rights of the person. The challenge now was to provide a convincing up-to-date Christian solution to problems Marxism had highlighted: labour–capital relations, work and property, exploitation and alienation.

John Paul II had never been an 'anti-communist'—condemning and combating communism were unnecessary. What *was* necessary was to find positive, liberating impulses to set against the negative, captivating resentments communist rulers used as tools of power. Communism could not be intimidated by confrontation or appeased by diplomacy. Nor could it be supplanted by some other ideology which would merely repeat its mistakes. But it *could* be undermined through the power of values—by the kind of moral victory over hatred and fear which ultimately became a political victory.

In the nineteenth century, under Pius IX, the Church had put its faith in the established order and resisted even sensible social changes. Under Leo

XIII, it had begun to react to the spiralling crisis. Yet *Rerum novarum* appeared a full quarter-century after *Das Kapital*, when it was too late for Catholics to recapture worker allegiance. Popes from Leo XIII on were well aware that the root cause of unrest lay in abusive capitalism which elevated selfish interests above community values—even Pius XI, the harrier of communists, admitted socialism's 'parent' was liberalism. While the Popes had urged social improvements, however, they had opposed changes to the social order.

That was the harmonious, organic vision which Émile Durkheim called 'Solidarism', and which led Leo XIII to compare the body politic to the 'symmetry of the human frame'.[5] 'Solidarism' was the antithesis of class struggle and proletarian revolution. It was an inadequate panacea for modern conflicts. The Popes had not healed the historic rift between paternalistic Christian ethics and rebellious secular radicalism. Instead, they had contributed to it.

'Solidarism' and 'Solidarity' were separated by nearly a century. In between lay the 'social charity' and distributive justice of the pre-war Popes, and the dreamy talk of their post-war successors of overhauling the world's social and economic structures. John Paul II had thrown the Church's authority into building bridges across the age-old rift: non-violent action, human dignity, the rights of conscience, absolute values. His 'solidarity' invoked the once-distrusted ideals of the French Revolution—liberty, equality and fraternity, or in Polish *wolność, równość, braterstwo*. It gave all three, however, a richer, deeper Christian interpretation, one which went beyond the civic, political and secular dimensions of 1789. It was on the half-forgotten ideal of *braterstwo*, unfulfillable without a moral consensus, that the main emphasis came to rest. No political system could build 'fraternity': attempts to do so had led to the horrors of totalitarianism. However, this did not mean it should be abandoned as a moral and spiritual postulate in people's minds.

The wheel had turned full circle from the time when Pope Gregory XVI had denounced the 'absurd and erroneous' idea of liberty of conscience championed by Lamennais and his disciples, and when Marx and Engels had identified the Pope as a 'power of the old Europe'. In Marx's day, opposing the Church had been justified as a means of ridding humanity of bondage and tutelage. The communist experience, on the other hand, had transformed the Church into a symbol of freedom. It had forced the Church to take its stand alongside common humanity.[6]

In *Redemptor hominis*, his first encyclical, John Paul II had spoken of a Church impelled by false ideologies to become 'more and more the custodian and champion of freedom'.[7] He added that the Church respected the solutions humanity had worked out for the world's problems. It did not reject any system *a priori*. All systems required 'continual revision', however, and an alertness to their original ideals. This had been the aim of philosophers like Leszek Kołakowski and Jan Patočka. It was the mission of John Paul II to recall the true values and positive aspirations which had been present in both liberalism and socialism, and to restore a sense of balance to contemporary society and culture.

That at least summed up John Paul II's response to communism. Would the identification of Christian ethics with justice and freedom survive in the changed conditions of a post-communist Eastern Europe? In 1989, the Pope could be forgiven for allowing the euphoria to sweep him along in its wake. What lay ahead was a 'world without frontiers', he told young people at Santiago de Compostela, a world which proclaimed Christ the 'Redeemer of mankind, the Centre of history, the Hope of nations, the Saviour of peoples'.[8]

The euphoria was destined to vanish. The preoccupations of the 1980s were not those of the 1990s. The new world now in place was symbolized by bloody conflicts from Bosnia to Tajikistan—by security anxieties, economic hardships, political feuds, social frustrations. The 'transition' so confidently predicted turned out to be never-ending, a trek between unmarked points on a compass, from an uncertain present to an undefined future.

In September 1993, when its citizens voted former communists back to power, in the latest of a string of similar ex-communist triumphs all over Eastern Europe, Poland's economy was growing by 7 per cent annually, while its private sector provided two-thirds of all jobs. Yet macroeconomic statistics were misleading. Surveys portrayed an apathetic, embittered society. Three million Poles, 15 per cent of the workforce, were officially unemployed, with 2 million more affected by early retirement or short-time working. Half the population was living below the social minimum, compared to a few per cent a decade before. The most important reasons cited in opinion surveys for the victory of Poland's Democratic Left Alliance were the 'neglect of ordinary people' by Solidarity-led governments and the view that 'life was generally better' under communism. Even in 1997, when a new coalition, Solidarity Election Action, finally ousted the ex-communists from power, half the population could see no essential difference between the former system and the present one. Although 74 per cent of Poles preferred current conditions, one in five said they would be happier with things as they used to be. As late as April 1998, the Polish Sejm was still debating whether to condemn communism, and if so how and why. More than half of all citizens believed General Jaruzelski had been right, in retrospect, to impose martial law.[9]

All over Eastern Europe, the Catholic Church became a factor in political disputes. In 1990, the Pope had warned Czech priests and nuns not to allow the Church to 'close in on itself'. He had listed the 'immense historic tasks' the Church now faced. It had to 'give life' to Catholic parishes in the light of Vatican II, renew religious orders and revive seminary vocations, provide education and catechesis, encourage the reintegration of lay movements, revive ecumenical bonds and assert its presence in public life. 'The Church's solidarity with the persecuted has strengthened its moral authority', he added. 'You hold in your hands the capital of merits amassed by those who sacrificed their life and freedom. This is truly a rich inheritance. Do not squander it!'[10]

The inheritance was quickly scattered in bitter struggles over the future shape of State and society, and the Church's place within them. Perhaps this was unavoidable. Under communism much had been said about reforms to political and economic life, but little about reforming the Church to face the demands of a pluralistic environment. The half-century had shown that the Church's greatest danger lay not in persecution, but in indifference. The spirituality of life on the margins could hardly be expected to survive the advent of democracy, when local conflicts over issues from education to property restitution soon overshadowed the Church's wider social mission.

In Poland, opinion surveys showed a sharp decline in the Church's public standing. This was not matched by any crisis of faith. Church attendance remained high; and though priestly vocations fell from their 1985–87 peak, this reflected a return to normal levels from the inflated figures of the previous decade. The problem was not with religiousness, but with the Church itself.

Under communist rule the Bishops' Conference had negotiated agreements discreetly and arbitrarily behind closed doors. Now every issue had to be dragged through the mud of public debate, mediated by assertive politicians and often unsympathetic media. Polish citizens now had other outlets for their social, cultural and political interests. Catholic media and educational institutions were no longer regarded as the country's best.

After decades of communism, furthermore, many Catholics saw the world in naive ideological categories and attempted to find in Christianity a new political blueprint. Some seized on an American model of 'democratic capitalism', with its idealistic vision of a society combining religion and morality with democracy and prosperity. Others relived the pre-war dream of a corporatist State in which the Church's position was constitutionally guaranteed.

Perhaps John Paul II had not foreseen the rise of post-communist nationalism. Eulogizing the 'nation', with its language and culture, had helped release identities and loyalties from communism's cultural straitjacket. The Pope had drawn on Romantic tradition—on images of national consciousness permeating Eastern Europe's pre-communist art and literature. He had not done so at the cost of ethnic minorities—on the contrary, he had encouraged smaller groups to reassert their identities too.

Yet the Pope's idealization of nationhood raised retrospective questions. He had personally witnessed the crimes attributed to nationalism in the Second World War—at the hands not only of Germans, but also of Serbs and Croats, Slovaks and Ukrainians, even Poles and Lithuanians. Had he failed to anticipate how the mood engendered by his own populism could be abused for aggressive ends—how the inspirational language of the 1980s could become the inflammatory rhetoric of the 1990s? Or had he, in reality, anticipated the nationalist passions which would erupt after communism's collapse, and attempted to calm their excesses by encouraging tolerant forms of national reawakening?

Whatever the truth, the Pope realized soon enough that a different language was needed for societies jealous of their new-found emancipation.

When the Polish bishops visited Rome in January 1993, he urged them to keep their distance from political parties. That October, he called on the bishops of Lithuania to recognize Vatican II's 'power of renewal'. In November he challenged the Hungarian bishops to help lay Catholics contribute more actively to Church life.

In April 1993 it took a papal letter to resolve long-running Catholic–Jewish disputes over a Carmelite convent at Auschwitz, and a ground-breaking papal appeal to generate Church concern for Eastern Europe's hard-pressed Gypsies.

In Albania, a country threatened by powerful neighbours and internal anarchy, he invoked Mary, the patron of 'good counsel'. In Latvia, he urged the Church not to 'limit itself' to the memory of past persecutions. In war-ravaged Croatia, he won praise for urging all national groups to 'forgive and ask forgiveness'. In Bosnia, he braved assassination threats to bring a message of peace and reconciliation.

In more substantive tasks, however, little headway was made. In *Ut unum sint* (25 May 1995), John Paul reaffirmed the Church's 'irrevocable' commitment to ecumenism. Catholics, he added, still hoped for 'full communion' with Orthodox Christians, and believed the example of Sts Benedict, Cyril and Methodius could provide a basis for ecumenical dialogue.[11] Yet the approaches initiated by Borovoi and Kotliarov at Vatican II had yet to yield fruit. Orthodox leaders accused the Pope of undoing the conciliatory work of John XXIII and Paul VI. They saw the post-communist revival of Greek Catholic Churches as a challenge to Orthodox jurisdiction, and accused Catholics of proselytizing in traditionally Orthodox territories. Historic enmities impeded co-operation in a post-communist reconstruction of faith and morals.

The Pope made slow progress in his quest for East–West unity even within his own Church. Questionnaires to 23 Bishops' Conferences before a special Rome Synod in December 1991 asked which problems were shared by the Church on both sides of Europe. There was no final document: views and perspectives remained far apart.[12] Western Catholics had trouble understanding why suffering and persecution were rooted in the East European identity. East Europeans had difficulty appreciating why apparent doctrinal abstractions mattered in the West. Nor did East European Church leaders entirely understand each other. The ethical values elaborated under communism did not translate easily into post-communist conditions.

The Pope's fourth pilgrimage to Poland in 1991 took the Ten Commandments as its theme. Its aim was to secure the Christian foundations for a new society. That meant looking carefully at the key Polish dilemma—how to create a strong, united homeland from the ruins of occupation and repression. He had come this time not to protect society from the State, but to strengthen the bonds between them. He spoke of a Poland in which State institutions shunned for centuries enjoyed authority and legitimacy again, of a stable, democratic order based on authentic values.[13]

The Pope blamed the re-election of former communists two years later on the 'ineffectiveness' of post-Solidarity politicians. The Democratic Left Alliance's victory, he added, did not mean a 'return to communism': it merely reflected the fact that Poland's only 'political class' for 50 years had been communist. It *was*, however, a reminder of Poland's 'atavistic failing'—an 'exaggerated individualism which leads to fragmentation and division', whose strength lies 'in opposition, not in the constructive propositions that lead to successful government'.[14]

The Pope returned to Poland again in May 1995 for a one-day visit only. At Zywiec he admitted he had 'many thoughts and feelings' on seeing the mountains of southern Poland which he had once visited so often as a priest, bishop and cardinal. At Bielsko-Biała he recalled his earliest childhood connections with the birthplace of his father Karol and elder brother Edmund, who had died there from the scarlet fever contracted from a patient while the younger Karol was still a schoolboy in nearby Wadowice.

This time, the Pope talked about individual consciences, about the need for committed Christians to remain steadfast against a background of competing interests and opinions. Post-communist changes, he acknowledged, had brought a 'programmed laicization of society', attempts to drive believers 'to the margins of social life'.[15]

This was an exaggeration; but it also reflected his bitterness. In a March 1996 questionnaire, most Poles thought the Pope's most important concern was abortion, whereas only one in ten believed it was human rights. Fewer than a third could even remember when he had been elected, and most appeared confused about his role in relation to Solidarity. Half believed he had played no role in the collapse of communism or were undecided about it. Although 90–94 per cent cited him as an authority, evidence suggested it was an abstract authority—that of a national symbol with little direct relevance to real life. Two-thirds of Poles believed John Paul II was above criticism.[16]

Had Karol Wojtyła revealed himself to the sceptical generation of the 1990s? Had the man who moved the world as a champion of freedom and human rights yielded to the remorseless pressure of a technological age?

In *Sollicitudo rei socialis*, the Pope had drawn attention to the twin dangers of 'super-development' and 'under-development'.[17] Yet if the 1987 encyclical had believed an end to East–West competition would improve the Third World's lot, it was wrong. Although the Cold War had diverted resources, it had also given the West a motive for helping poorer nations. By the mid-1990s, as aid budgets were slashed amid famine and genocide, John Paul might well have wondered whether the collapse of communism had not created a monster world—a world of extremes of wealth and poverty, opportunity and disadvantage, constrained only by the unreliable and inconsistent dictates of goodwill and conscience, a world in which the Church's voice was weak and intermittent, drowned out by the rival cacophonies of consumption and squalor.

The wings of Liberation Theology had been clipped in the 1980s. But exploitation and indignity were just as alive in the 1990s. Visiting Central America in February 1996, the Pope admitted the region still faced 'serious injustice and discrimination'. En route to El Salvador, however, he admitted he had come to bury an old ghost. 'Today, after the fall of communism, Liberation Theology has collapsed as well', he said. 'The bishops have confirmed that these ideologies are now neither a power nor a problem. There are other issues to be resolved, especially a genuine social justice.'[18]

The Guatemalan Church's human rights office released its latest figures at the time of the visit: 1,030 'political killings' in 1995 alone. Press reports said the Church was now concerned just as much with the spread of religious sects.

By then, the new *Catechism of the Catholic Church* had further restricted the option of armed struggle endorsed in Paul VI's *Populorum progressio*. It pointed out that although citizens could not follow government directives which contradicted the moral order, for armed resistance to be considered legitimate five conditions must be met:

(1) there is certain, grave and prolonged violation of fundamental rights; (2) all other means of redress have been exhausted; (3) such resistance will not provoke worse disorders; (4) there is well-founded hope of success; and (5) it is impossible to foresee any better solution.[19]

If John Paul II had underestimated something in the 1990s, it was the staying-power of ideology, as well as the powerful lobbies which now competed for his ear. Communism had collapsed; liberal capitalism was resurgent; and the apparent moral equivalence assigned to both in *Sollicitudo rei socialis* had provoked outraged reactions in some Western quarters. In *Centesimus annus* (1 May 1991), he had attempted to set the record straight.

The Pope called the encyclical a 're-reading' of *Rerum novarum*, whose centenary it marked. In 1891, a traditional society had been giving way to a new one, he pointed out, whose two classes were already separated by a deep chasm. Against this background, Leo XIII had shown how peace had to be built on a foundation of justice. He had created a 'lasting paradigm' by making the Church's social doctrine central to its mission.[20]

Centesimus annus then launched into a diatribe against 'socialism', in which past and present were fused indistinguishably. Leo XIII had recognized the harshness of working-class conditions, the encyclical acknowledged. He had, however, denounced socialism's 'simple and radical solution'—the suppression of private property. John Paul II was speaking in the past tense, as if this kind of socialism were a historical phenomenon. He now switched to the present. Socialism's fundamental error was anthropological, *Centesimus annus* continued. It viewed—and still viewed—the individual as a 'molecule' with no free choice or personal autonomy, and made him totally dependent on the 'social machine and those who control it'. Its mistaken conception of humanity derived from its atheism—an atheism closely connected to the 'rationalism of the Enlightenment' which viewed human and social reality in a mechanistic way. It was from the same atheistic source that socialism had chosen—and still chose—class struggle as its means of action.[21]

What should be offered in its place? Pius XI had talked of a conflict which 'abstains from enmities and mutual hatred', and 'gradually changes into an honest discussion of differences founded on a desire for justice'.[22] That was what John Paul now suggested.

The wars which had ravaged twentieth-century Europe, the encyclical went on, had been caused by 'militarism and exaggerated nationalism'. But their deeper causes had been a conception of human freedom which became detached from 'obedience to truth', and a self-love which led to an 'unbridled affirmation of self-interest'. The post-war period had been one of 'non-war rather than genuine peace'. While Soviet ideology had provided doctrinal justification for a new war, 'fought with enormous bloodshed in various parts of the world', other countries had made positive efforts to rebuild 'a democratic society inspired by social justice', by preserving free-market mechanisms, and ensuring 'steady and healthy economic growth' through a stable currency and social harmony.[23]

The Pope made a passing acknowledgement of UN efforts to combat Third World problems. He also listed the danger posed by 'systems of national security', which risked destroying freedom and values to protect against communism. And he criticized affluent societies which sought to defeat Marxism 'on the level of pure materialism'.

There were, however, several points on which *Centesimus annus* was inaccurate and ahistorical.

For one thing, it distorted the relationship between socialism and liberalism in Leo XIII's teaching, by giving the impression that socialist agitation had disrupted the continuity of reform. It made no more than a single concluding reference to the 'ideology of liberalism'. Yet Popes down to Pius XI had seen this as the root cause of both socialism and communism. The very opening premise of *Rerum novarum* had been the need to remedy the 'greed of unchecked competition' and 'hard-heartedness of employers'. Three years before, Leo XIII had subjected liberalism to his strongest denunciations, blaming it for the very same crimes against Church and religion which *Centesimus annus* now one-sidedly attributed to socialism.[24]

For another, the encyclical failed to make sensible distinctions between socialism past and present. Leo XIII had blamed 'crafty agitators' for 'perverting men's judgements' and 'stirring revolt', and had accused socialists of acting against 'natural justice'. He had also commended the notion of a 'Christian state' and condemned governments who 'put God aside'.[25]

Yet not even Leo XIII had branded socialism atheistic. Instead, he had more readily laid the charge of spreading atheism at the door of liberal capitalist states, accusing them of 'setting aside the ancient religion' and spreading 'moral degeneracy'.[26]

Centesimus annus also distorted Leo XIII's conception of State and society in an effort to portray *Rerum novarum* as a forerunner of late twentieth-century theories of limited government. It depicted the 1890s Pope as an early exponent of the 'option for the poor' and claimed to have traced the origins of 'solidarity' to what Leo XIII had called 'friendship'. This was crude revisionism. The purely material notion of poverty in *Rerum novarum* had little in common with the wider conception John Paul had helped pioneer. *Centesimus annus* said nothing about the Church's dilemmas in responding to early worker movements. It threw little if any light on the causes and consequences of nineteenth-century radicalism.

The encyclical continued with a special chapter on 1989. Communist regimes had fallen, it noted, largely because they violated worker rights and were economically inefficient. The 'true cause' of their collapse, however, was the void brought about by atheism. Marxism had promised to uproot the need for God in human hearts. Yet the events of 1989 exemplified the 'Gospel spirit'. They were a warning to 'those who, in the name of political realism, wish to banish law and morality from the political arena'.

The Pope then turned to the legitimacy of private property, and its limitations in Church teaching. It was the human person, rather than labour and capital, who was becoming the decisive factor in production. 'Many people, perhaps the majority', he acknowledged, 'do not have the means which would enable them to take their place in an effective and humanly dignified way within a productive system.' Yet the free market offered the 'best instrument for utilizing resources' and 'effectively responding to needs'.

It could not satisfy all human needs. Nor could the 'absolute predominance of capital' if it contradicted the 'free and personal nature of human work'. The aim should be 'a society of free work, of enterprise and participation', where the market was 'appropriately controlled by the forces of society and the State'.[27] Strong nations should help weaker ones; there should be concern for the environment; the post-modernist view of life as just a 'series of sensations' should be avoided.

The Pope then returned, however, to the key question: 'Can it be said that, after the failure of communism, capitalism is the victorious social system, and that capitalism should be the goal of countries now making efforts to rebuild?'

> The answer is obviously complex. If by 'capitalism' is meant an economic system which recognizes the fundamental and positive role of business, the market, private property and the resulting responsibility for the means of production, as well as free human creativity in the economic sector, then the answer is certainly in the affirmative ... But if by 'capitalism' is meant a system in which freedom in the economic sector is not circumscribed within a strong juridical framework which places it at the service of human freedom in its totality, and which sees it as a particular aspect of that freedom, the core of which is ethical and religious, then the reply is certainly negative.[28]

Communism's collapse had 'removed an obstacle' to tackling problems of exploitation and alienation. It had not, however, resolved them. Nor would a 'radical capitalistic ideology' which refused even to recognize them. The Church would go on raising its voice against injustice and oppression, but it had no models to present. To those seeking a 'new and authentic theory and praxis of liberation' it could only offer its social teaching, as well as its concrete commitment to the struggle against 'material and moral poverty'.[29]

The encyclical reiterated the Church's acceptance of democracy 'inasmuch as it ensures the participation of citizens in making political choices'. If it was not rooted in 'a correct conception of the person', however, democracy easily turned into 'open or thinly disguised totalitarianism'.

The same was true of the economy. Although the State had to safeguard individual freedom, private property, a stable currency and efficient services, it could not guarantee the right to work. It must avoid the 'excesses and abuses' of the modern 'Social Assistance State', which had corroded social responsibility. Protecting human rights was more the responsibility of groups and associations.

It would be claimed that *Centesimus annus* marked a turning point. In *Laborem exercens* and *Sollicitudo rei socialis*, the Pope had attacked the 'error of economism' wherever it appeared. In the new encyclical, however, he came down less even-handedly, criticizing negative aspects of capitalism, but condemning socialism *in toto*. In this way, he drove a final papal nail into the coffin of Liberation Theology, and of any other movement which attempted 'an impossible compromise between Marxism and Christianity'.[30]

Centesimus annus endorsed the efficient, wealth-creating mechanisms of the market economy, on the precondition that they were based on values. Yet these 'values' were only vaguely spelt out. The encyclical urged companies to be guided not only by profit, but by 'human and moral factors too'. It called for a 'change of lifestyles, models of production and consumption, and the established structures of power'. When it came to filling out these pious exhortations, however, it had little to offer other than an appeal to 'mutual understanding and knowledge', helped by 'sensitivity of consciences'.[31]

John Paul's use of concepts was confusing too. He distinguished what he called 'new capitalism' from 'primitive capitalism', but appeared unsure whether capitalism in either form signified a 'model of economic organization' or 'social system'. As for ideologies, the encyclical later talked interchangeably of 'socialism', 'communism', 'Marxism' and 'Marxism-Leninism', making no attempt to clarify their historical and political contexts.

The encyclical's image was of a society based on charity, family bonds and intermediate associations—a society not unlike that conjured up in the nineteenth-century teachings of Leo XIII. Trade unions merited only a brief mention in this vision of a future society and were recast in a paternalistic pre-war mould. Their function was not only to defend workers' interests: it was also to help workers 'participate honestly in the nation's life and assist the path of development'.

For all its references to culture and society, however, the view of the person set out in *Centesimus annus* was overwhelmingly economic. It was the 'radical reordering of economic systems', the text made clear, which was the key priority after communism—not social recovery, moral renewal, human rights or the rule of law.

In *Laborem exercens*, the Pope had examined the 'pathologies' of both communism and liberalism, criticizing attempts from any quarter to 'ideologize' ideas and values. In *Centesimus annus*, however, he had come close to making this mistake himself, by using ill-defined concepts as the hub of his new world vision. Issuing the encyclical in 1991, the Pope appeared to have assumed ideology was at an end. He had failed to anticipate how rapidly the 'free market' would assume ideological dimensions. If *Centesimus annus* had been intended to correct the imbalances in *Sollicitudo rei socialis*, it had merely done so by substituting new imbalances of its own.

The years 1989–93 were a time of disorientation in Eastern Europe, as inexperienced, impressionable new élites trumpeted fashionable libertarian ideas, and concern for the poor and marginalized was scorned as communist-tainted and retrograde.

The Pope said he particularly wanted to make Catholic social teaching 'known and applied' in the region, to help post-communist countries overcome their 'lack of direction'. However, he also recognized something else: Western societies risked seeing the collapse of communism as a 'one-sided victory of their own economic system'.[32]

Perhaps it was a belated realization that *Centesimus annus* had itself contributed to this 'one-sided victory' which afterwards made selfish individualism the Pope's main preoccupation. In *Veritatis splendor* (6 August 1993), he deplored the creeping abandonment of a sense of good and evil, even within the Church. Many currents of modern thought, the latest encyclical argued, had either lost touch with the transcendent or become 'explicitly atheist'. The resulting crisis of truth was becoming a crisis of human nature.

> Today, when many countries have seen the fall of ideologies which bound politics to a totalitarian conception of the world—Marxism being the foremost—there is no less grave a danger that the fundamental rights of the human person will be denied and that the religious yearnings which arise in the heart of every human being will be absorbed once again into politics. This is the risk of an alliance between democracy and ethical relativism, which would remove any sure moral reference point from political and social life.[33]

In *Evangelium vitae* (25 March 1995) the Pope warned against societies which became no more than 'a mass of individuals placed side by side but without any mutual bonds'. When everything was 'open to bargaining' and it was left to the law to define good and evil, the 'structures of sin' spoken of in *Sollicitudo rei socialis* put down deeper roots.

Some people, he said, believed moral relativism to be a precondition of democracy, claiming the idea of binding moral norms led to authoritarianism and intolerance. They were wrong. Democracy could not be 'idolized' to make it a 'panacea for immorality'. It was merely a 'system', a means to an end. The Church welcomed the 'almost universal consensus' about the desirability of democracy. It was a positive 'sign of the times'. But democracy would always stand or fall on the values it embodied and promoted.[34]

By the mid-1990s, John Paul II seemed to have moved a long way from the joy and hope of Vatican II. His view of the world had always been tinged with apocalyptic anxieties. Hitherto he had combined these with humour and a communicable enthusiasm. Now, his pessimism was reasserting itself. As he passed his 75th birthday, visibly frustrated at his own frailty, the self-assurance of a prophetic witness gave way to the severity of a stern teacher.

Those who expected the triumphalism to continue, however, were in for some surprises. In an apostolic letter, *Tertio millennio adveniente* (10 November 1994), John Paul unveiled preparations for the Third Millennium which fifteen years earlier he had anticipated in *Redemptor hominis*. Jubilee years in the Old Testament, he pointed out, had been intended to restore equality and freedom. They had been a time of justice and reconciliation, when the riches of creation were again shared by all. As the Church approached the year 2000, its first priorities would include restoring unity among Christians. It would also, however, be a time for 'looking with eyes of faith' at the modern calamities which had highlighted the world's need for purification. The best preparation would be a fresh commitment to Vatican II and the new evangelization inaugurated by Paul VI in *Evangelii nuntiandi*.

Although the approaching Millennium had been a 'hermeneutical key' to his own pontificate, the Pope said, all twentieth-century Popes had in some way anticipated it. Pius X and Benedict XV had done so by trying to forestall the tragedies of the First World War, Pius XI by contending with hostile regimes in Germany, Russia, Italy, Spain and Mexico. Pius XII had offered guidelines for a new world order after the horrors of World War II, while John XXIII and Paul VI had also tried to extrapolate a 'just system' from Catholic social teaching.[35]

Yet while the Church honoured its modern martyrs, it should also examine its own record in a spirit of penance. 'The Church should become more fully conscious of the sinfulness of her children', *Tertio millennio adveniente* continued, 'recalling all those times in history when they departed from the spirit of Christ and his Gospel and, instead of offering to the world the witness of a life inspired by values of faith, indulged in ways of thinking and acting which were truly forms of counter-witness and scandal.'[36]

The letter singled out 'intolerance' and 'violence' in the service of truth. It also listed Church leaders' shared responsibility for 'secularism and relativism', the 'lack of discernment' shown towards human rights violations by totalitarian regimes, and Christian involvement in 'grave forms of injustice and exclusion'. *Gaudium et spes* had urged an 'open, respectful and cordial dialogue', as well as a 'courageous witness to the truth'. This joint Vatican II injunction remained as valid as ever.[37]

The Pope called for a 'daily commitment to transform reality' to bring it closer to God's plan. The Millennium should also remind the Church of its 'option for the poor and outcast', in a world marred everywhere by 'intolerable social and economic inequalities'. 'With the fall of the 'great anti-Christian systems' of Nazism and communism, the liberating message of the Gospel was again urgently needed.[38]

A year later, the Pope again urged the Church to recognize its members' 'weaknesses, mediocrity, sins and at times betrayals'. This was sensitive ground in Eastern Europe. Investigations in the former East Germany suggested the Stasi secret police had only partially infiltrated the Church. In Czechoslovakia, on the other hand, up to 10 per cent of priests were estimated to have informed for the Státní Bezpečnost (StB). Even in Poland, where 'Department Four' records were illegally shredded, priests had had to be screened after 1989. Yet some Church leaders were vigorously against admitting fault, and resisted suggestions that the Pope had made the need for *metanoia* a Millennium theme.[39]

They were equally surprised when, in a rare interview, the Pope appeared to go back on the anti-socialist strictures of *Centesimus annus*. Communism's expansion, he reminded a Polish-Italian politician, Jaś Gawroński, had resulted from 'a certain type of unbridled, savage capitalism which we all know well'. Leo XIII and Marx had both correctly blamed the nineteenth-century's social realities on 'the system and principles of ultra-liberal capitalism'. This also explained why so many workers and intellectuals, Poles included, had initially supported communism. Of course, it had been legitimate to fight against the unjust totalitarian system, the Pope continued.

> But what Leo XIII says is also true, namely, that there are some 'grains of truth' even in the socialist programme. Obviously, these grains should not be destroyed or lost. Today, an accurate and objective view is needed, accompanied by a keen sense of discernment. The extreme champions of capitalism, in whatever form, tend to disregard the good things achieved by communism: the struggle against unemployment, the concern for the poor.[40]

The Pope contrasted communism's 'social concern' with capitalism's 'individualism'. The communist version had been 'tragically flawed', he stressed, exacting a 'high price' in inertia and passivity.

Yet the price of transition to a new system had been high too—'an increase in unemployment, poverty and misery'. The Church accepted the basic principles of capitalism, since they broadly conformed with natural law. However, it condemned the abuses of 'unbridled capitalism'—injustice, exploitation, violence, arrogance.

> In my opinion, at the root of many serious social and human problems troubling Europe and the world today are the degenerate aspects of capitalism. Naturally, modern capitalism is no longer that of Leo XIII's time. It has changed, and in large part due to socialist thinking. Capitalism today is different; it has introduced some social safety-net; thanks to the work of trade unions it has enacted a social policy; it is checked by the State and by trade unions. In some countries of the world, however, it has remained in its 'unbridled' state, almost as it was in the last century.[41]

The reference to 'grains of truth' was nothing new. Even in his 1937 diatribe, *Divini redemptoris*, Pius XI had acknowledged that 'like every other error, communism contains some element of truth'.[42] This added weight to claims that the interview remarks reflected John Paul's true thinking.

In *Tertio millennio adveniente*, the Pope again appeared to retract the anti-socialist focus of *Centesimus annus*. The latter encyclical had shown how everything written about communism in *Rerum novarum* had been vindicated, he noted.[43] This was strange wording. In reality, Leo XIII had not used the word 'communism' in his 1891 text. The Pope's implication seemed clear. Contrary to what *Centesimus annus* had claimed, Leo's denunciations had to be seen as applying to modern-day communism rather than to today's much-modified socialism.

The Pope went back on *Centesimus annus* in another way too—by defending the much-contested dual rejection of 'liberal capitalism' and 'Marxist collectivism' in *Sollicitudo rei socialis*. The 1987 encyclical had 'systematically reformulated' the Church's social doctrine against a background of East–West confrontation, he noted. It had also shown that peace was linked with 'the safeguarding of human dignity and rights' in labour–capital relations.[44]

'What we refer to as communism has its own history. It is the history of protest in the face of injustice, as I recalled in the encyclical *Laborem exercens*—a protest on the part of the great world of workers, which then became an ideology', the Pope recalled the same year. 'But this protest has become part of the teaching of the Church ... This teaching is not limited to protest, but throws a far-seeing glance towards the future.'[45]

All in all, Catholics could not be blamed for thinking they had been left with confused signals. Had John Paul II really endorsed capitalism at all?

It was left to the new *Catechism of the Catholic Church* to set the record straight.

> The Church has rejected the totalitarian and atheistic ideologies associated in modern times with 'communism' or 'socialism'. She has likewise refused to accept, in the practice of 'capitalism', individualism and the absolute primacy of the law of the marketplace over human labour. Regulating the economy solely by centralized planning perverts the basis of social bonds; regulating it solely by the law of the marketplace fails social justice ...[46]

With that sense of catholicity now restored, John Paul II's pontificate took on a new lease of life. When he returned to Poland on 31 May 1997, for his longest pilgrimage to date, he was given a rapturous reception. This time, the Pope stayed aloof from his homeland's bitter political disputes and avoided angry denunciations of declining moral standards. Instead, he rekindled the optimism of his early years, with a message of renewal for a society still deeply unsure of its values and priorities.

The eleven-day visit drew unprecedented crowds and was applauded equally from Left and Right. The Pope's themes ranged from ecumenical reconciliation to defence of life and loyalty to the Church—a loyalty, he said, which should endure the 'limits and imperfections' of the 'sinful and weak beings' who led it.[47]

There were two topics, however, which predominated. One was East–West unity. At Gniezno, the Pope held a meeting with the presidents of Poland, Germany, Ukraine, Hungary, Lithuania, Slovakia and the Czech Republic, to mark the thousandth anniversary of the martyrdom of St Adalbert in 997. Even after the Berlin Wall had fallen, he said, another 'invisible wall' still divided Europe. It was a wall in human hearts—'made out of fear and aggressiveness, lack of understanding for people of different origins, colours and religious convictions, a wall of political and economic selfishness, of weakening sensitivity to the value of human life'.

Yet the wall could be breached, the Pope insisted, by a return to Gospel values, by ensuring that 'no nation, not even the least powerful' was excluded from Europe's development. Preaching before the saint's relics, John Paul recalled that he had outlined his pontificate's 'programme' at Gniezno eighteen years before in 1979. 'Here, in this place, I repeat the cry I made then', he added. 'In the name of respect for human rights, in the name of liberty, equality and fraternity, in the name of solidarity among mankind, in the name of love, I cry out: Do not be afraid! Open the doors to Christ!'[48]

The second theme was social justice. World hunger remained a 'great challenge and indictment' for Christians, the Pope told worshippers in Wrocław. It required efforts to ensure 'elementary solidarity' prevailed over the 'unrestrained desire for profit' which disregarded inalienable human rights. Human freedom needed defending 'in a social context permeated by ideas of democracy inspired by liberal ideology'. The Church was still having to defend itself against charges that it was itself an enemy of that freedom.

The Pope returned to the subject in the depressed region of Legnica, at a Mass for 300,000 on an airfield previously used by the Warsaw Pact's Northern Army Group. Post-communist Poland, he said, needed a 'message of justice'. Many of the problems he had highlighted in 1979 were now 'even more acute'. It was a time of extreme poverty and the hopelessness of unemployment. Sharing the Eucharist would stand as an 'accusation' for those were led by 'visions of immediate profit at the expense of others'.

Historians might well have felt a sense of *déjà-vu*: the Pope's depiction of conditions was strikingly similar to what had been said by Leo XIII a whole century before.

> Every day we become aware of how many families are suffering from poverty. How many single mothers are struggling to take care of their children! How many old people are abandoned, without means to live! In institutions for orphans and abandoned children there is no lack of those without enough food and clothing. How can we fail to mention the sick who cannot be given proper care because of the lack of resources? On the streets and squares the number of homeless people is increasing. Alongside the problem of unemployment, there is also the attitude of those who consider the worker as a tool of production, with the result that man is insulted in his personal dignity. This phenomenon of exploitation is often manifested in conditions of employment in which the worker not only has no guaranteed rights but is subjected to such an atmosphere of uncertainty and fear of the loss of his job that he is in practice deprived of any freedom of decision. This exploitation is also often seen in the fixing of work schedules which deprive the worker of the right to rest and provide for the spiritual good of his family. It is often associated with inadequate pay, together with a negligence in the areas of insurance and health assistance.[49]

While copiously quoting from his other writings, the Pope hardly mentioned *Centesimus annus*. A misgiving that he had allowed the Church to ignore the lessons of the intervening century may well have been what now impelled him to go further. Visiting France that August, he beatified the radical nineteenth-century reformer Frédéric Ozanam (1813–53), the one-time associate of Lamennais and the 'social Catholic' journal *L'Avenir*, who had sympathized with the 1848 revolutionaries and proclaimed that the downtrodden needed 'not alms but proper institutions'.[50]

In Brazil the following October, he delivered a rap across the knuckles to complacent Latin Americans. Over the previous decade, countries in the region had boosted their GNP by 10 per cent. In Brazil alone, however, 7,000 homeless children were estimated to have been killed by death squads in 1995–97, with the tacit approval of middle-class society. A million more were involved in the growing market for child prostitution. Brazil's bishops, some of whom had criticized the Vatican's stance in the 1980s, had spoken out against 'barbaric brutality' by the police, accusing the State of protecting human rights only for the richest third of the population. Corruption was rampant; landless peasants still being massacred; women from poor families forcibly sterilized.[51]

During four days in Rio de Janeiro, the Pope stressed the importance of the family. It was, he told Brazilians, the 'fundamental community of life and love' from which all other forms of society derived. He warned of threats posed by 'hedonistic mentalities, unhealthy ambition and egoism', and called for 'just laws which will fight against poverty and the plague of unemployment'. He again urged the authorities to meet the 'challenge of gigantic proportions' posed by the 'unequal and unjust division of economic resources'.[52]

John Paul made no public mention of Liberation Theology. But there were signs that, barely eighteen months after his last lacklustre visit to Central America, even this was being reconsidered.

Fr Hans-Peter Kolvenbach, the conservative Dutchman picked to put the Jesuits in order in 1983, called for a 'new theological inspiration' to counter the 'neo-liberal' elevation of economic necessity over human dignity. The course taken by Liberation Theology in the 1980s had 'genuinely exhausted itself', Kolvenbach added. Church leaders had exposed its 'many mistakes': their critique had been 'fully justified'. It had, however, been 'deeply rooted in the Gospel' and the 'real life of the people of God'—at a time when many Christians believed the Church had become too remote from local conditions. 'We must remember the human person, including the poor person, lives not only on bread but also in his own culture', the Jesuit Father-General declared. 'A theology of liberation is more needed today than ever—but a renewed liberation theology, in a different form than previously.'[53]

Kolvenbach was just one of many once-subservient Church leaders who had become increasingly outspoken as John Paul II entered old age. It was with pressure like this to back him up that the Pope soon extended *Tertio millennio adveniente*'s call for penance into a series of pre-Millennium initiatives. The records of the Inquisition and Holy Office were made available to historians, while Church commissions began re-examining the work of past reformers. Meanwhile, the disputed record of Pius XII was hauled into the open with a 'Reflection on the Shoah' published in March 1998 by the Vatican's Papal Commission for Religious Contacts with Judaism. This went some way towards acknowledging the Church's inadequate reaction to the slaughter of the Jews and was accompanied by declarations of regret by individual Bishops' Conferences.

As archives were opened, more details emerged of the Vatican's game of wits in Eastern Europe during the 1980s. Mystery still surrounded the St Peter's Square shooting of May 1981, as fresh allegations of Soviet involvement continued to be met by insistent Russian and Bulgarian denials. Italian intelligence services confirmed, however, that murderous plots had indeed existed. Bugging devices were said to have been placed in Cardinal Casaroli's dining room by his nephew's Czech wife, a KGB agent.[54]

Further afield, communist regimes remained defiantly in power in Vietnam, North Korea and China. The Beijing government was still smarting over the Catholic Church's links with 'colonialists and imperialists', as well as Pius XII's 'breathing of hatred' for Mao's revolution in 1949. It was ready to 'improve relations' with the Vatican, the regime said; but only if Rome stopped recognizing Taiwan and 'intervening in China's internal affairs under the pretext of religion'.[55]

That still left Cuba, the only communist state the Vatican had consistently maintained ties with. In November 1996, desperate to break the hopeless isolation brought by US sanctions and Russian cold-shouldering, Fidel Castro headed to Rome and handed the Pope a contrite invitation. John Paul finally arrived, after protracted negotiations, on 21 January 1998. The atmosphere was one of bitter pathos mixed with nostalgia for history's might-have-beens.

The world's media compared the expectations aroused by the Cuba visit to those of the Pope's very first Polish pilgrimage. In reality, the priorities had evolved along with the passing epoch. The Pope had come to help Castro help himself—not by confronting and discrediting the Cuban revolution, but by suggesting how it might still rediscover its moral impulses after forty years of totalitarian abuse.

That meant seeking common ground at a point where communism and Christianity overlapped. There were two figures in particular who embodied a 'synthesis of Christian faith and Cuban culture'. One was the nineteenth-century architect of Cuban nationhood, Fr Felix Varela y Morales, who had worked among the poor of New York after being forced to flee the Caribbean island. Varela had viewed democracy, the Pope recalled, as the system 'most in harmony with human nature'. The other was the revolutionary poet José Martí, an icon of Latin American communists, who had died resisting Spanish rule in 1895. Martí had been 'an enlightened man', the Pope said, 'compact in his ethical values, animated by a spirituality largely rooted in Christianity'.[56]

The Pope urged modern rulers—Castro included—to remember that the State could not make either 'atheism or religion one of its political ordinances'. It had to distance itself from 'all extremes of fanaticism or secularism'. Meanwhile, he again spoke of a world divided between rich and poor, in which the globalization of capital was eroding self-determination and self-esteem.

> Various places are witnessing the re-emergence of a certain capitalist neo-liberalism that subordinates the human person to blind market forces and conditions the development of peoples on those forces. From its centres of power, such neo-liberalism often places unbearable burdens upon less favoured countries. As a result, the wealthy grow ever wealthier, while the poor grow ever poorer.[57]

That at least was an observation with which Castro fully concurred. But there were some dilemmas, the Pope implied, which would go on defying permanent solution. The greatest challenge, he told Cubans in Revolution Square, Havana, remained as it had always been: how to find a 'freedom based on truth' which could coexist with social justice and solidarity, and allow the human person 'initiative for personal development' without 'imprisoning him in his own egoism'. For Christians, the 'freedom of the children of God' was not only a 'gift and a task': it also served as a model, an 'invaluable witness', for the liberation of the human race.

For all its latter-day uncertainties, John Paul's pontificate was destined to the remembered for its dramatic images: the red-clad figure emerging into the arc-lights of a balcony in St Peter's Square in October 1978; the agonized grimace captured on a distorted face by a fast-moving TV camera in May 1981; the sunlight that played on decorated balconies in Gdańsk during the triumphant Workers Mass in June 1987.

Images were the Pope's trademark. When more than a million young people had flocked to Jasna Góra for World Youth Day in August 1991, the words of St Paul's Letter to the Romans had been read in Russian: 'What you received was not the spirit of slavery to bring you back into fear' (Romans 8:15). Five nights later, a coup by Soviet hardliners failed humiliatingly when a dense summer fog blocked the advance of tanks on the Moscow parliament. Many Russians attributed it to God's intervention. But the clash of lost tanks against half-hidden barricades had been a reminder of the fragility of Europe's post-communist order.

At his Youth Day vigil, the Pope had meditated on the three promises ascribed to the Virgin Mary in the Old Slavonic 'Call of Jasna Góra': *Tebje prjestojim, pametiwiji, Jesm bydeszte*—'I am standing by you, remembering, watching.' They were words of grace, he added, as well as words of eternal vigilance.

St John's Revelation captured the unending cosmic struggle of good with evil, John Paul continued. Its first portent was the image of Mary—'a woman clothed with the sun, with the moon under her feet and on her head a crown of twelve stars', crying out in the pangs of childbirth. Its second was the Evil One, the 'great red dragon, with seven heads and ten horns', who waited to devour the child who would 'rule all the nations with a rod of iron' (Revelation 12:1–5). With or without communism, the Pope cautioned his youthful audience, the struggle would continue to the end of time. The two nights of Bethlehem and Golgotha would remain embedded in the Christian consciousness.[58]

Communism had produced its saints. Bishop Vilmos Apor of Győr, the brave Hungarian killed by a Red Army soldier's bullet, who had deplored Pius XII's lack of wartime guidance, was beatified in November 1997. Bishop Eugen Bossilkov of Bulgaria, the show-trial victim whose executed remains had never been recovered, was similarly honoured in March 1998. Six Catholic Cardinals—Wyszyński, Beran, Mindszenty and Stepinac, the Czech Štěpán Trochta and the Romanian Iuliu Hossu—were also being considered for beatification. So were at least twenty bishops, including fourteen Greek Catholics from Romania and Ukraine. Poland's Fr Popiełuszko was also high on the list. So was a Czech, Fr Josef Toufar, tortured to death in 1950 after being accused of fabricating a 'miracle' at his church.

Meanwhile, former communist rulers had turned to the Church, as the bond between religion and nationhood reasserted itself. The president of independent Lithuania, Alfonsas Brazauskas, who led his republic's Soviet Communist Party through its 1989 break with Moscow, had become a practising Catholic. President Eduard Shevardnadze of Georgia, Soviet Foreign Minister in the 1980s, had been baptized in 1992. Before being ousted in 1991, Gorbachev had admitted he too was baptized as a child. So, by popular reckoning, were most former communists, prompting the question whether godlessness had ever really taken root at all. Lenin, the Soviet Union's atheist mastermind, was married in a Russian Orthodox church nineteen years before leading the Bolshevik revolution. Stalin, who presided over the greatest persecution in Christian history, trained for the priesthood at a Georgian seminary. His much-married daughter, Svetlana, became a regular guest at European convents after being received into the Catholic Church at a London seminary in 1982.

There was, all the same, a strange lightness in attitudes to the communist past. Stalin's purges in the Soviet Union had assumed the proportions of genocide, aimed not against races or classes, but against every perceived opponent without distinction. The Soviet campaign to exterminate the 'kulaks' had cost 6.5 million lives, with 'terror famines' of the early 1930s leaving another 8 million dead. Seven million more had been shot in a fresh campaign from 1935. Of the 12 million detained in 1938, a high proportion had died in incarceration. Once figures were added for the rest of Eastern Europe, communism's peacetime death-toll could be conservatively estimated at 25 million people. When China and the Third World were also included, the probable total soared to 95 million.[59]

Most were left to lie, however, unaccounted for in their mass graves, or where they fell in the dust and silt of distant Siberia and the Asian steppe. Their persecutors lived in comfortable retirement, often with honours for past 'services'. Maybe this was the price to be paid for communism's mostly peaceful overthrow; it was also a sign that temporal justice and satisfaction were beyond reach. Whole generations were condemned to go on living with the consequences of decisions taken by those who had believed themselves masters of history. Yet there were no great periods of mourning and soul-searching. There were few trials and sentences. All that could be done was to muddle through, relentlessly building and rebuilding on the broken bodies and spirits of the past.

The system of power devised by Lenin and Stalin had been unparalleled in human history. It had left society permeated at every level by terrorized dreams and deceptions. While many had opposed the system, many others had seen it as the promise of the future. And there had been no rational criteria for determining who stood in either camp.

Whereas Nazism had required fear and obedience, communism had demanded positive approval. It had claimed a right of possession not just over the bodies, but over the very minds and souls of its subjects. By promising absolute good, it had removed all sense of evil, in this way unleashing the primal instincts usually constrained by law and ethics.

Nazism had drawn its strength from a myth of racial superiority and lust for power, which fed on human and national weaknesses. Communism's legacy was more complex. It had thrived on arrogance and greed as well; but it was also based on a false world vision, a corrupted system of values and ideas. A path had been found from Nazism through admissions of guilt and acts of penance. The path from communism had required much more—a metamorphosis from illusion to reality.

Of course, the communism of the 1980s had been a far cry from the communism of the 1930s. Perhaps this was why many still believed the motor of revolt had been largely economic—and that better material conditions would satisfy East European aspirations. In reality, the communist experience taught deep lessons about human nature—about the despicable wickedness and glorious heroism of which human beings were simultaneously capable. For the modern world especially, it highlighted a crucial truth—that it was not only poverty but indignity too which provided fertile ground for destructive demagogues. If that truth was forgotten, the world would go on being powerless before ideologies which tried to find short-cuts to an earthly utopia.

'The real reason for the existence of Poland', the Romantic poet Zygmunt Krasiński wrote in 1847, 'is to realize on earth the kingdom of heaven, to merge politics and religion, to found the future church of humanity.'[60] That was the messianic spirit which Pope John Paul II had been raised on—the messianism of nations consigned to perpetual vulnerability on Europe's eastern margins, prey to Russian aggressiveness and Western indifference, condemned to go on yearning for revolutionary panaceas and miracle solutions to their own backwardness.

In the 1950s, Wojtyła might well have agreed with Jung that it was the vices of Western Man 'disguised under the mask of good manners at the international level, which the communist world is flinging back in his face shamelessly and methodically', and 'the grimacing face of his own shadow that Western Man sees leering at him from the other side of the Iron Curtain'.[61]

By the 1990s, he would also have concurred with Brother Albert, the character of his own play, that not even the Church could offer ultimate answers. There would, in the end, be various paths to God. But for all the 'great, just anger' of humanity, there would be no worldly liberation. The Church had to go on fighting for justice, for a dignity worthy of humanity. But it was destined never to achieve them. All that could be hoped for, as Brother Albert realized, was 'a failure which transforms itself into the Cross, a captivity which becomes freedom in Christ'—and a confidence that the mystery of faith would always endure against impossible odds.

In the meantime, the world would continue awaiting the Counsellor promised at the Last Supper in St John's Gospel. As Karol Wojtyła once wrote, human beings would always face a free choice between good and evil, between the salvation offered by the Holy Spirit, and the 'dead works' of sin and ruin.

Notes

1. Exchange of addresses (1 December 1989) in *The Pope Teaches*, no. 12 (London: Catholic Truth Society, 1989), pp. 369–73.

2. Gorbachev's column in *La Stampa* (3 March 1992); Catholic News Service (19 March 1997). The Pope described Gorbachev as 'a man of integrity, committed to principles and very rich in spiritual terms', who had spoken 'of the importance of prayer and the inner side of man's life': *The Tablet* (7 March 1982).
3. 'Speech to clergy, religious and committed laity', Holy See Press Office (21 April 1990); *National Catholic Register* (6 May 1990).
4. Jonathan Luxmoore and Jolanta Babiuch, 'Eastern Europe: the Catholic alternative', *The World Today*, vol. 46, no. 4 (April 1990), pp. 70–3.
5. Leo XIII, *Rerum novarum* (15 May 1891), no. 15.
6. From the first paragraph of *The Communist Manifesto*, published in February 1848; Gregory XVI, *Mirari vos* (15 August 1832), no. 14. In his 1994 book, John Paul II condemned the 'pure rationalism' of the Enlightenment for 'expelling God from the world', as well as the anti-religious excesses of the French Revolution. 'On the basis of this, there was a proclamation of Liberty, Equality and Fraternity. The spiritual patrimony and, in particular, the moral patrimony of Christianity were thus torn from their evangelical foundation. In order to restore Christianity to its full vitality, it is necessary that these return to that foundation': John Paul II, *Crossing the Threshold of Hope* (London: Jonathan Cape, 1994), p. 52.
7. *Redemptor hominis* (4 March 1979), no. 41.
8. Address in St James cathedral, Compostela (19 August 1989).
9. Figures from Jolanta Babiuch, 'Church and society in post-communist Eastern Europe', *The World Today*, vol. 50, no. 11 (November 1994), pp. 211–15; Ośrodek Badań Opinii Społecznej, survey in *Gazeta Wyborcza* (10 October 1997); *Rzeczpospolita* survey (13 December 1997).
10. 'Speech to clergy', op. cit.
11. *Ut unum sint* (25 May 1996), nos 52–54, 60–61.
12. *Catholic International*, vol. 3, no. 4 (February 1982), pp. 152–3.
13. *National Catholic Register* (23 June 1991).
14. *La Stampa*, interview (2 November 1993).
15. Homily at Skoczów (22 May 1995); *National Catholic Register* (25 June 1995).
16. Centrum Badań Opinii Społecznej, survey (21-25 March 1996); in Jolanta Babiuch and Jonathan Luxmoore, 'Popierają, ale czy rozumieją', *Rzeczpospolita* (11 June 1996).
17. *Sollicitudo rei socialis* (30 December 1987), nos 28–33.
18. Katolicka Agencja Informacijna bulletin (Warsaw: 12 and 22 February 1996).
19. *Catechism of the Catholic Church* (London: Geoffrey Chapman, 1995), no. 2243, p. 484.
20. *Centesimus annus* (1 May 1991), nos 4–5.
21. Ibid., nos 13–14.
22. Pius XI, *Quadragesimo anno* (15 May 1931), no. 114.
23. *Centesimus annus*, nos 17, 19.
24. Leo XIII, *Libertas praestantissimum* (20 June 1888), nos 10, 19–20.
25. Leo XIII, *Sapientiae Christianae* (10 January 1890), nos 1–3; *Rerum novarum*, no. 2.

26. Ibid., nos 1–2; *Libertas praestantissimum*, no. 10.
27. *Centesimus annus*, nos 24, 26.
28. Ibid., no. 35.
29. Ibid., no. 42.
30. Ibid., no. 26.
31. Ibid., nos 35, 52, 58.
32. Ibid., no. 56.
33. *Veritatis splendor* (6 August 1993), no. 101.
34. *Evangelium vitae* (25 March 1995), nos 69–70.
35. Apostolic Letter, *Tertio millennio adveniente* (10 November 1994), nos 21–22.
36. Ibid., no. 33.
37. Ibid., nos 33–36. Vatican II's Dogmatic Constitution had also acknowledged that the Church 'clasping sinners to her bosom, at once holy and always in need of purification, constantly follows the path of penance and renewal': *Lumen gentium* (21 November 1964), no. 8.
38. *Tertio millennio adveniente*, no. 57.
39. *Respekt* (Prague), no. 52 (January 1994); Catholic News Service (28 July 1994; 3 April 1996); *Catholic International*, vol. 8, no. 3 (March 1997), pp. 104–5. See also *Redemptor hominis*, no. 88; *Ut unum sint*, no. 11.
40. *La Stampa*, interview, op. cit.; *The Pope Teaches*, no. 11 (1993), pp. 337–8.
41. Ibid., p. 339.
42. Pius XI, *Divini redemptoris* (19 March 1937), no. 24.
43. *Centesimus annus*, no. 27.
44. *Tertio millennio adveniente*, no. 22.
45. John Paul II, *Crossing the Threshold*, op. cit., pp. 130–1.
46. *Catechism*, no. 2425.
47. Greeting to pilgrims, Jasna Góra, Holy See Press Office (4 June 1997).
48. Homily in St Adalbert's Square; Message aux présidents, Gniezno: Holy See Press Office (3 June 1997).
49. Homily at Legnica Airport: Holy See Press Office (2 June 1997).
50. Quoted in Jan Kracik, 'Patron otwartych dróg', *Tygodnik Powszechny* (24 August 1997).
51. Catholic News Service (19 September 1997); Jonathan Luxmoore, 'Pope John Paul's liberation theology', *The Tablet* (11 October 1997).
52. Homily in Rio de Janeiro: Holy See Press Office (4 October 1997).
53. Ecumenical News International (24 September 1997).
54. For example, *Rzeczpospolita* (Warsaw: 10 January and 8 April 1988).
55. From a government policy statement: *Rzeczpospolita* (17 October 1997).
56. Address to people of culture, Havana University: Holy See Press Office (24 January 1998).
57. Homily in Havana: Holy See Press Office (24 January 1998).
58. Homily at Jasna Góra: Holy See Press Office (15 August 1991).
59. Figures from Jonathan Luxmoore, 'Life after communism', *The Tablet* (22 August 1992); Robert Conquest, *The Harvest of Sorrow* (London: Arrow Books, 1988), pp. 299–308, and *The Great Terror: A Reassessment* (London: Pimlico,

1992), pp. 484–9. Figures for China (65 million dead), Korea (2 million), Kampuchea (2 million) and other countries are given in Stéphane Courtois et al., *Le livre noir du communisme: crimes, terreur, répression* (Paris: Robert Laffont, 1997).

60. In a letter to Bronisław Trentowski; in Andrzej Walicki, *Philosophy and Romantic Nationalism* (Oxford: Clarendon Press, 1982), p. 289.

61. Quoted in Patrick Michel, *Politics and Religion in Eastern Europe* (London: Polity Press, 1991), p. 180.

Bibliography

Papal documents

Pius VI	*Diu satis* (15 May 1800)
Gregory XVI	*Mirari vos* (15 August 1832)
Pius IX	*Qui pluribus* (9 November 1846)
	Nostis et nobiscum (8 December 1849)
	Quanta cura (8 December 1864)
Leo XIII	*Quod apostolici muneris* (28 December 1878)
	Rerum novarum (15 May 1881)
	Immortale Dei (1 November 1885)
	Libertas praestantissimum (20 June 1888)
	Sapientiae Christianae (10 January 1890)
	Graves de communi (18 January 1901)
Pius XI	*Nos es muy conocida* (28 March 1927)
	Quadragesimo anno (15 May 1931)
	Non abbiamo bisogno (29 June 1931)
	Dilectissima nobis (3 June 1933)
	Mit brennender Sorge (14 March 1937)
	Divini Redemptoris (19 March 1937)
Pius XII	*Summi pontificatus* (20 October 1939)
	Mystici corporis (29 June 1943)
	Humani generis (12 August 1950)
	Luctuosissimi eventus (28 October 1956)
	Laetamur admodum (31 October 1956)
	Datis nuperrime (5 November 1956)
John XXIII	*Ad Petri cathedram* (29 June 1959)
	Grata recordatio (26 September 1959)
	Princeps pastorum (28 November 1959)
	Mater et magistra (15 May 1961)
	Aeterna Dei sapientia (11 November 1961)

	Pacem in terris (11 April 1963)
Paul VI	*Ecclesiam Suam* (6 August 1964)
	Mense Maio (29 April 1965)
	Christi Matri (15 September 1966)
	Populorum progressio (2 March 1967)
	Octogesima adveniens (14 May 1971)
	Evangelii nuntiandi (8 December 1975)
John Paul II	*Redemptor hominis* (4 March 1979)
	Dives in misericordia (30 November 1980)
	Egregiae virtutis (31 December 1980)
	Laborem exercens (14 September 1981)
	Slavorum apostoli (2 June 1985)
	Dominum et vivificantem (18 May 1986)
	Sollicitudo rei socialis (30 December 1987)
	Euntes in mundum (25 January 1988)
	Magnum baptismi donum (14 February 1988)
	Centesimus annus (1 May 1991)
	Veritatis splendor (6 August 1993)
	Tertio millennio adveniente (10 November 1994)
	Evangelium vitae (25 March 1995)
	Ut unum sint (25 May 1996)

Papal encyclicals and documents from the nineteenth and twentieth centuries are quoted from Claudia Carlen Ihm (ed.), *The Papal Encyclicals* (New York: McGrath Publishing Co., 1981); or Sidney Z. Ehler and John B. Morrall (eds), *Church and State Through the Ages* (London: Burns and Oates, 1954); or Catholic Truth Society Publishers, London. All quotations from the documents of the Second Vatican Council and subsequent decrees are taken from Austin Flannery (ed.), *Vatican Council II: The Conciliar and Post-Conciliar Documents*, vols 1 and 2 (New York: Costello, 1982 and 1988). Other Vatican or Church documents are cited from David O'Brien and Thomas Shannon, *Renewing the Earth: Catholic Documents on Peace, Justice and Liberation* (New York: Image Books, 1977); or Michael Walsh and Brian Davies (eds), *Proclaiming Justice and Peace* (Mystic, CT: Twenty-Third Publications, 1991).

Karol Wojtyła's early books, *Miłość i Odpowiedzialność* (Love and Responsibility) and *Osoba i Czyn* (The Acting Person), as well as his articles and papers, have been retranslated from the Polish original to avoid the anomalies and inconsistencies in published English-language editions.

Other sources

Agocs, Sandor, *The Troubled Origins of the Catholic Labour Movement 1878–1914* (Detroit: Wayne State University Press, 1988).

Agostino, Marc, *Le Pape Pie XI et l'Opinion* (Rome: École Française de Rome, 1991).

Alexander, Stella, *Church and State in Yugoslavia Since 1945* (Cambridge: Cambridge University Press, 1979).

Alexander, Stella, *The Triple Myth: A Life of Archbishop Alojzije Stepinac* (New York: Columbia University Press, 1987).

Anderson, John, *Religion, State and Politics in the Soviet Union and Successor States* (Cambridge: Cambridge University Press, 1994).

Assmann, Hugo, *Theology for a Nomad Church* (New York: Orbis Books, 1976).

Baersdorf, Otton (ed.), *Papiestwo wobec Sprawy Polskiej w latach 1722–1864* (Wrocław: Polska Akademia Nauk, 1960).

Bardecki, Andrzej, *Kościół Epoki Dialogu* (London: Veritas, 1967).

Bardecki, Andrzej, *Zawsze jest inaczej* (Kraków: Znak, 1996).

Beeson, Trevor, *Discretion and Valour* (London: Collins, 1982).

Bernhard, Michael H., *The Origins of Democratization in Poland* (New York: Columbia University Press, 1993).

Bernstein, Carl and Politi, Marco, *His Holiness: John Paul II and the Hidden History of Our Time* (New York: Doubleday, 1996).

Berryman, Philip, *Liberation Theology* (London: I. B. Tauris, 1987).

Bethel, Nicholas, *Gomułka: His Poland and His Communism* (London: Longman, 1969).

Blet, P., Graham, R., Martini, A. and Schneider, B. (eds), *Actes et documents du Saint-Siège relatifs à la seconde guerre mondiale* (Vatican City, 1967–82).

Bonhoeffer, Dietrich, *Letters and Papers from Prison* (London: SCM Press, 1953).

Boniecki, Adam (ed.), *Kalendarium życia Karola Wojtyły* (Kraków: Znak, 1983).

Boniecki, Adam (ed.), *Notatki Rzymski* (Kraków: Znak, 1988).

Bonino, José Miguez, *Doing Theology in a Revolutionary Situation* (New York: Fortress Press, 1975).

Bourdeaux, Michael, *Land of Crosses* (Devon: Augustine, 1979).

Buttiglione, Rocco, *Il Pensiero di Karol Wojtyla* (Milan: Jaca Book, 1982).

Calvez, Jean-Yves, *Le Deuxième Concile du Vatican* (Rome: École Française de Rome, 1989).

Casula, Carlo Felice, *Domenico Tardini 1888–1961: L'azione della Santa Sede nella crisi fra le due guerra* (Rome: Edizioni Studium, 1988).

Catechism of the Catholic Church (London: Geoffrey Chapman, 1994).

Chadwick, Owen, *The Popes and European Revolution* (Oxford: Clarendon Press, 1981).

Chadwick, Owen, *The Secularization of the European Mind in the 19th Century* (London: Canto, 1990).

Charlton, Michael, *The Eagle and the Small Birds: Crisis in the Soviet Empire from Yalta to Solidarity* (London: BBC Books, 1984).

Charta 77 Foundation, *A Besieged Culture: Czechoslovakia Ten Years After Helinski* (Stockholm, 1985).

Chelini, Jean, *L'Église sous Pie XII* (Paris: Fayard, 1989).

Chudzik, Wanda, et al. (eds), *Uroczystości milenijne 1966 roku: sprawozdania urzędów spraw wewnętrznych* (Warsaw: MSW, 1996).

Cianfarra, Camille M., *The Vatican and the Kremlin* (New York: E. P. Dutton, 1950).

Clauss, Manfred, *Die Beziehungen des Vatikans zu Polen wahrend des Zweites Weltkrieges* (Cologne: Bohlan Verlag, 1979).

Congregation for the Doctrine of the Faith, *Instruction on Certain Aspects of the Theology of Liberation* (6 August 1983).

Congregation for the Doctrine of the Faith, *Instruction on Christian Freedom and Liberation* (22 March 1986).

Conquest, Robert, *The Great Terror: A Reassessment* (London: Hutchinson, 1986).

Conquest, Robert, *The Harvest of Sorrow* (London: Hutchinson, 1990).

Cooney, John, *The American Pope: The Life and Times of Francis Cardinal Spellman* (New York: Times Books, 1984).

Coppa, Frank J., *Cardinal Giacomo Antonelli and Papal Politics in European Affairs* (New York: State University Press, 1990).

Corley, Felix, *Religion in the Soviet Union: An Archival Reader* (London: Macmillan, 1996).

Corradini, Carlo, *Atteggiamenti del PCI verso la Chiesa Cattolica e la religione* (Rome: Rovigo, 1978).

Courtois, Stéphane et al., *Le livre noir du communisme: Crimes, terreur, répression* (Paris: Robert Laffont, 1997).

Csimadia, Andor, *Rechtliche Beziehungen von Staat und Kirche in Ungarn vor 1944* (Budapest: Akadémiai Kiadó, 1971).

Cywiński, Bohdan, *Rodowody niepokornych* (Warsaw: Biblioteka Więzi, 1971).

Cywiński, Bohdan, *Doświadczenie Polskie* (Warsaw: *samizdat*, 1987).

Cywiński, Bohdan, *Ogniem Próbowane: I was prześladować będą* (Lublin: Redakcja Wydawnictw, 1990).

Daniel-Rops, Henri, *L'Église des Révolutions: Un combat pour Dieu* (Paris: Fayard, 1964).

Davis, Nathaniel, *A Long Walk to Church: A Contemporary History of Russian Orthodoxy* (San Francisco: Westview Press, 1995).

Delzell, Charles F. (ed.), *The Papacy and Totalitarianism Between the Two World Wars* (New York: John Wiley, 1974).

Dmowski, Roman, *Polityka polska i odbudowanie państwa* (Warsaw: Parzyński, 1925).

d'Onorio, Joël-Benoît (ed.), *Le Saint-Siège dans les relations internationales* (Paris: Éditions du Cerf, 1989).

Douglas, J. Bruce and Holloubach, David (eds), *Catholicism and Liberalism* (Cambridge: Cambridge University Press, 1994).

Dumitru-Snagov, I., *Le Saint-Siège et la Roumanie moderne* (Rome: Editrice Pontificia Università Gregoriana, 1989).

Dunn, Dennis, *Détente in Papal–Communist Relations* (Boulder: Westview, 1979).

Dunn, Dennis, *Religion and Nationalism in Eastern Europe and the Soviet Union* (London: Rienner, 1987).

Dupuy, André, *La Diplomatie du Saint-Siège* (Paris: Tequi, 1980).

Dybciak, Krzysztof, *Karol Wojtyła a literatura* (Tarnów: Biblos, 1993).

Ehler, Sidney Z. and Morrall, John B. (eds), *Church and State Through the Ages* (London: Burns and Oates, 1954), pp. 281–5.

Eisler, Jerzy, *Marzec 1968* (Warsaw: Państwowe Wydawnictwo Naukowe, 1991).

Ellis, Jane, *The Russian Orthodox Church: A Contemporary History* (Bloomington: Indiana University Press, 1986).

Falconi, Carlo, *The Popes in the Twentieth Century* (London: Weidenfeld and Nicolson, 1967).

Falconi, Carlo, *Pope John and His Council* (London: Weidenfeld and Nicolson, 1964).

Falconi, Carlo, *The Silence of Pius XII* (London: Faber and Faber, 1970).

Fedorowicz, Tadeusz, *Drogi Opatrzności* (Lublin: Norbertinum, 1991).

Filipiak, Maria and Szostek, Andrzej (eds), *Obecność: Karol Wojtyła w Katolickim Uniwersytecie Lubelskim* (Lublin: Redakcja Wydawnictw, 1987).

Fletcher, William, *Religion and Soviet Foreign Policy* (Oxford: Oxford University Press, 1973).

Fredro-Boniecki, Tadeusz, *Zwycięstwo księdza Jerzego* (Warsaw: Nowa, 1990).

Friedlander, Saul, *Pie XII et le IIIe Reich—Documents* (Paris: Éditions du Seuil, 1964).

Friszke, Andrzej, *Opozycja polityczna w PRL 1945–1980* (London: Aneks, 1994).

Friszke, Andrzej, *Oaza na Kopernika: Klub Inteligencji Katolickiej 1956–1989* (Warsaw: Biblioteka Więzi, 1997).

Frossard, André, *Be Not Afraid!* (New York: St Martin's Press, 1984).

Gadille, Jacques (ed.), *Les Catholiques Libéraux au XIXe siècle* (Presses Universitaires de Grenoble, 1974).

Galter, Albert, *The Red Book of the Persecuted Church* (Maryland: Newman Press, 1957).

Gannon, Robert, *The Cardinal Spellman Story* (London: Robert Hale, 1963).

Garaudy, Roger, *From Anathema to Dialogue* (London: Collins, 1967).

Gibellini, Rosino, *The Liberation Theology Debate* (London: SCM Press, 1987).

Gorbachev, Mikhail, *Perestroika: New Thinking for Our Country and the World* (London: Collins, 1987).

Gowin, Jarosław, *Kościół po Komunizmie* (Kraków: Znak, 1995).

Gruber, Helmut, *Red Vienna: Experiment in Working Class Culture 1919–1934* (New York: Oxford University Press, 1991.

Gutiérrez, Gustavo, *The Power of the Poor in History* (London: SCM Press, 1983).

Hales, E. E. Y., *Pope John and His Revolution* (London: Eyre and Spottiswoode, 1965).

Hanák, Péter (ed.), *The Corvina History of Hungary* (Budapest: Corvina, 1988).

Hanson, Eric O., *The Catholic Church in World Politics* (Princeton: Princeton University Press, 1987).

Havasy, Gyula (ed.), *Martyrs of the Catholics in Hungary* (Budapest: privately published, 1993).

Hebblethwaite, Peter, *The Catholic–Marxist Dialogue and Beyond* (London: Darton, Longman and Todd, 1977).

Hebblethwaite, Peter, *John XXIII: Pope of the Council* (London: Geoffrey Chapman, 1984).

Hebblethwaite, Peter, *Synod Extraordinary* (London: Darton, Longman & Todd, 1986).

Hebblethwaite, Peter, *Paul VI: The First Modern Pope* (London: HarperCollins, 1993).

Heer, Frederick, *Europe, Mother of Revolutions* (New York: Praeger, 1972).

Hemmerling, Zygmunt and Nadolski, Marek (eds), *Opozycja demokratyczna w Polsce 1976–1980* (Warsaw: Wydawnictwa Uniwersytetu Warszawskiego, 1994).

Holmes, J. Derek, *The Papacy in the Modern World* (London: Burns and Oates, 1981).

Hosking, Geoffrey (ed.), *Church, Nation and State in Russia and Ukraine* (London: Macmillan, 1991).

Houtart, François and Rousseau, André, *L'Église face aux luttes révolutionnaires* (Brussels: Éditions Vie Ouvrière, 1972).

Houtart, François and Rousseau, Andre, *L'Église et les mouvements révolutionnaires* (Brussels: Éditions Vie Ouvrière, 1972).

Hruby, Peter, *Fools and Heroes: The Changing Role of Communist Intellectuals in Czechoslovakia* (London: Pergamon, 1978).

Ijjas, József, et al., *Ensemble pour une bonne cause: L'État socialiste et les Églises en Hongrie* (Budapest: Corvina, 1978).

Istranin, Veki, *Stepinac: un innocente condannato* (Vicenza: Edizione Lief, 1982).

Jaruzelski, Wojciech, *Stan Wojenny—dlaczego* (Warsaw: BGW, 1992).

John XXIII, *Journal of a Soul* (London: Geoffrey Chapman, 1965).

John Paul II, *Mężczyzna i Niewiasta Stworzył Ich* (Lublin: Redakcja Wydawnictw, 1987).

John Paul II, *Wierzę w Boga Ojca Stworzyciela* (Rome: Libreria Editrice Vaticana, 1987).

John Paul II, *Crossing the Threshold of Hope* (London: Jonathan Cape, 1994).

Kaariainen, K., *Atheism and Perestroika* (Helsinki: Suomalainen Tiedeakatemia, 1993).

Karon, Anna, *Dramat spotkania z Bogiem i z człowiekiem w myśli Karola Wojtyły* (Kraków: Wydawnictwo Naukowe PAT, 1994).

Karpiński, Jakub, *Portrety Lat: Polska w odcinkach 1944–1988* (London: Polonia, 1989).

Keogh, Dermot, *Ireland, the Vatican and the Cold War: The Case of Italy* (Washington, DC: Wilson Center, 1992).

Kertzer, David I., *Comrades and Christians: Religion and Political Struggle in Communist Italy* (Cambridge: Cambridge University Press, 1980).

Kijowski, Andrzej, *Gdybym był królem* (Poznań: W Drodze, 1988).

Kirk, John M., *Politics and the Catholic Church in Nicaragua* (Gainesville: University Press of Florida, 1992).

Kline, George L., *Religious and Anti-Religious Thought in Russia* (Chicago: University of Chicago Press, 1968).

Kłoczowski, Jan Andrzej, *Więcej niż Mit: Leszka Kołakowskiego spory o religię* (Kraków: Znak, 1994).

Kobler, John F., *Vatican II and Phenomenology: Reflections on the Life-World of the Church* (Dordrecht: Martinus Nijhoff, 1985).

Kołakowski, Leszek, *Kultura i fetisze* (Warsaw: Państwowe Wydawnictwo Naukowe, 1967).

Kołakowski, Leszek, *Main Currents of Marxism* (New York: Oxford University Press, 1981).

Konrád, György, *Antipolitics* (New York: Harcourt Brace Jovanovich, 1984).

Korec, Jan, *Od babarskej noci* (Bratislava: Lúč, 1991).

Kosík, Karel, *Dějiny filosofie jako filosofie: Filosofie v dějinách českého národa* (Prague: CSAV, 1958).

Kozak, E., *Jan Patočka: Philosophy and Selected Writings* (Chicago: University of Chicago Press, 1989).

Közi-Horváth, József, *Cardinal Mindszenty* (Devon: Augustine, 1979).

Kraus, Johann, *Im Auftrag des Papstes in Russland* (Siegburg: Steyler Vertrag, 1970.

Kuroń, Jacek, *Wiara i wina: do i od komunizmu* (Warsaw: Nowa, 1990).

Kuroń, Jacek, *Gwieżdny Czas* (London: Aneks, 1991).

Kwitny, Jonathan, *Man of the Century* (New York: Henry Holt, 1997).

Kydryński, Juliusz (ed.), *Młodzieńcze lata Karola Wojtyły* (Kraków: Oficyna Cracovia, 1990).

Lacroix-Riz, A., *Le Vatican, l'Europe et le Reich* (Paris: Armand Colin, 1996).

Lancaster, Roger N., *Thanks to the Cross and the Revolution: Popular Religion and Class Consciousness in the New Nicaragua* (New York: Columbia University Press, 1988).

Lane, Christel, *Christian Religion in the Soviet Union: A Sociological Study* (London: Allen and Unwin, 1978).

Leahy, William and Massini, Anthony (eds), *Third Session Council Speeches at Vatican II* (New York: Paulist Press, 1966).

Lenin, Vladimir Ilich, *Collected Works* (Moscow: Progress Publishers, 1972).

Lesourd, Paul, *Entre Rome et Moscou: Le jésuite clandestin* (Paris: 1976).

Levinas, Emmanuel, *De Dieu qui vient à l'idée* (Paris: Librairie Philosophique, 1986).

Levine, D., *Churches and Politics in Latin America* (London: Sage, 1980).

Lewy, Guenter, *The Catholic Church and Nazi Germany* (London: Weidenfeld and Nicolson, 1964).

Lipski, Jan Józef, *KOR* (Warsaw: Wydawnictwo CDN (*samizdat*) 1983).

Luukkanen, Arto, *The Party of Unbelief: The Religious Policy of the Bolshevik Party 1917–1929* (Helsinki: Studia Historica, 1994).

Mackiewicz, Józef, *W Cieniu Krzyża* (London: Kontra, 1972).

McLellan, David, *Marxism and Religion* (London: Macmillan, 1987).

Macqua, Mireille, *Rome–Moscou: L'Ostpolitik du Vatican* (Louvain-la-Neuve: Cabay, 1984).

McSweeney, Bill, *Roman Catholicism: The Search for Relevance* (Oxford: Basil Blackwell, 1980).

Magister, Sandro, *La politica vaticana e l'Italia 1943–1978* (Rome: Editori Riuniti, 1979).

Manfredini, Enrico, *Giovanni Battista Montini* (Brescia: Istituto Paolo VI, 1985).

Maritain, Jacques, *True Humanism* (London: Centenary Press, 1939).

Maritain, Jacques, *Man and the State* (Chicago: University of Chicago Press, 1951).

Masaryk, Tomáš, *Modern Man and Religion* (London: Allen and Unwin, 1938).

Mazowiecki, Tadeusz, *Drugi Twarz Europy* (Warsaw: Biblioteka Więzi, 1990).

Medvedev, Roy, *Let History Judge* (New York: Columbia University Press, 1989).

Micewski, Andrzej, *Cardinal Wyszyński* (San Diego: Harcourt Brace Jovanovich, 1984).

Micewski, Andrzej, *Kościół-Państwo 1945–1989* (Warsaw: Wydawnictwo Szkolne Pedagogiczne, 1994).

Michel, Patrick, *Politics and Religion in Eastern Europe* (London: Polity Press, 1991).

Michnik, Adam, *Kościół, Lewica, Dialog* (Paris: Instytut Literacki, 1977).

Michnik, Adam, Tischner, Józef and Żakowski, Jacek, *Między Panem i Plebanem* (Kraków: Znak, 1995).

Mieszczanek, Anna (ed.), *Krajobraz po szoku* (Warsaw: Przedświt, 1989).

Milcent, Ernest, *A l'Est du Vatican: La papauté et les démocraties populaires* (Paris: Cerf, 1980).

Mindszenty, József, *Memoirs* (London: Weidenfeld and Nicolson, 1974).

Misner, Paul, *Social Catholicism in Europe: From the Onset of Industrialisation to the First World War* (London: Darton, Longman and Todd, 1991).

Modras, Ronald, *The Catholic Church and Anti-Semitism: Poland 1933–1939* (London: Harwood, 1994).

Molony, John M., *The Emergence of Political Catholicism in Italy* (London: Croom Helm, 1977).

Montclos-Alix, Christine de, *Les Voyages de Jean-Paul II* (Paris: Centurion, 1990).

Mulazzi-Giammanco, Rosanna, *The Catholic–Communist Dialogue in Italy* (New York: Praeger, 1989).

Nichols, Aidan, *Rome and the Eastern Churches: A Study in Schism* (Edinburgh: T. & T. Clark, 1992).

Nielsen, Niels (ed.), *Christianity After Communism: Social, Political and Cultural Struggle in Russia* (San Francisco: Westview, 1994).

Niewęgłowski, Wiesław (ed.), *Moje spotkania z Janem Pawłem II* (Warsaw: Wydawnictwo Rok, 1991).

Nitecki, Piotr, *Znak Zwycięstwa* (Wrocław: Wrocławskiej Księgarni Archidiecezjalnej, 1991).

Novak, Michael, *The Catholic Ethic and the Spirit of Capitalism* (New York: Free Press, 1993).

Papee, Kazimierz, *Pius XII a Polska 1939–1949: Przemówienia, Listy, Komentarze* (Rome: Editrice Studium, 1954).

Papeloux, Léon, *Les Silences de Pie XII* (Brussels: Vokaer, 1980).

Papużyński, Andrzej, *Filozofia społeczna papieża Jana Pawła II* (Warsaw: Nauk Społecznych PZPR, 1988).

Passelecq, Georges and Suchecky, Bernard, *L'Encyclique Cachée de Pie XI* (Paris: Éditions de Découverte, 1995).

Pattee, Richard, *The Case of Cardinal Aloysius Stepinac* (Milwaukee: Bruce, 1953).

Pehe, Jiri (ed.), *The Prague Spring: A Mixed Legacy* (New York: Freedom House, 1988).

Pekař, Josef, *O smyslu českých dějin* (Prague: Rozmluvy, 1990).

Pelikan, Jaroslav, *Confessor Between East and West* (Grand Rapids: William B. Eerdmans, 1990).

Piasecki, Bronisław, *Ostatnie dni Prymasa Tysiąclecia* (Rome: Dom Polski, 1982).

Pieronek, Tadeusz (ed.), *Duszpasterski Synod Archidiecezji Krakowskiej 1972–1979*, vols 1–3 (Kraków: Kuria Metropolitana, 1985).

Pieronek, Tadeusz and Roman Zawadzki (eds), *Karol Wojtyła jako Biskup Krakowski* (Kraków: Papieska Akademia Teologiczna, 1988).

Pilch, Andrzej, *Studencki ruch polityczny w Polsce w latach 1932–1939* (Kraków: Zeszyty Naukowe, 1989).

Pithart, Petr, *Dĕjiny a politika* (Prague: Prostor, 1990).

Piwowarczyk, Jan, *Wobec nowego czasu* (Kraków: Znak, 1985).

Plongeron, Bernard (ed.), *Pratiques Religieuses dans l'Europe révolutionnaire 1770–1820* (Turnhout: Brepols, 1987).

Pollard, John F., *The Vatican and Italian Fascism 1929–32: A Study in Conflict* (Cambridge: Cambridge University Press, 1986.

Pontifical Council for the Instruments of Social Communication, *Communio et progressio* (29 January 1971).

Pospielovsky, Dimitry, *The Russian Church Under the Soviet Regime* (New York: St Vladimir's Seminary Press, 1984).

Pospielovsky, Dimitry, *A History of Marxism-Leninism, Atheism and Soviet Anti-Religious Policies* (London: Macmillan, 1987).

Poulat, Emile, *Catholicisme, démocratie et socialisme* (Paris: Casterman, 1977).

Purdy, William, *The Church on the Move* (London: Hollis and Carter, 1966).

Rabinbach, Anson, *The Crisis of Austrian Socialism: From Red Vienna to Civil War* (Chicago: University of Chicago Press, 1983).

Raina, Peter (ed.), *Kardynał Wyszyński*, vols 1–5 (Warsaw: Książka Polska, 1993–96).

Raina, Peter (ed.), *Kościół-Państwa w swietle akt wydziału d/s wyznań* (Warsaw: Książka Polska, 1994).

Raina, Peter (ed.), *Kościół w PRL—Dokumenty 1945–1989* (3 vols; Poznan: W Drodze, 1994–96).

Raina, Peter (ed.), *Rozmowy z Władzami*, vols 1–2 (Warsaw: Książka Polska, 1995).

Rakowski, Mieczysław, *Jak to się stało* (Warsaw: BGW, 1991).

Ratzinger, Josef and Messori, Vittorio, *The Ratzinger Report* (San Francisco: Ignatius Press, 1985).

Ravitch, Norman, *The Catholic Church and the French Nation* (London: Routledge, 1990).

Read, C., *Religion, Revolution and the Russian Intelligentsia* (London: Macmillan, 1979).

Rhodes, Anthony, *The Vatican in the Age of the Dictators* (London: Hodder and Stoughton, 1973).

Rhodes, Anthony, *The Power of Rome in the Twentieth Century* (London: Sidgwick and Jackson, 1983).

Riccardi, Andrea, *Il Vaticano e Mosca* (Rome: Editori Laterza, 1992).

Riccardi, Andrea, *Il Potere del Papa: da Pio XII a Giovanni Paolo II* (Rome: Editori Laterza, 1993).

Rolicki, Janusz, *Edward Gierek: Przerwana dekada* (Warsaw: Wydawnictwo Fakt, 1990).

Rossler, Roman, *Kirche und Revolution in Russland* (Cologne: Bohlan Verlag, 1969).

Ryn, Zdzisław, *Cierpienie ma tysiąc twarzy: Jan Paweł II i chorzy* (Kraków: Znak, 1988).

Ryszka, Czesław, *Charyzmat apostoła* (Kraków: Wydawnictwo Apostolstwa Modlitwy, 1986).

Ryszka, Czesław, *Papież końca czasów* (Bytom: Oficyna Wydawnicza 4K, 1995).

Sacred Congregation for Religious and Secular Institutes, *Le Scelte evangeliche* (January 1981).

Schatz, Klaus (ed.), *Vaticanum I 1869–1870,* Band III: *Unfehlbarkeitsdiskussion und Rezeption* (Paderborn: Schoningh, 1994).

Schmidt, Stjepan, *Augustin Bea: The Cardinal of Unity* (New York: New City Press, 1992).

Schneider, Burkhardt, *Pius XII: Friede, das Werk der Gerechtigkeit* (Göttingen: Musterschmidt Verlag, 1968).

Secretariat for Unbelievers, *Humanae personae dignitatem* (28 August 1968).

Senarclens, Pierre de, *Yalta* (Paris: Presses Universitaires de France, 1984).

Stacpoole, Alberic (ed.), *Vatican II by Those Who Were There* (London: Geoffrey Chapman, 1986).

Stankiewicz, Ewa, *Dar . . . powtarzamy te dni: Dokumentacja III Pielgrzymki* (Poznań: Pirobud, 1991).

Stehle, Hansjakob, *Eastern Politics of the Vatican 1917–1979* (London: Ohio University Press, 1981).

Stone, Norman, and Strouhal, Edward, *Czechoslovakia: Crossroads and Crises 1918–1988* (London: Macmillan, 1989).

Styczeń, Tadeusz, *Solidarność Wyzwala* (Lublin: Towarzystwo Naukowe, 1993).

Swieżawski, Stefan, *Wielki przełom 1907–1945* (Lublin: Redakcja Wydawnictw, 1991).

Swieżawski, Stefan, *W nowej rzeczywistości 1945–1965* (Lublin: Redakcja Wydawnictw, 1991).

Swieżawski, Stefan, *Owoce życia 1966–1988* (Lublin: Wydawnictwo KUL, 1993).

Synod of Bishops, *Ratione habita* (28 October 1967).

Synod of Bishops, *Ultimis temporibus* (30 November 1967).

Synod of Bishops, *Convenientes ex universo* (30 November 1971).

Synod of Bishops, *Final Report* (7 December 1985).

Szajkowski, Bogdan, *Next to God . . . Poland* (London: Pinter, 1983).

Szczesniak, Bolesław (ed.), *The Russian Revolution and Religion: Documents Concerning the Suppression of Religion by the Communists 1917–1925* (Indiana: University of Notre Dame Press, 1959).

Szulc, Tad, *Pope John Paul II: The Biography* (New York: Scribner, 1995).

Tajne dokumenty Biura Politycznego: PZPR a Solidarność (London: Aneks, 1992).

Tajne dokumenty Państwo-Kościół 1980–1989 (Warsaw: Aneks and Polityka, 1993).

Tajne dokumenty Państwo-Kościół 1960–1980 (London: Aneks, 1996).

Tambora, Angelo, *Chiesa cattolica e Ortodossia russa: due secoli di confronto e di dialogo* (Milan: Edizioni Paoline, 1992).

Tanalski, Dionizy, *Bóg, Człowiek i Politika: człowiek w teorii Jana Pawła II* (Warsaw: Książka i Wiedza, 1986).

Taras, Raymond (ed.), *The Road to Disillusion* (New York: M. E. Sharpe, 1992).

Tardini, Domenico, *Pio XII* (Vatican: Tipografia Poliglota, 1960).

Taylor, Myron (ed.), *Wartime Correspondence Between President Roosevelt and Pope Pius XII* (New York: Macmillan, 1947).

Teilhard de Chardin, Pierre, *The Phenomenon of Man* (London: Collins, 1983).

Tejchma, Józef, *Pożegnanie z władza* (Warsaw: Wydawnictwo Projekt, 1991).

Thils, Gustav, *Le Statut de l'Église dans la future Europe politique* (Louvain-la-Neuve: Librairie Peeters, 1991).

Timberlake, Charles (ed.), *Religious and Secular Forces in Late Tsarist Russia* (Seattle: University of Washington Press, 1992).

Tischner, Józef, *Polski kształt dialogu* (Paris: Éditions Spotkania, 1981).

Tischner, Józef, *Myslenie według wartości* (Kraków: Znak, 1982).

Trasatti, Sergio, *La croce e la stella: La Chiesa e i regimi comunisti in Europa dal 1917 a oggi* (Milan: Mondadori, 1993).

Turowicz, Jerzy, *Kosciół nie jest Łodzia Podwodna* (Kraków: Znak, 1990).

Urban, George, *End of Empire: The Demise of the Soviet Union* (Washington: American University Press, 1993).

Vardys, V. Stanley, *The Catholic Church, Dissent and Nationality in Soviet Lithuania* (Boulder: East European Monographs, 1978).

Vatican Council II, *Lumen gentium* (21 November 1964).

Vatican Council II, *Unitatis redintegratio* (21 November 1964).

Vatican Council II, *Nostra aetate* (28 October 1965).

Vatican Council II, *Christus Dominus* (28 October 1965).

Vatican Council II, *Gaudium et spes* (7 December 1965).

Vatican Council II, *Dignitatis humanae* (7 December 1965).

Vatican Council II, *Presbyterorum ordinis* (7 December 1965).

Vorgrimler, Herbert, *Commentary on the Documents of Vatican II* (London: Burns and Oates, 1969).

Walicki, Andrzej, *Philosophy and Romantic Nationalism* (Oxford: Clarendon Press, 1982).

Walsh, Michael, *John Paul II: A Biography* (London: Harper Collins, 1994).

Wenger, Antoine, *Rome et Moscou 1900–1950* (Paris: Desclée de Brouwer, 1987).

Wenger, Antoine, *Les Trois Rome: L'Église des années soixantes* (Paris: Desclée de Brouwer, 1991).

Wesołowski. W., *Losy Idei Socjalistycznych i Wyzwania Wspolczesności* (Warsaw: Polskie Towarzystwo Współpracy, 1990).

Wojtyła, Karol, *Katolicka Etyka Społeczna* (Lublin: *samizdat*, 1953–55).

Wojtyła, Karol, *Miłość i Odpowiedzialność* (Lublin: Towarzystwo Naukowa Katolickiego, 1960).

Wojtyła, Karol, *Osoba i czyn* (Kraków: Polskie Towarzystwo Teologiczne, 1969).

Wojyła, Karol, *U podstaw odnowy: studium o realizacji Vaticanum II* (Kraków: Polskie Towarzystwo Teologiczne, 1972)..

Wojtyła, Karol, *Znak ktoremu sprzeciwiać się będą* (Warsaw: Pallottinum, 1976).

Wojtyła, Karol, *Aby Chrystus się nami posługiwał* (Kraków: Znak, 1979).

Wojtyła, Karol, *Poezji i Dramaty* (Kraków: Znak, 1979).

Wojtyła, Karol, *Wykłady lubelskie* (Lublin: Wydawnictwo Towarzystwa Naukowego, 1986).

Wojtyła, Karol, *Nauczyciel i Pasterz: listy pasterskie, komunikaty, Zarządzenia 1959–1978* (Rome: Ośrodek Dokumentacji, 1987).

Wojtyła, Karol, *Brat Naszego Boga* (Kluczbork: Antykwa, 1996).

Wolf, Larry, *The Vatican and Poland in the Age of the Partitions* (Boulder: Westview, 1988).

Wołkowski, Józef (ed.), *Teologia wyzwolenia a szanse dialogu* (Warsaw: Instytut Wydawniczy Pax, 1988).

Wyka, Kazimierz, *Patrząc ku młodości* (Kraków: Uniwersytet Jagielloński, 1955).

Wyszyński, Stefan, *A Freedom Within: The Prison Notes of Stefan Cardinal Wyszyński* (London: Hodder and Stoughton, 1985).

Wyszyński, Stefan, *Un évêque au service du peuple de Dieu* (Paris: Éditions Saint-Paul, 1970).

Żakowski, Jacek, *Ćwiartki wieku: rozmowy z Jerzym Turowiczem* (Kraków: Znak, 1990).

Zieliński, Zygmunt and Wilk, Stanisław (eds), *Kościół w II Rzeczpospolitej* (Lublin: Wydawnictwo KUL, 1980).

Zizola, Giancarlo, *Il microfono di Dio: Pio XII, padre Lombardi e cattolici italiani* (Milan: Mondadori, 1990).

Zizola, Giancarlo, *The Utopia of Pope John XXIII* (New York: Orbis Books, 1978).

Zmijewski, Norbert, *The Catholic–Marxist Ideological Dialogue in Poland 1945–1980* (Aldershot: Dartmouth, 1991).

Journals and periodicals

Aneks (London).
Ateismo e Dialogo (Rome).
Cahiers de l'Est (Paris).
Catholic International (Baltimore).
Chronicle of the Catholic Church in Lithuania (New York).
Communist Affairs: Documents and Analysis (London).
Concilium (Utrecht).
La Documentation Catholique (Paris).
East European Quarterly (Boulder).
Journal of Contemporary History (London).
KAI Biuletyn (Warsaw).
Krytyka (Warsaw).
Listý (Bratislava).
The Month (London).
National Catholic Register (Hamden).
Occasional Papers on Religion in Eastern Europe (Princeton).
Orientierung (Zurich).
Das Östliche Christentum (Würzburg).
L'Osservatore Romano (Rome)
The Pope Teaches (London).
Powściągliwość i Praca (Warsaw)

Radio Free Europe/Radio Liberty Situation Reports (Munich)
Religion in Communist Lands (London).
Religion, State and Society (Oxford).
Slavic Review (Stanford).
Spotkania (Lublin).
Studie (Rome).
Survey (London).
The Tablet (London).
Tygodnik Powszechny (Kraków).
The Ukrainian Review (London).
Więź (Warsaw).
The World Today (London).
Znak (Kraków).

Index